THE PRACTICE OF MANPOWER FORECASTING:

A COLLECTION OF CASE STUDIES

The Jossey-Bass/Elsevier
International Series

 Elsevier Scientific Publishing Company
Amsterdam

THE PRACTICE OF MANPOWER FORECASTING

A Collection of Case Studies

EDITED BY

BASHIR AHAMAD
Canadian International Development Agency, Ottawa

AND

MARK BLAUG
University of London Institute of Education

 Jossey-Bass Inc., Publishers
San Francisco · Washington 1973

THE PRACTICE OF MANPOWER FORECASTING
A Collection of Case Studies
        by Bashir Ahamad and Mark Blaug

For the United States of America and Canada:

Jossey-Bass, Inc., Publishers
615 Montgomery Street
San Francisco, California 94111

For all other areas:

Elsevier Scientific Publishing Company
335 Jan van Galenstraat
Amsterdam, The Netherlands

Library of Congress Catalogue Card Number LC 72-83197

International Standard Book Number ISBN   0-87589-153-5

Manufactured in The Netherlands

FIRST EDITION

Code 7238

The Jossey-Bass/Elsevier International Series

Studies on Education

List of Contributors

BASHIR AHAMAD
Canadian International Development Agency

MARK BLAUG
University of London Institute of Education

KENNETH GANNICOTT
Directorate for Scientific Affairs
Organisation for Economic Co-operation and Development

KEITH HINCHLIFFE
Ahmadu Bello University, Nigeria

GEORGE PSACHAROPOULOS
Higher Education Research Unit
London School of Economics and Political Science

MAUREEN WOODHALL
University of Reading and
University of London Institute of Education

Foreword

This book comes from the L.S.E. Higher Education Research Unit and is one of a series on problems of educational planning.

The Unit, which has some twenty full-time research staff working on half a dozen projects, has been seeking to continue and develop the kind of research that was done for the Robbins Committee on Higher Education. Our particular interest is in economic and statistical aspects of national educational policy, and within this broad field we have focused on studies of the economics of qualified manpower; cost of higher education; computable models of student numbers; and the study of educational structures. Inevitably, we have always had a special interest in manpower forecasting. The Robbins Committee took the view, for a number of reasons, that the scale of expansion of higher education should be based on demand for places rather than on the demand for graduates emerging from higher education. Part of the reason for this was the uncertainty of manpower forecasts, and so the Unit has throughout its existence given attention to research on manpower needs.

It would, I think, be fair to say that our confidence in conventional methods of forecasting manpower needs has decreased over the years. But, at the same time, we continue to regard this side of educational planning as vital and we shall persevere with our investigations of it. At this stage, it seemed desirable to review experience with manpower forecasting in different contexts, and this is the purpose of the present volume.

The case studies in the volume illustrate that manpower forecasts have been used for a wide variety of policy decisions ranging from short-term labour market adjustments to long-term educational planning. The objectives of such forecasts are not always explicitly specified and there appears to be an implicit assumption that any forecast is better than no forecast at all. The authors found evidence, however, that some forecasts supported what subsequently turned out to be a wrong policy decision. The forecasting models adopted in this area are crude and no allowances are made for the unavoidable uncertainty of the future course of events. This determinism is particularly unsatisfactory because of the lack of adequate data about the current stock of manpower and its utilization.

The authors argue that the manpower forecasting models currently used are much more satisfactory for making short-term rather than long-term forecasts, which is to say that so far they have not proved to be particularly useful for educational planning. They suggest that forecasting should be an on-going activity in which short-term forecasts are continuously being revised and up-dated. But more importantly, they argue that manpower forecasting models must become optimizing models, in which the costs and benefits of different types of manpower are explicitly introduced, if they are to have relevance for educational decision-making

The conclusions of the authors are on the whole discouraging from the point of view of traditional methods, and we shall hope in our work over the next few years to contribute towards better techniques.

C. A. Moser
Director of the Unit

Author's preface

This is a book of ten case studies by six authors with an introduction and a conclusion by the two editors who are also among the authors of the case studies. All six authors participated in the discussion of every chapter, including the first and the last, but only the editors take final responsibility for the conclusions. No effort was made to produce absolute uniformity in treatment among the case studies. To have secured this kind of unanimity would have deprived the case studies of their individual flavour.

This book is the second publication resulting from co-operation between the Higher Education Research Unit at the London School of Economics and the Research Unit on the Economics of Education at the University of London Institute of Education. Mr. Ahamad and Mr. Hinchliffe were formerly Research Fellow and Research Officer at the Higher Education Research Unit. Dr. Psacharopoulos is a former Senior Research Officer there and now a Lecturer in Economics at the London School of Economics. Professor Blaug, Mr. Gannicott and Miss Woodhall are, respectively, Head of, and Research Officers at, the Research Unit on the Economics of Education. Earlier versions of Chapter 9 on scientists and engineers in Britain and Chapter 10 on teachers in England and Wales appeared in *Higher Education Review*, Autumn 1969 and Summer 1970, respectively, and Chapter 5 on Thailand in *Journal of Development Studies*, November 1971. We wish to thank the editors and publishers of the journals for permission to reprint them.

We wish to thank Mr. P. Armitage, Mr. R. Layard and Mr. G. Williams for helpful comments on an earlier draft of the book; Miss Christine Buchta and Miss Anne Usher for typing a manuscript that was written in many hands; and the Social Science Research Council for financing this study as part of its programme grant to the Higher Education Research Unit for a series of manpower studies.

Contents

1. Introduction

The years following World War II witnessed an unprecedented educational explosion the world over, in consequence of which there soon emerged an equally unprecedented interest in educational planning as an integral feature of central economic planning. Within a decade or so, the rapidly growing literature on the subject developed its now characteristic economic bias, its emphasis on numbers rather than on the quality of education and its controversial flavour dominated by a peculiar jargon. In a nutshell, three different criteria were advanced, all of which purported to offer guide-lines to public authorities in planning education to achieve economic objectives. The first, known as 'the social demand approach', proposed that educational expansion should be geared to the demand of individual households for education. The other two — 'rate of return analysis' and 'the manpower forecasting approach' — suggested instead that educational expansion should somehow be geared to the demand of employers for labour. The manpower forecasting approach, in particular, appeared to provide a simple and intuitively appealing method of determining the level of investment in education that is required to achieve specified economic growth targets. For that reason alone it has proved in practice to be the most popular of all approaches to educational planning and its popularity has been particularly striking in underdeveloped countries.

The manpower forecasting approach to educational planning has, however, received much criticism, particularly from the advocates of rate of return or cost-benefit analysis. The motivation for our study grew out of a desire to shed some light on this inconclusive debate. After 20 years of experience in manpower forecasting, we felt that the time was ripe to ask a few pertinent questions. Have manpower forecasts been as inaccurate as the opponents of the method suggested they would be? Since long-term forecasts are obviously less accurate than short-term forecasts and since most manpower fore-

1

casts are long-term forecasts, what use have they been in formulating policy? Can past experience provide any guide to the limitations of various forecasting models, and in particular can it provide any indication of what type of model is most suitable for planning purposes? Has the experience with manpower forecasting in under-developed countries been better or worse than that in developed countries?

In order to try to answer these and similar questions, we decided to make a detailed analysis of the forecasting work of a number of countries. We chose countries which have had a fairly long record of manpower forecasting: the United States, Canada, Britain, Sweden and France in the developed world, and India, Thailand and Nigeria in the underdeveloped world.[1] Our omission of the centrally planned economies of Eastern Europe is unfortunate but the well-known difficulties of obtaining information about these countries forced us to abandon earlier plans to include a communist country. We tried to cover a wide variety of forecasting methods and examined forecasts for the labour force as a whole as well as those for specific occupations, such as scientists, engineers, teachers and doctors.

A central difficulty in discussing the validity of the manpower forecasting approach is that the single rubric 'manpower forecasting' in fact covers a multiple of diverse activities. The first step in evaluating a manpower forecast is to ask for what purpose it was made. Our initial aim was to try to evaluate the usefulness of long-term manpower forecasting as a tool for educational planning. Our central concern, therefore, is with national manpower planning, not company manpower planning, and with a particular kind of national manpower planning. In the course of our analysis we came across a number of nation-wide forecasts which were designed, not for planning education, but as aids to what has come to be called 'an active manpower policy', that is, to provide information for training and retraining programmes, career counselling, vocational guidance, and a wide variety of schemes to eliminate structural and regional unemployment. Such forecasts tend to be short-term (1—2 years) or medium-term (3—5 years) rather than long-term (10—20 years) as is the case with most forecasts geared to the educational system. To

---

[1] The absence of other African countries in our sample was deliberate. R. Jolly of the Institute of Development Studies, University of Sussex, is in the midst of a similar evaluation exercise as ours confined to tropical Africa. Excellent evaluations of the manpower forecasting work of the three East African countries are already in print: Rado (1967) and Skorov (1967).

have considered these types of forecasts would have unduly lengthened our study; nevertheless, in the case of Canada we have included an evaluation of some medium-term manpower forecasts that were designed to improve general manpower policies. Elsewhere, however, our primary interest is that of evaluating national manpower forecasts for purposes of educational planning.

Why make manpower forecasts?

The growing interest in manpower forecasting in the 1950's and 1960's derived from three quite different sources: there were those interested in linking educational expansion to what were called the 'manpower requirements' of a growing economy; there were others who realized that target-setting for GNP eventually entailed a translation of these targets into their individual components, one of which was the manpower structure associated with different levels of output; lastly, there were those concerned with vocational counselling and placement services who felt that manpower forecasting could provide a rational basis for their activities. All these strands contributed to the practice of manpower forecasting but it is easy to see that they involve quite different considerations. Nevertheless, we can discern a common theme, namely, the belief that shortages and surpluses of different types of manpower tend to persist side by side in all economies, whether planned or unplanned. Such imbalances are undesirable from the point of view of individuals, since they suffer losses not only in earnings but also in morale, status, wealth, and so on. These imbalances are also undesirable from the point of view of society since the growth of the economy may be restricted by shortages of particular kinds of manpower. Thus, the attempt to eliminate such imbalances by deliberate manpower planning can make a contribution both to individual and to social welfare.

The simultaneous existence of shortages and surpluses suggests that the problem calls for the re-allocation of manpower from some uses to others. This could be brought about by retraining existing manpower so as to increase the number of workers with skills in high demand and to reduce the number with skills in low demand. But this may be a lengthy process and, in the meantime, the pattern of demand and supply is continually changing. Thus, it seems desirable to gear retraining plans as well as the size and structure of the educational system as closely as possible to the future demand for manpower. The point of making manpower forecasts, therefore, is to

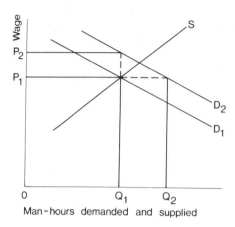

Figure 1.1. Demand for and supply of a particular type of manpower

ensure that new supplies of manpower become available at the same time that new demands materialize; in this way, manpower imbalances may be eliminated or at least minimized.

It will be clear that the argument for making manpower forecasts is based on the implicit assumption that rigidities in the economy restrict the price—quantity adjustments that form the cornerstone of standard economics. To illustrate the argument, let us consider the usual demand-supply relationships of elementary price theory. Assume in Figure 1.1 that the market demand curve for a particular type of manpower — that is the curve showing the amount of manpower demanded by all employers at various wage rates — is given by D_1, and that the supply curve — showing the amount of that type of manpower supplied at various wage rates — is given by S. Assume also that the market is initially in equilibrium with a ruling wage of OP_1 and an employment of OQ_1, determined by the intersection of D_1 and S. Assume now that the demand curve shifts to D_2 because of, say, an increase in the demand for the goods of industries employing this type of manpower. The immediate effect of this change is that employers increase their demand for manpower at the ruling wage OP_1 to OQ_2. Before suppliers of manpower can react to the change, a shortage of manpower measured by (OQ_2 − OQ_1) exists at the ruling wage OP_1.

Economic theory assumes that such a shortage is only a temporary phenomenon and that the labour market can be relied upon with a short time-lag to restore the system to equilibrium (see Arrow and Capron, 1959). Competition among employers for the limited man-

4

power supplied will tend to drive wages up.[2] As wages rise, the quantity demanded falls since some empoyers will be able to substitute other types of manpower for the one in question, or other factors of production for labour; if we assume that the supply of labour is fixed in the short-run at OQ_1, then the wage rate will be driven up to OP_2 and the system will be in short-run equilibrium. At the same time, the higher wage rate will in the longer term encourage the additional supply of manpower along the given supply curve S. Thus the wage—employment adjustment process continues until the system is once more in long-run equilibrium with a new wage rate and employment level determined by the intersection of the new demand curve D_2 and the supply curve S.

There are two critical assumptions in this standard argument: the first is that the labour market produces the right signals in situations of disequilibrium and that the participants in the market — employers and employees - react to these signals; the second is that factors of production — including different types of manpower — can be easily substituted for one another. In the real world, however, there may be rigidities in both the labour market and in the production of goods and services which restrict the adjustment process. For example, if employers have a strong bargaining advantage in the labour market, the shortage of manpower may not lead to a rise in wages with the result that output will be restricted; similarly, if the given type of manpower is a necessary input in the production process, then factor substitution is limited and output is again restricted. In both these cases, adjustments must then take place in product markets through the pricing mechanism.

Rigidities may exist in the labour market for a large number of reasons. Cultural factors and habits often limit the mobility of manpower between areas or between jobs. Similarly, poor labour market information about earnings, employment vacancies and manpower availabilities may substantially lengthen the time taken for the participants in the process to react to signals. Institutional controls — for example the restriction of manpower in certain professions — and monopoly practices by employers may also hinder the functioning of the labour market. Finally, the training periods of some types of

---

[2] Occupational wage rates may be held constant while employers relax minimum hiring standards for jobs, that is, they hire men with lower qualifications for a given job. In consequence, a worker with a given qualification finds himself earning more than before. In that sense, wages per man of a given quality increase.

manpower — particularly highly specialized manpower — are so long that supply may never be able to catch up with demand and hence labour markets may be in a continuous state of disequilibrium.

Rigidities in the production process govern the ease with which one type of manpower can be substituted for another and these may be more critical than rigidities in the labour market. We can certainly help to improve the workings of the labour market by trying to remove some of the existing rigidities: but even if we could get the market to work perfectly, output may nevertheless be restricted by limited substitution possibilities in the production process. Substitutability is not of course solely a question of how effectively one type of manpower performs a given set of tasks relative to another; it is also a question of how much it costs to hire the two types of manpower. A measure of substitutability is therefore a function of relative earnings. It is possible to define this measure precisely but it is not easy to quantify it. The standard definition of the so-called 'partial elasticity of substitution' is the percentage change in the relative quantities employed of two types of manpower (or of any two factors of production) due to a 1 per cent change in the relative earnings (strictly speaking, the relative marginal products) of the two types of manpower *at a given level of output.* If this elasticity is infinite, it follows immediately that the demand curves for both types of manpower are horizontal lines: a small increase in their relative earnings will lead instantaneously to zero employment. Conversely, if the elasticity of substitution is zero, the demand curves are vertical lines and output cannot be increased unless additional quantities of that type of manpower are hired. Of course, these are really polar extremes and most cases will fall somewhere in the middle. It is not difficult to see that the long lead-time required to produce highly qualified manpower creates no problems whatsoever if the elasticity of substitution for highly qualified manpower is a very large number. On the other hand, if it is a low number, particularly if it is less than one, supply constraints on a particular type of manpower will tend to cause skill bottlenecks which may limit the potential growth of output.

To sum up then there are two main reasons why we try to make manpower forecasts: (i) the labour market may function imperfectly and with extremely long time-lags and (ii) the elasticity of substitution may in fact be zero or nearly zero; the former does not imply the latter but the latter almost always implies the former. *In all cases,* what we do is try to forecast shifts in the demand and supply curves for different types of manpower and hence to identify future long-run equilibria. The forecasts provide a basis for planning education and training facilities in the effort to ensure that new manpower supplies become available at the same time that new demands materialise.

Long-term or short-term forecasts?

It seems obvious that if we wish to influence the supply of manpower with different types of education at a given point in time, investment plans may have to be made operational several years earlier. The planned changes in supply may necessitate the construction of new buildings, the provision of new books and equipment and the training of new teachers; these constraints introduce a considerable time-lag in the production of manpower with highly specialized skills. In addition, students normally have to choose their fields of specialization a long time before they enter the labour market. Thus it seems reasonable to assume that manpower forecasts should be long-term if they are to be useful for planning formal education.

The critics of long-term manpower forecasting argue that the necessary changes in manpower supplies are usually marginal and can therefore be made with the existing educational facilities. Moreover, although there is little doubt that the lead-time for student choice may be very long in some fields — for example, in the case of doctors — this may be less true for other types of manpower. Thus it is not clear that early specialization in schools will necessarily increase the productivity of individuals when they join the labour market: early specialisation may simply reflect rigidities in the educational system. If this were the case, then the necessity for long-term forecasting could be largely eliminated by reducing the amount of early specialization in schools: changes in demand could then be met by influencing the careers of students already in the educational pipelines.

These criticisms are sound so far as they go, but they ignore the fact that long-term forecasts may also provide valuable information for decision-making by individuals. If students choose careers only on the basis of current labour market information, they may find that the market situation has been considerably altered by the time they join the labour market. For example, students may choose a type of education in which wages are currently high, but they may find that when they actually join the labour market, wages are low because of over-adjustment to the excess demand. This would be unimportant if education could be completely general so that manpower could be perfectly flexible — which seems unlikely in practice especially for highly qualified manpower — and if students regarded their first employment as only temporary. But if students consider that their first employment should be fairly secure for a number of years, then the estimates of future prospects should cover a reasonably long time-horizon.[3]

In a similar way, employers may plan their investment in physical capital on the basis of current labour market information. For example, employers may plan to invest in equipment for which the necessary manpower is in excess supply and hence for which labour costs are currently low; but they may find that, because of over-adjustment to the excess supply, wages have risen by the time the equipment is installed and hence that profit expectations are disappointed. Similarly, current shortages of manpower may have a retarding effect on the adoption of new and more efficient techniques of production. Thus for efficient investment planning, firms ought to be interested in the manpower demand and supply situation, not only when new equipment is installed, but over the lifetime of the equipment. If this is so, long-term manpower forecasts clearly form one of the prerequisites of efficient decision-making.

There is little doubt, however, that because of the uncertainty of the future and the compounding of errors over time, long-term forecasts will tend to be subject to larger errors than short-term and medium-term forecasts. This implies that the information provided by long-term forecasts can only be used for planning purposes as a broad indicator of the future course of events. We have the paradoxical situation that manpower forecasting should be long-term to be really useful for educational decisions but, unfortunately, highly accurate forecasting is only possible in the short-term or medium-term. As we shall see in a moment, it is this paradox which makes it so difficult to evaluate manpower forecasting in practice.

Manpower forecasting in practice

Manpower forecasting in the framework of standard economics involves identifying the variables which generate changes in both the demand for and supply of different types of manpower. To forecast

---

[3] However, the estimates of future prospects would have to include a great deal more than what is usually conveyed by manpower forecasts to be really useful to students (see Blaug, 1970, p. 164).

changes in the demand for manpower we need to forecast changes in the level and composition of final demand for goods and services, changes in technology and their effects on the substitutability between factors of production, changes in inter-industry demands for intermediate goods, changes in prices, and so on. To forecast changes in the supply of manpower we need to forecast changes in population, changes in labour force participation rates, changes in wages and salaries, changes in the costs of education, and so on. The construction of such a fully specified forecasting model would be an exceedingly complex task and in fact an impossible one, given existing data and our limited knowledge of the workings of labour markets.

In practice, forecasts of the demand for manpower, in the economist's sense of the term 'demand' as a function of price, are seldom made. More typically what is done is to make forecasts of manpower 'needs' or 'requirements' on the assumption that all relative prices, wages and salaries remain constant. These manpower needs or requirements are sometimes unwittingly confused with demand in the economist's sense, but they are usually defined as the amount of manpower needed or required to achieve given objectives or standards. The concept is therefore a technological rather than an economic one: for example, the needs or requirements for teachers may be defined as the number of teachers needed to achieve certain educational standards, but these do not necessarily correspond with the number of teachers who will be offered employment at prevailing salary scales.

Herbert Parnes, on the other hand, draws a distinction between 'needs' and 'requirements': 'A country's "needs" for education . . . depend upon the criteria selected and even then can be ascertained only in reference to a host of competing needs', but 'the only meaningful way in which a country can ascertain its educational "requirements" is to establish certain targets for social and economic development and to see what these necessitate in the way of education' (Parnes, 1962, p. 12). Parnes seems to argue that requirements form a subset of needs and refer only to those needs which can actually be met with the resources available at a particular point in time; the calculation of these available resources constitutes the subset of 'requirements'.

Parnes defines manpower requirements as 'the functional (occupational) composition of employment that will be necessary if certain social and/or economic targets are to be achieved' (pp. 17—18). He suggests that it is easy to illustrate and defend the concept for

9

particular types of manpower (for example, for doctors) but he admits that for most types of manpower there is 'no unique relation between output in an industry and either the total labour force of that industry or its occupational composition' (p. 18). If this is so, it follows that manpower 'requirements' cannot be optimal or even strictly necessary for achieving given objectives: they merely represent one possible way of meeting the given objectives and are contingent upon assumptions made about the existing state of technology. In other words, they may be more properly described as feasible technological requirements.

It is apparent that this technological concept of requirements can only be translated into the standard economic conception of demand if we assume that the elasticities of substitution between different factors of production are all zero or close to zero. In all such cases, a change in relative wages has either no effect or very little effect on the demand for manpower, so that the level of employment is in fact technologically determined. Although this seems a plausible general assumption to make in the short run, it is highly unlikely that the manpower structure of any economy is rigidly determined in the long run. If shortages and surpluses of particular types of manpower persist, employers will tend to alter the composition of their capital stock so as to use less of the manpower in short supply and more of that in excess supply. Even if this proved to be impossible for technical reasons, the rise in the price of goods that made intensive use of expensive manpower in short supply, would lead to commodity substitution in favour of other goods. In consequence, the manpower structure of the whole economy would tend to change in the long run, even if it remained unchanged within every industry.

The controversy about the validity of the technological approach — which forms a central part of this book — may be resolved by estimating elasticities of substitution. Since the denominator of the expression for the elasticity of substitution involves relative marginal products and since marginal products are simply derivatives of a production function, statistical estimates of the elasticity of substitution involve statistical estimates of a production function. But the statistical and economic problems of estimating production functions are formidable (for an excellent survey, see Walters, 1968, Ch. 10) and so far few of the production functions that have been estimated have taken explicit account either of the occupational or the educational composition of the labour force.[4]

By way of a short cut, Bowles (1969, pp. 42—50) has estimated partial elasticities of substitution between three types of manpower by directly estimating the relationship between employment and earnings; these estimates turned to be very high implying great ease of substitution between different types of manpower. However, Psacharopoulos and Hinchliffe (1971) using the same method but a larger sample obtained different results: although their estimates were greater than unity — implying some substitutability — they were much lower than those by Bowles. In both cases the standard errors of the estimates were large so that the results are consistent with either low or high substitutability; moreover, both analyses were based on international cross-section data on earnings and employment which may not be directly comparable. The net result is that these studies provide no definite evidence on the presence of rigidities in the production process.

Be that as it may, forecasts of manpower requirements are usually compared with estimates of the amount of manpower expected to be available[5] on the basis of existing educational plans. The differences between the two are then interpreted as shortages and surpluses of manpower and these are used to identify the necessity for changes in current educational plans. The comparison appears to provide not only an indication of which types of education should be expanded, but also an indication of the numerical size of the necessary expansion.

The various possible steps in the calculation of manpower requirements and availabilities are illustrated in Figure 1.2. On the requirements side, manpower forecasts are usually obtained by the fixed — coefficients method: this is a simple extension of the so-called Leontief production function in which inputs are assumed to be used in fixed proportions in the production of output. The fixed — coefficients approach provides a particularly simple method of obtaining

---

[4] The standard method of dealing with the educational composition of the labour force is to construct a labour-augmenting index of years of schooling, weighted by the earnings differentials associated with different years. This begs too many questions because it assumes that earnings reflect the marginal productivity of schooling, which is precisely one of the things we want to discover when we estimate production functions. For a somewhat less than successful attempt to estimate production functions, where labour is suitably disaggregated by levels of education, see Layard et al. (1971).

[5] In the literature, this is normally referred to as manpower supply, even though it is not 'supply' in the economist's sense.

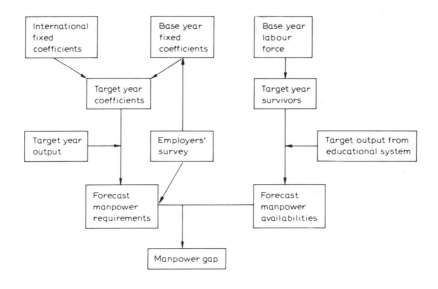

Figure 1.2. Calculations of manpower requirements and availabilities.

manpower forecasts. Since

$$\text{manpower input} = \left(\frac{\text{manpower input}}{\text{output}}\right) \text{output}$$

forecasts may be obtained by making separate forecasts of the manpower input per unit of output (i.e. the fixed coefficients) and the level of output.

An important assumption in this approach is that the fixed coefficients, or reciprocals of the labour-productivity coefficients, are independent of the level of output. But this assumption seems inplausible in the light of empirical evidence. For example, using data for the UK for the period 1924—50, Salter (1966, pp.122—124) found that labour productivity (for an aggregated measure of labour) and output were closely related: industries which recorded large increases in labour productivity also tended to record large increases in output, and vice versa. Salter argued that the saving in unit costs which accompanies increases in labour productivity lead to lower product prices and hence to the expansion of output.

Problems also arise in attempting to forecast changes in labour productivity over time. We still know very little about the factors which cause changes in labour productivity, so that forecasts are generally made by the simple extrapolation of past trends. But

12

Kendrick's analysis (1961) suggests that rates of change of labour productivity differ substantially but unsystematically between industries and within industries at different points in time. A preferable alternative involves an examination of the distribution of existing techniques of production across firms: at any point in time, firms producing the same output will differ in the techniques they employ because of such factors as differences in the age structures of their plant and equipment. Thus forecasts of labour productivity may be derived from observations for firms using 'best practice' techniques (Salter, 1966). However, this involves making assumptions about the speed with which other firms adopt these techniques.

Measures of output are not always meaningful for manpower analysis. Ideally, output should be measured in terms of physical units but such measures are only possible for specific products. More usually, output is measured in terms of market values obtained by weighting physical quantities with market prices. But this is not possible for goods or services which are not sold commercially as, for example, government services. In this case, the usual procedure is to base the value of output on the cost of the factor inputs: thus output is implicitly related to employment and hence to labour productivity.

As in the case of forecasts of manpower requirements, forecasts of the amount of manpower estimated to be available do not take direct account of the effects of prices and hence of market adjustments which may take place. Forecasts of manpower availabilities are generally derived by correcting the base year manpower stock for losses through mortality and retirement and by adding the expected manpower outputs from the educational system. But the effects of the mobility of manpower already in the labour force — either directly through job changes, or indirectly through a retraining programme — are seldom taken into account. This means that educational plans which are drawn up on this basis may over-estimate the change in investment necessary for different types of education since part of the forecast shortages and surpluses will tend to be eliminated by on-the-job training and by employers' retraining schemes.

The MRP method for forecasting manpower requirements

In order to set the scene for our case studies, we now discuss the methods that have been used in making manpower forecasts. Our discussion here is necessarily brief since more detailed discussions of various aspects of the methods appear in later chapters.[6] Let us first consider one of the best known applications of the fixed-coefficients method to manpower problems, the so-called 'MRP approach' which was pioneered by Parnes in the OECD Mediterranean Regional Project (see Parnes, 1962). The aim of the method is to make simultaneous forecasts of manpower requirements in all occupations and then to translate these into educational requirements. In the first stage, forecasts of occupational requirements are obtained by multiplying the projected level of employment in each industry by the projected occupational structure of each industry and summing over all industries. If we let L refer to manpower and Y refer to output and use the subscripts i and j to refer to occupation and industry respectively, then employment in a given occupation is denoted by

$$L_i = \sum_j \left(\frac{L_{ij}}{L_j}\right) \left(\frac{L_j}{Y_j}\right) (Y_j)$$

where L_{ij} is the amount of manpower in a given occupation and industry. Thus forecasts of occupational requirements are derived by making separate projections of:

(i) the occupational structure of each industry (i.e. L_{ij}/L_j)
(ii) labour productivity in each industry (i.e. Y_j/L_j); and
(iii) the level of output in each industry (i.e. Y_j).

If we let the subscript k refer to education, then in the second stage, educational requirements are given by

$$L_k = \sum_i \left(\frac{L_{ik}}{L_i}\right) (L_i)$$

where L_{ik} is the amount of manpower in a given occupation with a given level of education. The coefficients L_{ik}/L_k and L_{ij}/L_j are both proportions and hence they are constrained to sum to one over all educational levels and over all occupations respectively.

Since forecasts are made separately for the occupational structure, for labour productivity and for output in each industry, the method assumes implicitly that these are all independent. But this does not seem to be realistic. If the level of output increases, this may mean — for some industries — that average costs fall because of economies of scale and external economies. Thus more efficient but more expen-

---

6 Other discussions may be found in Mehmet (1965), Goldstein and Swerdloff (1967) and Blaug (1970, Ch. 5).

sive capital equipment, requiring different types of manpower, can now be adopted in the production process; in addition the new machinery may be labour-saving so that labour productivity may rise.

The method also assumes that the occupational structure of an industry and the educational structure of an occupation are determined by the state of technology in the industry: in effect, this means that there can be no substitution between occupations in the production of output, and that there can be no substitution between different kinds of education in the performance of the operations or functions that define a given occupation. It appears unrealistic to assume that the manpower structure of the economy is rigidly determined, and it is mainly for this reason that the MRP approach has been severely criticized (see Hollister, 1966).

The assumption of rigid occupational and educational coefficients is equivalent to an assumption that the employment of manpower is independent of the supply: thus if the supply of manpower in a given occupation or education changes, it has no effect on the amount of manpower employed. This assumption may be realistic in the short run since firms may not be able to substitute one type of manpower for the other in the face of a given capital stock. But in the long run, firms will clearly be able to choose their equipment so as to utilize more of the manpower in excess supply and hence to reduce average costs. An alternative is that firms may upgrade occupations by employing the manpower in excess supply in jobs which were previously performed by similar but less skilled manpower.

For example, suppose that the supply of engineers increases, because of say an expansion in university places, while the demand remains constant, then the wage of engineers will tend to fall. In the long run, employers will tend to substitute engineers for other types of manpower — e.g. scientists — and in this way average labour costs may fall. If the excess supply is large, and the price is low enough, employers will also tend to employ engineers to perform jobs which were previously performed by less skilled manpower, e.g. technicians.

In the original application of the method in the Mediterranean Regional Project, only limited account was taken of the supply effects and hence of substitution possibilities (Hollister, 1966, pp. 20—24). In several of the applications discussed in this book, some attempt has been made to incorporate such effects via 'sensitivity analysis', that is by projecting the various coefficients on the basis of alternative assumptions about the values of the critical variables. The importance of supply effects and of substitution possibilities depends critically on the level of occupational and educational disaggregation in a forecast. When applied to France, for example, the occupations used were mainly broad aggregates, though special forecasts were also made for some highly qualified occupations. In Canada and the United States however, the projections covered the entire range of occupational classes for which data existed. The advantage of the latter approach is that projections for detailed occupations are more useful for general manpower planning; however, it seems reasonable to assume that the greater the detail, the greater the scope for substitution possibilities and hence the greater the size of likely forecasting errors.

In the United States and France, the projections of output by industry were obtained using an inter-industry input—output model of the economy. Forecasts of final demand — consumption and investment — were first obtained by a variety of methods including the use of econometric models and these were then translated into output by means of a projected inter-industry input—output table. The advantage of this approach is that more accurate and internally consistent forecasts of output are obtained, but these still have to be transformed into forecasts of employment by industry by making assumptions about productivity changes. In a recent application for Canada, projections of output by industry were obtained by the simple extrapolation of past trends, but these were modified to take account of existing expectations about future developments. Projections of labour productivity were obtained in a similar way; but because of the uncertainty about future productivity changes, two alternative assumptions were derived thus providing two projections of employment in each industry.

The MRP method is also fairly expensive to apply because of the data requirements. Manpower data are required cross-classified by occupation and industry and by education and occupation and preferably for a number of time periods. Normally, such data are available only in census years at decennial intervals and hence are often quite out of date. In addition, the education, occupation and industry classification systems used have changed so much from one census to the other that such data are not usually directly comparable over time. Data are also required for output and total employment by industry for a number of time periods. Input—output tables tend to provide more accurate projections of output and hence are preferable to simple estimates of real domestic product by industry. But input—output tables are expensive to compile and are usually available only for one time period, if at all.

Forecasting manpower requirements for specialized occupations

Because of the difficulty of translating multi-occupation forecasts of occupational requirements into educational requirements, separate forecasts are often made for specialized occupations which are closely linked to specific types of education and training. This is usually the case for highly qualified manpower for which a university degree or a similar qualification is generally considered to be essential; scientists, engineers, teachers and doctors are among the occupations for which separate forecasts are often made.

The method used is usually the basic fixed-coefficients method in which separate projections are made for the manpower input per unit of output and the level of output: in this context, the method is often described as the 'labour-output ratio' or 'physical norms' method. A variation of this method is to forecast the manpower input per member of the total labour force, together with the total labour force derived from projections of total output and labour productivity: this is often referred to as the 'density ratio' method. One of the troublesome problems in this approach is to obtain a satisfactory measure of output. In the case of scientists and engineers, output is usually measured in terms of value added, but in the case of doctors and teachers, this method cannot be used; since medical and educational services are rarely sold on a purely commercial basis, value added is usually measured in terms of the costs of factor inputs and is therefore implicitly related to the manpower inputs. Hence for forecasting the number of doctors and teachers, output has to be measured in physical units; in the former case, total population, and in the latter case, pupils in school, tend to be used as proxies for output. Note however that these measures may be only poor approximations: for example in the case of doctors, output should really be measured by the number of persons treated with different diseases, and this number will depend not only on total population but also on the age structure, sex composition, standard of health, and so on.

Forecasts of the manpower input per unit of output are sometimes derived on the basis of desired norms or targets. For example, in an application of the method to teachers in England and Wales forecasts were based on a desired pupil—teacher ratio. The desired ratio was based on an *assumed* relationship between the average size of class and the proportion of oversize classes, and between the pupil—teacher ratio and the average size of class. In this way, the target ratio was derived from the desirable educational objective of eliminating oversize classes; if the supply of teachers were increased, then the desirable objective would be achieved.

In some cases, the target ratio is obtained from time series observations by taking either the maximum ratio observed, or by extrapolating the observations over time: the former method was used in forecasting the ratio of general practitioners to patients for Britain in 1975, while the latter has been used in other forecasts of the doctor—population ratio. But since the rationale for specialized occupation forecasting is that a given occupation is associated with a specific educational qualification, then unless unemployment of doctors existed at various points in time, the observed ratios would have been partly determined by the supply of doctors. Thus if disequilibrium situations exist — for example if there is a shortage of doctors — the use of the observed ratios may implicitly assume that the existing disequilibria will continue to exist in the future. The use of specific observed ratios as the desired target ratio may be particularly misleading in this respect.

The same kinds of methods have been used to forecast the density ratio for scientists and engineers in a number of the countries we have studied. In some cases the ratio has been assumed to remain constant but this was mainly because of lack of enough information, while in others the forecast ratio was based on the extrapolation of past trends: the problems of extrapolation of existing disequilibria which we discussed above thus equally apply in this case.

Other methods

The methods of manpower forecasting described so far assume the existence of adequate manpower data in the country concerned. For example, in the MRP method, detailed data on the occupational structure of industries and on the educational structure of occupations are necessary before forecasts can be made; similarly, in the density ratio method, satisfactory forecasts can only be made if numerous time—series or cross-section observations are available. These data requirements are often met only in highly developed countries so that alternative methods usually have to be used in developing countries. One approach is to collect the relevant data from existing firms; but this may be costly and may provide a poor indication of the future because of the generally rapid changes taking place in developing economies.

A simpler method is to try to use data from a similar economy at a point in time when its stage of development was in some sense comparable to the current stage of the country concerned. A variant of this method is to estimate the relationship between the manpower structure of an economy and its stage of development, using currently available data for different countries. Several applications of the latter approach appear in the literature: Rado and Jolly (1965) have applied to Uganda a simple model proposed by Tinbergen for relating educated manpower to GNP per capita; Horowitz *et al.* (1966), Layard and Saigal (1966) and OECD (1970) have used a more disaggregated model in which the relationship between the proportion of manpower of a given type is related to output per man.

The rationale of the method of international comparisons is the notion that all economies will tend to follow a reasonably well defined development path, so that the experience of developed countries may provide useful planning indicators for developing countries. This is only strictly valid if we assume that at any point in time all countries are on the same aggregate production function — though, of course, at different points on the function. In practice this depends on such factors as time lags in the application of the best practice techniques of production across countries, the age of the existing capital stock, intercountry differences in the composition of national output, capacity utilization, and so on. Another assumption implicit in this approach is that the relationship between education and economic growth is uni-directional, that is that education is a cause of economic growth. But in fact since education is also a result of economic growth, the resulting statistical estimates will tend to be biased.

Forecasts of manpower requirements may be obtained by simply asking existing employers what their manpower requirements will be at some time in the future. The method is sometimes used for obtaining forecasts of total employment, but more often it is limited to estimating requirements for employees with specific educational qualifications. It is worth noting that unless employers are asked to forecast their requirements at various wages, the forecasts cannot be interpreted as forecasts of manpower demand.

Several well known problems exist in the design and execution of any survey and these all apply to the employer forecasting method. These problems include ensuring adequate coverage of all firms, minimizing non-response and biased responses, asking meaningful and properly worded questions, and so on. In the employer forecasting method, some of these become particularly important. For example, if employers are simply asked to predict their manpower 'requirements', then we have no way of ensuring that they will all make the same assumption about the future course of events; hence their forecasts may be inconsistent. Even if we specified the assumptions to be adopted about the growth rate in different industries, firms may nevertheless make inconsistent assumptions about their individual shares in the market. Another problem is that we must decide how to weight the responses of the different firms in deriving the forecast of the total: some employers may base their forecasts on clearly specified development plans while others may base them on pure guesswork.

The employer forecasting method assumes that firms can foresee the effects of technological change on their required inputs. In effect this means that firms must be able to estimate the possibilities of substituting one type of manpower for the other in the future production of output. It is mainly because of these difficulties that the employer forecasting method has not in fact proved to be a popular way of estimating future manpower requirements.

Types of forecasts

Having briefly described some of the forecasting methods that are in use, we turn now to the problem of evaluating the accuracy of manpower forecasts. In the literature on manpower forecasting, the words 'forecast', 'projection' and 'prediction' have been used interchangeably to describe the estimated future quantity of manpower. The words have apparently been used to mean quite different things, but only a few authors have taken the trouble to spell out precise definitions.

For example, Blaug has defined a 'forecast' as 'a prediction that depends on the achievement of definite growth targets, that is, a statement of what would happen if economic growth were deliberately manipulated by government policy', and a 'projection' as 'the outcome of purely spontaneous forces, that is, *what will happen* in the normal course of events in an unplanned economy' (Blaug, 1970, p. 138). Meltz and Penz suggest that a 'forecast' depends 'upon an expectation that the complete set of assumptions upon which it has been made will be fulfilled', whereas a 'projection' is 'not a statement of what will happen, nor about what should happen . . . [but simply] . . . a statement of what could happen under given conditions' (Meltz and Penz, 1968, p. vii). Stone draws the same sort of distinction but employs a different terminology: a 'projection' is 'a possible picture of our economic future as detailed and complete as we can make it ...' while a 'prediction' says '. . . what is actually likely to happen' (Stone, 1970, p. 44). Parnes argues that 'it is necessary to distinguish first between an unconditional forecast to *predict* what the manpower structure at some future date will be, and a statement of what the future manpower structure *must* be if certain production targets are to be achieved. The estimates of future manpower requirements in the MRP reports are of the latter variety' (Parnes, 1962, p. 157).

Although these definitions differ slightly in detail, the authors all seem to be trying to draw a distinction between:

(i) outcomes which seem likely to happen *if* a specified course of action is taken; and

(ii) outcomes which seem actually likely to happen: the two are equivalent only if the course of action specified in the former is actually undertaken.

For example, we may estimate a future outcome, A, if real GNP grows by 8 per cent per annum; but if the most likely rate of growth of real GNP is 4 per cent per annum, the estimate A is clearly not the most likely outcome.

The reason for the distinction seems to centre on the degree of control exercised by planning authorities. Some outcomes are closely dependent on policy actions while others can be influenced by policy only to a limited extent. Thus, in the former case, we might derive the estimated outcomes associated with different policies, so that planners can choose the policy which will bring about a desirable outcome: in the latter case, however, we might try to predict the future value of a variable over which the state has little control but which affects another variable that is controlled by the state.

Some examples may help to clarify the distinction. The future demand for doctors in Britain can be directly influenced by the British Government since the supply of health services is almost exclusively in the hands of the state. On the other hand, the future demand for doctors in the United States depends partly on the price of medical care and on the level of incomes, and cannot therefore be directly controlled by the state; but we may nevertheless be interested in forecasting demand in order to plan the future supply of doctors which is regulated by state governments.

This distinction is to some extent arbitrary since control by the state exists to varying degrees over most economic variables. But it provides a convenient means of classifying forecasts into those in which the effects of policy are known to be large, and those in which the effects of policy are small or unknown. The problems of evaluation are different in the two cases: for example, in the first case we can try to estimate how much of an observed discrepancy between forecast and outcome arose because of wrong policy assumptions. For this reason, we feel that it is desirable for us to devise a shorthand method of describing the two types of estimates. 'Projection', 'forecast' and 'prediction' do not seem to be useful for this purpose since there is already much confusion in the literature about their respective meanings. We intend to use all three words interchangeably to describe the future value a variable is estimated to take. In addition, we define the following special cases:

(i) A *policy conditional forecast*[7] specifies the value of a dependent variable Y, given the value of an independent variable X, which is assumed to be determined by policy. Policy conditional forecasts may be based on a rule of thumb, or on judgement, or on an explicitly specified model, or on any combination of the three. For example, a policy conditional forecast of the requirements for doctors in Britain may be based on a rule of thumb that one doctor can treat the complaints of, say, 1,000 patients per year, or on a professional judgement of the medical needs of the population, or on a statistical model relating the requirements for doctors to the incidence of various diseases.

(ii) An *onlooker forecast*[8] specifies the likely value of a dependent variable Y on the assumption that all independent variables continue to change in the future as they did in the past. It is true that an onlooker forecast is strictly conditional on assumptions that are made about the development of exogenous variables, that is, variables over which the planner has no direct control. Nevertheless, we shall reserve the use of 'conditional' for the case defined in (i). Onlooker forecasts may also be based on a rule of thumb, or on judgement, or on an explicitly specified model, or on any combination of the three.

(iii) We define an *optimizing forecast* as one which will maximise (or minimize) a given objective function. Optimizing forecasts are generally obtained as solutions of programming models in which we specify an objective function involving the relevant variables and the constraints operating on them. For example, we may derive a set of

---

7 Tinbergen (1963, p. 13) has defined such a forecast as a 'plan'.
8 See Frisch (1961).

optimizing manpower forecasts by maximizing output measured by the contributions of the various types of manpower, given the constraints on the availability of manpower. In practice, however, manpower forecasts have not been derived from such models and they are therefore often not optimizing forecasts even though it is sometimes claimed that they are optimal in some sense.

On the evaluation of forecasts

Friedman (1966, p. 2) has argued that 'the only relevant test of the *validity* of a hypothesis is comparison of its predictions with experience'. Thus to test the validity of a hypothesis or model, we simply compare the forecasts of the model with actual outcomes. If the two differ, we reject the hypothesis; but if they are the same, we can only tentatively accept the hypothesis since future evidence may disprove it. For this reason, empirical evidence can never *prove* the validity of a hypothesis, but if the predictions turn out to be correct a large number of times, we develop greater confidence in its validity. Empirical testing also provides a means of identifying the sources of inaccuracy in a forecast, that is, why it differed from the outcome, and hence forms a basis for improving the model.

In the social sciences, hypotheses are seldom exact since human behaviour depends on a large number of factors which we do not fully understand or which are not easily measured. In this sense, models of human behaviour provide only approximations to actual behaviour and necessarily include unpredictable elements consisting of the effects of omitted variables. These effects are usually assumed to follow a random process: thus we often cannot reject or tentatively accept a hypothesis only on the basis of a few observations, since any observed inaccuracy may be a chance occurrence. Instead, we need to test the significance of the difference between forecast and outcome using statistical methods in an effort to minimize the probability of rejecting the hypothesis when it is true or of accepting it when it is false. The moment we allow for the presence of random disturbances in a quantitative model, the question of accuracy takes on new meaning. The existence of random disturbances means that a forecast will almost always differ from the actual outcome: but the forecast can only be regarded as inaccurate if the differences are statistically significant.

This concept of inaccuracy raises an important problem in the evaluation of forecasts, since we can always ensure that a model gives accurate predictions by including a sufficiently large disturbance term. But such a model is rarely useful for policy purposes because we have purchased accuracy at the expense of simplicity. Theil (1966, p. 2) has suggested that 'a forecast is useful when it reduces the level of uncertainty as to the actual outcome below the level of uncertainty that prevailed before the forecast was made'. Theil uses the term 'uncertainty' to mean the unpredicted variation or the variance of the disturbance term in the model: thus, using this criterion, we would choose between two accurate forecasting models on the basis of their deviations from predicted values, or, more accurately expressed, the variance of the disturbance term. Even if only one model is available, we can still test its past empirical performance by comparing its predictions with those of a naive 'no change' model. This in effect provides a test of whether or not the forecasts of the model have reduced the uncertainty below that which would have existed if we had only used current information.

This point is worth emphasizing to illustrate further the ambiguity of judging a forecast solely in terms of accuracy. Even a perfectly accurate forecast based on pure guesswork may be less useful for planning and policy than an inaccurate forecast obtained from a well-specified model. In the latter case, we are in a position to learn from our mistakes and to go on improving the quality of our forecasts, whereas in the former case we can only hope that we shall be as lucky next time.

Accuracy as a criterion for evaluating forecasting models, is entirely relative to the purposes for which forecasts are made. Cairncross (1969, p. 809) has argued that a forecast '. . . has to be judged in terms of the policy advice to which it leads, and not in terms of the accuracy of the forecast itself'. In other words, a forecast which reduces the uncertainty of a future outcome to a level that dictates a unique decision is clearly useful for policy purposes. On the other hand, if the range of uncertainty in the forecast is so large that contradictory policy decisions are compatible with it, then the forecast may be of little use for planning purposes. To take a concrete example, suppose that we are considering an expansion of higher education up to 1980 and we know that we must build new universities if we want to increase the number of graduates by more than 20 per cent; in these circumstances, it is of little use to be told that the demand for graduates by 1980 will be either 5 per cent or 40 per cent greater than it now is. All that this tells us is that the decision to build new universities may be the right one or the wrong one, which is something we already know before making the forecast. However,

24

the information that the future is as uncertain as this does have the virtue of warning us against taking irreversible decisions that commit substantial resources. If it costs nothing to make forecasts, little harm is done by even so inaccurate a prediction, particularly if it constitutes a first stage in a continuous activity which promises eventually to produce more accurate forecasts.

Strictly speaking, to assess the seriousness of inaccuracy in a forecast, we need to know the planner's preference function, as Theil (1966, p. 19) has emphasized; that is, we need to know the loss-value that is being attached to error. It is always possible, after all, to improve a forecast by collecting a vast amount of new information, but the costs of the improvement may far exceed the benefits of increased accuracy. Thus we need to look at the construction of a forecasting model in a cost-effectiveness framework by comparing the cost of making decisions without information about the future with the effectiveness of whatever information is provided.

The question we must ask ourselves therefore in trying to evaluate manpower forecasts is not whether or not they have differed from the outcome, but whether they have been sufficiently accurate for the purposes at hand. An inaccurate forecast that leads to an erroneous policy decision may be much worse than ignorance of the future, especially if the latter would have led to postponement of the decision. It is pointless to argue in general that forecasting is a desirable activity because there can be no harm in trying to reduce the uncertainty of the future. The question is whether we have actually succeeded in doing so without deceiving ourselves that the future is more certain than it actually is. We will see that it is not an easy question to answer decisively.

2. Canada

by Bashir Ahamad

The current interest of the Federal Government of Canada in manpower planning and employment policy can be traced back to the late fifties when the growth rate of the economy slackened and unemployment increased considerably. Structural unemployment became the focus of attention: several economists argued that the causes of unemployment were to be found in the functioning of the labour market, producing pockets of unemployment side by side with shortages of particular types of manpower. Their arguments were strengthened by empirical estimates of the contribution of labour to economic growth based on the methods developed in the US by Denison (1962): the estimates suggested that the quality of the labour force, as measured in terms of educational attainments, had limited the potential growth of the Canadian economy, (Bertram, 1966, p. 5).

As a result, the Economic Council of Canada recommended in its *First Annual Review* (1965) that there should be increased emphasis on education and training and that a separate authority should be set up for the systematic study of the various aspects of manpower and its utilization. The Council suggested that the objectives of this authority should be to co-ordinate the Federal Government's manpower programmes and employment policy in order to bring about a better matching of the demand and supply of labour in specific localities and occupations. This implies the removal of obstacles, both financial and institutional, to desirable labour mobility and the provision of adequate information about job opportunities in different areas and occupations.

In response to the Council's recommendation, the Federal Government created the Department of Manpower and Immigration in early 1966. The Department's jurisdiction was defined to include the operation of the Adult Occupational Training Act 1967, the Manpower Mobility Program, immigration control, the provision of labour market information through the Canada Manpower Centres, and so on. It is important to note, however, that planning formal education comes under the jurisdiction of the ten provincial governments: since the distinction between education and adult training is ill-defined, there is clearly ground for disagreement between the various governments on the division of responsibility. In contrast, the provincial governments may, and many have, set up their own authorities for dealing with manpower and employment problems. It is obvious that the objectives of the various governments will frequently conflict and in consequence so will the education and training programmes of the provincial governments and the Federal Government.

Canada's relatively small population of 20 million people is unevenly distributed over its vast land area and both population concentration and economic growth have broadly tended to follow the pattern of development of Canadian exports (Caves and Holton, 1959). In the post-war period, the once important primary industries — agriculture, forestry, fishing and mining — have become relatively less important: their share in total output has declined considerably and so have their absolute levels of employment. This has created severe employment problems in the areas particularly dependent on primary industries and hence has emphasized the need for an active manpower policy. But these employment problems cannot be easily solved because of the similarly uneven spatial development of the secondary and tertiary sectors of the economy.

The sheer physical size of Canada and the severe regional disparities in income and industrial structure are only some of the factors which limit the effectiveness of manpower policy in the country. Since the Canadian economy is highly influenced by that of the United States, partly because of its proximity to that country and partly because of the importance of the US both as a supplier of physical capital and as a market for exports, manpower policy has to be closely related to developments across the border. The existence of the French and English cultures is a further complication. Manpower programmes and policies must therefore take due account not only of economic factors but also of sociological and psychological barriers to the mobility of labour.

In order to achieve its operational aims, the Department of Manpower and Immigration has tried to improve its information about the current labour market situation and to broaden its basic research programme. The Canada Manpower Centres are scattered all over the country and they provide one of the best potential sources of information on current labour market shortages and surpluses; but their coverage of the market is still somewhat limited in that the *employed* labour force seldom seek their services. Current information on job vacancies is also collected at regular time intervals in a survey of employers.

The research programme in the Department covers a fairly extensive range of topics. These include cost-benefit analyses of manpower training programmes, specific occupation and industry studies, the impact of technological change, the economic determinants of immigration, the special employment problems of Canadian Indians and Eskimos, projections of occupational requirements, and so on. Manpower forecasts thus form part of the input for making decisions for manpower programmes though, as we shall see later on, they are used only as broad indicators of what the future may hold.

Forecasts of occupational requirements are often made in special industry, occupation or area studies but they form only a small part of such analysis. However, two special studies were designed expressly to provide projections of manpower requirements in all occupations in the Canadian economy. These are the studies with which we shall be concerned here.

Canada's manpower requirements in 1970

The aim of the study by Meltz and Penz (1968), entitled *Canada's Manpower Requirements in 1970*, was to determine the manpower implications of potential output projections for 1970 prepared by the Economic Council cf Canada in its *First Annual Review*. The Council's projections were medium-term and were based on the assumption that the economy would be operating close to its potential in 1970: the Council assumed that an unemployment rate of 3 per cent would be consistent with the assumption of maximum potential output. No account was taken of short-term fluctuations or cyclical effects so that the projections for a particular year like 1970 may be expected to deviate substantially from observations for that year. For example, it was clear in early 1970 that the unemployment rate for that year would be considerably higher than the 3 per cent rate assumed by the Council and this will, in turn, have affected the level of actual output in 1970.

The manpower projections in question were made in a crude and fairly mechanical way. For this reason, Meltz and Penz emphasized that the projections of manpower requirements did not necessarily represent the best way of meeting the goals proposed by the Council and hence that they could not be regarded as optimal in any sense. In effect, the projections provided only one of many equally reasonable ways of looking at the likely course of events. In our terminology, these are therefore 'policy conditional forecasts' since they are based on the goals proposed by the Council; but they are only one of the set of outcomes consistent with these goals.

The method used in the study broadly followed the MRP method (see Chapter 1). Projections of employment were made for each of 15 industries and these were translated into occupational requirements in 13 groups on the basis of the occupation—industry matrix, projected from past observations. Projections of educational requirements were obtained from the projected occupational requirements by making assumptions about the appropriate educational structure of each occupation.

Projections of employment by industry

Let us begin by considering the projections of employment. In its *First Annual Review*, the Economic Council of Canada prepared employment projections for four sectors in the economy: agriculture, public administration, community services and commercial non-agriculture. Total employment in these four sectors was derived from demographic projections on the basis of specified assumptions about fertility, mortality and net immigration; these were then transformed into labour force projections by applying projected age and sex specific participation rates and finally into employment estimates after allowing for a 3 per cent unemployment rate.

Various methods were used to disaggregate the total projections into projected employment in each of the four sectors. These were based on variations of the method of logarithmic trend extrapolation, except in the case of the commercial non-agriculture sector which was treated as a residual category. Meltz and Penz regarded this particular sector as far too heterogeneous for making manpower projections and they therefore further disaggregated its employment into 12 sub-sectors. Their method involved fitting regression equations of the form.

$$\frac{y_j}{y} = \alpha_j + \beta_j\, t + \gamma_j\, u + \delta_j\, u^2$$

where y = total employment in the commercial non-agriculture sector, y_j = employment in the jth sub-sector, t = time, u = the total unemployment rate (entered twice to allow for a non-linear relationship between y and u) and α_j, β_j, γ_j and δ_j are parameters for the jth sub-sector. The unemployment rate was used as a cyclical adjustor and also to ensure that the projections were consistent with the Economic Council's assumed unemployment rate of 3 per cent.

The equations were estimated using time-series data for both 1946-63 and 1952-63; the regressions where run in a step-wise manner by first including only t as the independent variable, then t and u, and finally t, u and u^2. The authors tried to choose the particular regression equation to be included in their analysis on the basis of three criteria: (a) a maximum coefficient of determination (R^2); (b) a Durbin—Watson statistic close to 2; and (c) a reasonable projection in the light of other qualitative information.

The coefficients of determination varied enormously for the two time periods and both within industries and between industries: for example, in the mining industry it varied from 0.01 to 0.57, while in finance it varied from 0.93 to 0.98. Similarly, the Durbin—Watson statistics and the projected levels of employment varied considerably for the two series. Because of the large unexplained variation in these results, the authors decided to use the equations only for the later time period. They argued that this was reasonable partly because of the greater reliability of more recent data and partly because of the unusual economic fluctuations in the immediate post-war period.

The difficulty the authors faced may be more clearly illustrated by considering some of the results in detail (see Table 2.1). The variation in the projections for 1970 is particularly striking both in percentage and absolute form. The range is more than 200,000 which is roughly 10 per cent of the maximum projection.

The authors were well aware of the difficulty of interpreting these results and suggested that the projections must be used with caution. From our point of view, the results are valuable in demonstrating that employment models based on the simple extrapolation of past trends may be highly sensitive to changes in the time period considered and in the variables included in fitting the regression line. In the absence of properly specified structural models, the true range of possibilities may be far wider than it is commonly believed to be on the basis of the standard errors of the regression estimates. Thus caution is advisable in the case of forecasts based on regression analysis: the use of fairly sophisticated statistical analysis may create the mistaken impression that such forecasts are highly reliable.

TABLE 2.1.

COEFFICIENTS OF DETERMINATION, DURBIN–WATSON STATISTICS
AND PROJECTIONS FOR THE MANUFACTURING SECTOR, CANADA, 1970

Time period	Equation	Coefficient of determination	Durbin–Watson statistic	Projected employment for 1970	
				Percentage	Thousands
	(1)	0.84	0.69	30.96	1,797
1946–63	(2)	0.83	0.71	30.53	1,772
	(3)	0.82	0.73	30.54	1,773
	(1)	0.56	1.53	32.94	1,912
1952–63	(2)	0.66	1.80	34.43	1.999
	(3)	0.62	1.85	34.65	2,011

Source: Meltz and Penz (1968), p. 12.
Note: Equation (1) includes only t; equation (2) includes t and u; and equation (3) includes t, u and u^2.

Projections of the occupational structure of industries

In Canada, data on the labour force cross-classified by occupation and industry are available only in census years. However since classifications of industries and occupations differ substantially from one point in time to another, such data are not directly comparable from one census to the other. To facilitate comparisons, the Dominion Bureau of Statistics has prepared tables which allow the conversion of existing census data from one classification basis to another. Thus before making projections of the occupational structure of each industry Meltz and Penz had to re-classify existing census data on a common basis to provide the necessary time-series (Meltz, 1969). The bases chosen were the 1951 census occupational classification and the 1948 Standard Industrial Classification; conversion tables for the more recent classifications were not available at the time the study was made.

It is important to note that the conversion procedure relates only to existing data and because of conceptual differences between the censuses, the data are still not strictly comparable. For example, in censuses before 1951 occupations were defined with respect to an individual's usual type of work; in the later censuses, however, occupations were defined with respect to the job held in the week

31

immediately preceding the census. Similarly it is clear that the work functions in any given occupation have changed over time so that the same occupation title might have had significantly different meanings at different points in time. Finally methods of data collection have been considerably improved over the years: differences in observations might have arisen because of improved classification procedures or reduced ocing errors, and so on. These limitations are important because of the long time lag between censuses and hence the likelihood of substantial changes in definition, concept and measurement from one census to the other.

In the above study, the census data for 1931, 1941 and 1961 were reclassified on the classification bases used in the 1951 census. These provided only four observations from which the occupational structure of each industry could be projected for 1970. For this reason the projections were obtained by visually fitting the 'best' straight line through the observations: the authors used as their informal criteria both the visual minimization of the deviations of the observations from the chosen line, and the consideration of special industry factors. Because of the subjective element in the second of these criteria, and because there are clearly a number of possible 'best' lines or curves that 'fit' the data, it is important for planning purposes to know what effects another chosen line would have had on the results: in other words it is important to investigate the sensitivity of the occupational requirements' projections to changes in the assumptions about the occupational structure of industries. The authors did not, however, carry out any sensitivity tests, and this necessarily limited the potential usefulness of their results for planning purposes.

Projections of the educational structure of occupations

Two alternative methods were used for making projections of educational requirements: the first involved projecting the educational structure of the stock of manpower, while the second involved projecting the educational structure only for new entrants to the labour force. In the latter case, the number of new entrants to each occupation was determined by subtracting the 1961 manpower stock, corrected for attrition from mortality and retirement from the occupational requirements in 1970.

In the first method census data were again used, although this time only for 1941, 1951 and 1961. In this case the problems of data comparability were much more serious than those in the occupation—industry data: for 1941 and 1951 the data referred to years of schooling whereas in 1961 they referred to the highest level of education attained. The authors assumed that the two concepts were directly comparable but they recognized that this introduced a bias into their projections. Once again the projections were made through the three census points in a fairly arbitrary manner.

In the second method, the projected manpower requirements for the 13 occupation groups were disaggregated into individual occupation classes. For those occupations for which data were available for more than one census, the disaggregation was carried out by projecting (a) the trend in the share of each occupation class in the relevant occupation group; or (b) the logarithmic trend in the size of the occupation class itself; or (c) the trend in the share of the occupation class in the total labour force. For those occupations for which data only existed for 1961, a complex weighting system based on the educational requirements and sizes of the various occupation groups was used.

The education and training required by employers of new entrants in the various occupational classes were estimated with the help of the Manpower Training Branch in the Department of Manpower and Immigration. The authors recognized that the specification of such requirements was an enormously difficult task and that there would clearly be large errors in the estimates. But they argued that in aggregating the educational requirements of the various occupation classes to arrive at the requirements for 13 occupation groups, many of the errors would cancel out. This is certainly true if the errors in the estimates can be assumed to be random: but if substantial non-random biases exist, the errors in aggregation can of course be cumulative.

Evaluation of the study

The projections obtained in the study represent the occupational and educational structure of the labour force required on the basis of assumptions about the structure of output and technology. They can only be interpreted as manpower demand projections if we make the restrictive, and perhaps unrealistic, assumption that the elasticities of substitution between the various types of manpower are approximately zero (see Chapter 1).

The authors of the study were perfectly frank about the limitations of their work and they suggested that it should be considered as experimental, providing only crude guidelines for decision-making.

33

This is the more so in that the projections refer only to Canada as a whole. Because of the wide regional disparities in income and output, manpower planning in Canada must clearly have a strong regional bias. National projections may provide reasonable planning guidelines for the more highly developed provinces but they may well be of less relevance in the less developed areas in which the more important and pressing manpower problems will tend to occur.

The empirical results of the study are perhaps more difficult to evaluate than its meaning for policy purposes. In theory, it is perfectly possible to analyse the projection errors of this study in order to determine which assumptions were wrong and to calculate their effects on the results. Such analysis obviously requires that the model employed be explicitly specified. In the present case, it is possible to determine the part of the total projection errors due to (a) erroneous projections of industrial employment, (b) wrong assumptions about the occupational structure of industries and (c) wrong assumptions about the educational structure of occupations; but we cannot then determine, say, how much of the error in the projected occupational structure was due to a mis-specification of the underlying model and how much was due to errors of judgement by the authors.

The time interval and classification problems already mentioned limit the possibility of empirically testing the results. Nevertheless there are clear signs that projections will be some way off the mark. For example, the projection of the total labour force used in the study was based on an Economic Council of Canada Staff Study made in 1963 (Denton *et al.*, 1965). The projection was revised upwards in 1967 after a more detailed study of trends in immigration and female participation rates (Illing *et al.*, 1967); it was further revised in 1968 on the basis of the results of the 1966 population sample census (George and Gnanasekaran, 1968). Thus it is clear that the manpower projections need to be substantially revised in an upwards direction.

Similarly, some of the assumptions made by the Economic Council of Canada in arriving at the projections in its *First Annual Review* have already been revised in subsequent Reviews (Economic Council of Canada, 1967); others still need revision. For example, the depressed state of world wheat markets since the mid-sixties suggests a more rapid decline in agricultural employment than had been previously assumed. Similarly, the tariff reductions under GATT in recent years, new oil discoveries in Alaska, the recent restrictions on Federal Government employment, and so on, will all affect the projections.

34

All of this suggests that attempts to test the empirical performance of the projections cannot really give much insight into their usefulness for planning. The real test is whether or not they made a contribution towards decision-making. This question may be postponed until we have looked at an attempt to improve on the work of Meltz and Penz.

A projection of manpower requirements in 1975: Canada and its regions

The more recent study by Ahamad was described as . . . an exploration of how the growth of the Canadian economy is capable of affecting the structure of the future requirements for manpower' (Ahamad, 1969, p. i). It followed the same basic methodology as the previous study but with some important modifications. Its purpose was to provide projections of manpower requirements in more than 200 occupation classes and groups; but no attempt was made to translate these into education and training requirements. Projections were made not only for the country as a whole but for each of the five economic regions: an attempt was also made to adjust the projections in accordance with 'informed opinion' about likely developments in each region. There was also much more emphasis on the substantial limitations of existing data and the enormous uncertainty involved in making the projections: some attempt was made to investigate the sensitivity of the projections to changes in the basic assumptions and to design a sensitivity scale for the guidance of planners. Finally the data used were classified on the occupational and industrial classifications used in the 1961 census, so that the projections made are comparable with current data published by the Dominion Bureau of Statistics.

As in the previous study, the method adopted was essentially that of the MRP: projections of employment were made for 12 industries and these were translated to occupational requirements in more than 200 occupation classes and groups. The minimum level of detail used corresponds to the three-digit classification in the International Standard Classification of Occupations. One of the major criticisms of this approach is that it assumed that the occupational structure of an industry is determined primarily by the state of technology in that industry and hence that the various types of manpower are used in rigid proportions (see Chapter 1). The author of this study took note of this criticism but denied its validity in view of the fact that an occupational category, as it is usually measured, in fact includes manpower with a wide variety of educational qualifications. Thus changes in relative wages may generate adjustments, not in the relative numbers employed in the different occupational categories, but in the relative numbers employed at different levels *within* the same categories.

Ahamad noted that the process of matching individuals and jobs is a very complex process about which we know very little. He argued that individuals possess characteristics which are necessary for the efficient performance of the duties, operations or work functions which are required for the production of output. An individual's occupation is defined in terms of the work he does and it is therefore determined with reference to his most important duty or operation. In adjusting to price changes, an employer may change the job of an individual and hence the particular combination of duties performed by the individual; but in doing so, his *most important* duty, which determines his occupation, may not be changed.

The point is that the assumption of a fixed occupational structure does not necessarily imply a rigidly determined manpower structure: since occupations are heterogeneous there may be a great deal of flexibility within occupations. The model outlined by the author is untested and may be invalid. But it does serve to suggest that the substitutability arguments against manpower forecasting may well have been exaggerated; at the same time, however, it highlights the difficulty of using manpower forecasts for educational policy.

Projections of employment by industry

Ahamad derived employment projections at the national level for almost all industries from independent projections of output and labour productivity; the latter was measured in terms of both output per man and output per man-hour but the two measures did not yield significantly different results. For public administration and fishing, the productivity approach did not provide a realistic method for making projections: in public administration, estimates of output are prepared from estimates of employment, while in fishing, employment and output are primarily determined by the weather and other vagaries of nature. In these two industries, employment was projected by making a direct extrapolation of the trend. This was also done in projecting employment by industry for each region, since estimates of output by industry and region were not available.

Obtaining an adequate time-series of employment by industry

presented a serious initial problem. In Canada, annual employment estimates are available from either a survey of the labour force or a survey of establishments. The former is based on a 1 per cent sample of households and has been extensively re-designed recently to improve its coverage (Fellegi *et al.*, 1967). The survey of establishments covers only paid employees in all firms with 15 or more employees but only about 10 per cent of those with less than 15 employees. The two surveys also differ markedly in concept; and a recent study has shown that even when the estimates have been corrected for coverage and concept, the substantial difference between them — 177,000 people — still remains unexplained. The employment estimates from the establishment survey were used in the Ahamad study because of the greater reliability of the industrial disaggregation; data from the labour force survey were however used to fill in the gaps in coverage.

The author felt that the seven observations which were all that were available since 1961 were too few for making the projections to 1975. However, quarterly estimates for the period 1961—64 suggested that the trends in industrial employment under the pre-1961 classification closely followed those under the new; estimates for the period 1953—60 were obtained by assuming that this relationship also held for that period.

These difficulties in a country with a well developed statistical system illustrate some of the enormous practical difficulties which exist in obtaining adequate time-series data. Ahamad emphasized these by making two alternative projections of employment for each industry.

Initially, projections were obtained by visually fitting the 'best' straight line through the logarithms of the observations. An attempt was also made to take account of special circumstances in certain industries: for example, the Economic Council of Canada (1967) has argued that much of the expansion in the manufacturing sector in the period 1961—66 was associated with the increasing use of capacity rather than with the growth of capacity itself. The initial projections were circulated to a number of economists in universities, industry and government departments; they were then modified to conform with some of the opinions expressed about the course of future developments. The modifications in question were quite large for the primary industries, particularly in some regions.

The extent of the modifications and the range of the two alternative projections for Canada are reproduced in Table 2.2. The range between the alternatives varies enormously from 45.2 per cent in fishing and trapping to —3.9 per cent in services.

TABLE 2.2

PROJECTED EMPOYMENT BY INDUSTRY, CANADA, 1975 (THOUSANDS)

Industry	Initial projections	Final projections Alternative (1)	Alternative (2)	Alternative 1 / Alternative 2 x
Agriculture	419.2	430.0	372.7	115.4
Forestry	78.0	73.3	61.0	120.2
Fishing and trapping	18.5	24.4	16.8	145.2
Mining, etc.	130.1	155.4	133.4	116.5
Manufacturing	1998.6	2000.8	1889.0	105.9
Construction	497.6	479.0	539.7	88.8
Transportation, etc.	656.0	627.8	681.3	92.1
Public utilities	86.1	85.6	81.5	105.0
Trade	1418.5	1353.0	1416.5	95.5
Finance, etc.	394.7	368.8	388.3	95.0
Service	2646.4	2630.0	2736.3	96.1
Public administration	502.8	598.0	·	·
Total	8847.0	8926.0	8914.4	100.0

Source: Ahamad (1969), p. 67.
Note: Only one projection was made for Public administration because of the difficulty in specifying a reasonable alternative.
· = not applicable

The final projections were based mainly on judgement and hence any empirical test of the forecast can tell us nothing about the basic quantitative model used. However, the large range in the alternative projections serve at any rate to emphasize the limitations of unique projections of employment by industry for planning purposes.

Projections of the occupational structure of each industry

As in the case of the Meltz and Penz study, the census data for 1941 and 1951 had to be re-classified on the basis of the classifications used in the 1961 census before projections could be made. As we noted in our earlier discussion, the procedure deals only with the re-classification of existing data so that differences in definition, concept and data collection may have introduced considerable biases in the time-series. Ahamad argued that the errors tend to some extent to cancel out one another in using the proportion that each cell in the occupation—industry matrix formed of total industry employment, but not sufficiently to eliminate all biases (Ahamad, 1970, p. 5).

38

The re-classification of the data is time consuming and therefore had to be limited to the occupation—industry matrix for the whole country — this alone took about six months — and the re-classification was not carried out for the regional matrices. For Canada as a whole, projections of the occupational structure of each industry were once again made by visually fitting the 'best' straight line through the logarithms of the observations. Since this was not possible for the five economic regions, Ahamad made the assumption that the rate of change of the occupational structure for a given industry for 1961—75 would be the same in every region as in Canada as a whole. For example, the rate of change in the proportion of managers in agriculture in Ontario was assumed to be the same as the rate of change in this ratio projected for all of Canada.

Thus the projected occupational requirements in each region depend on (a) the occupational structure in 1961; (b) the projected change in the national occupational structure; and (c) the projected industrial structure. It follows that the projected differences in the regional occupational requirements will depend on projected differences in the regional industrial structures and the 1961 observations of the differences in the regional occupational structure of each industry. Thus one of the weaknesses of the method is that it assumes that regional disparities will be reduced only as the industrial structures of regions change; it therefore takes no account of government policy designed to reduce regional disparities in other ways.

A further difficulty in obtaining regional projections in this way, as Ahamad noted, is that the method provides unrealistic results if the regional and national occupational structures of a particular industry are substantially different. This is certainly true of the primary industries so that the results had to be considerably altered on the basis of judgement. For example, the mining industry in the Prairie region is dominated by the oil industry while that of the Atlantic region is more traditional: professional and technical occupations form a much larger proportion of employment in the former, so that technical change will tend to have quite different effects on both structures.

Sensitivity analysis

Ahamad recognized that a unique projection of the occupational structure of each industry may not be of much use for planning purposes. He therefore attempted to investigate the sensitivity of the occupational projections to changes in both the occupational structure of industries and the industrial structure of employment.

For manpower planning purposes, the focus of attention is the projected manpower requirements in any occupation. If we let y_j be employment in the jth sector and a_{ij} be the proportion that employment in the ith occupation and jth sector forms of total employment in the jth sector, then manpower requirements in the ith occupation (x_i) will be given by

$$x_i = \sum_j a_{ij} y_j \quad (i=1 \ldots n, j=1 \ldots m)$$

that is, by the cross-products of the occupational structure and industrial employment summed over all industries. Since a_{ij} is a proportion, it follows that $0 \leqslant a_{ij} \leqslant 1$. Industrial employment may be considered to be similarly constrained within given limits; for example, total employment ($\Sigma_j \gamma_j$) may be constrained to equal the projected labour force less a projected or assumed level of unemployment.

Suppose that we change a given a_{ij}, say, a_{ik} by $\alpha\, a_{ik}$ then the corresponding change in the occupational requirements (x_i) is given by

$$\Delta x_i = \sum_{j/k} a_{ij} y_j + (a_{ik} + \alpha\, a_{ik}) (y_k) - \sum_j a_{ij} y_j$$

$$= \alpha\, a_{ik}\, y_k$$

The proportional change in x_i is given by

$$\frac{\Delta x_i}{x_i} = \alpha \left(\frac{a_{ik}\, y_k}{x_i} \right)$$

and hence depends on α and $a_{ik} y_k / x_i$. The latter represents the ratio of employment in a particular cell in the occupation—industry matrix to total employment in that occupation: it represents what might be called the 'degree of manpower concentration' of a given occupation across industries. Now, the smaller the 'degree of manpower concentration' and the more even the distribution of occupations across industries, the smaller will be the proportional change in the projected requirements. In other words, the projected requirements in occupations which are evenly distributed over industries will tend to be fairly insensitive to changes in the occupational structure coefficients. For example, the projection for the occupation, typists, which is fairly evenly distributed over industries will tend to be less sensitive to changes in the coefficients than the projection for the occupation, university teachers, which appears only in the service industry.

The proportional change in a_{ik}, i.e. α, is also important in determining $\Delta x_i/x_i$. Since $0 \leqslant a_{ij} \leqslant 1$, α will be small for large a_{ij} and large for small a_{ij}. For example, for $a_{ik} = 0.8$ the maximum possible range of α is from -1 to $+1/8$, while for $a_{ik} = 0.2$, α can vary from -1 to $+5$; in practice, of course, the *reasonable* range may be a good deal smaller. Thus the sensitivity of the projected occupational requirements will also depend on the size of a_{ik}, that is, on the relative importance of an occupation in any industry: the projection for occupations which are relatively important in a given industry will tend to be less sensitive to changes in the coefficients. For example, farmers form a large part of total employment in agriculture, so that the projection of farmers will be fairly insensitive to changes in the relevant coefficient; but millers form only a small proportion of employment in the manufacturing industry, so that the projection for millers will be highly sensitive to changes in the proportion.

The next step was to try to put these results in a meaningful form so as to provide some guidance for planning purposes. To do so the author constructed a sensitivity scale based on a_{ij} and $a_{ik}y_k/x_i$; this could not be done in an objective way and after some graphical experimentation, it was decided to assign a sensitivity scale to the projections on the basis of the figures in Table 2.3. The scale was based on the minimum value of $a_{ij}y_j/x_i$ for the given occupation and the size of the corresponding a_{ij}. The minimum value of $a_{ij}y_j/x_i$ for a

TABLE 2.3

SENSITIVITY SCALE FOR OCCUPATIONAL REQUIRE-MENTS, CANADA (percent)

Scale	Minimum $\dfrac{a_{ij} y_j}{x_i}$	Corresponding a_{ij}
A	2.0–	2.0–99.9
B	2.0–	0.0– 1.9
	1.0–1.9	20.0–99.9
C	1.0–1.9	2.0–19.9
D	1.2–1.9	0.0– 1.9
E	1.0–1.1	0.0– 1.9

Source: Ahamad (1969), p. 113.

41

given occupation reflects the distribution of the particular occupation over industries: if the minimum equals one, then the occupation appears only in one industry. Thus the scale is based on (a) consideration of the distribution of a given occupation over industries and (b) the relative importance of the occupation in the most important industry.

What the sensitivity scale says is this: the projections for occupations with an A or B scale value may give a fairly reliable indication of the range of likely developments; but the projections with a D or E value are highly sensitive to changes in the assumptions and may not provide a reliable guide for planning purposes. On this basis about 25 per cent of the projections can be considered to be fairly reliable while 35 per cent must be regarded as highly unreliable.

Ahamad concedes that the sensitivity scale is not completely satisfactory and that it would have been much better to investigate the variation in the projections to simulated changes in the coefficients[1]. The scale was based to some extent on personal judgement and to that extent there is an arbitrary element in it. However, it does serve a useful purpose in encouraging a more sophisticated interpretation of the degree of reliability of manpower forecasts.

Further testing of the model and results

Throughout the study, Ahamad tried to assess the reliability of the results by comparing them with other projections. For example, the projection of total output was compared with a projection of GNP made by the Economic Council of Canada. An attempt was also made to test the underlying model by making projections for past census years and by comparing these with actual observations.

One of the basic assumptions of the MRP approach to manpower forecasting is that the occupational structures of occupations change only slowly over time in response to technical change. Ahamad argued that if this assumption is valid then an observed occupation—industry matrix should provide a reasonable basis for projections of derived occupational requirements. He therefore derived 'projections' for 1951 by using the occupational structures observed in 1941 with the industrial structure observed in 1951; these were then compared with actual employment in each occupation in 1951 to provide an indication of the predictive accuracy of the 1941 occupation—industry matrix. Similarly, the accuracy of the 1951 matrix in

---

[1] See Ahamad and Scott (1972) for an improvement in this method.

predicting occupational employment in 1961 was tested in the same way.

The results of the two exercises are given in Table 2.4. This shows the distributions of the projection errors (in both absolute and percentage form, irrespective of signs) for all occupations included in the study. For both years, about one-third of the absolute projection errors fell in the range ± 1,000; in only 10 to 15 per cent of the projections were the errors greater than ± 15,000: the latter were

TABLE 2.4

DISTRIBUTIONS OF PROJECTION ERRORS CANADA 1951 AND 1961

Absolute error			Percentage error		
Range (numbers)	1951 per cent	1961 per cent	Range	1951	1961
0— 999	33.1	35.3	0— 4	16.9	18.1
1000— 2499	19.8	22.0	5— 9	14.5	20.4
2500— 4999	10.7	15.6	10—14	17.8	12.8
5000— 9999	15.7	12.1	15—19	8.0	10.0
10000—14999	5.0	4.6	20—24	12.1	6.4
15000—	15.7	10.4	25—	30.7	32.2
Total	100.0	100.0	Total	100.0	100.0

Source: Ahamad (1969) p. 120, and Ahamad (1970)
Note: Figures are based on 121 and 173 occupation classes and groups for 1951 and 1961, respectively.

associated with the larger occupation groups, so that even here the percentage errors were relatively small. Similarly, roughly one-third of the percentage projection errors fell in the range ± 10 per cent while three-quarters of them fell in the range ± 25 per cent.

For planning purposes, absolute errors as well as percentage errors may be important; in any case, errors of these magnitudes will be acceptable for some purposes but not for others. Nevertheless, Ahamad concluded that the results provide strong support for the MRP model, especially since only 12 industries were included in the analysis.

Further tests were carried out by making projections for 1967 and by graphically comparing these with observations of employment in 12 occupation divisions obtained from the labour force sample survey. The comparison could only be approximate since data for 1967 include sampling errors and they differ in concept, definition and coverage from the data used for making the projections. The projections do however appear to be reasonably accurate (Ahamad, 1969, pp. 122—3).

Use of the projections

The projections of occupational requirements in 1975 represent the projected stock of manpower required in each occupation in that year. Ahamad then calculated the 'required manpower inflow', defined as the 1975 stock less the 1961 stock after correcting for attrition from mortality and retirement in the period to 1975. The required manpower inflow thus represents the amount of manpower which has to be provided in each occupation if the assumed technological manpower requirements for 1975 are to be met. The required manpower inflow concept is set out in tabular form in Table 2.5.

The table presents an attempt to separate out the different manpower flows which contribute to the stock at any given time. It shows that there are several different sources from which the manpower requirements in 1975 may be met: by new entrants to the given occupation, by government planned occupational mobility; by free market occupational mobility, by inter-regional migration and by immigration. This emphasizes the fact that the required manpower inflow cannot simply be equated with educational and training requirements since the manpower gap in an occupation may be completely filled by the working of the labour market without the need for policy intervention.

Ahamad comments that:

'Our knowledge of the working of the labour market and hence about the potential manpower available from the various sources is incomplete. There is therefore clearly a risk that intervention may occur when it is not needed, or that policy measures may be inadequate. Thus there may be over- or under-adjustment, and manpower gaps may still appear in the future. The development of more reliable and appropriate indicators of current occupation shortages and surpluses thus become important in detecting at a fairly early stage those occupations in which maladjustment is taking place so that the necessary corrective action may be taken' (Ahamad, 1969, p. 151).

44

TABLE 2.5

REQUIREMENT AND RESOURCES FOR A GIVEN OCCUPATION AND REGION, CANADA, 1975

Requirements		Resources	
Manpower requirements 1975		Additions less withdrawals from labour force 1961—75	
less:	1961 manpower stock less mortality and retirement 1961—75	plus:	Entrants from re-training programmes, 1961—75
		plus:	Market transfers from, less market transfers to, other occupations, 1961—75
		plus:	Migration from, less migration to, other regions, 1961—75
		plus:	Immigration to, less emigration from Canada, 1961—75
Equals:	Required manpower inflow 1961—75	Equals:	Additional manpower resources 1961—75

Source: Ahamad (1969) p. 140

General assessment

The two studies we have examined here were highly experimental and were partly aimed at throwing up important issues for future research. The first provided only national occupation projections and an attempt was made to translate these into educational requirements. The second proceeded a step further and provided regional projections; no attempt was made to translate these into education and training requirements since it was felt that knowledge of the sources of manpower supply to the various occupations is far too incomplete to allow this.

Both studies suffer from several important limitations. First of all, the projections were based on simple time extrapolations of observations which represent the interaction of both demand and supply effects. For this reason the projections represent *ex-post* realizations rather than *ex-ante* demand. They have been interpreted as providing technical manpower requirements and hence are based on the assumption that the manpower structure of the economy is largely determined by the state of technology.

This fixed—coefficients approach has been criticized on the grounds that it assumes an implausible degree of rigidity in the manpower structure of an economy. But it cannot be denied that the approach provides a useful first approximation for building quantitative models. The effects of price changes and' of substitution possibilities — and of course of omitted variables — can be introduced in the model by assuming different values for the fixed coefficients. In this way we can provide a range of possible outcomes and hence improve the usefulness of the forecasts for planning and policy.

In the second place, the models used are only partial representations of the economy and they ignore the strong interdependence that exists between manpower variables and the economic structure of a country. Ahamad made some attempt to allow for this through the introduction of judgement and qualitative economic information. The disadvantage of such an approach is that it necessarily introduces arbitrary elements into the forecasts; but since quantitative models are merely simple approximations of reality and not fundamental laws which behaviour *must* follow, we obviously can never exclude the use of judgement in making forecasts, or indeed in any economic analysis. Several Federal Government departments in Canada are currently jointly engaged in building a medium-term input—output model of the economy. This suggests that partial models of the economy may be less of a problem in the future.

The adequacy of available data also seemed to present enormous problems in the two studies. Differences in concept, definition, classification and coverage were often large enough to invalidate the numerical significance of the projections. Annual estimates of employment were available from two surveys but these differed considerably. Data on detailed occupations were only available for census years, at ten-year intervals, and only three or four of the most recent censuses were believed to be adequate for projecting the occupational structure of each industry. Trends were therefore difficult to establish and this must have contributed to large projection errors. More numerous, accurate and up-to-date time-series data will probably considerably improve the reliability of future projections.

Associated with this problem is the need to provide projections at a sufficiently disaggregated level that they can be useful in the decision—making process. Decisions have to be made at the national level but also for smaller regions and for specifically defined skills. The broad projections made so far can only be of indirect use for decision-making in the solution of particular manpower problems.

Even in making aggregate projections, several technical problems remain to be solved. For example, total employment projections have been obtained from output projections on the basis of projections of labour productivity; but labour productivity appears to grow at substantially different rates at different points in time so that such projections are necessarily subject to large error.

In Ahamad's study, it was explicitly recognized that the projected occupational requirements cannot be easily related to educational and training requirements. The fact that the projected requirements can be met from a variety of sources complicates the direct usefulness of the projections in formulating policy.

It is clear that decision-making for manpower policy and programmes is a complex process and it is therefore extremely difficult to separate out the effects on official policy — if any — of a forecasting exercise. This is true in Canada not only because of the difficulty of co-ordinating the policies of the Federal Government with those of the provincial governments but also because the continuous flow of current information undoubtedly has an independent impact on decision-making. The Canada Manpower Centres provide most of the information about current labour market trends, especially for local areas and for specific skills. The Department of Manpower and Immigration tries to co-ordinate all the information available in the Centres — both qualitative and quantitative — in order to make decisions about grants under the Adult Occupational Training Act 1967, immigration control, career counselling, and so on. Although these data are close to particular labour markets, they suffer from cyclical and other short-term and spatial fluctuations, and their coverage tends to be mainly restricted to the unemployed. Medium-term projections provide a longer-term and wider perspective for checking decisions made on the basis of current information. But other research activities in the Department, for example cost-benefit analyses of manpower training programmes, special occupation studies, and so on, may have a similar influence on decision-making.

Perhaps the main conclusion we can draw from Canadian experience with the MRP manpower forecasting model is that the application of the model is still fraught with important practical problems. It seems clear that the model can provide only an experimental basis for investigating some of the effects of the changing structure of the economy on the structure of employment. Forecasts based on the model may be very approximate and hence can be used only as broad indicators for planning purposes: for this reason, it seems important that such forecasts should not form the sole basis for formulating policy and that they should be properly integrated with other kinds of analysis in order to arrive at the best policy decisions.

3. The United States

by Kenneth Gannicott and Mark Blaug

When Boulding in 1953 condemned manpower forecasting as 'facistic and communistic and unfitting company for the minds of the young' (Boulding, 1953, p. 30), the practice of manpower forecasting was still an infant industry in the United States. It is clear that this condemnation has not deterred most practitioners of the art: the number of American forecasts of future manpower requirements sharply accelerated during the 1960's as part of an unprecendented interest in manpower planning. A growing number of books and articles have attempted a preliminary evaluation of the federal manpower programme (Wolfbein, 1967; Mangum, 1969; and Somers and Wood, 1969) but almost without exception these studies have concentrated on assessing what might be called the social welfare aspect of manpower policy; the creation of education, training and employment opportunities for disadvantaged and low-income groups. But the 1960's were also a time of considerable federal concern with alleged shortages of qualified scientific, health and teaching manpower. Increasingly, the simultaneous shortage of technically trained manpower and the high unemployment rate of poorly educated workers came to be heralded as twin manifestations of a 'manpower revolution.' The shock of the initial Russian space successes and America's subsequent decision to put men on the moon before 1970 added force to earlier beliefs about a prevailing shortage of scientific and engineering manpower. At the same time, the concern of the Kennedy administration with the apparently intractable unemployment problem, and the finding that the unemployed were largely high school drop-outs, created fears of a new era of general unemployment that would prove resistant to the Keynesian measures advocated by the Council of Economic Advisers. These fears of accelerating economic and technological change generated a demand for a variety of warning systems, manpower forecasts and forecasts of the economic and social impact of technology.

The reduction in unemployment since the 1964 tax cut has taken some of the heat out of the structural debate but the concern with monitoring the future supply and demand of educated manpower remains. The increased federal intervention of the last few years, whether arising from 'Great Society' welfare and education programmes, the manpower demands of the Vietnam War, or the disbursement of R & D funds, has encouraged the development of manpower forecasting. The persistent theme of these forecasts of the need for more and better education and training at all levels provided the backdrop for the National Defense Education Act of 1963 (and its later expansion) and of the Higher Education Facilities Act of that year. In turn, the welfare and education oriented policies of the 'New Frontier' and the 'Great Society' have themselves encouraged forecasting activities so as to evaluate the feasibility of these programmes. The Vocational Education Act of 1963, Section 5(a) 4, requires state vocational boards, in co-operation with the public employment service, to make available 'occupational information regarding reasonable prospects of employment in the community and elsewhere'. Similarly, the Manpower Development and Training Act of 1962 requires the Secretary of Labor to present annually to the President 'a report pertaining to manpower requirements, resources, use and training'.

Despite this burgeoning federal interest in forecasting manpower requirements, academic economists in America have for the most part either ignored the activities of their government colleagues or treated their efforts with extreme cynicism. This is not because of any lack of interest in the subject of educated manpower: that growth industry of the 1960's, the economics of education, testifies to their concern. But opinions about the manpower forecasting approach have ranged from the mildly critical flavour of two recent symposia on the subject (March, 1966 and *Journal of Human Resources*, Spring, 1967) to Anderson and Bowman's scathing dismissal of planners who ignore the adjustment mechanism of markets as mere 'technicians' (Anderson and Bowman, 1967, p. 35). Not that such criticism has emanated only from academic economists. A federal investigation into its own projections resulted in an extremely critical review of the state of the art.[1] The report concluded that

---

[1] This was carried out by a Working Group on Manpower Projections of the President's Committee on Manpower (1967). The Committee, with the Secretary of Labor as chairman, is composed of the heads of various federal agencies whose activities have a significant impact on the demand, supply and utilization of labour. The Committee assists the Secretary of Labor in carrying out federal functions under the Manpower Development and Training Act of 1962.

49

many projections gave insufficient recognition to the critical role of the assumptions used, that projections were often made on a hasty *ad hoc* basis to guide immediate policy determination, and that poor communications between different agencies resulted in duplication of (often inconsistent) projections. Moreover, the Working Group demonstrated that insufficient attention had been paid to providing alternative projections, to estimating the range of uncertainty of the projections and to problems of evaluation by objective standards. Among its particular recommendations, the Group called for a strengthening of the data base so as to clarify the relationship between school enrolments, degrees, job requirements and occupational mobility (Working Group on Manpower Projections, 1967, pp. 11—18). Indeed, one member of the Group, in a personal comment on the Group's report, concluded that the fundamental problem was that 'the demands . . . made upon economics and statistics for reasonable projections in the manpower area have probably outrun the ability of these disciplines to supply them' (Lukaczer, 1968, p. 247).

Our purpose here is to carry out a further technical assessment of some of these projections. We write from a frankly sceptical viewpoint. We believe that our evaluation lends strong support to the Working Group's comments; it demonstrates that recent projections have done little to allay those criticisms. This does not mean that we shall simply tread the same ground as the Group: the Group's survey was necessarily very general and we have instead based our assessment on a detailed evaluation of a limited number of projections. At the same time, our purpose is a little different from that of such writers as Lee Hansen and Cartter, whose analyses of manpower projections for specific occupational groups have usually been part of an investigation into the meaning and size of shortages of these groups (Hansen, 1965 and 1967; Cartter, 1966). Our concern is rather with the development of manpower forecasting as such and the role it has played in the United States in the last 10 years. Nevertheless, it will be obvious how much this paper owes to the pioneering work of Hansen and Cartter and in what follows we shall draw liberally upon their work.

One reason for our particular focus is that there has been a change in the nature of American manpower projections since about 1960. Most recent American work in this field starts from a demographic projection and works through labour force estimates, unemployment levels and productivity assumptions to reach an estimate of GNP. This is a 'supply side' or 'capacity approach' and is entirely consist-

50

ent with the characteristic American attitude towards educational and manpower planning: the supply of labour is taken as the independent variable and the problem is to assess the implications of the growth of the labour force for GNP. This is precisely the opposite method from, say, that of the MRP where a target rate of growth of GNP is taken as exogenously determined and the labour supply required to attain that growth rate is calculated.[2] We would expect, therefore, that U.S. efforts in this field would fall in the category of what we have called 'onlooker forecasts'. Earlier American work was definitely of this sort. Harris' attempt to predict the future supply and demand of college graduates (Harris, 1949) and Wolfle's estimate of future needs for scientists (Wolfle, 1954) were pioneering efforts. A postmortem of these projections demonstrated their uniform tendency to under-estimate future enrolments (Rivlin, 1961); even Wolfle's estimate, which was closer than most, under-estimated bachelor's degrees 10 years later by about 15 per cent and doctorates by over 50 per cent.[3] But as Folger pointed out in his survey of these early efforts, such projections reflected the prevailing attitudes of the 1950's: 'planners concentrated on the immediate and more easily defined problems of enrolment increases and needs for money'; this

---

[2] Of course, no sensible country would choose a target rate of growth of GNP completely independent of plausible labour force and productivity estimates. In this sense, American practice in deriving the 'resource potential' of the economy is no different from anyone else's. Nevertheless, there is a profound difference of emphasis between the American practice of calculating a 'full employment GNP', whatever that may be, and the British attempt in 1964 to conform to the OECD target rate of increase of GNP of 4 per cent per year, culminating in a projected shortfall of manpower of 200,000. Was the assumption of 4 per cent growth unrealistic?; if not, where were the extra 200,000 workers supposed to come from?

[3] An interesting example of projections which had a better record of accuracy is the *Occupational Outlook Handbook* which the Bureau of Labor Statistics has been publishing biannually since 1937. The *Handbook* is a compilation of employment projections for many different occupations together with much useful information on salaries and promotion prospects, and is widely used for vocational counselling. They are certainly 'onlooker forecasts': the BLS makes no judgement of its own, implicit or otherwise, about the desirability of students entering one field rather than another. Using 1960 census data to test the predictions of the 1949 *Handbook*, Goldstein (1963, p. 1137), showed that the *Handbook* was successful in three out of four cases in projecting both the direction and relative magnitude of changes in employment by occupation and industry. He admits, however, that the broad categories used in the projections (a five-point scale ranging from 'no-growth or decline' to 'rapid growth') may conceal larger errors.

51

was consistent with the idea that 'people should be free to choose the field of work they want to enter and with the implicit assumption that these choices would generally lead to an adequate distribution of persons to jobs' (Folger, 1967, p. 204).

Although the same basic methodology is used in more recent work, there has been a strong shift of emphasis towards 'policy conditional forecasting' in our sense of the term: instead of assessing the likely outcome of autonomous supply changes, the focus has shifted to the forecasting of manpower 'requirements', so that they can be analysed in terms of available resources. The usual implication is that if resources do not meet requirements, something must be done on the supply side to remedy the situation. In short, there has been a growing tendency to regard the demand for labour as given, instead of examining the way supply and demand will reach an equilibrium through changes in wages and costs. In part, this is in the nature of the beast: the 'capacity approach' implicitly includes some estimates of prospective demand, since labour force participation rates, unemployment rates and productivity assumptions are dependent on such estimates. Moreover, the switch in emphasis is hardly surprising when one considers that forecasts do not compare objective supply and demand, but supply and the value-laden concept of 'requirements' or 'needs'. Insofar as this comparison simply represents the priority accorded to economic growth and anything believed to contribute to it, it is not of course applicable only to America. But we shall try to show that the result in the United States has been the emergence of a hybrid which embraces the language and method of Parnesian manpower forecasting without, however, assigning any precise role to a central forecast of requirements in a country where educational planning is decentralized and where the expansion of tertiary education is more or less determined by the private demand of students.

This does not mean that there is difficulty in discovering the stated objectives of the forecasts: the many reasons why the federal government has embarked on an ambitious programme of manpower forecasts are implicit and obvious from what has been said earlier. We can even, following Goldstein (1966, p. 17), make these objectives explicit and classify them formally as (1) planning educational programmes and estimating what expansions in enrolments must be provided for in order to meet future needs for trained workers; (2) evaluating the feasibility of launching new programmes requiring skilled personnel; (3) vocational guidance of individuals; and (4) developing manpower programmes and policies. The real difficulty, as Mangum points out, is that to 'naively expect to evaluate manpower programs (in America) by the goals enumerated as motivation for legislative action . . . would assume a cold rationality that the legislative process neither aspires to nor attains' (Mangum, 1969, p. 7). The growth of forecasts of manpower requirements in the United States is instead much more usefully understood as part of what Siegel has described as the trend towards a 'monitored' economy, in which the federal government exercises an increasingly more positive and wider co-ordinating role. The main characteristic of the 'monitored' economy, according to Siegel (1966, pp. 272–77) is

'the use of government power to define a comprehensive master objective or small cluster of dominant "national goals", to set "targets" relating thereto, and to pursue these aims with deliberativeness . . . primarily by exhortation of the private sector. In the "monitored" economy, formal detailed planning is not attempted for society, although quantitative and other simplified forecasting "models" may be used as aids in public and private policy design. Heavy stress continues to be placed there on private initiative and money incentives, and wide latitude remains for freedom of economic choice and action . . . On the whole, the people may seem, like Macbeth following the dagger, to be marshalled where they were already going. The targets indicate general directions rather than personal quotas . . . and projections that are judged desirable are expected to derive a self-fulfilling impetus from the responses of the private sector, and corrective private responses are expected to be induced by the announcement of national prospects regarded as objectionable. In addition, government has to "plan" its own complements to such private responses, which may not be deemed sufficient for attainment of established national targets'.[4]

It is this increasing federal involvement which accounts for the shift from onlooker to policy conditional forecasts. Moreover, Siegel's analysis exemplifies Mangum's warning about naively expecting to evaluate American manpower programmes in terms of their stated

---

[4] Siegel's article was not concerned so much with manpower forecasts as with the 'meaning and use of productivity statistics in the light of policy requirements concerning employment and wage price stabilization in our evolving economy'. We believe that many of his comments on productivity statistics also apply to manpower forecasts. Even the lengthy quotation above does not really do justice to his subtle analysis of the changing federal role and its impact on statistical requirements, and the reader is referred to the original article.

objectives. He shows clearly the open-ended nature of the federal role and the extent to which its involvement in the outcome of a forecast is so much more indirect, diffuse and dependent on moral suasion than is the case in, say, Britain or Sweden. It is precisely because the federal government has to be ready 'to "plan" its own complements' to a very wide variety of possible 'corrective private responses', that federal agencies will feel the need for many more 'quantitative and other simplified forecasting "models"' than if the targets were precise, the planning process institutionalized and decision-making centralized. To carry this paradox to its logical conclusion, there is virtually no limit to the amount of 'monitoring' the various federal agencies will feel it necessary to carry out, and the collection of manpower data and the construction of 'models' will then come to be undertaken for their own sake. Manpower forecasting thus becomes an end in itself, and the 'objectives' classified above by Goldstein are revealed as simply the rationalization of an activity pursued for quite different reasons. This does not imply that the authors of such forecasts do not genuinely believe that their work contributes to these ostensible objectives. But it does mean that there will almost certainly be no critical test of that belief, and where the carrying out of an activity is itself sufficient justification for that activity, we should not be surprised if the forecasts come ultimately to lack any operational content.

But we have said enough by way of introduction: it is time to get down to cases. We start by analysing the economy-wide forecasts in the Manpower Reports of the President 1963 and 1965; we move on to consider some attempts to forecast the supply and demand of particular categories of high-level manpower and we conclude by looking at some recent developments. It may be thought contentious to concentrate on the work of the Bureau of Labor Statistics of the Departmen of Labor, but we have not been comprehensive because no useful purpose is served by discussing all the many forecasts that have been made by academic research workers and private organizations. Instead we concentrate on the best examples of the art.

The Manpower Reports of the President 1963 and 1965

As we indicated earlier, the first stage of Department of Labor forecasts is to project the growth of the total labour force on various assumptions about the future level of employment, the size of the armed forces, and so on and to assess the implications for the rate of growth of GNP. The scheme below summarizes the various steps in the calculation:

(1) Total population by age and sex × Participation rate for each age-sex group = Total labour force
(2) Total labour force − Armed forces = Civilian labour force
(3) Civilian labour force − Unemployment = Employed civilian workers
(4) Employed civilian workers × Average hours of work per year = Total manhours worked
(5) Total manhours worked × Money value of output per manhour = GNP.

Once the future level of economic activity has been calculated, the next step is to distribute the production and employment estimates among the various industrial sectors. As the 1963 Manpower Report points out, this was done in a variety of ways. In some industries, future activity levels were estimated by analysing their past relationship to GNP or one of its major components, such as personal consumption expenditures. In most industries, however, the method seems to have been to use regression techniques to analyse the past relationships between employment in each industry and total employment. These regressions were then modified after discussions with industry and union representatives. The results are shown in Table 3.1.

Let us leave analysis of this table on one side for a moment and turn to the derivation of employment by occupation. The method was straightforward. Occupational ratios − the fraction of employment in a specific occupation in the total employment of the industry in the base year 1960—were multiplied by the industry employment estimates for 1970 and 1975. This gives the number of workers required by 1970 and 1975 in each occupation in each industry of the economy. The numbers in a given occupation in each industry were then summed to give the total number of workers in that occupation. The results are shown in Table 3.2.

One feature of the tables is immediately obvious. They both reflect the anxiety felt at this time (1963) about the predicted slow rate of growth of employment in manufacturing industry and about the different opportunities for professional and technical occupations on the one hand, and unskilled blue-collar workers ('operatives and kindred'), on the other. Table 3.1 indicates that apart from transportation and mining, employment in manufacturing industry was expected to be the slowest growing of all major sectors during

TABLE 3.1

EMPLOYMENT BY MAJOR INDUSTRY DIVISION, UNITED STATES, 1960—75

Industry division	Employment (millions)			Percentage change 1960—75
	1960 actual	1970 projected	1975 projected	
Manufacturing	16.8	19.2	20.3	21
Contract construction	2.9	4.0	4.4	52
Mining	0.7	0.7	0.7	—
Wholesale and retail trade	11.4	14.0	15.6	37
Government	8.5	11.5	12.8	51
Service and miscellaneous	7.4	10.2	11.9	61
Transport and public utilities	4.0	4.4	4.5	13
Finance, insurance and real estate	2.7	3.5	3.9	44
Total	54.3	67.7	74.2	37

Source: Department of Labor (1963), p. 95.
— = nil or negligible.

TABLE 3.2

EMPLOYMENT BY MAJOR OCCUPATIONAL GROUP, UNITED STATES, 1960—75

Major occupation group	Number (millions)			Percentage change 1960—75
	1960 Actual	1970 Forecast	1975 Forecast	
Professional, technical and kindred	7.5	10.7	12.4	65
Managers and proprietors	7.1	8.6	9.4	32
Clerical and kindred	9.8	12.8	14.2	45
Sales workers	4.4	5.4	5.9	34
Craftsmen and foremen	8.6	10.3	11.2	30
Operatives	12.0	13.6	14.2	18
Service workers	8.3	11.1	12.5	51
Labourers, except farm and mine	3.7	3.7	3.7	—
Farm workers and managers	5.4	4.2	33.9	—28
Total	66.7	80.5	87.6	31

Source: Department of Labor (1963), p. 100.
— = nil or negligible.

56

the forecast period. Similarly, Table 3.2 suggests that while employment of high-level occupations will rise by 65 per cent between 1960 and 1975, employment of the blue-collar workers, the largest occupational group in absolute terms, will rise by the smallest percentage increase except for agricultural workers.

But how reliable were these findings? Testing their reliability is extremely difficult as the Manpower Report supplies little data other than those already given. It is, for instance, virtually impossible to test the industry employment forecasts. We have already indicated that these were calculated by a variety of methods, but even in the technical appendix there is nothing to indicate the projected composition of final demand, the productivity measures used, and the results of the regression equations. To go back one stage, these estimates depend in the final analysis on the successful projection of total population. As we shall see in Chapter 8, projecting total population even a few years ahead can be a very hazardous business. How much more difficult then to predict participation rates! Yet there is no indication in the Manpower Report of the sensitivity of the employment forecasts to the labour force estimates. This was a serious omission, for only a year later the Bureau of the Census published revised population growth figures. Although revisions in the projection of total population in 1970 were expected to bring a 350,000 reduction in the 1970 labour force, this was more than offset by an expected increase of 650,000 from higher labour force participation rates for women (Cooper and Johnston, 1965, p. 14). The net change in the labour force was thus only 300,000, not a significant difference in a total of some 86,000,000. But can we always be sure that such errors will be self-cancelling?

Assessing the method of deriving occupational employment is a little easier since it was based on the assumption, standard in manpower forecasting, of fixed occupational-input coefficients. The rationale for this method was summed up in an earlier BLS study: 'the occupational composition pattern of each industry reflects its technology and the institutional arrangements affecting the organization to work in the firms that make up the industry . . . these factors tend to impose certain optimum patterns of quantitative relationship among the occupations employed in the individual plants and the entire industry (Department of Labor, 1955, p. 2). But the word 'optimum' is quite illegitimate. The 1963 Manpower Report suggested that one of the factors influencing occupational composition patterns would be 'the supply of workers expected to be available' (Department of Labor, 1963, p. 123). If the observed 1960 occupational inputs do reflect changing relative supplies of various types of labour, using these ratios to derive manpower requirements for 1970 and 1975 will introduce an unknown bias into the forecasts. The authors of the 1963 Report would no doubt agree with Goldstein and Swerdloff (1967, p. 21) that although the numbers in each occupation are affected by past supply, 'patterns change relatively slowly and so a pattern can be used for 10 or 15 years if allowance is made for changes likely to take place'. But this begs the whole question. Especially at a time when we believed that occupational changes were going to be rapid, it is precisely this 'allowance' which the forecast ought to indicate.

Some light can be shed on this question if we move on to consider the conversion of these occupational forecasts into educational requirements in the 1965 Manpower Report.[5] The derivation of educational requirements from forecasts of the occupational structure is one of the weakest links in the manpower forecasting chain. The usual procedure is to apply the amount of education associated with each occupation in the base year of the forecast occupational distribution and the BLS used a variant of this standard method. The procedure in the 1965 Report was to derive the 1975 occupational requirements as described earlier, and apply to these the amount of education attained by the 25—34-year-old age group in 1960. The justification for this was that 'the amount of education indicated for this age group reflected actual current employer requirements'. The reason for choosing this particular age group was that 'the educational attainment of these recent entrants to the labour force will represent the average educational attainment of the entire labour force in 1975' (Department of Labor, 1965, p. 56). But precisely how will the 40—49 age group be representative of the 'average educational attainment' of the labour force in 1975? What do we mean by average in this context? The modal age group of the American labour force is 30—39-years-old and the mean number of years of education in 1962 of the American male labour force is 10.7 (Denison, 1967, p. 107). This is just a little less than the average

---

[5] The occupational forecasts in the 1965 Report were not exactly the same as those in the 1963 Report. The estimates presented in 1965 had been adjusted to take account of the revised population estimates mentioned above but the changes were masked because the 1965 estimates were not given in precise numerical terms but in general terms such as 'average growth', 'faster than average', and so on. The method of deriving occupational employment in the 1965 Report was nevertheless fundamentally the same as in 1963, and it is less repetitious to consider both together.

years embodied in the 40—49 age group. So in what sense is this age group representative? To reiterate: what the BLS has in fact done in a very roundabout way is to derive 1975 educational requirements by applying the projected average level of educational attainment in 1975 to the forecast occupational distribution in that year. Presumably, the rationale for this procedure is the attempt to build into the forecast not only the rising educational level of the labour force, but also the finding that this rise had been widely distributed among occupational groups and was not simply the result of a shifting occupational distribution. As Folger and Nam put it: 'between 1940 and 1960 about 85 per cent of the rise in educational attainment may be attributed to increased educational levels within occupations, and only about 15 per cent to shifts in the occupational structure from occupations requiring less education to occupations requiring more' (Folger and Nam, 1964, p. 29).

The Department of Labor seemed unaware that there are two equally plausible hypotheses to explain Folger and Nam's data. One explanation is that the generally rising demand for better educated workers reflects the growing requirements for specific skills. That is to say, changing productive processes require a shift in the education associated with each occupation. This hypothesis is implicit in the Manpower Report's declaration that 'in every broad occupational group, the requirement seems to be for more and more education and training' (Department of Labor, 1965, p. 56). But even if this is true, it is not what the Department has in fact measured. The Department centred its forecasting effort on the occupational distribution but Folger and Nam's evidence of a dominating shift in the occupation—education relationship implies that, even if the future occupational distribution is correctly estimated, only a small fraction of the total relationship between output and educational input is thereby identified. Thus, far from successfully incorporating Folger and Nam's findings, the Manpower Report almost entirely failed to account for them simply by placing the entire emphasis of the forecast on shifts in the occupational structure.

The other, equally plausible, explanation of Folger and Nam's figures casts even greater doubts on the Report's methodology. This hypothesis suggests that the rising educational level of the labour force may be quite unrelated to the production requirements of the economy, being related instead 'to a subtle change in the educational standard of living of the population . . . rooted in but now developing independently of the changes in occupational structure' (Folger and Nam, 1964). This suggests that what we have been observing over the past few years is not a demand—inspired shift in the occupational distribution requiring increased levels of education, but instead a relative upgrading of skill requirements by employers because of a supply—inspired rise in educational attainments. In these circumstances, *absolute* levels of educational attainment are a necessary but not sufficient condition for occupational entry: an individual's job prospects depend upon his *relative* attainment. This means that an unemployed Negro high school dropout may have difficulty in finding a job not because the job he seeks requires the training implied by the completion of high school but because a growing proportion of his fellow job applicants have a high school diploma. Heller, the ex-chairman of the Council of Economic Advisors, has pointed out that the 'highly educated manpower bottleneck argument arrives at its alarming conclusion by projecting to new situations a perfectly static set of educational requirements' (Heller, 1966, p. 138). He might well have added 'and so does the uneducated unemployment argument'. If there is no *absolute* level of educational requirements that are closely geared to and can be derived from the occupational distribution, of what possible relevance is a forecast of such requirements?

Folger and Nam's data do not allow us to choose between these hypotheses, or to say how much of the change in the education of the American labour force reflects increased skill requirements for specific occupations and how much the availability of better educated workers for the same jobs. In any event, supply and demand factors are not as easily disentangled as many manpower forecasters seem to think. Denison has provided a very suggestive interpretation of how these factors were woven together in the past. He summarizes that the upgrading of the labour force 'led to changes in the whole organization of production as among occupational groups in order to take advantage of a labour supply of higher quality. Second, advances in technology have been such as to shift the pattern of demand towards occupations requiring more education' (Denison, 1964, p. 38). He suggests that although upgrading of labour may have been a prerequisite for these advances, the fact that income differentials by years of schooling have not declined, despite the great upgrading of the labour force, is presumptive evidence for the view that the shift in occupational composition could not have been solely a response to supply factors. Denison's argument provokes a further comment. What warrant is there actually for thinking that workers are fitted to jobs, rather than jobs to workers? The standard presumption in the manpower literature, and one that is certainly implicit in the Manpower Reports, is that occupational requirements are determined by technical considerations and that educational requirements come later in the chain of causation because men have to be fitted to a predetermined occupational structure. Plausible as this relationship may sound, there is no evidence to support it. It is almost as plausible to assume that employers hire workers to fulfil a given set of tasks and then develop a job structure to suit the labour they have hired, rather than the other way round. Or, as a further plausible alternative, it is possible that occupation and education are simultaneously determined in the recruitment process. Recent empirical evidence on the effects of automation supports these doubts about a simple relationship between occupation and education. One such study suggests that during the 1950's and 1960's changes in occupational composition resulted from changes in the industrial mix rather than as a consequence of one skill level replacing another (Jaffe and Froomkin, 1968, pp. 78 and 79). They concluded not only that 'the rate of change in output per worker contributes little toward explaining changes in occupational composition', but that 'even in these industries . . . undergoing the most rapid technological changes, one-half to three-quarters of the manual workers had less than a high-school education (suggesting) that modern advancing technology does not necessarily require workers to have more formal schooling'.

Our dismissal of the Department of Labor line of argument should not be taken to imply complacency about the unemployment of the poorly educated. Nor do we suggest that the problems of the unemployed school dropout or older worker will simply melt away provided aggregate demand is pushed high enough. The person with less education will always find his position precarious. The recent changes in employment in manufacturing bear this out. The gloomier prognostications of the Manpower Reports of 1963 and 1965 in fact turned out to be unfounded: 'growth of the economy since 1963 has led to a dramatic reversal in the sluggish performance of manufacturing employment . . . between 1963 and 1965 manufacturing employment increased by about a million workers, with most of the increase occurring in 1965 . . . since then employment in manufacturing has continued to increase — achieving new records in 1966 and 1967' (Alterman, 1968, p. 12). Nevertheless, there were already signs in 1967 of a slackening of the rate of economic growth, and during that year, in contrast to the early years of the sixties, there were few additional opportunities for unskilled and semi-skilled workers. The 1968 Manpower Report correctly pointed out that this characterized the vulnerability of less skilled workers to any slowdown in overall economic activity and that their changes for new job opportunities depended largely on sustained economic growth. But what has this to do with forecasting the occupational structure for 15 years ahead, as the earlier Manpower Reports suggested? Manpower forecasting, with its definition of future demand for personnel as those workers with the education and skills to perform certain jobs, and its complete neglect of the capacity of labour markets to reconcile discrepancies between labour supplies and labour demands is at best an irrelevant attempt to tackle the issues of more education for blacks, retraining older workers, minimizing high school dropouts, and so forth.

Forecasts of high-level manpower

Before turning to forecasts of particular occupational groups, we consider an attempt by two staff members of the Bureau of Labor Statistics to forecast the employment outlook for college graduates in general up to 1975 (Rosenthal and Hedges, 1968). The calculation of employment in 1975 followed the standard BLS method described earlier so we need say no more on that score. Essentially, the forecast consists of a comparison of expected total output of graduates in 1975 with projected job openings.

TABLE 3.3

PROJECTED OPENINGS FOR COLLEGE GRADUATES, UNITED STATES, 1966—75 (thousands)

	Net growth employment	Replacement employment	Total employment	Total supply
All occupations	3,800	2,400	6,200	6,400
Professional, technical and kindred workers	2,700	1,600	4,300	·
Managers	550	350	900	·
Salesworkers	250	100	350	·
Clerical	175	175	350	·
Others	125	175	300	·

Source: Rosenthal and Hedges (1968), Table I.
· = not applicable.

Taking supply and demand at face value, the implication is that there will be some graduate unemployment in 1975. But it was only in 1965 that the Department of Labor declared that 'the demand of em-
62

ployers for better trained personnel appears to be insatiable' (Department of Labor, 1965, p. 56). Was the 1965 forecast wrong? Or was it so successful in persuading students to go to college that shortage has turned into imminent surplus? Or is this latest forecast wrong? A closer examination suggests that the BLS does not in fact expect any general graduate unemployment. This is partly because 'the requirement projections are based heavily on past utilisation patterns (and) . . . are somewhat understated for occupations for which shortages existed in the past' and partly because the increasing supply of graduates, so far from being out of work, will 'alleviate long-term shortages in teaching, engineering, science and health occupations' (Rosenthal and Hedges, 1968, pp. 9—11).

If there were shortages in the past, it is quite correct to try to allow for them when calculating current employment: there is no point in projecting today's disequilibrium into the future[6] . Unfortunately, the treatment of shortages in this forecast is far from clear. The authors' belief that 'keen competition for engineers may widen the gap between their earnings and those in other occupations requiring similar abilities, resulting in an increase in the proportion of engineering graduates who actually enter the field' (Rosenthal and Hedges, 1968, p. 9) is almost certainly quite correct. But if the labour market is likely to function as efficiently as this in the future, why did it not operate like that in the past to alleviate those 'long-term shortages[7] ? '

Further doubts are raised if we turn to the actual calculation of 'net growth employment' in Table 3.3. It is clear that the BLS has tried not to fall into the same trap as Harris (1949), who predicted a surplus of college graduates at the end of the 1960's. He estimated that in 1940, 70 per cent of all employed college graduates were in professional and related occupations, and assumed that 70 per cent of future graduates would seek similar professional employment. If forced into other occupations by an increasing number of graduates, the 'surplus' would have to settle for lower status jobs and would

---

[6] But see p. 207 in Chapter 8 on Swedish manpower forecasts.

[7] Compare this study with a more recent forecast of the supply and demand for college graduates (Folger et al., 1970). This also used the basic BLS model as benchmark data, but subjected the findings to a critical analysis of the way supply and demand adjust to each other. The result is a sophisticated attempt to set a manpower forecast in the context of manpower adjustment mechanisms such as occupational and geographical mobility, the raising of entry standards, international migration, and substitution of different educational levels.

become dissatisfied and under-utilized. What Harris did not see was the growing acceptance of college as preparation for a wide variety of occupations outside the professions. In fact, the proportion of 25—34-year-old male professional and technical workers who are college graduates rose from 58 per cent in 1950 to about 63 per cent in 1965; for proprietors, managers and officials the proportion rose from 15 per cent tot 30 per cent; and for sales workers the proportion of male college graduates doubled from 14 per cent to 28 per cent. It is not surprising, therefore, that the employment figures in Table 3.3 allow for an increase in the proportion of graduates in those occupations. But this immediately brings us back to the problems of the previous section when we discussed Folger and Nam's findings: does the employment of an increasing proportion of graduates in these occupations reflect the growing needs for specific skills or does it reflect a supply-inspired relative upgrading of skill requirements? To put the argument crudely, it must surely be true that a far higher proportion of the graduates working in 'salesworker', 'clerical' and 'other' occupations are doing jobs where their qualifications, however useful in themselves, are not directly required for satisfactory performance in those jobs. If this is so, it is clear that the proportion of graduates actually observed in these occupations is as much the outcome of their supply in the past as of the demand for qualified manpower. The implicit assumption in comparing 'total employment' with 'total supply' (Table 3.3) must be that total employment is demand-determined. But what if it is biassed by supply effects, as we have suggested? We discuss the problem of identifying supply and demand more fully in our next forecast: suffice it to say for now that ignoring the interaction of supply and demand introduces a bias into the forecast besides which the problem of allowing for past 'shortages' pales into insignificance.

Forecasts of scientists and engineers

Forecasts of scientists and engineers in America are legion. We select three for consideration to illustrate some of the typical problems encountered. Two of the forecasts were carried out by the Bureau of Labor Statistics for the National Science Foundation in 1961 and 1963. The first, *The Long-range Demand for Scientific and Technical Personnel*, describes the methodology and presents some preliminary estimates. These were amplified in the second report, *Scientists, Engineers and Technicians in the 1960's*, and it is convenient to treat them as one forecast. We contrast the BLS' work with

64

the third forecast, *Demand for Engineers, Physical Scientists and Technicians — 1964*, which was one of a series carried out by the Engineering Manpower Commission.

Formidable problems of evaluation arise from the self-defeating nature of the BLS forecast. Independent forecasts of both supply and demand for technical manpower were made to illustrate the relation between them as it would be if no special effort had been made to influence the supply of labour. At the same time, the forecast was explicitly intended to influence students' choices. The result, as the report itself points out, was that 'it is unlikely that deficits of the magnitude projected . . . will be clearly observable in 1970 . . . accommodations to the existing manpower situation will occur each year, and adjustments will be made by employers' (BLS — NSF, 1963, p. 1). It may be true that the purpose of the forecast is fulfilled if employers and students change their actions and a deficit does not occur. But the report expressed no concern over the fact that this rendered the original forecast untestable: we can only conjecture what the outcome would have been had the forecast not influenced labour responses.

The method of calculating future demand is familiar, for the BLS used a variant of the 'density ratios' technique — more fully described in Chapter 8[8] — which has also been used in Britain and the U.S.S.R. Although the calculations were made separately for private industry, universities and colleges and State and Federal government, the method used in each sector was essentially the same. This consisted of establishing ratios of scientists and engineers to total employment in each sector during the period 1951—59[9], extrapolating these ratios to 1970, and applying them to independent projections of total employment in each sector for 1970. We have already commented on the derivation of total employment, so we need say no more here. The interest in this particular forecast lies rather in the derivation of the ratios of technical manpower. But let us leave that for one moment and return to the question of supply effects which we raised earlier. As these forecasts are merely extrapolations of past employment trends, they are presumably forecasts of future employment. But the reports complicate the issue by talking interchangeably and confusingly of 'employment', 'demand',

---

[8] See p. 216 in that chapter for a discussion of the assumptions implicit in the method.

[9] 1954—9 for private industry; 1957—58 for colleges and universities; and 1951—9 for State and Federal government.

'requirements' and 'needs'. The BLS cannot mean 'demand' in the economist's sense of the word, for nowhere (either in this forecast or those considered earlier) is there a reference to relative prices of labour. Rather, the BLS seems to have had in mind the Parnesian concept of 'technical requirements', that is to say the 'functional (occupational) composition of employment that will be necessary if certain social and/or economic targets are to be achieved' (Parnes, 1963, p. 76). For example, it points out that its estimates 'represent the scientific and technical manpower needs in 1970 that are expected under a given set of assumptions as to economic growth and institutional change; . . . since the projections of requirements were developed independently of supply considerations, they represent the number of persons required by 1970, not the number who will actually be employed' (BLS — NSF, 1963, pp. 4—5). However, the BLS concedes that its projected requirements were in fact based on past employment: to the extent that 'there were shortages in the period concerned, past employment reflects supply rather than demand' (BLS — NSF, 1963, p. 5). If past employment really does reflect supply as well as demand, what sense is there in deriving future requirements, allegedly determined by purely technical considerations, from that employment trend? In short, what these reports do is to project employment, whose level is determined by the interaction of supply and demand, as though it were determined by demand alone. Figure 3.1 illustrates this.

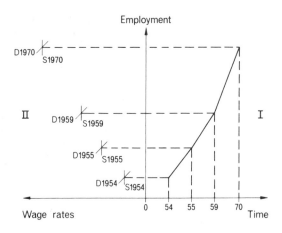

Figure 3.1. Demand, supply and employment of engineers, United States, 1954—1970.

66

The forecasters actually observed the rising trend of scientific employment over time (quadrant I), and projected this trend to 1970 as though it were rising demand. But the BLS admits that these employment points were determined by supply—demand interactions, as shown in quadrant II of Figure 3.1. Certainly one can extrapolate employment trends to 1970, but this does not help in identifying 'demand' or 'requirements' in that year.

After our lengthy digression to discuss precisely what it is that is being forecast, let us return to the question of the validity of the projected ratios of technical manpower. The rationale for the method is simple: 'it is reasonable to expect a close relationship between the number of scientific and technical workers employed in each industry and total employment in that industry, since the occupational composition of each industry reflects not only its technology but also a variety of institutional factors' (BLS — NSF, 1961, p. 3). The main conclusion from our postmortem on the use of the density ratios method in Sweden (see below Chapter 8) is the extreme sensitivity of the results to quite minor changes in the precise data and time period used in calculating the trend. It is not possible to test the results of the BLS forecast in quite the same way, as we do not yet have 1970 data on the employment of scientists and engineers. But some simple sensitivity analysis is possible nonetheless.

The BLS carried out two intensive studies of the chemical and electrical equipment industries to see whether the density ratio method forecasts for 1970 stood up to closer analysis. While the estimates for the chemical industry were thought to be reasonable, those for electrical equipment were believed to be vast over-estimates. The 1954—9 period has been one of rapid growth of scientific and engineering employment in electrical equipment, and the conclusion of the special study was that this was unlikely to be sustained up to 1970. Accordingly, a new ratio of scientific to total employment in electrical equipment was derived: 10.2 per cent instead of the 12.1 per cent initially projected. It is interesting that in this industry the ratios method was abandoned and a new estimate derived after 'discussions with company officials' (BLS — NSF, 1961, p. 23), yet on the first page of the same report the BLS dismissed surveys of employers' opinion because of the many practical and conceptual problems with regard to such surveys. Much more important, however, is the fact that this new ratio implied that the total number of engineers required by 1970 in electrical equipment would be 186,000 instead of 222,000, a reduction of 34,000, or almost 13 per cent of the total projected deficit of engineers in 1970. The magnitude of this adjustment, stemming from only one industry study, does little to increase one's confidence in the meaningfulness of the projected deficit. Moreover, Hansen has shown that the projected deficit is very sensitive to recent changes in scientific employment. In the 1961 BLS — NSF study, 'based on bench-mark data up to 1959 and extrapolation of their current trends, projected engineer requirements for 1970 totalled 1,484,000, whereas in the second (of the two forecasts being considered) based on bench-mark data up to 1970 and extrapolation of then current trends, projected engineer requirements were 1,375,000. This is a difference of over 100,000 on a net change in the total number of engineers of 552,000 from 1960 to 1970, or a variation of almost 20 per cent' (Hansen, 1967, p. 204).

We shall say little about the supply estimates of these forecasts. Hansen has already shown that they were derived from mistaken beliefs about the proportion of degree to non-degree entrants and of retention rates for enrolled engineering students (Hansen, 1967, pp. 204—6). However, there is one intriguing feature which deserves amplification. We have already commented on the similarities between Swedish and American experience with the density ratios method of forecasting requirements: there is also an interesting similarity in their supply estimates. We shall see in the Swedish chapter that in its 1962 forecast of engineers, the Labour Market Board projected an increasing proportion of qualified engineers in the occupational category of engineer. We argue that the Board confused occupational with educational classifications, and that one plausible explanation of the observed constant proportion of qualified engineers, despite the diffusion of better educated people in the working population, was the movement of educated engineers into line management or supervisory occupations. Hansen has shown (1967, pp. 204—5) that the BLS made almost exactly the same error. The projections of supply for the 1960—70 period imply that the ratio of degree to non-degree among new entrants into engineering during 1950—60 had been 4 : 1, and that this ratio was assumed to hold for 1960—70. But, as Hansen points out, 'we know from the population censuses that the proportion of engineers having completed four or more years of college . . . hovered in the 50 to 55 per cent range from 1940 to 1960; the exact percentages for 1940, 1950 and 1960 are 50, 53 and 56 per cent respectively. If during the 1940's the ratio of degree to non-degree holders had been 4 : 1, then, given that new entrants during the decade comprised 40 to 50 per cent of the stock of engineers at the end of the decade, the proportion of engineers with four years of college should have risen far more dramatically from 1940 to 1950 than it did, and similarly for 1950 to 1960'. The result, as in Sweden, was an almost certain gross over-estimates of the proportion of engineers with degrees, simply because neither forecast sufficiently recognized that someone doing an engineering job does not necessarily have to have an engineering degree. Once this distinction, and the tendency of better educated engineers to move into managerial positions, is recognized, the paradox of a small change in the overall percentage of degree holders disappears, despite the fact that a large proportion of new entrants is better educated.

Running through all the BLS forecasts so far considered has been the persistent problem of the relationship between occupation and education. As we have seen, some of the methods used for translating one into the other have been so suspect as to make it doubtful if the results are at all meaningful. But this is not a problem that afflicts only the BLS. The forecast of engineers and scientists carried out by the Engineering Manpower Commission in 1964 founders for the same reason. (The Commission in fact carried out a series of forecasts for technical manpower, but we have chosen just one of them to compare with the BLS approach).

The Commission's 10-year forecast relied on an unconditional employers' survey. The BLS had dismissed this method as unreliable, and the reasons for such scepticism soon became obvious. The differences between the forecast of 1964 and a similar one two years previously exemplify the tendency of employers to base such long-term unconditional forecasts on their recent short-term experience. The pessimistic forecast of employment growth from 1964 to 1973 as compared to the optimism of the 1962—71 forecast is almost certainly a result of the downturn in hiring activity in 1963. What reliability can we put on one forecast rather than the other?

In spite of its methodology, the forecast has been taken seriously and 'employers' opinion' has often been cited in support of the idea of a shortage of scientists and engineers. Instead of dwelling on the general problem of methodology in the area of attitude surveys, we shall examine one particularly vulnerable aspect of this forecast, namely the way in which the sample estimates of new engineering graduate requirements were grossed up to derive new graduates required in the total economy between 1964 and 1973. The report uses a simple equation for the grossing-up exercise[10], and arrives at a total new graduate requirement of 451,000 compared with a supply of 390,000 new engineering graduates for the decade. A closer look suggests that the figure of 451,000 is quite misleading. When we turn to the actual questionnaire we find that employers were asked to estimate 'engineering graduates (employed in all activities including supervision and management)', and also 'non-graduates'; a footnote defines non-graduates as men 'lacking an engineering degree but whose experience and training permit them to hold positions normally requiring such a degree' (Engineering Manpower Commission, 1964, p. 78). Having said this, they then arbitrarily excluded non-engineering graduates from the forecasting equation as if such people were of little importance. Yet in 1960 about 5,500 such graduates were estimated to have entered engineering, compared to 32,000 with engineering degrees (BLS — NSF, 1963, pp. 23 and 24). Slighting the role of these non-engineering graduates helps of course to explain why the proportion of degree-holding engineers among the survey respondents (83.7 per cent) was so much higher than the proportion of total engineers with degrees in the population (55 per cent in the 1960 Census). To sum it up, this is a forecast of the requirements for those people the Engineering Manpower Commission designates as 'engineers'. But having had enough confidence in businessmen to have asked them how many engineers they were going to hire, why not extend this confidence to the labelling of the occupation 'engineering'. Are we forecasting requirements for people with degrees or jobs to be filled by people? Since the Engineering Manpower Commission is composed of representatives of profes-

---

[10] $G_y = \frac{EP}{ep}g_y + N\left(\frac{EP}{ep}g_y\right)$ where

G_y = New graduates required by the total economy for any given year between 1964 and 1973.

E = Number of individuals in total population who identify themselves as engineers.

P = Proportion of E with degrees.

e = Engineers employed by responding organizations.

p = Proportion of engineers with degrees among respondents.

g_y = New graduates required by the survey group for any given year 1964—73.

N = Proportion of engineering graduates who do not enter the profession.

That is, new graduates required equals the ratio between all engineers with degrees in the population and the number of engineers with degrees in the sample *times* the new engineering graduates required by employers in the sample *plus* the engineers produced who will not enter the profession.

sional engineering societies, their procedure may not be wholly inexplicable, but it hardly contributes to a rational discussion of engineering manpower.

Conclusions

What lessons can we draw from all this? We are well aware of the smallness of our sample: there are many other forecasts and projections we could analyse, but we believe that our choice demonstrates the problems most typically encountered, and nothing is added by being comprehensive.[11] We are aware too that, as we have not yet reached the terminal date of many of these forecasts, we have not carried out a definitive analysis of accuracy in the way that we did in Britain and Sweden. Nevertheless, our analysis gives a sufficient basis for drawing some tentative conclusions.

Some of the criticisms we made of earlier forecasts have to some extent been rectified by recent developments. One problem which was apparent in the Manpower Reports of 1963 and 1965 was the difficulty of forecasting employment in the various industrial sectors. The method of extrapolating the past ratio between the individual sectors and projected total employment was fundamentally a fairly crude technique, and its deficiencies have become evident in the last few years. As we saw earlier, the industrial composition of employment in 1970 was projected largely on the evidence of a downturn in manufacturing employment from 1957 to 1963. The resulting pessimistic predictions for manufacturing employment were soon seen to be unfounded.[12] In recent years the Bureau of Labor Statistics has been working with other federal agencies in the Interagency Growth Project, an attempt to use an input—output model to project the level and composition of final demand and to derive industry employment requirements by using projected input—output coefficients

---

[11] There are two or three major omissions, nonetheless. Forecasts of doctors are described elsewhere in this book. Forecasts of teachers have been omitted simply because we have nothing to add to Cartter (1966). One major forecasting exercise by the National Planning Association deserves separate analysis and could not be satisfactorily handled within the framework of this chapter. The interested reader is referred to Lecht (1968).

[12] This does not deny the fact that there may be a long run shift from manufacturing employment to services. But the forecasts of its timing and impact were grossly exaggerated.

71

and labour productivity ratios. We can summarize the work in the following steps:

(1) Projected real national output in 1970 is derived from projections of the labour force, hours of work and productivity and based on assumptions of unemployment and the size of the armed forces. Two alternative assumptions of the rate of unemployment (3 per cent and 4 per cent) in 1970 were used.

(2) Real GNP is distributed among major categories of final demand. These categories include personal consumption expenditures, private domestic investment for plant and equipment, residential construction, federal, state and local expenditures, and net exports. Alternative assumptions were used here also: the 'high durables' alternative assumes that the increase in expenditure on consumer durable goods and capital goods will remain at almost the same high rates as in the mid-1960's; the 'high services' alternative assumes that capital expenditures will fall as a proportion of GNP.

(3) Major components of final demand are distributed into detailed items such as food, clothing, medical care, machine tools, etc. These detailed estimates for consumer demand, government expenditures, etc., are classified by producing industry and then aggregated to obtain the 'bill of goods' in 1970 for the end products or services of each of the 87 industries in the input—output system.

(4) The interindustry production relationships in (3) are multiplied by appropriate ratios of employment per dollar of output to derive an interindustry employment table.

(5) The input—output coefficients and the productivity ratios in the base year (1958) are extrapolated to the terminal year (1970) and stage (4) is repeated so as to derive the interindustry employment table for the terminal year.

This is an extremely brief summary of a very ambitious project. However, stages (1) to (3) follow standard input—output methodology, so we shall say no more about that. It is stages (4) and (5) which are of particular interest for manpower forecasting.[13] In many respects, the Interagency Growth Project is a major advance in forecasting industrial employment. It provides more consistent estimates of final demand and interindustry relationships than the usual study-by-study approach in which little recognition is given to the interrelationships in an economy; it makes possible an analysis of the impact of changing defence expenditures, of alternative fiscal policies

---

[13] A full description of all the stages is given in Department of Labor (1967).

72

on the structure of employment, of the impact of foreign trade and many other questions; and it uses alternative assumptions for the first time in any BLS forecast.

But the acid test for manpower forecasting is the success with which stages (4) and (5) can be performed. The successful implementation of stage (5) requires not only the projection of input—output coefficients over a 12-year period from 1958 to 1970, but also the projection of changes in productivity between 1963 and 1970. Input—output coefficients can change over time because of changes in technology, substitution of one type of material for another, changes in product mix and industry integration, and so on. The report stresses that these changes were not derived by simple extrapolation of past trends but were modified by detailed industry studies. But the two industry studies described, so far from increasing one's confidence in the reliability of the projected coefficients, merely demonstrate the magnitude of the problem. For example, the special study of the textile industry implied that a successful projection of the 1970 coefficients would have to take account of the substitution of synthetics for natural fibres, substitution of noncellulosics (such as nylon) for cellulosics (such as rayon), and the increased use of chemicals (Department of Labor, 1967, p. 90). When economists are only just beginning to congratulate themselves on being able to predict GNP two years ahead (Zarnowitz, 1968), what evidence is there for thinking that changes such as these can be foreseen 12 years in advance? Similarly, what reliability can be placed on the projection of the 1957—63 productivity trends to 1970? Predicting productivity changes is the Achilles heel of manpower forecasting and the Interagency Project is no exception. Kutscher and Jacobs (1967) carried out a sources-of-change analysis of the factors affecting the Interagency employment projections and their findings demonstrate the extreme sensitivity of these projections to assumptions about future changes in labour productivity. They show that under the 'high durables' assumption of the model, employment in trade and services would grow as a proportion of total employment; manufacturing would retain its share; and agriculture, mining, transport and public utilities would decline in importance. More importantly, they show that 'the changes in relative shares of these sectors are primarily due to variations in the movement of unit labor requirements rather than to changes in the structure of final demand. While final demand changes for major sectors (except agriculture) show little variation from the average, unit labor requirements vary from declines 30 per cent more than the average to 15 per cent less than the average'. Similarly, *within* the manufacturing sector, 'for 13 out of 20 industries the divergence of unit labor requirements from the average is greater than for final demand, and in general, the direction of changes in unit labor requirements determines the direction of changes in relative employment' (Kutscher and Jacobs, 1967, p. 12). The Interagency Project is a very sophisticated way of projecting changes in final demand: the implication of Kutscher and Jacobs' findings is that this still leaves unresolved the major problem in forecasting future industrial employment.

One other recent development by the Bureau of Labor Statistics deserves special mention. One of the most fundamental problems of all the forecasts reviewed in this chapter is that quite apart from technical aspects of their construction it is hard to see what possible basis they could form for policy. Actual decisions on education and training programmes in the United States are made at local level and a national forecast can provide at best only a general guide to area trends. Indeed, a national forecast could be positively misleading: the whole point of the manpower legislation of the early and mid-1960's was that the impact of automation, unemployment and lack of schooling made itself felt unevenly across the country and among occupational groups. It is difficult to see how any of the forecasts reviewed here can be said seriously to contribute to the ostensible objectives classified earlier in this chapter without a recognition of this fact. Now, with *Tomorrow's Manpower Needs*, the BLS is beginning to tackle this problem. In many respects this work represents the culmination of the BLS forecasting work over the last ten years. The BLS has not itself attempted to construct forecasts for any particular state or region; rather it uses a combination of all the methods we have already reviewed to produce a national forecast that state and local forecasting agencies can draw upon for benchmark data. It uses a synthesis of detailed industry and occupation studies, input—output analysis and regressions relating employment to different combinations of real GNP, unemployment and the size of the armed forces, not only to forecast employment in different industries in 1975 but to project the occupational structure of the economy through a new industry—occupation matrix.

For all its technical virtuosity, the result is disappointing. Despite the use of an input—output table, this latest forecast fails to incorporate two of the most promising developments of the Interagency Project. Where are the alternative assumptions of unemployment and growth of demand for consumer durables and capital investment that

74

figured so prominently and usefully in that project? Why is there no analysis of the sensitivity of the forecast of requirements, along the lines suggested by Kutscher and Jacobs? But the main reason for doubts about this latest forecast is that it runs the risk of repeating at state and local level precisely those errors we have identified in the national forecasts. For example, the BLS offers two main methods for local forecasters, taking national data as the starting point. For each method, employment estimates by industry and area are derived by extrapolating to the target year the past ratio of area employment in an industry to national employment in that industry: area occupational requirements are then derived through use of the national industry—occupation matrix. This can be done either by applying 1960 and 1975 national industry—occupation patterns to the appropriate area—industry—employment estimates, or by developing an area—industry—occupation matrix and applying to this the change forecast for the national matrix between the base and target years. In the final analysis, therefore, such local forecasts will depend for their accuracy on the national matrix. There is no need here to repeat the doubts expressed earlier. Suffice it to say that the BLS cannot really be said to have learned the limitations of assuming fixed occupational input coefficients when its handbook for state practitioners flatly declares that 'each industry in the economy requires a specific mix of occupations' (BLS, 1969, Vol. IV, p. 9).

To be sure, the BLS has learned some lessons from those early efforts. The Interagency Project and *Tomorrow's Manpower Needs* are impressive statistical achievements that go some way towards remedying important deficiencies. But in weighing the balance of evidence it is difficult to escape the judgement that the effort which went into these forecasts was a waste of resources. In her review of college enrolment projections, Rivlin (1961) concluded that they had all been so far off the mark that nothing was to be gained by fitting yet more trend lines to the same set of basic data. Rivlin's conclusion applies to the work of the Bureau of Labor Statistics. Over the last ten years the BLS has continually refined its statistics and data, using better and better forecasting techniques, but these techniques are being applied to a model that experience has shown to be inadequate. There is no need to reiterate some of the technical criticisms we have made of BLS forecasts: the precise meaning of 'requirements', supply effects, projecting productivity changes, and so on; all these are a recurring theme of this book, and American experience here is no different from anyone else's. The difficulty in the United States goes beyond this. We asserted in the introduction that the BLS had taken over the techniques of Parnesian manpower forecasting without ever systematically evaluating their relevance to the particular problems of the U.S.A. The result has been the blanket application of an exclusively demand oriented outlook to a country where all the evidence — from Folger and Nam, Jaffe and Froomkin, to Denison — suggests that the concept of an appropriate job for a given level of education is meaningless. The consequence of this in turn has been that the forecasts, far from shedding light on popular fears of a shortage of high-level manpower in conjunction with the unemployment of the poorly-educated, have instead reinforced and perpetuated those groundless fears. It is not enough to assume, as seems to be implied by the latest work from the BLS, that forecasting errors will be reduced if only the data and statistics can be refined. What is needed is what the BLS has not carried out in the ten years we have reviewed — a fundamental assessment of the relevance and objectives of the manpower requirements approach itself.

4. France

by George Psacharopoulos

Manpower forecasting in France is an integral part of economic planning as a whole. Therefore, we shall first describe briefly the general Plan as the framework within which the manpower forecasts are made.

Economic planning has been practised in France since 1946 and although the details of the planning technique have changed over time, the fundamental objective of each Plan remains the same: how to co-ordinate the conflicting interests of different government departments and business firms into a course of action that is consistent with the attainment of national goals. But what are these national goals?

It is difficult to specify the welfare function of French planners, since political, economic and social considerations are all fused into what is called 'the final Plan'. Let us assume for the purposes of discussion, that the planners attempt to maximize a welfare function with a single argument, namely, the rate of growth of the economy as a whole. In this case, the planning process starts with a rather mechanical projection of the rate of growth of the economy in the future, that is on the assumption that no action is taken by the planning authority. Assume that the result of this projection, which is mainly based on extrapolation of past time trends, is a rate of growth of 4 per cent. The question the planner asks is: How can we interfere with the spontaneous course of events in order to raise the rate of growth to, say, 6 per cent? In our language, the planners begin with an 'onlooker forecast', to which they then add a 'policy conditional forecast'.

There are two polar cases in economic planning. At one extreme is mandatory planning, consisting of exact guide-lines which firms must follow with sanctions for non-conformity to the plan. At the other end of the spectrum is indicative planning, which can best be described as providing general guidelines for firms to follow if they wish; there are no sanctions for those who insist on going their own way. French planners place themselves at the middle of these two extremes. They call their kind of planning *active* planning; that is, although there are no sanctions for firms that refuse to follow the Plan, the Government can take certain policy measures to try to ensure its implementation. Moreover, since the plan is itself produced by the wide participation of employers and workers, its implementation is to some extent ensured as soon as it is drawn up.

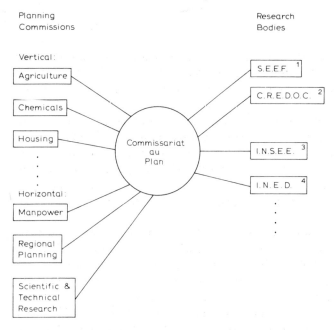

Figure 4.1. The organization of French Planning.

Notes: [1] Service des Etudes Economiques et Financières

[2] Centre de Recherche et de Documentation sur la Comsommation

[3] Institut National de la Statistique et des Etudes Economiques

[4] Institut National d'Etudes Démographiques

Figure 4.1 gives a sketch of the organization of French planning. The Planning Office (Commissariat au Plan) is responsible for the elaboration of the Plan but very little work in this respect is done in the Office itself. What is unique about the French Plan is that its elaboration takes place mainly in outside units. There are two kinds of outside units: (a) research units to which a particular task is assigned (e.g., projections of consumer demand for the target year), and (b) the so-called Planning Commissions. Each Commission deals with a particular section or subject and their role lies in adding the expert opinion of their members to the planning process. There are two kinds of Commission, the vertical ones and the horizontal ones: vertical Commissions specialize in one particular sector, while horizontal Commissions have a cross-sectoral character. It is through these Commissions that the French Plan involves all parties concerned in a co-ordinated effort to agree on the outlines of the Plan.

The planning process starts with the research bodies analysing the future potential of the economy in accordance with past trends. For example, consider the preparation of the Fourth Plan which covered the period 1962—65. The first step involved the determination of a feasible range fo growth of output. This resulted in the Plan being based on three alternative annual rates of growth of output, 3 per cent, 4.5 per cent and 6 per cent. This work was done in the research bodies mentioned above. Three alternative forecasts of the economy for 1965 were made on the basis of these alternative rates.[1] These capacity output figures are supplied next to the Planning Commissions who modify them according to their own criteria. The main criterion used in the Planning Commission is expert opinion and judgement. The modified production figures are supplied back via the Commissariat to the research bodies, while all three units involved (Commissariat, Commissions and research bodies) agree on a given course of events. This successive iteration between the units responsible for the elaboration of the Plan is the principal methodological characteristic of French planning techniques.

Manpower forecasting within the French Plan

The objective of manpower forecasting within the French Plan is to specify the number and kinds of people required to achieve the economic goals set out in the Plan.[2] These manpower forecasts take the form of occupational and educational distributions of the labour force in the target year. But manpower forecasts are also made for a date beyond the target year of the Plan on a preliminary basis, in order to provide guidelines for planning the educational system. For example, although the Fifth Plan covers the period 1965—70, manpower forecasts were also made for the year 1978.

---

[1] There was also a more distant forecast for 1970 to take into account conditions beyond the target year of the Plan.

[2] '... de savoir si les hommes, tels qu'ils étaient formés, étaient dans les proportions convenables pour l'exécution du Plan économique' (Vimont et al., 1966, p. 483).

There are four distinct phases in French manpower forecasting for the target year of the Plan; (a) the total supply of manpower, (b) employment by sector, (c) the occupational distribution of the labour force by sectors of employment, and (d) the educational distribution of the labour force within a given sector and occupation.

Figure 4.2 gives an oversimplified but illustrative view of how phases (a) and (b) above are carried out. Phases (c) and (d) are a simple sequence of phase (b) and are not presented on the diagram.[3]

As shown in Figure 4.2, the starting point of the manpower forecast is a population forecast (Box 1). This population forecast

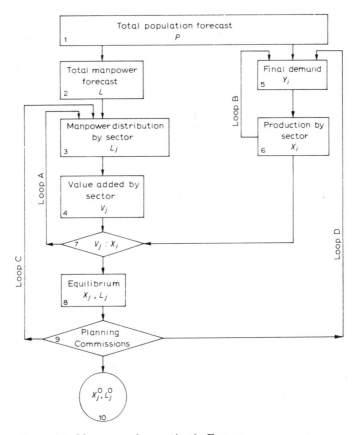

Figure 4.2. Manpower forecasting in France.

---

[3] The methodology used in the last two phases will be examined later in this chapter.

serves a double purpose. First, it provides the basis for estimating the total labour force, (L) in the target year of the Plan (Box 2). Second, it serves as a basis of the forecast of final demand (Y_i) in the target year (Box 5). The total manpower forecast derived in Box 2 is distributed by economic sector (Box 3). The number of people employed in each sector determines further the capacity output (value added, V_j) by sector in the target year (Box 4).

The next step consists of determining whether demand is consistent with supply. For this purpose production (X_i) is estimated (Box 6) on the basis of the previously forecast final demand (Box 5). If the value added in any given sector as determined by the supply conditions is not consistent with the demand for the product of this sector (Box 7 comparison), successive iterations take place (loops A and B) until a consistent pair of production and manpower values by sector is reached (Box 8).

Once this is reached, it is transmitted for comment to the Planning Commissions (Box 9). If the opinion of the experts in the Commission differs from that in the research bodies which provided the preliminary forecasts, further iterations take place (loops C and D) until a set of values is reached (Box 10), which represents the final production and manpower figures (X_j^O, L_j^O) selected by the planning authorities. It is this particular figure of employment by sector (L_j^O), which will be further analysed by occupational and educational categories.

Figure 4.2 was presented in a computer flow chart form for easy understanding. It should be emphasized, however, that the final solution is not the result of a computer program. Each step involves successive feedbacks and iterations which are performed by different people in different departments, employing diverse methodologies. By way of summary, these methodologies consist of a mixture of: (1) no change assumptions over the period of the plan; (2) forecasts based on past time trends; (3) international comparisons; (4) input– output techniques; and, above all (5) experts' opinions and judgement. In the following, we shall try to identify which methodology was mainly used for which purpose.

Population forecasting and the estimate of the total labour force follow a straightforward demographic procedure. Since the labour force within the period of the Plan consists of persons already born when the forecasts are made, the age-cohort method is used. The forecast is based on mortality rates by age and net migration estimates. The latter are derived by extrapolation of observed trends. Mortality rates are assumed to be the same as the observed rates for

81

each age group. The total supply of manpower in the target year is found by applying labour force participation rates by age and sex to the population forecast derived above. Labour force participation rates have been assumed to be the same as the observed rates for the 25—60 age group. Lower participation rates than those observed were used for age groups below 25 and over 60 in order to reflect a longer schooling period for the former and an earlier retirement age for the latter.

Forecasting employment by sector

As already mentioned, there is no unique methodology for forecasting employment by sector in the target year. The methodology ranges from arbitrary estimates: input—output techniques, international comparisons and extrapolation of past trends. To illustrate this, we discuss the methodology used for the various sectors in the preparation of the Fifth Plan. In agriculture, it was assumed that the active population would decline by 115,000 persons annually in the 1962—70 period. This is a higher value than the rate of decline observed in the period 1954—62 (95,000 per year). The reason for the adoption of the higher figure was that, in the opinion of the planners, older persons would retire earlier in the future because of the impact of recent policies designed to accelerate the movement out of the agricultural sector. Employment in services was estimated as a function of a previously forecast demand for services in the period of the Plan. In manufacturing, employment was estimated using a more complex model the highlights of which are presented below.

The object of the exercise was to provide a set of equilibrium values of output (X_j) and employment (L_j) for the target year (Box 8 in Figure 4.2). The first step consisted of estimating the distribution of total manpower by sector based on the extrapolation of past trends and international comparisons. The methodology consisted of observing the trends and employment by sector in ten countries and for 25 sectors. The function fitted was

$$L_{jc} = f(L_c) \tag{1}$$

where L_{jc} is employment in sector j in country c, and L_c is total labour force in country c. The forecast was based on the positions on the curve of technically more advanced countries (Box 3).

Once the number of people employed in the target year by sector was determined, the next step was to estimate the value added by sector (V_j) (Box 4). This was estimated on the basis of the following equation

$$V_j = (V/L)_j L_j \qquad (2)$$

where L_j is the previously derived employment in sector j, and V/L is a productivity coefficient for the sector in question. Productivity coefficients in a given sector were obtained on the basis of past trends, the experience of other countries and the possible introduction of new techniques. The result of this step (Box 4) is a value added and employment forecast by sector in the target year.

It should be obvious from the above that the value added and employment forecast derived represent the supply side. Therefore, the next step consists of checking whether this supply output is consistent with demand. For this purpose the demand side has to be estimated independently.

Consider, as an illustration, the preparation of the Fourth Plan which covered the period 1962 to 1965. The first step consisted of examining the target year (1965) equilibrium:

$$X + M = (C + I + E) + AX \qquad (3)$$

where X is production, M is imports, C is consumption, I is investment, E are exports, and A is the technological coefficients matrix of the input—output table. What equation (3) says in words, is that the total supply of goods and services in the economy should be equal to the demand for these goods and services. The three terms in parenthesis on the right-hand side of equation (3) represent the final demand, whereas the last term represents inter-industry demand. Twenty-nine sectors were distinguished.

Forecasts of the final demand component were made first. Consumption and investment were split into a private and public component, that is

$$Y = C_{pr} + C_{pb} + I_{pr} + I_{pb} + E \qquad (4)$$

where Y is final demand, and the subscripts pr and pb mean private and public, respectively. Private consumption for the target year was obtained on the basis of income elasticities of demand and population projections. Public consumption and investment were obtained directly from the expenditure programmes of the various ministries. Private investment was obtained by three different methods. For the chemical industries and machine tools it was determined on the basis of incremental capital—output ratios. For some large sectors (like transport), it was obtained by simply asking the experts in that sector what they thought they might invest over the period of the Plan. Finally, investment in smaller sectors was determined in proportion to the predicted sales of the sectors and investment—sales ratios as established by previous studies. Exports were predicted by extrapolating past trends. Exports to the Common Market countries were estimated on the additional assumption that the clauses of the Common Market Agreement would come into effect.

Once the value of the final demand (Y) was known, the volume of production by sector was determined using the input—output table as follows:

$$X = [I - A] - 1 . Y \tag{5}$$

It should be noted that the calculation of investment depends upon the value of output which is the unknown in our case. Therefore, the above calculation was repeated in an iterative procedure (Loop B) until consistent values of X and I were obtained. The calculation of imports was done on the basis of trend extrapolations and as a function of the total GDP.

The past experience of the economy and the available resources indicated that it would be plausible to examine the above equation on the basis of three alternative rates of growth of output: 3.0, 4.5 and 6.0 per cent. The result of this preliminary exercise was that the range of growth of output was narrowed down to between 5.0 and 5.5 per cent.

These preliminary employment and production forecasts by sector were then supplied to the Planning Commissions. The members of the Commission of each sector consist of professionals, trade unionists and experts of that sector and also of staff members of the Planning Office. The Commissions were given the government targets and asked for their opinions and in particular to formulate estimates of their own production, imports, investments, exports and interindustry demand. They were also asked to specify the personnel necessary to carry out the targets they set. The methodology used for the formulation of the Commissions' targets is more or less the same as that described in the preliminary work. The main difference is the experts' opinion which counts heavily and thus can supersede a production target derived on the basis of more sophisticated techniques.

The next step consists of the horizontal Manpower Commissions gathering the employment forecasts of each separate sector and attempting to make them consistent with one another. 'In the event of any disparities between the total manpower requirements and the available supply as shown by population forecasts, the problem is referred to the Planning Commissioner and the Commissions are asked to revise their objective or their hypotheses, in order that the volume of manpower used may correspond to the supply available' (Fourastié, 1963, pp. 66—67).

Forecasting the occupational distribution of the labour force

It was on the occasion of the preparation of the Fourth Plan in the early sixties that forecasts by skill level were made for the first time in France. The target year of the forecasts was 1965, although tentative forecasts were made also for the occupational distribution of the labour force in 1975. Seven occupational categories were used within a given sector, as follows:

(1) Administration and business executives
(2) Engineers
(3) Technicians and draughtsmen
(4) Foremen and supervisors
(5) Clerical staff
(6) Skilled operatives
(7) Semi-skilled and unskilled operatives.

The forecast was based on two base year sample surveys (1952 and 1957) of the occupational distribution of the labour force by sector of economic activity in firms employing more than 10 persons. The technique used was linear extrapolation of the 1952—57 trend to 1965 and to 1975. For agriculture and services, experts' opinions were used as these two sectors were not covered by the base year surveys.

In the Fifth Plan a more sophisticated technique was used. The forecasts for 1970 and 1978 were based on two occupational sector matrices in 1954 and 1962; the base year matrices were derived from a 1/20 sample of the 1954 and 1962 censuses. The 1954 census distinguished 41 sectors and 1,200 occupations, while the 1962 census used the same sector classification but a different occupational classification. For the purpose of the 1954 to 1962 comparisons, occupations were regrouped and the forecasting exercise was performed at the level of 41 sectors and 105 occupations. Total employment within a sector in the target year was distributed by occupation on the basis of the following alternative assumptions: (1)

85

H_1 (minimum assumption) — the occupational structure within a given sector remain unchanged over the period of the Plan; in other words, the percentage distribution of persons employed by occupation within a given sector in 1962 was directly applied to the total employment by sector in 1970; (2) H_2 (average assumption) — the percentage distribution of occupations within a given sector in the target year was reached by a linear extrapolation of the 1954 to 1962 distribution;[4] (3) H_3 (maximum assumption) — the occupational distribution by the target year would change at double the observed rate of change in the 1954 to 1962 period; and (4) H_4 (modified assumption) — the occupational distribution was determined in this case by taking into account the opinion of the Planning Commissions of the various sectors. H_4 was considered to be most realistic by the planners.

The base year actual employment figures and the target year forecasts according to the alternative hypotheses are presented in Table A4.1, in the appendix. Table 4.1 presents the most likely

TABLE 4.1

FORECAST RANGE FOR SELECTED OCCUPATIONS, FRANCE, 1970

Occupation	Most likely forecast H_4 (1)	Forecast range (2)
Farmers	2,930,900	60,500
Production workers	7,706,600	361,900
Scientific and technical personnel	933,500	279,600
Teachers	652,400	111,000
Clergy	128,300	110,000

Source: Table A4.1
Note: Col. 2 is the difference between the maximum and minimum predicted values for a given occupation.

---

[4] There were two exceptions to the linear extrapolation. Certain occupations representing a small absolute number of employees would disappear by 1970 if linear extrapolation were used for these occupations; hence, the average rate of decline between 1954 and 1962 was used. Furthermore, unskilled workers would appear in unrealistically large numbers by 1970, if linear extrapolation were used; this is due to the change in the census classification between 1954 and 1962. Therefore, a constant percentage of labourers in certain sectors was used, a weak growth in others and a decline in services.

forecast for selected occupations based on the assumption H_4, along with the forecast range (difference between the maximum and minimum values of a forecast under any of the four alternative assumptions). This table shows that the forecasting range varies widely, the narrowest one corresponding to farmers. On the other hand, the forecasting range of clergy was almost equal to the absolute value of the forecast itself.

The number of persons employed by occupation, as derived on the basis of the above assumptions represent, in the words of the French planners, 'labour requirements due to economic needs'. To that one must add the number of people who will be replaced during the period of the Plan, in order to arrive at the total number of people to enter each occupation by the target year; replacement referred to death and retirement, by occupation.

The mortality rates observed in the 1952—56 period were applied to the number of persons already employed in 1962 by age, sex and occupation. The following assumptions were used regarding retirement: no persons aged 75 will be active in any occupation; men will start to retire at the age of 60, with the exception of certain occupations where retirement age is specified by law; and the higher the level of education women have, the longer they will remain in the labour force.

Forecasting the educational distribution of the labour force

In the Fourth Plan, the educational distribution of the seven occupations used for the forecast were based on the vectors of schooling shown in Table A4.2 in the appendix. The percentage distribution of educational attainment within a certain occupation was based on trend extrapolation between two points in time, 1952 and 1957. Once again, for agriculture and services, experts' judgements were used.

In the preparation of the Fifth Plan, a different classification system was used. The criterion for the educational level assigned to a certain occupation was the level usually required for people entering this occupation (Table A4.3 in the appendix).

For the purpose of forecasting the educational distribution of the labour force, three major occupational groups were distinguished:

(1) Occupations such as doctors, engineers and nurses which present no particular problem in assigning appropriate educational qualifications (30 per cent of the labour force in France).

(2) Qualified workers (40 per cent of the labour force). Three sample surveys of firms employing 10 persons or more in 1952, 1957 and 1961 have shown that the percentage of qualified workers rose by less than 0.5 per year. For the purpose of the forecast, a 0.5 per year rate of growth was assumed for this kind of occupation as a whole. The distribution of qualified workers within each sector was assumed to be the same as in 1962.

(3) For unqualified workers and farmers (30 per cent of the labour force), educational norms were established after consultation with the experts in the various Planning Commissions. These norms were usually higher than the observed educational background of this part of the labour force.

The results of the forecasts for the 1966 to 1970 period were that 32 per cent of the new recruits to the labour force should have at least a secondary school degree (i.e. a degree or, at least, the bacca-lauréat) and that 45 per cent of the labour force should be qualified workers. The first percentage is consistent with current policy in France to orient 33 per cent of each age group to secondary education and above. The second percentage, however, is higher than the one stipulated in the current educational reform.

The accuracy of manpower forecasts in France

Two types of comparisons between actual and predicted employment are presented in this section. The first type of comparison deals with employment forecasts by sector in the Second and Third Plans. The second type of comparison deals with employment forecasts by occupation in the Fifth Plan.

Table 4.2 gives the actual and predicted employment for ten sectors in the Second Plan. The number of employed persons in the base year of the forecasts (1952) appears in column 2, in order to give an idea of the size of the sector. Predictions and realizations for the target year (1957) are given in terms of indices relative to the base year (columns 3 and 4).

For the sake of the comparisons in this section, let us define the percentage prediction error (E) of employment in a given sector or occupation (j), as

$$E_j = \left(\frac{P_j - A_j}{A_j} \right) 100$$

where P_j is the predicted and A_j is the actual value. Therefore, a positive sign of the error would mean over-estimation and a negative sign under-estimation of the value of the variable being predicted.

Looking at column 5 of Table 4.2, we see that the error ranges from an over-estimation of 7.7 per cent in the textile industries to an under-estimation of 14.0 per cent in liquid fuels. Employment was exactly predicted only in the wood and furniture industries. Out of the remaining nine sectors, employment was under-estimated in seven cases, while over-estimation was observed in only two cases.

The last three columns of Table 4.2 present a comparison of production figures as predicted in the Second Plan and their actual values. It will be remembered that employment forecasts in France largely depend on production forecasts. Therefore, the examination of how well production was predicted will give us a clue in evaluating the manpower forecasts. As shown in column 8 of Table 4.2, the errors in the production forecasts have varied from an under-estimation of 29.3 per cent in the chemical industries to an over-estimation of 20.3 per cent in liquid fuels. One interesting point to observe is that production figures appear with higher prediction errors than employment figures. Moreover, in the case of liquid fuels, employment was *under*-estimated by 14.0 per cent while production was *over*-estimated by 20.3 per cent. This is a reflection of the diverse methods and continuous reconciliation of different figures that is so essential an element of French manpower forecasting techniques. In consequence, employment forecasts are not very sensitive to production forecasts.

Table 4.3 presents a comparison of employment forecasts and realizations in the Third Plan. In this case, over-estimation rather than under-estimation is the rule, both in the employment and production figures. It is interesting to observe that while production errors are less on the average than in the previous Plan, employment errors are higher than before. For example, employment in the vulnerable sector of liquid fuels has been under-estimated by 14.0 per cent in the Second Plan and over-estimated by 40.7 per cent in the Third Plan. And this in spite of the fact that production in this sector was more accurately predicted in the Third Plan ($E = -5.0$ per cent) than in the Second Plan ($E = 20.3$ per cent).

Tables A4.4 to A4.7 in the appendix present comparisons of employment forecasts and realizations by occupation in the Fifth Plan.[5] An outline of the methodology used in obtaining the forecasts

---

[5] This set of comparisons draws heavily on Vimont (1970).

TABLE 4.2

ACTUAL AND PREDICTED EMPLOYMENT BY SECTOR, SECOND PLAN, FRANCE, 1952 AND 1957

Sector	Actual employment 1952 (thousands)	1957 employment index (1952 = 100)			1957 Index of production (1952 = 100)		
		Forecast	Actual	Percentage prediction error	Forecast	Actual	Percentage prediction error
(1)	(2)	(3)	(4)	(5)	(6)	(7)	(8)
Coalmining	238	89	92	− 2.7	106	103	2.9
Gas	35	90	93	− 3.2	146	139	5.4
Electricity	77	108	102	5.9	136	141	− 3.9
Liquid fuels	48	105	122	−14.0	140	116	20.3
Iron and steel	136	99	103	− 3.9	129	129	− 0.4
Mechanical and electrical engineering industries	1,115	111	113	− 1.3	130	155	−16.1
Chemical industries	175	100	107	− 6.5	130	184	−29.3
Textile industries	506	96	89	7.7	113	132	−14.8
Leather	135	93	103	−10.2	115	116	− 0.9
Wood and furniture	178	97	97	—	113	132	−14.4

Source: based on Fourastié (1963), p. 75.

Note: Figures in columns 2, 3, 4, 6 and 7 are rounded to the nearest unit. Estimates in columns 5 and 8 are based on exact figures.

— = nil or negligible.

TABLE 4.3

ACTUAL AND PREDICTED EMPLOYMENT BY SECTOR, THIRD PLAN, FRANCE, 1956 AND 1961

Sector	Actual employment 1956 (thousands)	1961 employment index (1956 = 100)			1961 Index of production (1956 = 100)		
		Forecast	Actual	Percentage prediction error	Forecast	Actual	Percentage prediction error
(1)	(2)	(3)	(4)	(5)	(6)	(7)	(8)
Electricity	124	102	107	−4.2	141	146	−3.4
Petroleum — liquid fuels	59	137	97	40.7	150	158	−5.1
Solid mineral fuels	231	102	91	12.7	106	101	5.0
Extraction of other minerals and ores	54	100	91	9.9	127	126	0.8
Pottery — building materials	246	105	101	4.7	128	125	2.4
Glass — chemicals — rubber	330	103	108	−4.6	145	190	−23.7
Production of metals	220	106	107	−1.4	144	146	−1.4
Mechanical and electrical engineering industries	1,775	116	105	10.0	142	138	2.9
Textile industries	566	104	93	12.4	135	120	12.5
Clothing	482	105	99	6.1	130	113	15.0
Leather	205	103	96	7.3	120	104	15.4
Wood	230	96	96	0	120	131	−8.4
Paper and board	108	108	109	0	135	147	−8.2
Graphic arts	167	101	105	−3.8	119	130	−8.5
Other industries	141	103	114	−9.6	134	128	4.7

Source: based on Fourastié (1963), p. 76.

Note: See Table 4.2.

was given above. Out of the four alternative assumptions discussed, H_4 was adopted for the evaluation. This is the employment forecast as amended by the Planning Commissions.

The target year of the Fifth Plan is 1970 but recent manpower observations are available only for 1968 from a manpower census. As the French Plan does not produce figures for the intermediate years, it was necessary to estimate the implications of the 1970 predictions for 1968 in order to compare it with the actual employment given in the census. This interpolation for 1968 was done by means of two alternative methods:

Prediction method 1: Employment in 1968 was obtained by backward extrapolation of figures on the basis of the average rate of growth of employment in the 1962—70 period.

Prediction method 2: It was assumed that the planners perfectly predicted the absolute size of the labour force in 1968. Therefore, an evaluation based on the figures derived according to this method would check only how well the percentage distribution of the labour force was predicted.

As it is shown in Table A4.4, the size of the labour force was under-estimated by 228,200 people, or by 1.1 per cent. This under-estimation was due to two factors: first, the end of the war in Algeria and the repatriation which followed; and, second, the length of military service was reduced in France during the period of the Plan. Contrasting the predicted numbers of persons in different occupations with actual numbers, we observe a range of error of −15.9 per cent in the case of teachers to 7.1 per cent in the case of the armed forces. Standardization of the forecasts for the actual size of the labour force (Table A4.5) seems to improve the forecast of the absolute number of employed persons in 11 out of the 16 occupations we have distinguished, while the error in the percentage distributions is reduced only in seven cases.

Tables A4.6 and A4.7 present prediction and realization comparisons for particular occupations. Architects appear to have been under-estimated by 62.7 per cent while university teachers were over-estimated by 20.6 per cent. The conclusion we reach from these tables is that the finer the occupational classification used, the higher is the prediction error.

In order to have a summary measure of the error in each forecast of the appendix tables, let us define the root—mean—square prediction error (RMS) of a prediction as

92

$$\text{RMS} = \sqrt{\frac{1}{n} \sum_{j=1}^{n} E_j^2}$$

where E_j is the previously defined percentage prediction error in sector or occupational group j and n is the number of sectors or occupational groups distinguished in the prediction. Table 4.4 shows that the root-mean-square prediction error of the three types of forecasts we examined above is 6.9 per cent, 12.7 per cent and 6.6 per cent respectively.

TABLE 4.4

ROOT—MEAN—SQUARE ERROR OF SELECTED MANPOWER FORECASTS IN FRANCE

Subject of forecast	Error (per cent)
Employment by sector (Second Plan)	6.9
Employment by sector (Third Plan)	12.7
Employment by occupation (Fifth Plan)	6.6

Source: based on Tables 4.2, 4.3 and A4.4.

An evaluation of the French manpower forecasts

One could summarize the characteristics of the manpower techniques employed in France as follows:

(a) No unique 'model' is used for manpower forecasting. In contrast, a variety of models covering different stages in the planning process are used.

(b) Experts' opinion and judgement are used in every stage of the planning process along with the partial models mentioned above. If the models seem to give implausible forecasts, employment estimates according to the judgement of the planners supersede those of the models.

(c) Continuous iteration at every stage of the planning process assures that manpower forecasts are consistent with other orders of magnitude of the French economy.

At first sight it seems that it is very easy to criticise the forecasting techniques presented above. One could suggest marginal improvements at every stage of the process. Yet, it must be remembered that the French planners use every piece of statistical information available and they are aware of the weaknesses of their techniques. As better statistical material becomes available, the methodology is expanded and improved.[6]

One might be tempted to think that the technique used in employment forecasting in France is that of the 'manpower requirements' type (see Chapter 1), where economic goals are set first and then the employment forecasts are estimated conditional on the realization of economic forecasts. A careful inspection of the technique reveals that this is not true. Employment forecasts and production by sector are determined simultaneously by the iterative process discussed above.

One must not go to the other extreme, however, and think that this simultaneity implies optimization in an economic sense. The costs involved in the creation of the skills set out in the Plan are not taken into account. It is only in this sense that the French employment forecasting techniques may be considered as falling broadly within the manpower requirements approach.

Attempting to trace the source of errors in the French manpower forecasts, we have a case of *embarras du choix*. There are three main sources of error: methodology, data and judgement. From the point of view of data, French planners have done their best with the statistical information they have at their disposal. From the point of view of methodology, we have classified French manpower forecasting as coming close to the manpower requirements approach and the literature is rich in the weaknesses of this approach.[7] In our opinion, it is the role of judgement in French forecasting that must be mainly blamed for the prediction errors presented above.

The reason is that the two first sources of error (data and methodology) are closely related. The manpower requirements approach has been popular around the world because it is not data demanding. Had the French had age-earnings profiles by educational level, they could have attempted alternative approaches like rate of return analyses or linear programming. Moreover, it should be remembered that judgement overrides model solutions in France. Whatever number the model yields, this number will be modified in the final Plan if the members of the particular Commission find this number implausible.

Remember also that manpower forecasts in France are conditional

---

[6] On contemplated future improvement in the French manpower forecasting techniques, see Vimont (1970).

[7] For example, see Blaug (1970), Chapter 5.

on production and productivity targets. In the Second Plan, the root—mean—square error of production forecasts by sector was 14.2 per cent. The corresponding figure for the Third Plan was 10 per cent. Table A4.8 in the appendix presents the record of predicting the productivity change by sector between 1959 and 1965 in France. The percentage prediction errors range from + 64.2 per cent in the case of printing and publishing to −36.8 in military construction. The overall percentage error in productivity forecasting was 30 per cent (or 1.22 per cent in absolute terms).

In view of the above record, should one give a pass or a fail to French manpower forecasting techniques? Obviously, the answer to this question involves a judgement about judgements! In order to avoid this, one must digress and present an objective reason why one *cannot* evaluate a manpower forecast by simply comparing the predicted and actual employment, as we have done above. One has to take account of the real wage of labour prevailing at the base and target years. Although a prediction may be accurate from the point of view of the number of persons employed, the 'manpower forecast' which is the basis of the prediction is not necessarily 'accurate' in any scientific sense of the term. This is the case where the real wage of the kind of labour predicted has changed between the base and target years. The following example will illustrate the case.

Let us assume that the purpose of the forecast is to predict the number of engineers required by the target year T. As is shown in Figure 4.3, the number of engineers in the base year t is 70,000 and a manpower forecast model generated a solution of 100,000 engineers required by the target year T. If this manpower forecast is actually implemented, we will not be able to observe in year T anything else

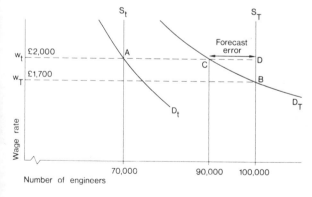

Figure 4.3. A manpower forecasting 'error'.

but 100,000 engineers employed. Should we conclude from that observation alone that the manpower forecast has been a good one? The answer is no. In order to evaluate the manpower forecast we must also look at the wages of engineers at the base and target years.

It would be helpful to remember that a manpower forecast deals with shifts of demand *at the same price.*[8] If the wage of engineers was £2,000 in the base year t then the full manpower forecast statement should read: 'By the target year T, the economy will require 100,000 engineers at a wage of £2,000 each'. Therefore, the manpower forecast leads to a predicted intersection of the supply and demand curves for engineers at point D.

Remember also that implementation of a forecast means a shift to the right of the (assumed for simplicity sake to be perfectly inelastic) supply curve for engineers. Therefore, although in year T we observe that prediction is equal to realization from the point of view of numbers, the manpower forecast itself (i.e. shift of the demand curve) has been wrong. (Point D was predicted instead of point C.) What has happened in this case is that the manpower forecast has over-estimated the requirements of the economy in terms of engineers by the target year T and more engineers were produced instead of the 'truly required' 90,000. The term 'truly required' is used in the sense of the number of engineers technically required, which can be absorbed by the market at the same wage rate. In this case, the over-estimation and consequent implementation of the Plan has led to a decrease in the wage of engineers to £1,700 by the target year T, at which wage all 100,000 engineers have been absorbed.[9]

The lesson from this example is that we can never judge a manpower forecast before looking at the new equilibrium wage as well. Therefore, in evaluating manpower forecasts one should make a double comparison:

(a) Prediction versus realization from the point of view of numbers employed, and

---

[8] At least if it is agreed that (1) there is a unique relationship between employment and wages paid to a particular type of manpower and (2) demand and supply are independent such that one can change without the other changing. It must be admitted that some manpower forecasters write as if they rejected both (1) and (2), in which case they would also reject the argument in the text that follows.

[9] This point is very different from the one raised by Blaug (1967, p. 267), as he was concerned with the error arising from a non-implemented manpower forecast.

(b) Real wages at the base and target year for the kind of labour which is the subject of the forecast.

In case the first comparison yields

prediction = realization

we have to distinguish three sub-cases:

$w_T = w_t$: Good manpower forecast (i)

$w_T < w_t$: Manpower requirements have been over-estimated and consequently earnings declined. (ii)

$w_T > w_t$: Manpower requirements have been under-estimated and consequently earnings have risen. (iii)

It is evident that these propositions will depend upon the elasticity of demand for the kind of labour predicted. The true manpower forecasting error will be greater (for any given wage discrepancy), the higher the elasticity of demand for that kind of labour. This is easily demonstrated by defining the manpower forecasting error as

$$\frac{\Delta N}{N} = M_L \left(\frac{\Delta w}{w}\right)$$

where M_L is the elasticity of demand for the kind of labour predicted, and $\Delta w/w$ is the percentage change of wages between base and target year.[10] Of course, data on earnings by educational qualifications are not available in France and therefore we cannot conduct the proper test.

In order to give an over-all evaluation of manpower forecasting in France, one can separate it into two parts: first, the preparatory work and second, the final numbers produced for inclusion in the Plan. When the consistency and sensitivity tests of the preparatory stage are borne in mind, manpower forecasting certainly helps in increasing the understanding of the relationship between manpower and the economy as a whole. One view is that the value of every plan lies more in the experience gained while it is elaborated than in the final numbers that are produced. In the case of manpower forecasting in France, the smell coming from the kitchen is preferable to the *plat-du-jour* served in the *grand salon*.

---

10 This difference in wages should be defined as

$$\Delta w = w_T - E(w_T) = w_T - w_t \, (1 + g_y + g_p)^{T-t}$$

where $E(w_T)$ is the expected wage in the target year, g_y is the real rate of growth of the economy between base and target year, and g_p is the annual rate of inflation between base and target year.

APPENDIX A4

TABLE A4.1

ACTUAL AND PREDICTED EMPLOYMENT ACCORDING TO ALTERNATIVE HYPOTHESES, FRANCE, 1954–78

INED No.	Occupational group	1954 actual employment	1962 actual employment	1970 forecast on alternative hypotheses				1978 forecast
				H_1	H_2	H_3	H_4	
(1)	(2)	(3)	(4)	(5)	(6)	(7)	(8)	(9)
01	Farmers and forestry workers	5175.4	3878.1	2969.5	2930.6	2909.5	2930.9	2183.0
02	Fishermen and merchant sailors	80.0	76.3	66.8	55.9	47.1	63.1	49.0
03	Production workers and craftsmen	6687.2	7050.4	7932.0	7782.6	7570.9	7706.6	8081.0
04	Drivers and conductors	319.4	413.4	460.5	527.5	595.6	532.6	652.0
05	Scientific and technical personnel (except managerial)	460.4	617.8	729.4	868.9	1009.0	933.5	1307.0
06	Administrative personnel (except managerial)	1506.8	1849.8	2284.1	2305.7	2333.9	2318.0	2733.0
07	Shopkeepers and sales workers	1664.1	1627.2	1791.5	1694.6	1614.4	1698.8	1783.0
08	Managerial personnel	303.8	377.6	445.0	502.7	565.5	499.8	639.0
09	Medical personnel and related workers	250.0	346.2	423.7	444.2	497.7	492.7	726.0
10	Teachers	360.5	505.9	644.2	697.1	755.2	652.4	845.0
11	Jurists	62.3	56.3	68.4	61.8	55.0	61.3	69.0
12	Artists	49.2	47.1	52.3	49.1	45.4	48.4	54.0
13	Workers in personal services (barbers, etc.)	106.3	128.8	157.1	159.4	160.2	154.7	200.0
14	Service workers in mixed enterprises, transport and communications	1298.5	1385.9	1514.2	1524.5	1507.0	1524.9	1686.0
15	Armed forces, policemen, firemen and customs officers	443.1	435.7	428.3	418.2	409.8	419.0	..
16	Clergy	177.0	158.5	198.0	142.2	88.8	128.3	..
	Total	18944.0	18955.0	20165.0	20165.0	20165.0	20165.0	21500.0

Source: Vimont and Dubrulle (1966), pp. 496–8.

.. = not available.

TABLE A4.2

RELATIONSHIP BETWEEN THE OCCUPATIONAL AND EDUCATIONAL DISTRIBUTION OF THE LABOUR FORCE, FRANCE

Occupation	Level of qualification	Number of years of formal schooling
Administrative and business executives	20 per cent very highly qualified	11
	40 per cent highly qualified	9
	40 per cent technicians	7
Engineers	50 per cent very highly qualified	11
	50 per cent highly qualified	9
Technicians and draughtsmen		7
Foremen and supervisors		5
Clerical staff	50 per cent	5
	50 per cent	4
Skilled operatives		3–4
Semi-skilled and unskilled operatives		0

Source: Fourastié (1963), p. 69.
Note: The number of years of formal schooling given starts after the end of the 'Observation Cycle'.

99

TABLE A4.3

EDUCATIONAL CLASSIFICATION USED IN THE FIFTH FRENCH PLAN

Level 1.   Employed persons in jobs normally requiring a degree
      (a) Law and business
      (b) Sciences
      (c) Literature
      (d) Health
      (e) All other subjects

Level 2.   Employed persons in jobs usually requiring two years of study beyond the·baccalauréat or the technician's diploma
      (a) Sciences
      (b) Law and business
      (c) Education
      (d) Social and sanitary services
      (e) Literature

Level 3.   Employed persons in jobs usually requiring the equivalent of the completion of secondary education
      (a) Agriculture
      (b) Manufacturing
      (c) Administration
      (d) Commerce
      (e) Social and sanitary services
      (f) All other subjects

Level 4.   Employed persons in jobs normally requiring a diploma equivalent to Certificat d'Aptitude professionnel or Brevet d'Etudes professionnelles et commerciales
      (a) Agriculture
      (b) Manufacturing
      (c) Electricity
      (d) Construction
      (e) Other industrial occupations
      (f) Administration
      (g) Commerce
      (h) Social and sanitary services
      (i) Other

Level 5.   Employed persons in jobs normally not requiring any qualification beyond completion of education to the minimum school leaving age.

ACTUAL AND PREDICTED EMPLOYMENT BY MAJOR OCCUPATIONAL GROUP, FRANCE, 1968.
PREDICTION METHOD 1

INED No.	Occupational group	Actual		Predicted		Percentage prediction error.	
		Thousands	Per-cent-age	Thousands	Per-cent-age	Thousands	Percentage
(1)	(2)	(3)	(4)	(5)	(6)	(7)	(8)
01	Farmers and forestry workers	3,090.2	15.45	3,144.8	15.90	1.77	2.90
02	Fishermen and merchant sailors	65.8	0.33	65.8	0.33	–	–
03	Production workers and craftsmen	7,445.9	37.23	7,529.8	38.07	1.13	2.28
04	Drivers and conductors	473.4	2.37	499.3	2.53	5.47	6.75
05	Scientific and technical personnel (except managerial)	893.0	4.46	840.9	4.25	– 5.92	– 4.71
06	Administrative personnel (except managerial)	2,309.4	11.54	2,196.0	11.11	– 4.91	– 3.73
07	Shopkeepers and sales workers	1,703.5	8.52	1,676.2	8.48	– 1.60	– 0.47
08	Managerial personnel	470.0	2.35	463.8	2.35	– 1.32	–
09	Medical personnel and related workers	507.0	2.53	450.0	2.28	–11.24	– 9.88
10	Teachers	721.9	3.61	607.3	3.07	–15.88	–14.96
11	Jurists	66.1	0.33	60.1	0.30	– 9.08	– 9.09
12	Artists	52.7	0.26	47.9	0.24	– 9.12	– 7.69
13	Workers in personal services (barbers, etc.)	148.8	0.74	147.6	0.75	– 0.81	1.35
14	Service workers in mixed enterprises, transport and communications	1,525.6	7.63	1,486.2	7.52	– 2.58	– 1.44
15	Armed forces, policemen, firemen and customs officers	395.1	1.97	423.0	2.14	7.06	8.63
16	Clergy	133.8	0.67	135.3	0.68	1.12	1.49
	Total	20,002.2	100.00	19,774.0	100.00	–1.14	–

Source: Cols. (1)—(6): based on Vimont (1970), pp. 13—4.

Col. (7) = (Col. 5 — Col. 3) x 100 of Col. 3.
Col. (8) = (Col. 6 — Col. 4) x 100 of Col. 4.
Note: See text for the prediction method used.
– = nil or negligible.

101

TABLE A4.5

ACTUAL AND PREDICTED EMPLOYMENT BY MAJOR OCCUPATIONAL GROUP, FRANCE, 1968.
PREDICTION METHOD 2

INED No.	Occupational group	Actual		Predicted		Percentage prediction error	
		Thousands	Per-centage	Thousands	Per-centage	Thousands	Percentage
(1)	(2)	(3)	(4)	(5)	(6)	(7)	(8)
01	Farmers and forestry workers	3,090.2	15.45	3,059.6	15.30	− 1.02	− 0.97
02	Fishermen and merchant sailors	65.8	0.33	64.9	0.32	− 1.37	− 3.03
03	Production workers and craftsmen	7,445.9	37.23	7,618.0	38.09	2.31	2.31
04	Drivers and conductors	473.4	2.37	516.5	2.58	1.10	8.86
05	Scientific and technical personnel (except managerial)	893.0	4.46	890.0	4.45	− 0.23	− 0.22
06	Administrative personnel (except managerial)	2,309.4	11.54	2,254.8	11.27	− 2.35	− 2.34
07	Shopkeepers and sales workers	1,703.5	8.52	1,689.2	8.45	− 0.84	− 0.82
08	Managerial personnel	470.0	2.35	483.4	2.42	2.85	2.98
09	Medical personnel and related workers	507.0	2.53	472.5	2.36	− 6.80	− 6.72
10	Teachers	721.9	3.61	632.5	3.16	− 12.38	− 12.46
11	Jurists	66.1	0.33	60.6	0.30	− 8.32	− 9.09
12	Artists	52.7	0.26	48.0	0.24	− 8.92	− 7.69
13	Workers in personal services (barbers, etc.)	148.8	0.74	151.2	0.76	1.61	2.70
14	Service workers in mixed enterprises, transport and communications	1,525.6	7.63	1,506.2	7.53	− 1.27	− 1.31
15	Armed forces, policemen, firemen and customs officers	395.1	1.97	421.2	2.10	6.60	6.60
16	Clergy	133.8	0.67	132.4	0.66	− 1.05	− 1.49
	Total	20,002.2	100.00	20,002.2	100.00	—	—

TABLE A4.6

ACTUAL AND PREDICTED EMPLOYMENT FOR CERTAIN OCCUPATIONS, FRANCE, 1968.
PREDICTION METHOD 1

INED No.	Occupational group	Actual		Predicted		Percentage prediction error	
		Thousands	Per-centage	Thousands	Per-centage	Thousands	Percentage
(1)	(2)	(3)	(4)	(5)	(6)	(7)	(8)
052	Engineers	194.0	0.97	177.6	0.90	− 8.45	− 7.20
053	Architects	11.0	0.05	4.1	0.02	−62.73	−60.00
054	Technicians	516.6	2.58	475.1	2.40	− 8.03	− 6.98
055	Draughtsmen	149.7	0.75	163.1	0.82	8.95	9.33
091	Physicians, surgeons, dentists, pharmacists, veterinarians	120.7	0.60	113.6	0.57	− 5.88	− 5.00
092	Midwives and nurses	148.2	0.74	130.0	0.65	−12.28	−12.16
096	Social workers	31.4	0.16	24.4	0.12	−22.29	−25.00
101	School teachers	507.6	2.54	411.6	2.08	−18.91	−18.11
104	University teachers	22.3	0.11	26.9	0.14	20.63	27.27
151	Officers	55.1	0.27	63.3	0.32	14.88	18.51
152	Other ranks	340.0	1.70	359.7	1.82	5.79	7.06

Source and note: see Table A4.4.

TABLE A4.7

ACTUAL AND PREDICTED EMPLOYMENT FOR CERTAIN OCCUPATIONS, FRANCE, 1968.
PREDICTION METHOD 2

INED No.	Occupational group	Actual		Predicted		Percentage prediction error	
		Thousands	Percentage	Thousands	Percentage	Thousands	Percentage
(1)	(2)	(3)	(4)	(5)	(6)	(7)	(8)
052	Engineers	194.0	0.97	171.8	0.86	−11.44	−11.34
053	Architects	11.0	0.05	15.8	0.08	43.64	60.00
054	Technicians	516.6	2.58	507.0	2.53	− 1.86	− 1.94
055	Draughtsmen	149.7	0.75	172.9	0.86	15.50	14.67
091	Physicians, surgeons, dentists, pharmacists, veterinarians	120.7	0.60	117.0	0.58	− 3.06	− 3.33
092	Midwives and nurses	148.2	0.74	138.0	0.69	− 6.88	− 6.76
096	Social workers	31.4	0.16	25.0	0.12	−20.38	−25.00
101	School teachers	507.6	2.54	421.0	2.10	−17.06	−17.32
104	University teachers	22.3	0.11	31.7	0.16	42.15	45.45
151	Officers	55.1	0.27	63.4	0.32	15.06	18.52
152	Other ranks	340.0	1.70	357.8	1.79	5.23	5.29

Source and note: see Table A4.4.

TABLE A4.8

ACTUAL AND PREDICTED RATE OF PRODUCTIVITY GROWTH BY
SECTOR, FRANCE, 1959—65

Sector	Actual	Predicted	Percentage prediction error
Food and beverages	4.3	3.9	− 9.3
Solid fuel	2.2	2.2	−
Gas	7.8	7.3	− 6.4
Petroleum products and natural gas	7.6	7.2	− 5.3
Construction materials	7.7	5.1	−33.8
Glass	5.1	6.0	17.6
Iron ore and metallurgy products	3.5	4.3	22.9
Non-ferrous metals	4.5	7.1	57.8
Primary metal products	3.2	4.7	46.9
Machinery and mechanical apparatus	4.2	5.1	21.4
Machinery and electrical apparatus	4.2	5.6	33.3
Automobiles and cycles	3.1	4.8	54.8
Military construction	3.8	2.4	−36.8
Rubber and chemical products	6.5	6.4	− 1.5
Textiles	5.3	5.2	− 1.9
Housing	5.0	5.4	8.0
Leather	3.7	4.3	16.2
Wood products	4.0	5.2	35.0
Paper	4.8	5.2	8.3
Printing and publishing	2.8	4.6	64.2
Plastics	6.4	5.2	−18.8
Construction and public works	4.5	5.1	13.3

Source: Vimont (1970), p. 21.

5. Thailand

by Mark Blaug

Educational planning, in the modern sense of the term, goes back in Thailand no further than 1962, when the Second Economic and Social Development Plan (1962—66) was launched. The Second Plan included a plan for the educational system as did the Third Plan (1967—71), which is now drawing to a close. These two educational plans were based on a variety of methods, including those of making long-term forecasts of manpower requirements. Between 1963 and 1967, five different groups prepared manpower forecasts for Thailand, some of which looked no further than 1970, while others projected manpower requirements up to 1986. Our task here is to assess the quality of these forecasts and, so far as it is possible, to compare prediction with outcome. We begin with a brief review of background data in order to highlight the problems of manpower forecasting in an economy such as that of Thailand, after which we will take up each of the five forecasts in turn. The question of the influence that these forecasts actually exerted on educational planning in Thailand will be postponed to the end of the chapter.

Background data

The Thai economy is essentially based on agriculture and more fundamentally on the production of rice: over 80 per cent of the economically active population is engaged in the agricultural sector; the rice crop alone accounts for 15 per cent of GNP and 85 per cent of exports. The last 15 years have seen the rapid development of light industry, construction and mining, together with some diversification of agricultural production. GNP passed the mark of £2,000m. in 1969, with per capita GNP at about £60. The rate of growth of GNP has averaged about 6 per cent over the decade 1953—63 but 8.5 per cent was taken as the target rate of growth in the Second Plan;

106

recent years have seen annual growth rates as low as 2 per cent and as high as 12 per cent. Total population now stands at about 35 million, with an annual growth rate well above 3 per cent.

One of the most remarkable features of the Thai economy — which is of some importance to our story — is the extent to which the city of Bangkok dominates its economic activity. Greater Bangkok contains 2.5 million people; the next largest city, Chiengmai, contains 150,000. Only 800,000 of the 14 million members of the labour force live in Greater Bangkok but more than a fifth of all manufacturing labour, more than a quarter of construction labour, nearly a third of transportation workers, just about a third of the workers in services and over half of the labour involved in the generation and distribution of power are employed in the metropolitan area (Muscat, 1966, p. 182). From a different point of view, the whole of the central government, all of the leading firms, 9 out of the Kingdom's 12 institutions of higher education, and 400 of the country's 1,600 secondary schools are located in Bangkok.

The broad outlines of the Thai educational system are conveyed by the 1969 enrolment pyramid (Figure 5.1). It is clear from the pyramid that about 20 per cent of children entering primary schools

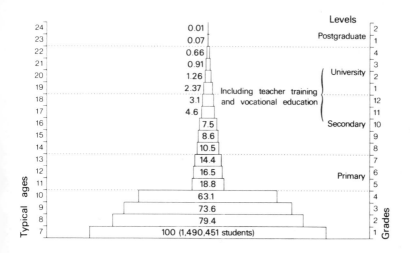

Figure 5.1. Educational enrolment pyramid, Thailand, 1969.

Source: Unpublished figures furnished by the Educational Planning Office of the Ministry of Education

Note: All years are expressed as percentages of enrolments in Primary Grade 1.

107

leave with only one year of education, although the most receive four years; thereafter, the pyramid tapers off rapidly. Half of the schooling at secondary levels is in fact provided by private rather than state schools. According to the 1960 Census of Population, 94 per cent of the total population over the age of 6 had only received primary schooling, about 5 per cent had at least received some secondary schooling and only 0.73 per cent had completed higher education. The educational structure of the labour force as distinct from the total population is revealed by the figures in Table 5.1.

TABLE 5.1

PERCENTAGE DISTRIBUTION OF EMPLOYED PERSONS BY EDUCATION AND SEX, THAILAND, 1966—67

Educational level	Male	Female
Primary and below	71.40	79.82
Academic secondary	16.17	9.64
Vocational secondary	2.58	3.34
Teacher training	0.60	2.20
University	6.15	4.11
Other	3.10	0.89
Total	100.00	100.00

Source: NSO (1968), Table 8A, pp. 39—40.
Note: The figures refer only to urban areas.

The table highlights the lack of information in Thailand about the rural labour force. The only available comprehensive source on the entire labour force of the kingdom is the 1960 Population Census. It does not, however, provide four-way tables of employment (i.e., by age, sector, occupation and education). These have to be extracted from the bi-annual Labour Force Surveys of Municipal Areas which cover only about 10 per cent of the economically active population and go no further than eight one-digit sectors and ten one-digit occupations. Vacancy statistics, even if taken at face value, are unreliable because of the extremely limited coverage of establishments to date. No serious efforts have been made to study the extent of under-employment of labour in farms or factories, and unemployment statistics, like statistics of employment, cover only urban areas. The only source of direct data on the productivity of labour in non-agricultural pursuits is the 1964 Industrial Census and there is no direct evidence whatever on past trends in output per worker in any

108

of the major sectors of the economy. Indeed, since the only population census is the one of 1960, there is no reliable information from which *trends* in labour force characteristics — shifts in occupational structure, changes in industrial composition, changes in participation rates by sex and age, etc. — can be determined.[1] The temptation, in these circumstances, to lean heavily on the slender reed of international comparisons is irresistible. It is a temptation, as we shall see, to which all the manpower forecasters in Thailand have in one way or another succumbed.

A few more words about the difficulties of manpower forecasting in Thailand are in order before we get down to cases. No figures have ever been published in Thailand on employment in the public, as distinct from the private sector, much less a breakdown of public employment by educational attainment. The figure would be difficult to estimate in any case because of the problem of defining 'public employment': the government owns shares in a large number of manufacturing companies but the percentage of shares held is not always disclosed. Perhaps a quarter of all university graduates and a quarter to a third of all secondary school graduates work for the government, that is, in the civil service, state enterprises, schools, universities, the armed forces and the police.[2] They do so at salaries that have been variously estimated to be as low as 25 per cent of the salaries offered to the same kind of labour in private industry (Silcock, 1967, pp. 292—300). They make up much of the difference, however, by holding two or three jobs simultaneously, frequently by working for themselves or their family. As a matter of fact, in the manufacturing sector, only half of the labour force are employees, the rest being 'own account workers' and 'unpaid family workers' (Muscat, 1966, p. 184). Of course, in commerce, self-employment and family employment is practically universal. In general, the widespread practice of carrying on jobs in two or more occupations and sectors within the one-digit classification — such as farm women becoming petty traders of non-agricultural goods in the off season — severely limits the usefulness of working with data on the occupational and sectoral composition of the labour force in Thai-

---

[1] For a more detailed analysis of the manpower data gap in Thailand, see Seal (1970).

[2] No official data are available on this question; the proportions cited are the estimates of H. F. McCusker who has examined the educational backgrounds of civil servants in a number of government departments in the course of preparing a doctoral dissertation on the manpower problems of the Thai government.

land (Muscat, 1966, p. 55). We mention this problem now because it is one which all the forecasters in Thailand have so far evaded. By itself, it may well be sufficient to render all their work meaningless for planning purposes.

The forecast of the Joint Task Force

The publication of the 1960 Population Census led almost immediately to a pronounced interest in manpower problems within the Thai government (Silcock, 1967, pp. 283—86). The result was the formation of the Joint Thai—US Task Force, which carried out a study in the incredibly short period of two months in 1963.[3] The Task Force was given extremely broad terms of reference which they interepreted themselves as implying that:

'priority should be given to: (1) . . . work in the development of over-all manpower requirements at two specific target dates, i.e. 1966 (end of current six-year economic development plan) and 1980 (sufficiently long-range to give the widest lattitude in educational planning) and (2) assessment of the current educational system's capacity to supply manpower for economic and social development at the suggested target dates . . . The exercise would develop areas of student supply in surplus, or in shortfall, which would then suggest the possible alternatives in adjusting the educational system to supply the educated manpower at each educational level in the accepted projections of manpower demand at the target dates' (Task Force, 1963, I, p. 2).

However, despite this fairly clear statement of intentions, subsequent remarks show that the Task Force was willing to consider labour market policies, changes in salary structure and out-of-school training schemes as perfectly legitimate ways of meeting shortfalls or gluts of particular types of manpower (Task Force, 1963, I, pp. 3—6). We may conclude, therefore, that the Task Force left the

---

[3] The Task Force consisted of E. W. Burgess, C. Brembeck and W. J. Platt of AID (US Agency for International Development) and eight high-ranking Thai officials. Apart from the two-volume publication that we will cite, there is also a one-volume version in Thai and English, published by the Educational Planning Office of the Thai Ministry of Education in 1967 and separate but related accounts of the study by W. J Platt and C. Brembeck in Adams (1964), pp. 103—53).

110

ultimate purpose of its forecasts deliberately vague: significant shortages or surpluses by 1966 or 1980 would demonstrate that 'something' must be done but that 'something' might be the provision of more or less places in the educational system or the enactment of measures to influence employers' behaviour and individual career choices.

The Task Force made 10 different long-term projections or forecasts of both supply and demand up to 1980, of which three also included short-term predictions up to 1966. We start with a supply projection No. 1 which assumes that the fraction currently enrolled in schools in each age group will remain the same in the future, absolute enrolments reflecting nothing else but the rate of growth of population. This provided a minimum baseline for all the other supply projections, at least if it were correct to assume that the birth rate would decline by one-third between 1960 and 1980.[4] Supply projection No. 2 assumes that the percentage of persons with different levels of education in the 1960 population will remain constant in the future or, in other words, that the stock of educated manpower will grow just as fast as population. Projection No. 3 assumes that the educational attainments of the population of the whole kingdom in 1980 will reach the levels attained in Bangkok—Thonburi in 1960, the outcome, say, of a deliberate policy of equalizing educational opportunities between urban and rural areas. Projections No. 4 and 5 assume fulfilment of the Karachi Plan target of 7 years of compulsory education by 1970 and 1980 respectively.

So far, these are merely alternative projections or forecasts of educational supply. With projection No. 6 we move to estimates of the future demand for educated manpower. Recalling the terminology of Chapter 1, 'onlooker forecast' No. 6 assumes that (a) the percentage of people in different occupations in different sectors with different levels of education in the whole of Thailand in 1980 will rise to the 1960 level for Greater Bangkok; (b) the share of the labour force employed in agriculture will fall from 81 per cent in

---

[4] The 1970 Census of Population will show whether this assumption is correct. However, most population experts working in Thailand doubt that the birth rate has significantly declined in the decade of the 1960's. There was some expectation in 1960 that Thailand would shortly adopt a family planning programme (Silcock, 1967, pp. 35ff) but the prospects of that happening still look uncertain 10 years later.

1963 to 70 per cent in 1980;[5] and (c) the economically inactive population will reach the same educational levels in 1980 as those achieved by the economically active population in 1960. 'Onlooker forecast' No. 7 adds to these resulting numbers a policy of 'up-grading' educational attainments within occupations of 2 per cent per year, that is, 2 per cent of the absolute number of people of different educational levels in 10 one-digit occupational categories; the only justification offered for this procedure is the statement that 'we selected 2 per cent per year upgrading of educational attainments as the contribution that added "human capital" would make to an overall required increase in productivity of 3 to 4 per cent per year' (Task Force, 1963, II, pp. 97, 108). Both forecasts No. 6 and 7 were made only for 1980 and not for 1966.

This brings us to demand forecasts No. 8—10 in which the authors themselves place greatest reliance; these were advisedly only short-term forecasts up to 1966. Let us explain how they were made. Output estimates by 11 sectors of economic activity for 1966 were made by the National Economic Development Board (NEDB) of Thailand. Having already accepted independent population and labour force projections up to 1966, the average increase of output per man employed in the period 1963—66 came to about 4 per cent per annum, compared with 3 per cent actually experienced in the late 1950's and early 1960's. In other words, either the output estimates were too optimistic or the labour force estimates were too pessimistic. Brushing over this difficulty, however, the Task Force now distributed the average 4 per cent increase in the productivity of labour over the 11 sectors by what they themselves describe as 'reasoned judgement and the experience of other countries' (Task Force, 1963, II, p. 106). Out of this came the so-called 'required employment levels by sectors' for 1966, which, as we are beginning to see, are generally on the low side because of the over-estimation of probable productivity improvements. It is worth noting that the Task Force treated agriculture as a residual, calculating its employment as the difference between total projected employment and the amount required by all other sectors, which gave a reasonable 1 per cent

---

[5] This assumption was defended by citing data for nine countries, only two of which are in Asia, and despite the fact that the share in question over the 16-year period 1947—63 declined only 4 percentage points in Thailand, falling from 85 to 81 per cent (Task Force, 1963, II, p. 103). Reasons for doubting that employment in agriculture as a proportion of total employment will significantly decline in the next 10 or 15 years are given by Muscat (1966, pp. 56—64).

productivity improvement for agriculture over the years 1960—66.

Next, the educational composition of the labour force by economic sectors in 1960 was applied to the 1966 sectoral employment estimates and then summed to form the total required stock of educated manpower in 1966, as the assumption that both the active and the inactive labour force would achieve the same level of education. After allowing for losses due to deaths and retirements, we finally arrive at the required educational output by 1966, which constitutes forecast No. 8. 'Onlooker forecast' No. 9 now adds to this the same upgrading assumption as forecast No. 7, namely 2 per cent per year. Lastly 'onlooker forecast' No. 10 treats only a part of the total labour force, namely, employment in five non-agricultural sectors which together accounted for over half of GNP in 1960. Here a number of special labour market surveys were used to provide more accurate indications of trends in occupational composition and these resulting employment estimates were then converted into educational requirements by using comparative international data borrowed from an OECD study (Parnes, 1962, pp. 110—1). The end-product yields estimates of requirements in four one-digit occupational groups specified by three levels of educational attainment.

The major recommendation that emerged from this entire exercise was the proposal to expand significantly the scale of secondary education. The authors admit, however, that 'our methods are not precise enough for us to say that . . . a deficit (of secondary graduates) will definitely prevent achieving desired economic growth. Over the short run, an economy can compensate somewhat for inadequate educational attainment of its manpower by such means as superior on-the-job training, borrowing techniques and know-how from abroad, reducing underemployment, and improvement in physical capital' (Task Force, 1963, I, p. 20). Unfortunately, what educational planners want to know is precisely whether it pays to 'compensate' in this way, that is to say, whether to take advantage of alternative possibilities of producing qualified manpower. On this crucial question the Task Force provides little guidance.

The report of the Task Force is full of very sensible proposals for educational reform: for example, the immediate introduction of automatic promotion in primary schools to eliminate mixed-age classes; the restrained, orderly extension of schooling opportunities at the lower levels rather than a pell-mell race to complete the Karachi Plan; the creation of a terminal type of secondary education in keeping with the needs of the two out of three students who complete secondary education but never gain admission to universities; not to mention numerous administrative recommendations (Task Force, 1963, I, pp. 27ff). And their list of educational data requirements says almost all that can be said on this score. But as a document designed to link education with economic development, it is extremely ambiguous.

Consider, first, forecasts No. 1 — 7 for 1980, of which the first five deal with the supply side and the last two with the demand side. We have described the last two as 'onlooker forecasts' but, in fact, it is not clear whether they amount to predictions of what will happen or what should happen. Forecast No. 6 assumes that the educational composition of the labour force in the whole kingdom in 1980 will resemble that of Greater Bangkok in 1960. The realism of this assumption cannot be tested because the 1960 Census failed to cross-classify the economically active population by sex and education. To our previous remarks on the economic dominance of Bangkok, we may now add evidence of its dominant educational role: of the 25,000 candidates sitting for their nationally administered secondary leaving certificates in 1968, 15,000 were studying in Greater Bangkok, of whom half had parents residing in the metropolitan area, the other half having been sent by their 'up-country' parents to study in Bangkok; in fact, in no region in Thailand do a majority of the parents send their children to local secondary schools. Having passed Maw Saw 5 examinations, a certain fraction of the successful candidates then sit for the Higher Education Entrance Examination; in recent years, over 85 per cent of these have come from families living in Bangkok. It is obvious, therefore, that to expect the educational gap between Bangkok and the rural areas to be closed in 20 years is a heroic assumption, roughly equivalent to assuming that the Outer Hebrides in 1990 will be like London in 1970. But waiving this point, the deeper question is: How is it to be accomplished? Suppose that educational facilities could be expanded in rural areas by 1980 to provide the same opportunities as existed in Bangkok in 1960 (the basis of projection 3). Suppose even that students would take up all the places provided. Can it be assumed that employers outside Bangkok would be able to absorb all the additional output by simply upgrading the mimimum hiring standards for jobs? Apparently, this is not what was intended in forecast No. 6. Upgrading at a rate of 2 per cent per year is added to forecast No. 6 to give a still larger forecast No. 7. But what are the policy variables that can produce the kind of economic growth in rural areas by 1980 to create the same job opportunities that are now available in Bangkok?

Consider now forecasts No. 8—10. These are quite clearly forecasts

114

of probable rather than desirable outcomes. Are they reasonable? The estimates in forecasts No. 8—10 are, in fact, annual averages of the flow demand, that is, additions to stocks, for the period 1960—66, making no allowance for a build-up to the 1966 target figure (Task Force, 1963, II, p. 96). The estimates were as shown in Table 5.2.

Let us take first the question of university graduates. The Task Force did not anticipate a serious shortage of graduates. Having

TABLE 5.2

ESTIMATED AVERAGE ANNUAL FLOW DEMAND AND SUPPLY AND
ACTUAL SUPPLY OF GRADUATES BY EDUCATIONAL LEVEL,
THAILAND, 1960—66

Levels of education	Demand			Supply		Shortages	
	Projection 8	Projection 9	Projection 10	Projection 5	Actual Supply	Estimated shortages[c]	Recalculated shortages[d]
University graduates	1,248	1,957	2,567	2,550	3,387[a]	17	−820
Secondary school leavers (12th Grade)	32,182	39,238	10,677	21,214	17,895[b]	18,024	21,343
Upper primary leavers (7th Grade)	154,141	116,345	—	85,800	115,249	30,545	1,096
Lower primary leavers (4th Grade)	621,707	877,002	—	665,100	743,750	211,902	134,252
Total	809,278	1,034,542	—	774,664	880,281	260,488	155,841

Source: Task Force (1963), II, pp. 24, 95; NEC (1969), pp. 48, 76, 98, 158—68.
Notes: [a]excludes recipients of diplomas or certificates from universities,   ies,
giving cumulated total of bachelor degrees issued divided by seven,
[b]includes equivalent levels of teacher training,
[c]highest estimated demand minus highest estimated supply,
[d]highest estimated demand minus actual supply.
— = nil or negligible.

seriously under-estimated their supply however, there should have been heavy graduate unemployment by 1966, at least if the demand projections were accurate. But the annual Labour Force Surveys of Municipal Areas have continued to report extremely low figures for unemployment all through the 1960's (about 1 per cent of the labour force). It is true that unemployment is not reported by educational levels but casual impression of the Thai economy does not suggest that graduate unemployment is now or ever has been a serious problem. We do not know, of course, what percentage of new graduates decided not to enter the labour force: labour force participation rates in Thailand are not broken down by educational attainments. We do know that roughly one-third of all graduates are women but female labour force participation rates are surprisingly high in Thailand: 85 per cent in the age range 15—65 as against 96 per cent for men (NEDB, 1967A, p. 14). The figures for graduates must be higher for both sexes than these over-all statistics. We are, therefore, driven to the conclusion that the Task Force seriously under-estimated the demand as well as the supply of graduates over a forecasting period as short as 3 years. The source of the downward bias on the demand side is undoubtedly connected with the optimistic view which the Task Force took of potential productivity improvements in the Thai economy.

Turning now to 12th grade leavers, we see that the shortage of middle-level manpower should have been even greater in 1966 than that predicted by the Task Force. There is no independent evidence which we can use to assess the accuracy of this prediction. What we can say is that the growth rate of the Thai economy did not slow down in the 1960's, despite this apparent massive shortfall of middle-level manpower.

The supply of both upper and lower primary leavers was badly under-estimated. This is extraordinary because, as we shall see later on, the steady growth rate of primary education is one of the few constants of the Thai educational system.[6] At any rate, the result of

---

[6] As Figure 5.4 shows, primary education had been growing at a constant rate between 1954 and 1963, whereas secondary education had been growing at a declining rate. The Task Force over-estimated the supply of secondary school leavers and under-estimated the supply of primary school leavers. Yet an almost perfect prediction of both for 1966 would have been produced by fitting $y_t = ab^t$ to primary school enrolments and $y_t = Ka^{b^t}$ (the Gompertz curve) to secondary school enrolments, where y_t = enrolments, t = time, a, b = constants and K = the asymptote of the Gompertz. It has not been possible to throw any light on the source of the bias in the Task Force's projections: they never explain precisely how they project supply.

this under-estimate of supply is practically to wipe out the prediction of a shortfall of 7th grade leavers but to leave substantially intact the prediction of a shortage of 4th grade leavers.

This is perhaps as far as we can go in assessing this pioneer forecast in Thailand. There would seem to be little point in reproducing their 1960—80 estimates, except to say that they probably over-estimated demand (which they have assumed will grow at an implausibly high figure of about 25 per cent per annum for secondary school graduates) and under-estimated supply (by assuming a one-third decline in the birth rate). The two biases reinforce each other and hence lead to the prediction of a serious shortage of middle level manpower throughout this 20-year period.

One more observation is in order. The Task Force noted that the government employs one out of three workers classified in the 1960 Census as 'employees', that is, all those that are economically active except 'own account workers' and 'unpaid family workers'. They remark on the fact that government salaries exert a strong influence on the total salary structure, although much less at the higher levels, and point out that entry points on government pay scales are principally based on educational qualifications. They then go on to remark that 'one could almost safely wager that a study of civil service employees in class (2), (1), and "special" would reveal a substantial number that are not working in their area of professional or trained competence' (Task Force, 1963, II, p. 69). If they are correct in this wager, they have inadvertently built this sort of malutilization into their projections and thus helped to perpetuate it. This is a difficulty which is not satisfactorily resolved anywhere in their document.

Later forecasts

The second major forecasting effort in Thailand, referred to hereafter as Secondary Education Programs (SEM), was carried out in 1964. It concentrated its efforts on secondary education in keeping with the central finding of the Task Force of a prevailing shortage of middle-level manpower. SEM's forecasting methodology, like that of the Task Force, consisted essentially of four steps: (1) projecting the total labour force up to 1986; (2) distributing it accordingly among major economic sectors; (3) distributing it further among major occupations within economic sectors; and then (4) translating this occupational composition into a corresponding educational struc-

117

ture. As they say: 'The general method just described above was chosen (in preference to the method of projecting GNP by sector) because the labour force projections upon which it was based were much more reliable than any GNP projections available in Thailand' (SEM, 1966, p. 29). Having no other data than those for 1960 by one-digit occupational categories and for 1963 by two-digit occupational categories, they proceeded by assuming that the ratio of the numbers in each two-digit category in 1963 to the numbers in each one-digit category in 1960 will remain the same up to 1986; in short, they assumed a constant internal composition of the occupational structure between 1960 and 1986 (SEM, 1966, pp. 29, 34). In projecting the change in the industrial composition of non-agricultural sectors up to 1986, they made use of a regression equation estimated by W. Galenson[7] from data for 25 countries (SEM, 1966, pp. 31, 204—5). In estimating changes in occupational composition within sectors, they employ Italy in 1963 as a model for Thailand in 1986, after rejecting the Philippines and Japan for vaguely stated reasons.

A critical point in any manpower forecast is the ultimate conversion into educational forecasts. SEM's method of handling this problem was pure guess-work: they divided all occupations into four categories — professional, technical, skilled and semi-skilled — and then arbitrarily postulated the amount of education required by each without so much as an explanation (SEM, 1966, pp. 36, 64—5). They added that 'since the manpower demands on the formal educational system are expected to be great, a much more concerted effort should be made to increase non-formal-on-the-job training and adult education programs' (SEM, 1966, p. 41; also pp. 65, 166). But in the absence of any quantitative targets for training and adult education programs, it is not clear how we are supposed to interpret the 1986 forecast of educational requirements.

The upshot of the entire exercise is a projection of middle level manpower shortages which even in 1965 posits a stock demand 9 times as large as the stock supply of secondary school leavers and which in 1986 will leave a gap of 3 million between demand and supply (see Figure 5.2). The report admits that 'it is obviously

---

[7] Of Galenson's 25 countries, only 2 are in Asia and only 5 are underdeveloped. Although the coefficient of determination for Galenson's basic regression is quite high, this was not true of some of his subsidiary regressions (standard errors of estimates or standard errors of coefficients were not reported for any of the equations). Nevertheless, these were also used by the authors of SEM.

118

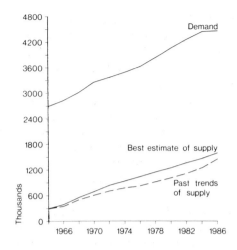

Figure 5.2. Estimated stock demand and supply of secondary school graduates, Thailand, 1965–1986.

Source: SEM (1966), Fig. 6.01, p. 169.

impossible for the schools to increase their enrolments instantly by such a tremendous amount. But the enrolment projection (to satisfy demand) does represent an ideal goal towards which the schools can aim' (SEM, 1966, p. 68). Why schools should aim at a clearly unattainable goal is not made clear. Is this a 'projection' of requirements? Clearly not. Is it a 'forecast' then or merely an expression of a pious hope? If the gap cannot conceivably be closed by the formal educational system, why bother to translate occupational requirements into formal educational qualifications? The difficulty, of course, is that the authors never explain how their forecasts are supposed to be used by educational planners.

Like the earlier Task Force study, SEM has wise things to say about the curriculum, about the problem of drop-outs and about space utilization in schools, but their manpower forecasts must be dismissed as meaningless. We turn without further ado to the forecast prepared in 1967 for the second Plan by V.R.K. Tilak of ILO and H.F. McCusker of the Stanford Research Institute (NEDB, 1967B). The method is essentially that of the MRP. They begin with the known productivity of labour (GDP per worker) in each sector in 1960 and the known GDP per sector in 1966. The object is the modest one of forecasting manpower requirements up to 1971. In effect, because of the lack of data about the sectoral labour—output

119

coefficients in 1966, the forecast involved an 11-year rather than a 5-year horizon. Between the given target growth rates of GDP laid down in the Second Plan (8.5 per cent) and the projections of the rate of growth of the active labour force (3 per cent), the increase in GDP per man during the plan period had to be 5.5 per cent (more than 2 per cent above the productivity improvements actually experienced in the 1960's). The problem was to distribute the over-all increase of 5.5 per cent among the various sectors of economic activity, the results depending very sensitively on the division of the labour force between agricultural and non-agricultural activity, which in turn depends critically on the extent to which farmers are sometimes engaged in non-farm activities. Once again, information about labour productivity by sectors in India, Pakistan and France was introduced to arrive at definite estimates (NEDB, 1967B, p. 19). Similarly, the results of the 1960 Census and the 1963 Labour Force Survey of Municipal Areas were used to provide occupational distributions of the labour force by 1971. Special adjustments were made, however, for (1) attrition from the labour force due to death and retirement; (2) current manpower shortages as revealed by vacancy statistics; and (3) 'modernization of employment'. Step (3) deserves separate comment. 'Modernization of employment' was calculated by using minimum-standards-of-service ratios for doctors, nurses and teachers, as well as 'the requirements of individual projects of government departments included in the Plan'. 'The government departments, the report noted, 'furnished data of their manpower needs according to the educational qualification of the personnel required at various levels' (NEDB, 1967B, p. 4). Apparently, the authors did not share the misgivings of the Task Force about the utilization of educated personnel in the civil service (see above). Nothing was said about the possibility of under-employment or malutilization of manpower. On the other hand, the authors did make purely arbitrary adjustments in some of the manpower ratios to allow for the existence of under-employment in the service industry (NEDB, 1967B, pp. 23—24).

After projecting school enrolments between 1967 and 1971, and after making certain assumptions about future labour force participation rates, they arrive at the conclusion that 89.5 per cent of the new entrants to the labour market over the plan period 1967—71 will have received some primary education, 9.6 per cent will have completed secondary education and 0.9 per cent will have completed university education (NEDB, 1967B, p. 1)[8]. These fractions pertaining to the supply of educated people are now applied to the 'forecasted' occupational composition of the labour force, that is, to the demand side. After still more ad hoc adjustments for particular occupations and disciplines (NEDB, 1967B, pp. 33, 37)[9], we arrive at a table of anticipated shortages over the Second Plan period 1967—71:

TABLE 5.3

SUM OF ANNUAL ANTICIPATED FLOW SHORTAGES OF EDUCATED PEOPLE, THAILAND, 1967—71

Categories of educated people	Number
1. University graduates in agriculture and animal husbandry	750
2. University graduates in forestry and fishing	420
3. Vocational school graduates in agriculture	—
4. Physicians and surgeons	900
5. Nurses	2,000
6. Engineers	310
7. Trained craftsmen in building construction, metal trades, electrical	10,000
8. Trained teachers	1,000
9. University graduates in science	1,600

Source: NEDB (1967B), Table V, p. 40.
— = nil or negligible.

---

[8] These figures for the whole of Thailand over the years 1967—71 may be contrasted with the actual figures for Bangkok in 1967 (see above, Table 5.1) as a dramatic illustration of the pull of the megapolis in Thailand.

[9] For example, 'Provision has been made for the modernization of employment structure. For example, it is necessary to increase the number of physicians and nurses to improve medical services to a desired standard. This is done by applying a certain percentage to the number of persons estimated to be employed in 1971, and the resultant number has been counted as a part of additional manpower requirement in those occupations'; or 'An exception has been made in regard to two occupational groups, namely (i) Chemists, physicists, geologists, etc. and (ii) Biologists, agronomists and related scientists. When based on Census figures, the estimate of requirements in these two occupations is quite low perhaps due to problems arising out of occupational classification in the Census; hence, an independent estimate has been made taking the requirements of the public sector ascertained separately and other considerations.' These quotations give a fair sample of the standards of reporting of this document.

121

This adds up to a total of 25,980 high-level and middle-level personnel in short supply, or an annual average of 5,200. Of these (4), (5) and (8) are entirely functions of given 'standards of service': these are not 'shortages' in the normal sense of the term, but simply represent the numbers of people whom the Thai government would like to produce for non-economic reasons. Of course, there is nothing wrong with this if the standard is clearly laid down and if evidence is adduced that the manpower in question is essential to reaching this standard. Unfortunately, neither condition is met in this document. The doctor—population ratio, for example, stood at 1:8,000 in Thailand in 1967 and this is arbitrarily raised to 1:7,000 by 1971 (NEDB, 1967B, p. 37), but we are not told where this figure comes from and what it has to do with standards of health; the only paramedical personnel mentioned in the document are nurses, and the question of hospital facilities is entirely ignored. Exactly the same point pertains to teachers. No one can quarrel with a country's choice of certain minimum educational standards, but where is the evidence that such and such teacher-pupil ratios are an important ingredient of that standard? At any rate, no such evidence exists for Thailand.

As for the rest, namely (1), (2), (3), (6), (7) and (9), all are well within the margin of error of such forecasts, with the possible exception of (7). That is to say, in each case except (7), the shortage is less than 5 per cent of the stock of such people in Thailand. The upshot of this forecasting exercise, therefore, is the finding that there may well be a significant shortage of skilled craftsmen over the Second Plan period. Strangely enough, however, earlier studies of a limited group of vocational schools in the Bangkok—Thonburi area had drawn attention to the incidence of heavy unemployment among vocational school graduates (see Task Force, 1963, I, pp. 38—9; SEM, 1966, pp. 26—28), so that even the shortage of craftsmen predicted by the NEDB team is somewhat suspect.

The fourth Thailand forecast, which seems to have actually attracted little attention in Thailand, was carried out in 1964 by G. Hunter for UNESCO and the International Association of Universities, as part of a large effort to assess the 'manpower needs' of the Asian region. Hunter (1967, p. 23) used the now discredited Harbison rule-of-thumb, namely that the output of high-level manpower should grow twice as fast and the output of middle-level manpower three times as fast as GNP (see Blaug, 1970, p. 73).

Hunter compares his own results with those of the Task Force and discovers that his estimates for university graduates are much higher, while his estimates for secondary school graduates are much lower than theirs. (Note: his estimates for secondary graduates are *lower*, even though he assumed they would grow three times as fast as GNP.) He attributes the discrepancy to the Task Force's assumption that the whole population of Thailand would, in 1980, have the same level of educational attainment as was observed in Greater Bangkok in 1960. This assumption, he points out, has far more effect on forecasts of secondary than of tertiary educated people, because the proportion of university graduates already working in Bangkok greatly exceeds the fraction of all secondary graduates working there. He concludes that a cautious expansion combined with quality improvements at the secondary level is called for (Hunter, 1967, pp. 66—67). There is little point in discussing his more detailed estimates by fields of specialization: these involve so many special personal judgements as to defy empirical assessment.

Our fifth and last forecast represents an unpublished ILO effort, which may be regarded as a purely academic exercise. This reviews all the data now available in Thailand for purposes of long-term manpower forecasting of the conventional type and then attempts to extend these by the judicious use of international comparative material. It begins by invoking two studies which regressed output per man per sector for some 30 countries around the world against the occupational and educational characteristics of the labour force by sectors (Horowitz *et al.*, 1966; Layard and Saigal, 1967). The first result is to show that the occupational distribution of the Thai labour force within sectors differs radically from the mean observations for 32 countries in the Layard—Saigal study, the second and the more sophisticated of the two studies just mentioned. This seemed to trouble the ILO experts and it is easy to see why: the variance around the mean in the Layard—Saigal regressions (as judged by the standard errors of the coefficients as well as by the R^2s and the standard error of the estimate) is considerable, which appears to support the idea that there is scope for substituting educated manpower within and between occupations, thus weakening the foundations of the manpower requirements approach. They then turn to the Horowitz figures, which involve a much simpler model of the determination of sectoral labour productivities than the Layard—Saigal study and which, by the way, does not include Thailand in its regressions. They derive the future occupational structure of Thailand under three assumptions: (1) that Thailand will correspond in 1971 to a group of countries in each of which output per man per sector in 1950 corresponded closely to that of Thailand in 1966; (2)

123

that Thailand in 1971 will be identical in the relevant characteristics to Japan in 1960; and (3) that Thailand in 1971 will correspond to the unweighted average occupational structure of a small group of countries in which the average productivity of labour in 1966 was similar to that prevailing in Thailand in the same year. All three assumptions yield figures radically different from those officially projected by the Thai government (see Table 5.4). Having come so far, however, they then throw it all away by admitting quite candidly that the observed international data which are the basis of their three projections are the outcome of both demand and supply forces (ILO, 1968, pp. 12—13).

TABLE 5.4

ADDITIONAL EMPLOYMENT BY MAJOR OCCUPATIONAL GROUPS, THAILAND, 1967—71 (thousands)

Occupations	Projection 1	Projection 2	Projection 3	Official Thai projections
Professional and technical	142	127	121	85
Administrative, executive and managerial	45	−209	136	30
Clerical	163	110	146	77
Sales	190	342	126	340
Manual	473	563	480	489
Miners and quarry- men	− 28	10	11	10
Transportation and communications	74	109	54	90
Craftsmen, production process workers	427	442	415	389
Services	139	222	144	133

Source: ILO (1968) Table 21, p. 42.

The last comment is worth emphasizing. There appears to be a widespread misunderstanding about the appropriate role of international comparative data in the field of manpower forecasting. What international comparisons can show is, not what would be an optimum occupational and educational structure for a country, but what is the range of feasible structures within which a national optimum might lie. In short, it is not on the least-squares regression line that we should concentrate but rather on the variance around the line.

The finding that there is considerable variance is a source of comfort, not a cause of worry. If the optimum utilization of educated people by occupation and by sector were indeed a knife-edge laid down by regression coefficients, economic development would be a virtual impossibility.

The ILO team proceed to recommend the approach adopted recently by OECD in its Argentina and Peru Reports, where, instead of attempting to forecast manpower requirements, they work forward from student supply projections: first estimating the future output of the educational system and then attempting to discover what sectoral growth rates, what changes in sectoral labour productivity and what occupational composition of sectors would be required to absorb that supply without serious educated unemployment. The great advantage of this approach is that far more is known about the dynamics of students flows through the education system than about the nature of the demand for people with various educational qualifications.

The ILO experts derive some assurance from the fact that the demand for doctors, engineers and technicians is easy to forecast because 'under the present educational system, the basic educational qualification is generally uniquely defined for these occupations' (ILO, 1968, p. 13). But a few pages later they face the fact that this amounts to an appeal to conventions as a way of solving the difficulties of manpower forecasting. They close by recommending 'A detailed study on the "optimum" qualifications for occupations, with the help of educational and vocational training specialists in Thailand' (p. 17). This is perhaps the most significant sentence in their study. One can only hope that this is where efforts in Thailand will be focussed in the future.

The problem of malutilization of manpower is crucial to any evaluation of forecasting methods. There is an understandable tendency among manpower planners to think of optimum utilization in physical terms, that is, as a perfect matching of skill requirements with skills imparted by the educational system. But the problem of utilization is a little more complicated than that. Employers do not care, and should not care, about a perfect fit between occupation and education but rather about the trade-off between jobs and men. Consider the following sentence in Thailand's Second Plan document: 'An insufficient supply of skilled personnel may have an upward impact on wages and prices and obstruct the achievement of Plan targets. Shortages of qualified manpower may not always be evident since available jobs are not kept vacant but are filled by less qualified hands, a situation which is not favourable to increases in productivity and output' (NEDB, 1967A, p. 59). To be sure, but what if 'less qualified hands' are cheaper? The statement just quoted practically implies the view that automobile mechanics should have university degrees because they would be more productive with than without them.

The impact of the manpower forecasts

The educational targets of the Second Plan appear to be based on the various manpower forecasts that have been made in Thailand: expansion of academic and vocational secondary education, expansion of teacher training, expansion at the higher levels in engineering, agriculture and medicine, but quality improvements at the expense of quantity in the social sciences (which covers almost half of all students in higher education). We should have to wait for the results of the Census of Population of 1970 to pass final judgement on all five forecasts. Nevertheless, a technical review of their methodology and a belated attempt to assess the accuracy of some of them, such as is attempted above, is likely to sap one's confidence in the appropriateness of these targets. We must avoid the danger, however, of giving credit where perhaps no credit is due. It is noteworthy that all the five manpower forecasts were initiated and sometimes carried out in all details by foreigners working in Thailand; although some of these were carried out under the auspices of the Manpower Planning Division of the National Economic Development Board, a key government ministry, it is probably fair to say that manpower forecasting never became an indigenous Thai activity, and that its results have always been taken with a grain of salt by Thai planners. What influence the manpower forecasts did have was largely by way of inhibiting the customary penchant of educational planners, Thai or otherwise, for higher education, encouraging instead an expansionist approach to secondary education and particularly vocational secondary education. Primary education, it appears, the Thais were determined to leave alone to grow at its 'natural rate', despite the fact that the 1963 Task Force had revealed a much greater absolute and relative shortage of primary school leavers or university graduates (see above, Table 5.2).

All this comes out nicely when we contrast the 'unplanned' 1950's with the 'planned' 1960's by looking at enrolment trends between 1954 (the earliest year for which reliable enrolment estimates are

available) and 1969. Figure 5.3 provides indices of absolute enrolments by the five main levels of the Thai educational system;

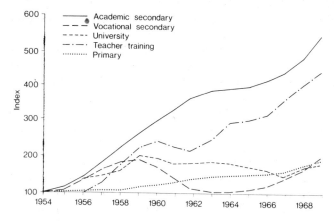

Figure 5.3. Indices of educational enrolments by level, Thailand, 1954—1969.

Source: NEC (1969) and unpublished data furnished by the Ministry of Education for 1954—57 and 1968—69.
Index: 1954 = 100 except for teacher training where 1956 = 100.

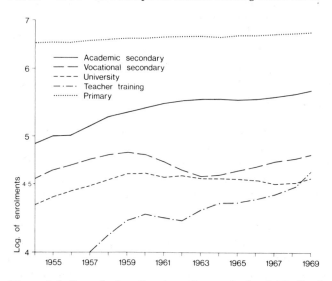

Figure 5.4. Log of educational enrolments by level, Thailand, 1954—1969.

Source: As Figure 5.3.
Note: The percentages in brackets are the implied average annual growth rates
over the 16-year period.

127

Figure 5.4 is a semi-logarithmic version of 5.3, allowing the direct comparison of growth rates of enrolments at the various levels. Certain broad trends stand out from these two charts.

First of all, it is evident that primary education has been kept on a steady growth path of 3.6 per cent (with upper primary growing at 9.8 per cent and lower primary at 1.4 per cent).[10] If we knew whether population in Thailand since 1960 had grown at 3.3 per cent, in accordance with official estimates, or at 3.5 per cent, as some alarmists suggest, we could say whether the proportion of the age group 7—14 enrolled in primary schools had actually risen or remained constant. The annual school census in Thailand does not report the ages of students by grades, but it is well known that the first four grades enrol more than a 100 per cent of the age group 7—11, the children in these grades being sometimes as old as 13 or 14 years. Even without this consideration, it is certain that the proportion of the age group 7—11 enrolled in the first four grades of primary schooling has been falling steadily. If population has been growing at 3.2 per cent, the birth rate has in fact been rising at an annual rate of 4.2 per cent; after deducting the infant mortality rate, the assumption of a constant proportion of the age group enrolled gives us a 3.8 per cent rate of growth of 7—11-year-old school children. Since enrolments in lower primary education have been growing at 1.4 per cent, it follows that the proportion of the age group 7—11 enrolled in school must have declined over time. However, when we add the growth rate of upper primary education, it leaves us unable to make definite pronouncements about the trend in the entire age group 7—14 enrolled in schools.

Secondly, it is obvious that university education has been held down below its 1950's growth rate, at least up to 1967, since when enrolments have risen sharply. The university figures for the 1950's include part-timers and those were the days when anyone with a secondary leaving certificate could get into some university, at least on a part-time basis. Part-timers were weeded out gradually between 1963 and 1967, which accounts for the absolute decline in university enrolments over those years. In 1968 and 1969, however, enrolments rose 7 and 15 per cent respectively, re-establishing the growth pattern of the 'unplanned' 1950's. Since the creation of the annual University Entrance Examination in 1963, university admissions have been tightly controlled in Thailand and hence the expansion of 1968

---

[10] It is obvious from these rates of growth that lower primary enrols about three times as many children as upper primary.

and 1969 must have had official approval. Yet all the manpower forecasts concurred in recommending a reduction in the university enrolment trends that prevailed in the 1950's. We are driven to the conclusion, therefore, that the Thai authorities are now ignoring these forecasts or that they have evidence which they have not revealed that the demand for university graduates has been underestimated in the past.

Thirdly, consider secondary education, the critical area in all these forecasts. Can we really discern much change after 1964, the first year when the manpower forecasts of impending shortages of middle-level manpower might have had some effect? The growth rate of academic secondary education had slowed down by 1963 and all we can discern in the figures is a slight acceleration since 1966. Where the significant change came was in vocational secondary education, which had been steadily declining from its peak of 1959; since 1964, vocational schooling and secondary teacher training have been the fastest growing sectors of the Thai educational system. There can be no doubt that this policy was the major outcome of the manpower forecasts we have been reviewing.

Some will find this a reason for congratulating the manpower forecasters in Thailand. But others, like the author, have severe misgivings about the advisability of expanding formal vocational education. Vocational secondary schools are inordinately expensive — the operating costs in Thailand run about 3 times, and the capital costs about 30 times higher than academic secondary schools — and they prepare students for an extremely narrow range of skills. Furthermore, they are unpopular with both parents and students and are generally regarded as providing a second-best chance of schooling at the secondary level; in other words, it appears that most graduates of vocational schools do not make use, and never intended to make use, of their acquired manual skills. One cannot substantiate these assertions here[11] they are offered merely as food for thought.

In conclusion

The record of the 3—4 year medium-term manpower forecasts in Thailand can only be described as poor to dismal. We can imagine

---

[11] The results of a cost-benefit analysis of educational investment in Thailand which reveals extremely low social and private rates of return to vocational secondary education will, it is hoped, be published shortly.

what we will say about the 20-year long-term forecasts when the time comes to assess these retrospectively. No doubt, there is considerable scope for improving the technical quality of medium-term manpower forecasting, but at best, the method itself seems so unreliable that it ought never to be given more than a subsidiary role in educational planning.

But if not manpower forecasting, then what else? This is a different question from the one we have been considering in this chapter — it ought to be possible to call an egg rotten even if one cannot actually lay eggs! — and this is not the place to do justice to this theme.[12] For the reader who insists on constructive criticism, we might suggest (1) follow-up studies of random samples of school leavers to see where they end up working; (2) job-analysis of a range of representative occupations in the public and private sector, as suggested in the ILO study we discussed above; and, (3) on a more exalted plane, rate of return analysis of educational investment, leading up to simplified linear programming models of the economy with education as one of the sectors of the model. In the meantime, while research is going forward, a whole host of labour market policies, out-of-school training schemes and curriculum changes suggest themselves to keep the educational system flexibly tuned to the labour market and to dispense with the necessity of having knowledge of the too distant future; this is merely to emphasize the *obiter dicta* recommendations of the Thai-U.S. Task Force (see above). In other words, the question: What are the ways, other than manpower forecasting, of peering into the future 5 to 10 to 20 years hence? is a false question. There are no such ways. Nor is manpower forecasting such a way, at least if we care about accuracy of prediction. But that does not mean that we cannot have educational planning. It only means that we shall have another kind of educational planning.

---

12 But see Blaug (1970), Ch. 7.

6. Nigeria

by Keith Hinchliffe

During the years since political independence in 1960, Nigeria, the most highly populated country in Africa, has seen many changes in both its political and economic structures. Politically, the period has been dominated by the inter-regional rivalries which led eventually to the attempted secession of the Eastern Region and consequently the civil war. Economically, Nigeria has been able to achieve a cautious but steady increase in national income and in fact has been one of the few developing countries in which the actual rate of economic growth has surpassed the planned rate. During the late 1960's, the civil war probably retarded the economic development of the country as a whole; but with renewed political stability and further exploitation of the oil reserves, Nigeria can expect rapid increases in economic development in the 1970's.

This chapter is directly concerned with only one feature of the economic structure — the labour force — and with the attempts which have been made to mobilize it for purposes of economic development. After ten years of such attempts in Nigeria, it is pertinent to consider some of the problems encountered and the progress that has been made. Not all the reports concerning the manpower situation in Nigeria have been forecasts of manpower requirements; many have been stocktaking exercises designed to provide knowledge of the structure of employment in the base year. In our assessment we cannot assume that a common objective existed for all studies and therefore the reasons for each study will be discussed before presenting its results.

Data Problems

To attempt detailed manpower forecasting requires a wealth of data concerning the likely future volume of output, its sectoral

131

distribution, the ratio of output to labour, the mix of occupations, etc., and to convert these forecasts to an educational plan requires knowledge of the educational attainments required for each occupation. In most developing countries few, if any, of these relationships are known and Nigeria is no exception. For manpower forecasting based on either the use of actual economic variables or on international comparisons, minimum data needs are the level of national income and the size of population. We shall begin by examining the measurement of these two quantities for Nigeria.

The Federal Office of Statistics issues estimates of Gross National Product, which are based on a study by Okigbo for 1957 (Okigbo, 1962). After considering Okigbo's methods and further information derived since 1957, Eke puts the possible error of these estimates at up to 30 per cent. He suggests that 'in Nigeria there are many reasons to make one . . . suspect of government statistics . . . . Some of the most unreliable data happen to be the most important for the estimation of the national product. Two of these are population statistics and agricultural output statistics' (Eke, 1966A, p. 337). Because of political wranglings, the 1962 Population Census had to be repeated in 1963 and the final results, giving a population size of 55.7 million, are still regarded as rather unsatisfactory. Other estimates for 1963 range from 40 to 50 million.[1] Okigbo, who made explicit use of population figures in building up some of the most important aggregates, accepted the 1952—53 population census figures and allowed for a 2 per cent growth per year over the next decade. His series gives a 1963 population of 37.43 million. The two most authoritative population estimates thus differ by 18 million.[2]

Similar reservations apply to the method used by Okigbo to estimate agricultural output. Since this figure is very important for the size of GNP, Eke's criticism of Okigbo's estimates is quoted at length:

'Okigbo's 1957 estimates were based on Federal Office of Statistics enquiries. These enquiries were themselves based on information gathered from field sampling in which stratified random sampling technique was used. The information gathered from the sampled households was grossed up to village totals on the basis of the ratio of number of informants to the number on the tax or

---

[1] For example, Eke (1966B) gives an estimate of 41.25 million.

[2] The new Second National Development Plan 1970—74 estimates the 1969—70 population at 64.5 million.

132

electoral rolls. The village totals were grossed up to stratum totals by reference to the estimated number of males aged 15 and over. This process snowballed until the regional totals were arrived at' (Eke, 1966A, p. 340).

It is obvious that the estimates of the size of population were crucial to this whole snowballing process. There are several other reasons why Okigbo's series cannot be regarded as highly accurate; for instance, many small service industries and many craft workers were omitted because of the difficulty of assessing output from people with multiple occupations.

This short description of the estimates of two leading economic aggregates indicates the kind of data problems for economic forecasting in general and for manpower forecasting in particular that are encountered in an economy like that of Nigeria. The problem then posed to planners in whether to depend upon personal judgement and the experience of other countries, so as to proceed immediately to manpower forecasting, or whether to start at the very beginning and first build up reliable data about the key relationships. Obviously there is a critical time factor involved, for in many countries the planners may be under pressure to produce a complete set of forecasts as quickly as possible so as to give some indication of the direction in which the educational system should move. This is understandable but the question still remains as to whether any value can be attached to such findings. The history of manpower forecasting exercises made in Nigeria mirrors this fundamental dichotomy.

The labour market

Before we turn to the actual manpower forecasts and educational plans which have been produced in Nigeria, it will be useful to present an overview of the total labour market situation in the mid—1960's, in order to illustrate the types of problems facing manpower planners in Nigeria. This section leans heavily on a report of Education and World Affairs (EWA, 1967, Ch. 1).

As stated previously, the exact size of the population of Nigeria is not known precisely, but most observers choose a figure of around 50 million for the mid 1960's which implies a total labour force of around 17.5 miilion. In disaggregating this labour force, EWA chose divisions corresponding to three productivity levels — high, inter-

133

mediate and low. The high productivity or modern sector employs around 4 per cent of the labour force or about 700,000 people of whom just over one-half are employed in private enterprise. The next level, the intermediate productivity sector, includes all those in small scale manufacturing and service industries. In this group there are perhaps 5 million workers, about 2 million of whom are engaged in cash crop agriculture. Finally, the low productivity sector contains a wide range of activities from subsistence farming to petty trading. In Nigeria, this sector probably covers about 12 million or 70 per cent of the total labour force.

Assuming, as does the EWA report, that the 15-year-old age group forms 2.5 per cent of the population or about 1,250,000, and allowing for participation rates of approximately 95 and 35 per cent for boys and girls respectively, new entrants to the labour force in 1965 would have been about 788,000 (allowing also for those who continue their education and those who enter the labour force after further education). Of these 788,000 young people about 420,000 had some primary and 55,000 some post-primary education. Assuming a 2 per cent a year attrition rate for existing members of the labour force, net additions in 1965 would have been about 440,000.

The next question to ask is what happens to these 15-year-olds when they arrive in the labour market. At present it is impossible to give an accurate answer, but rules-of-thumb based on past experience in Nigeria can present us with some reasonable approximations. One such rule-of-thumb used in the EWA report is that, for the high productivity sector, employment increases at most by only half the annual rate of growth of output. Therefore, if output increases by 5 per cent a year, new employment will increase by at most 2.5 per cent and on a base of only 700,000 this means less than 20,000 new jobs. Total employment intake for this sector, assuming 3 per cent attrition, would be around 40,000. In the non-agricultural, intermediate sector, the rule-of-thumb chosen is that the rate of employment growth is three quarters the rate of growth of output. Hence if 10 per cent (1,750,000) of the total labour force is in this sector and output grows by 5 per cent a year, new employment per year would be 100,000, allowing for 3 per cent attrition of the existing labour force. For the agricultural, intermediate sector and the low productivity sector, it is impossible to use even rules-of-thumb to gauge the annual rate of additional employment. Suffice it to say that if 140,000 people enter the high productivity and non-agricultural, intermediate productivity sectors, then around 650,000 jobs must be available in these sectors if all potential entrants are to find work.

Applying an attrition rate of 2 per cent to the farming and low productivity sectors, this means that 350,000 new jobs must be created each year in these sectors.

By presenting these employment intake figures in relation to the various levels of education which the potential labour force entrants possess, it is possible to indicate roughly the opportunities open to school leavers from each level. Table 6.1 gives a breakdown of labour force entrants into each sector in 1965 by levels of education.

TABLE 6.1
EDUCATIONAL LEVEL OF LABOUR FORCE ENTRANTS, BY SECTOR, NIGERIA, 1965

Educational level	Total	High productivity sector	Intermediate productivity sector (a)	Low productivity sector (b)
None	312,807	—	—	313,000
Primary dropout	274,149	—	—	274,000
Primary completer	146,495	—	85,000	61,000
Secondary modern and craft school	30,874	16,226	15,000	—
Secondary grammar forms I-V and equivalent	19.546	19,546	—	—
Tertiary — non-university	2,114	2,114	—	—
Tertiary — university	2,114	2,114	—	—
Total	788,000	40,000	100,000	648,000

Source: EWA (1967), Table IV-5.
Notes: (a) excluding the agricultural intermediate sector;
(b) including the agricultural intermediate sector.
— = nil or negligible.

As will be seen later, all manpower reports prepared in Nigeria during the 1960's have concentrated solely on the high productivity sector, neglecting 95 per cent of the labour force entrants, some of whom have six to nine years of formal education.

The Ashby Report

The idea of manpower forecasting as a tool for educational planning may be said to have been born in Nigeria in 1960 with the

135

publication of the Ashby Report. The terms of reference for the Commission were 'to conduct an investigation into Nigeria's needs in the field of Post Secondary and Higher Education over the next twenty years' (Ashby Report, 1960, p. 2). Evidence that education was seen to be of the utmost importance for economic growth in Nigeria is shown by the way in which the Commission based their recommendations solely on the manpower requirements estimates furnished by Harbison, which were especially prepared for the Commission. In passing, it is of further interest to note that as recently as 1960, members of such a Commission felt justified in stating 'we could have approached this task by calculating what the country can afford to spend on education and by proposing cautious, modest and reasonable ways in which the educational system might be improved within the limits of our budget. We have unanimously rejected this approach to our task' (p. 4). The educational system had to expand *at any cost*.

At the beginning of his report, Harbison was careful to state exactly what he was *not* doing, but he was not so careful to state precisely what he was doing: 'in this report, no attempt has been made to predict what the number of persons in the HLMP (high level manpower) category is likely to be in the next decade. Nor is this a manpower survey, because as yet the statistical information is lacking for such a survey. The report merely suggests minimum HLMP targets for the period 1960—70' (Ashby Report, 1960, pp. 52—53). These minimum targets, based on an annual rate of economic growth of 4 per cent, were divided first by 10 economic sectors and second by two manpower levels, the Senior category calling for a university degree and the Intermediate category for two or three years post-secondary education. The targets themselves were based on existing stocks and vacancies, interviews with officials and personal judgement, since a more precise approach was precluded by a lack of relevant data. Table 6.2 presents estimated stocks of high level manpower for 1960 together with the minimum targets for 1970.

Assuming a 4 per cent rate of economic growth, the target annual rates of growth for Senior and Intermediate category manpower were 8 and 13 per cent respectively. (This exercise was the origin of the now famous 'Harbison rules-of-thumb', to which we will return later, and which have been used extensively in many educational planning exercises since 1960).

On the basis of these targets for high level manpower, the Ashby Commission drew up educational targets for 1970 for the whole of the educational system and these were projected year by year in the

136

TABLE 6.2

ESTIMATED STOCKS AND TARGETS FOR HIGH LEVEL MANPOWER, NIGERIA 1960 AND 1970

Manpower category	1960 (estimated)	1970 (target)
Senior	13,675	28,875
Intermediate	11,075	37,275

Source: Ashby Report (1960) Tables A, B.

TABLE 6.3

COMPARISON OR ARCHER PROJECTIONS AND ACTUAL ENROLMENTS IN EDUCATION, NIGERIA, 1961–70

Educational level	1961	1963	1965	1966	1970
Primary					
Archer	2,879,000	3,347,000	3,669,000	3,767,000	4,125,000
Actual	2,803,000	2,896,000	2,911,000	3,026,000	
Secondary forms I—V					
Archer	59,980	79,970	109,506	127,240	188,530
Actual	59,512	88,132	128,160	149,018	
Secondary form VI					
Archer	..	3,075	4,240	4,840	5,639
Actual	1,332	3,621	4,815	5,995	
University (degree courses)					
Archer	..	..	5,950	..	9,400
Actual	2,480	4,622	6,866	8,221	

Source: Archer Report (1961), Ch. 1—4, 7.
Annual Abstract of Education Statistics, 1961, 1962.
Statistics of Education in Nigeria, 1963 and 1966.
.. = not available.

Archer Report of 1961. After modification by the Federal Government, the latter Report was used as a basis for educational expansion in the National Development Plan 1962—68. Table 6.3 presents the

137

projections together with actual enrolments over the period 1961 to 1966, while Table 6.4 presents actual and percentage projection errors. It is impossible to go beyond 1966 enrolments for the country as a whole due to the disruption caused by the war.

TABLE 6.4

ABSOLUTE AND PERCENTAGE PROJECTION ERRORS OF
ENROLMENTS IN EDUCATION, NIGERIA, 1960—66

Educational level	Absolute error	Percentage error
Primary	−741,000	−19.7
Secondary forms I—V	+ 21,778	+17.1
Secondary form VI	+ 1,155	+23.9
University	+ 916	+15.4

Source: As Table 6.3.
Note: Projection error = Projected − Actual.

As may be seen, most of the projections had been surpassed by 1966 except at the primary level, where in absolute terms the difference between projected and actual enrolments was very large. The Ashby Commission suggested that by 1970, 100 per cent of all children in the primary age group should be in school in the Eastern and Western Regions and 25 per cent in the Northern Region. Callaway has estimated, on the basis of the 1963 Census, that in 1966 the percentages of school age children attending primary schools were: North, 8.34; East, 62.47; West and Mid-West, 51.98 (Callaway, 1969, p. 202). Although use of the 1963 Population Census data probably leads to an under-estimate of the enrolment ratios, it is beyond doubt that none of these targets have come close to being achieved.

Expansion of enrolments at the secondary and university levels has been enormous since the Ashby Commission reported and the influence of the report may be gauged by comparing the periods 1956—61 and 1961—66. However, although enrolments at secondary and university level increased three times as much between 1961 and 1966 as between 1956 and 1961, the actual annual rates of growth indicate a more uniform increase over the whole ten year period (Table 6.5).

138

TABLE 6.5

EDUCATION ENROLMENTS, NIGERIA, 1956—66

Year	Educational level					
	Primary		Secondary		University	
	Enrolment	Annual per- centage rate of growth	Enrolment	Annual per- centage rate of growth	Enrolment	Annual per- centage rate of growth
1956	2,036,000	•	29,700	°	563	•
1961	2,803,000	•	60,842	•	2,480	•
1966	3,026,000	°	155,013	•	8,221	°
Increase						
1956—61	767,000	6.6	31,142	15.4	1,917	34.0
1961—66	223,000	1.5	94,171	21.0	5,741	27.0

Source: Callaway and Musone (1968), pp. 115, 117. *Statistics of Education in Nigeria*, 1963 and 1966.
• = not applicable.

Nigeria's introduction to manpower forecasting as a basis for forecasting educational requirements began, as we have seen, in a very simple and unsophisticated way by using highly subjective procedures. The Ashby Report was far more important for stressing the relationships between education and economic activity, for providing a rationale for wholesale expansion of educational facilities and for indicating the importance of gathering further statistical data on the subject, than it was for providing actual targets. It was on the recommendations of both Harbison and the Ashby Commission that the National Manpower Board was established in 1962 to further studies in the field of manpower planning.

The National Manpower Board

Since its foundation in 1962, the National Manpower Board (NMB) has produced ten reports in its series of Manpower Studies. The fundamental aims of this series have been twofold: first to carry out investigations of the actual employment and occupational structure of the labour force in a base year in selected sectors or industries, and second to forecast future labour requirements.

139

The chief areas of investigation, in addition to the actual fore-casting exercises, have included professional manpower, the man-power content of selected capital projects, the education and training content of occupations, and management and health manpower.[3] As well as these reports in the Manpower Studies series, the NMB has undertaken other investigations including rudimentary periodic as-sessments of unemployment and the compilation of a National Register of Students. Even a quick glance at the nature of the studies will indicate the manpower planning priorities as the Board has seen them. All ten refer to what has been called earlier the high-produc-tivity sector even though this sector employs only 5 per cent of the total labour force. This total preoccupation with the 'modern' sector and high level manpower has certain justifications: the desire for 'Nigerianization' of the top jobs in the private and public sectors, the fear of bottlenecks and critical shortages in high prestige and fast growing industries, and the potential advantages of leadership cadres with high spillover effects. On the other hand, such emphasis has resulted in a neglect of the other sectors of the economy and important questions such as the scope and extent of training and apprenticeship schemes in small workshops and enterprises which employ the bulk of the non-agricultural labour force have had to be bypassed.

However an appraisal of the work of the NMB must not only consider what it has not done but also, and more importantly, the relevance of, and the techniques used, in the studies which it has undertaken. From a manpower forecasting point of view the three most important studies have been — *Nigeria's High Level Manpower 1963—70*, *Sectoral Manpower Survey 1964* and *A Survey of Labour Force Requirements 1965*.

Nigeria's High Level Manpower 1963—70

This report, *Nigeria's High Level Manpower 1963—70*, was the most comprehensive manpower forecasting exercise undertaken in Nigeria in the 1960's. The most important part of the terms of reference was:

'To undertake an immediate survey to assess the present and future needs for high-level manpower both in public and private employ-ment in all occupations requiring university, professional, tech-

---

[3] For a complete annotated list, see Appendix 6.1 at the end of this chapter.

nical and craft training, throughout the Federation . . .'

At the same time, the Board expressed its reservations about attempting such an exercise given the paucity of basic statistics, but it realized that such questions were of immediate concern to the government.

The initial problem was to enumerate the level of total demand in 1963 for both the Senior and Intermediate categories of manpower. This was attempted by means of a questionnaire to all known firms and agencies employing ten or more persons. In terms of the NMB, total demand = reported employment + vacancies + 10 per cent for non-response. After deriving estimates of total stock and total demand in this fashion, the Board attempted to forecast future demand for 1968 and 1970. In all, three attempts were made to do this based on: (1) employers' estimates; (2) an envisaged, full employment economic structure for the forecast year, using 1963 skill mixes 'adjusted where suitable' (NMB, 1964, p. 11); and (3) recommendations from an International Manpower Seminar. These three approaches are reviewed below in more detail.

The returns received from employers, both public and private, for expected high level manpower demands year by year from 1963 to 1968 indicated overall annual rates of growth of 8.6 and 9.2 per cent at the Senior and Intermediate levels respectively. However, year by year estimated increases show great variability and appear to have no systematic pattern. The figures in Table 6.6 must cast great doubt on the reliability of employer forecasts even over a relatively short period.

TABLE 6.6

EMPLOYERS' ESTIMATES OF EXPECTED HIGH LEVEL MANPOWER EMPLOYMENT, NIGERIA, 1963—68

Year	Senior	Annual per-centage increase	Intermediate	Annual per-centage increase
1963	13,716	.	44,009	. ·
1964	16,496	20	49,878	13.0
1965	17,026	3	55,123	10.0
1966	18,077	6	59,892	8.5
1967	18,980	5	67,319	12.5
1968	20,137	9	68,329	1.5

Source: NMB (1964), Table 13.
· = not applicable

The Board, as well as noting the variations, regarded these expectations as being rather conservative since many firms were unable to forecast and some had no definite plans for the future. In these instances, requirements for 1968 were left at the 1964 level. Because of these considerations, as well as the need to consider new industries, the Board attempted to establish their own forecasts.

Many classic approaches to manpower forecasting were examined by the NMB. One method considered was an analysis of the volume and composition of trade, the rate of change of the national economic structure and the level of national income in relation to manpower stocks. Not surprisingly, this method was ruled out due to the lack of relevant data. A second method which they took note of was the analysis of the manpower situation in a country whose economy was similar to the one envisaged for Nigeria in 1968. This approach was also ruled out: 'while this method may seem attractive it is in practice fraught with basic difficulties because of the differences in the social, political and, indeed in the economic climate and in the financial and other resources available in different countries' (NMB, 1964, p. 11). What in fact the Board did was to envisage a 'realistic' economic structure for the forecast year and, in conjunction with this, a full employment objective. This exercise necessitated forecasting the level of high level manpower necessary to achieve full employment by the forecast year. The only indication given by the Board on exactly how they estimated requirements from this approach is given in the sentence: 'On the basis of existing skill mixes, suitably adjusted, the HLMP targets were then determined by occupations' (p. 11).

Without further details of the forecasting procedure, it is difficult to judge the actual method used. It would appear that the procedure was first to estimate the total full employment level in 1968 from the supply side. This total was then split among sectors according the their expected growth on the basis of existing labour-output ratios, and the HLMP targets for each occupation were determined according to 1963 occupational mixes. Although the report states that these mixes were 'suitably adjusted', it is unlikely that this was the case to any large degree, since no information was available in 1964 concerning changes in occupational mixes with relation to changing levels of output. Annual rates of growth that resulted from this method were 22 per cent for both the Senior and Intermediate manpower categories.

At the International Manpower Seminar, initiated to assess the Board's forecasts, it was suggested that the full employment objective was unlikely to be attained by 1968, and that it should therefore be dropped as a basis for forecasting the demand for high level manpower. The recommendation of the Seminar was that manpower requirements should be based on the experience of other developing countries which 'had shown that the growth in the level of employment was approximately equal to half of the growth rate of national income; and the rates of growth of the demand for Senior and Intermediate personnel were generally about two and three times the rate of growth of the national income respectively' (NMB, 1964, p. 11). From these 'Harbison rules', it was estimated that since national income in Nigeria was expected to grow at a rate of 4 per cent a year, total employment would increase by 2 per cent, the Senior category by 8 per cent and the Intermediate category by 12 per cent a year.

Although the Board had earlier rejected this type of international comparison approach, they now justified their acceptance of it by stating that its implications were very close to the forecasts made by the employers. Revised minimum targets were therefore drawn up on this basis. Table 6.7 gives a comprehensive summary of all the forecasts made in this survey.

TABLE 6.7

ALTERNATE ESTIMATES OF MANPOWER REQUIREMENTS, NIGERIA, 1968

| Base | Manpower category | |
	Senior	Intermediate
(1) 1963 Actual	13,716	44,009
(2) 1963 Demand	17,890	48,767
(3) 1968 Employer estimate	20,737	68,329
(4) 1968 Full employment target	48,264	129,260
(5) 1968 Revised minimum target	25,250	83,400
Annual rate of growth 1963—8		
(percentage)		
(1) − (3)	8.6	9.2
(2) − (4)	22.0	22.0
(2) − (5)	7.1	11.3

Source: NMB (1964), pp. 23, 37.
Note: 1963 demand allows for non-response and vacancies.

143

After assessing manpower requirements in 1968 (and also 1970), the Board turned to the supply side and by assuming the continuation of existing and planned educational schemes, assessed the likely number of additions to high level manpower stocks over the planned period. Bringing the supply and demand analyses together, the Board foresaw shortfalls in the Senior and Intermediate categories in almost a 1 : 10 ratio.

It will be useful at this point to consider the 'Harbison rules-of-thumb', used to formulate the final revised minimum targets, a little more closely since they dominated manpower forecasting exercises in Nigeria between 1960 and 1964.[4] At no time has empirical evidence, or even theoretical argument, been advanced for the justification of these 1 : 2 and 1 : 3 ratios between increases in national income and stocks of Senior and Intermediate high level manpower respectively. Indeed, the most comprehensive empirical study indicates that the ratios are more like 1 : 1 and 1 : $\frac{2}{3}$ (Netherlands Economic Institute, 1966). As for the impact of using the 1 : 2 ratio for senior high level manpower, Rado and Jolly have shown that its application to Uganda produces a ratio of university graduates to working population of 0.03 in only 31 years, a figure equivalent to that of the U.K. in the mid 1950's (Rado and Jolly, 1965, p. 232). As they point out, it appears unlikely that Uganda would need to reach such an educational level in order to attain Ghana's present level of output per head.

Considering the lack of evidence for these particular rules-of-thumb it is surprising that they have been applied at one time or another, not only to Nigeria, but also to three East African and seven South East Asian countries (see Blaug, 1970, pp. 73, 150). If many more countries adopt these ratios and plan their educational systems accordingly, the ratios will eventually become truisms but this will have nothing to do with manpower requirements.

The change in emphasis

Attempts at manpower forecasting up to 1964 in Nigeria were established on extremely precarious analyses based implicitly or explicitly on untested and generalized formulae. However, in building up data on the manpower situation in 1963, the National Manpower Board began to acquire the basis for more objective

---

[4] In 1969 the rules were still being utilized for forecasts of Intermediate manpower, and for non-graduate teachers and nurses.

144

analyses in the future. Indeed 1964 appears to have been a very significant year in the short history of manpower forecasting in Nigeria, since all the studies from that date until the Second National Development Plan 1970—74, have dealt with far more selective topics (see Appendix 6.1), the emphasis having shifted from macroeconomic studies to microeconomic studies. It appears to have been fully realized at this point that the tendency to approve indiscriminately of manpower forecasting in all forms was indefensible and that future efforts ought to be directed towards gleaning knowledge of key relationships, such as the composition of the labour force in different industries and its change with respect to varying levels and compositions of output. With regard to this task, two studies were published between 1964 and 1969; *Sectoral Manpower Survey 1964* and *A Survey of Labour Requirements 1965.*

Sectoral Manpower Survey 1964

In the introduction to the Sectoral Survey 1964, it was stated that in past forecasting exercises 'it was discovered that more detailed manpower data were needed for each sector of economic activity . . . As a result the Manpower Secretariat initiated in 1964 an establishment survey into four sectors viz. — Manufacturing, Mining, Construction and Electricity for collection of basic manpower statistics' (NMB, 1967, p. 1). The coverage of the Survey was intended to include all establishments employing 10 or more persons in each of the selected sectors, although it is probable that this aim was not achieved.

Although the basic aim of the survey was to collect data concerning the present state of the labour force composition, an attempt was made to go beyond this and acquire knowledge of the future demand for different types of manpower as seen by the employers. In Part A of the questionnaire used, data were collected on employment in 1963 and 1964 differentiated by nationality, and on vacancies at the start of 1964 plus statements as to the difficulty of filling particular occupations. The replies were broken down into four skill categories: A — Senior, requiring a university degree or similar professional qualification; B — Intermediate, requiring at least one year's specialized training after school certificate; C — Skilled, requiring an apprenticeship or craftsman training; and D — Residual, all other workers. This section of the questionnaire aimed at an assessment of the current stock of manpower and the employment trend for the two years 1963 and 1964. In addition it was hoped that

145

evidence of occupational patterns and skill mixes would be provided. Vacancies were interpreted as manpower shortages.

Part B was intended to provide items of information relevant to manpower forecasts. Establishments were asked to estimate the present degree of capacity utilization, so reflecting the effects of the general economic situation and allowing calculation of future manpower requirements assuming greater utilization of existing capacity. Finally, employers were asked to forecast likely changes in employment year by year for each skill category and also details of their own training facilities. In effect then the aims of the Survey were twofold, first to examine the composition of the labour force in 1964 and second to inquire as to the future manpower requirements as estimated by the employers.

Since this chapter is chiefly concerned with the evolution of manpower forecasting techniques in Nigeria, there is no need to present in detail the findings of this initial attempt to analyse the structure of employment in one year. Discussion is therefore limited to those parts of the inquiry which have obvious implications for past and future forecasting exercises. Initially however it is useful to present the skill mix ratios as they existed in 1964. This is done in Table 6.8.

These ratios were seen to be useful, as a first step, for indicating the manpower implications in the event of industrial expansion. It should be recalled that the Board in its study of *High Level Manpower 1963—70* largely based its own forecasts on the assumption of stable skill mix ratios. Such use of the ratios assumes (1) that they are the result solely of demand forces; (2) that in 1964 they were optimal in all sectors; and (3) that elasticities of substitution between skills are zero. On the other hand, Uganda in 1963 had an A : B manpower ratio of 1 : 2.4 and, rather than assume this constant over time, the planning authorities there quite arbitrarily decided that the ratio should become 1 : 4 by 1980 (Rado, 1967, Table 3). The use of either constant skill ratios or arbitrarily chosen new ones are unlikely to solve any manpower forecasting problems.

With regard to the rules-of-thumb used in the final version of the Board's *High Level Manpower 1963—70* forecast, the percentage increases in employment of Senior and Intermediate personnel between 1963 and 1964 were: manufacturing 5.5 and 9.7; mining 2.9 and 5.6; electricity 29 and 27; construction —3.8 and —3.0, respectively. The large differences between these growth rates indicate that employment patterns are far too complicated to be handled by simple formulae.

146

TABLE 6.8

SKILLS EMPLOYED IN FOUR SECTORS AS PROPORTIONS OF SENIOR
SKILL A, NIGERIA, 1964

Industry	Skill categories			
	A	B	C	D
Manufacturing	1	2.3	13.5	15.1
Mining	1	1.4	17.5	22.4
Construction	1	1.7	16.4	17.1
Electricity	1	1.2	7.5	13.3

Source: NMB, 1967, p. 9, 24, 43, 53.
Note: Skill category A requires a university degree or equivalent;
skill category B requires at least one year's specialized training after school
certificate;
skill category C requires an apprenticeship or craftsman training;
skill category D represents all other workers.

Finally, the likely accuracy of employer estimates of future manpower requirements may also be checked to some extent by the
Sectoral Survey. In the High Level Manpower 1963—70 report, firms
in the manufaturing sector estimated that their total level of employment would increase by 4,400 a year between 1964 and 1970. Actual
employment levels given in the Sectoral Survey for this sector for
1961, 1962, 1963, 1964 were 48,000, 58,000, 79,000 and 99,000
respectively — average annual increases of 17,000 a year. Once again
the use of employer estimates appears to be a dubious procedure.

The Sectoral Manpower Survey 1964, although only a short document, definitely indicated that past methods and assumptions used
for manpower forecasting in Nigeria needed re-evaluation. The subjective procedure used in 1960, and the employer forecasts and
rules-of-thumb used in 1964 cannot be accepted as reliable guides,
whilst any more complex method cannot be based on unproven
assumptions such as constant skill mixes over time. As a result of
these conclusions, it was decided to conduct further microeconomic
studies so as to build up the basic relationships already investigated
in the 1964 Survey.

A Survey of Labour Requirements 1965

The most recent report of the National Manpower Board is A Survey
of Labour Requirements 1965, published in 1969. This report fol-

147

lows on from the *Sectoral Manpower Survey 1964*, but extends its scope to eight sectors of economic activity, the four new ones being agriculture, commerce, transport and services. The aim of the report was 'to elicit relevant data on economic ratios and norms of manpower requirements desirable for effective and realistic planning' (NMB, 1969, p. 1). Data were collected by means of questionnaires and interviews in firms and agencies employing 10 or more persons. (This obviously limited the use of the survey in the agricultural sector.) The response rate was 76 per cent and covered 3,493 establishments.

The main body of the survey dealt with each sector in turn under the following headings:

(1) Level and structure of employment: devoted to a regional analysis of the sectors' development, size of firms, and the 1965 skill mix ratios compared, where possible, with 1963 and 1964 ratios.

(2) Anticipated growth and industrial pattern of employment: vacancies and anticipated manpower requirements for 1966 as seen by the employers, differentiated by sub-sector, region and manpower category.

(3) Prospects for future growth: degree of capacity utilization used to estimate the possible increase in employment with the existing capital structure. The assumption used was that the labour—output ratio is constant for all degrees of capacity utilization.

(4) Training facilities: finally employers were asked to list the types of training schemes undertaken by their enterprise and the number of persons engaged in them.

Two important analyses which may be performed using the replies are first, a comparison of skill mix ratios over time and second, a comparison of employers' estimates of employment changes for one year with those made in 1963 for a five year period, and also with the rules of the International Manpower Seminar.

As was stated earlier, it is very convenient in manpower forecasting to regard the skill mix ratios as stable, at least over the short-run. It is important therefore that this convention is tested on all possible occasions. But before the ratios operating in Nigeria in 1963, 1964 and 1965 in particular sectors are outlined, it is important to note that the two surveys involved did not in all cases refer to the same establishments. An instance of this may be indicated with reference to the manufacturing sector since, whereas in 1964 almost all the largest firms responded to the Survey, in 1965 this was not the case. If large firms have different skill ratios from smaller firms, as is likely to be the case, then the two studies are not fully comparable. Bearing

148

TABLE 6.9

SKILL MIX RATIOS IN FOUR SECTORS, NIGERIA, 1963—5

		Senior	Intermediate	Skilled	Residual
Manufacturing	1963	1	2.2	13.0	15.3
	1964	1	2.3	13.5	15.1
	1965	1	1.2	8.8	7.6
Mining	1963	1	1.4	17.0	22.0
	1964	1	1.4	17.5	22.4
	1965	1	0.97	47.6	11.5
Construction	1963	1	1.7	15.9	17.8
	1964	1	1.7	16.4	17.1
	1965	1	3.7	16.0	25.6
Electricity	1963	1	1.2	8.3	14.7
	1964	1	1.2	7.5	13.3
	1965	1	3.3	7.8	8.4

Source: NMB (1967), pp. 9, 24, 43, 53; NMB (1969), pp. 17, 23, 30, 39.
Note: For definitions of skill categories see note to Table 6.8.

this in mind, Table 6.9 shows the ratios in four economic sectors for 1963, 1964 and 1965, as indicated by the surveys.

Even allowing for a large degree of non-comparability of data between the years 1964 and 1965, the variations in skill mix ratios shown above certainly add weight to the arguments that estimates of future manpower requirements are on shaky ground if based on an assumption of constant mixes. The claim may be made that differences in coverage are so wide as to render comparisons meaningless, but if this is the case then the credibility given to either report must fall very low.

Turning to the employer forecasts of employment changes for 1966 over 1965, it is possible to compare these with earlier forecasts. In 1963, employers estimated that employment would increase by 8.6 and 9.2 per cent a year for Senior and Intermediate personnel respectively. Believing these expectations to be conservative, the NMB raised both percentages to 22. Finally the International Seminar agreed that, allowing for 4 per cent a year economic growth, total employment would increase at 2 per cent a year and Senior and Intermediate employment at 7.1 and 11.3 per cent respectively. In contrast to this set of estimates, employers in eight sectors in 1965 estimated that employment changes over the following year would be 4.48 per cent for total employment, 1.51 per cent at the Senior

149

level and −2.49 per cent at the Intermediate level. The 1965–66 figures therefore give little comfort to the previous forecasts and in particular are very much at variance with similar employer estimates made in 1963.

One final table showing all the estimates of rates of growth of high level manpower made during the 1960's clearly shows the lack of consensus and the unreliability of the forecasting procedures. The long run forecasts have generally been around 8 per cent a year for Senior and 11 per cent a year for Intermediate category workers, largely based on the 'Harbison rules-of-thumb', whereas the actual increase 1963–64 and the employers estimates for just one year have been far lower. These divergences were made even more important since the 1964 exercises were broken down by 44 occupations and forecasts made for each. Using uncertain and improbable assumptions originally developed for highly aggregate categories and applying them to finer sub-divisions where they are even more improbable than at the aggregate level gives the worst of all worlds.

TABLE 6.10

FORECASTS OF ANNUAL RATES OF GROWTH OF EMPLOYMENT FOR SENIOR AND INTERMEDIATE CATEGORIES, NIGERIA, 1960–68

Manpower category	Ashby (1960–70)	Source of forecast				
		Employers' forecasts (1963–68)	National manpower board (1963–68)	International manpower seminar (1963–68)	Employers' forecasts (1965–68)	Actual (1963–64)
Senior	8	8.6	22	7.1	1.5	4.9
Intermediate	13	9.2	22	11.3	−2.5	8.3

Source: See text.

Much of the effort devoted to manpower forecasting exercises between 1965 and 1969 was in preparation for the Second National Development Plan which was published late in 1970. The preceding discussion of the NMB's individual reports therefore must be supplemented by an analysis of the manpower sections of the new Plan and the use made in this of the earlier work.

150

The Second National Development Plan 1970—74

The first point to make about the new Plan is that the sections which deal with manpower implications are much more carefully presented and comprehensive in scope than any other manpower report previously presented in Nigeria. Of particular interest is the emphasis on the 95 per cent of the labour force who are not wage paid and who have not been included in any of the previous forecasting exercises. However, this point should not be made too strongly since it is still the case that the quantitative manpower forecasting techniques are unable to handle this group and that resort is made to general discussion of the employment creating possibilities of development projects and the crucial role of small, indigenous, non-agricultural enterprises. In passing it is worth stating that this new emphasis on people other than those who neatly fit into high level manpower categories is probably due to the enormous increase in school leaver unemployment witnessed over the 1960's and also to the problem of the demobilization of the rapidly inflated army.

Even with the new emphasis on the non-wage sector, it is still made clear in the Plan that whereas the modern sector is not able to provide a wide employment base, it is still strategic in the process of modernizing and diversifying the economy. From this argument it is a quick jump to the manpower requirements forecast.

The forecasting methodology used in the Plan involves a major difference from the techniques previously used. The 'Harbison rules-of-thumb' and employer forecasts are ignored and in their place is a muted version of the approach used in the Mediterranean Regional Project (see Chapter 1). Presenting the procedure as laid down in the Plan, first sectoral Gross Domestic Product estimates for the Plan period were used to estimate employment, assuming only slight changes in the pre-Plan relationships between trends in employment and output. To these sectoral employment estimates, occupational mixes taken from the *Survey of Labour Requirements, 1965* were applied to derive occupational totals and these were summed over all sectors. The resulting occupational requirements were meant at this stage to reflect the differential rates of employment growth by major industries. To allow for changes in the occupational structures of industries, two alternative estimates were made, first by allowing for a 10 per cent increase in the ratio of high level manpower to total wage employment during the Plan period, and second by providing a range of estimates based on changes in occupational mixes between 1963 and 1965. Of the general approach, the Plan states 'The procedures

151

adopted were in certain respects determined primarily by the fact that time and data were not available for making alternative estimates' (Federal Ministry of Information, 1970, p. 329). This implies that if more data had been available a more ambitious approach would have been used and also that the procedure actually used was within the limits provided by the availability of data. It may be assumed therefore that the planners were satisfied that their final results were legitimate forecasts. The data and assumed relationships which were used therefore should be looked at more carefully.

In terms of manpower statistics, the most important pre-requisite for the above forecasting method is an accurate description of the base year, in this case 1970, and reasonable data concerning the key relationships over the years immediately prior to this date. It is apparent from the previous discussion that no reliable time-series data on employment are available and indeed there has not even been a single, totally acceptable bench mark study. In the event, employment data were taken from several diverse sources including the NMB studies back to 1956, and these were adjusted where possible for differences in coverage. The resulting employment series by industry up to 1966 were then projected to 1969 on the basis of available measures of output and assumptions about the employment—output trends over the period. Once an estimate of the 1970 base figures had been arrived at, the GDP estimates up to 1974 were applied and, assuming a continuation of past employment—output trends, total employment was forecast for each sector in 1974.

At the next stage, the conversion of employment forecasts to occupational forecasts, first the occupational mixes in the *Survey of Labour Requirements 1965* were applied and second alternative estimates were derived on the basis of the 1963—5 changes. Enough has been presented earlier to show that either method was too cavalier for the sake of accuracy. If the enormous variations in skill mixes between 1963 and 1965, shown in Table 6.9, were due to differences in data coverage then there is nothing to be gained by analysing these variations; if the differences were actual ones, then they are so wide and erratic as to defy application of the 1965 mixes for five to ten years ahead. In fact, from the final results shown in Table 6.11, it is impossible to know which method was actually used. In addition to the difficulty of accepting the 1970 base figures and the assumptions concerning occupational mixes, it is rather interesting to note that the annual percentage increases in the senior and total employment categories are just about the same as the projected annual increase in GDP over the same period, 6.6 per cent. Whether

152

TABLE 6.11

ESTIMATED EMPLOYMENT IN SELECTED OCCUPATIONS IN MEDIUM
AND LARGE-SCALE INDUSTRY, NIGERIA, 1970 AND 1974

Manpower category	Estimated employment		Annual percentage increase 1970—74
	1970	1974	
Senior	45,654	58,861	6.6
Intermediate	126,879	159,257	5.9
Skilled	217,304	289,413	7.4
Residual	375,163	477,469	6.2
Total	765,000	985,000	6.5

Source: Federal Ministry of Information (1970), p. 330.

this is by design or accident is unclear.

From a methodological point of view, the 1970 forecasting exercise is certainly superior to the 'Harbison rules-of-thumb' and employer estimates, yet the scanty statistical basis for the calculations must still leave us pessimistic about its accuracy and usefulness. This leads to the question of the actual aims of this particular forecasting exercise. The Plan itself states that 'the procedure adopted was intended to be a general technique of determining the employment impact of the Plan. It will be used essentially as a framework within which to study estimates of direct employment creation of individual investment projects' (Federal Ministry of Information, 1970, p. 329). At the end of this separate analysis for the wage sector, we are back to the point made at the beginning of this section that the main aspect of manpower policy in the Plan is employment creation.

This new emphasis is, or rather could develop into, a major advance but on the other hand the educational system has been totally neglected. Assumptions concerning the occupational—educational relationships which have been prevalent in Nigeria throughout the 1960's have not been emphasized in this chapter, but in fact with the exception of Manpower Study No. 7 (see Appendix A6) all the work of the NMB seems to have assumed that occupational and educational categories are, or can be made, synonymous. It seems unfortunate therefore that no further thought has been given to this question in the latest exercise, and that while the occupational categories remain, there is no mention at all of their transformation into educational categories. In fact the sections of the Plan which are concerned with education show no indication that a major manpower forecasting exercise is reported elsewhere.

Conclusion

Manpower forecasting in several different guises has existed in Nigeria for over a decade. To what extent the whole effort has been of use depends on one's criterion of success and on the time period of concern. Different reports have had different aims and consequences and therefore it is impossible to use a single type of quantitative criterion as a success indicator. As to the actual middle-run forecasting exercises, the Ashby Report was more important as a spur to rapid educational development than it was for the precise figures it gave, and the highly ambitious *Nigeria's High Level Manpower 1963—70* must be regarded as a failure in terms of the methodologies used and the highly disaggregated and detailed forecasts it provided. The high costs and low returns, at this moment in time, of going one stage further than data collection and forecasting the future demand and supply situation, persuaded the NMB that much more groundwork had to be done. As a result, the general macroeconomic studies were seen to be of little use and more detailed micro studies were given emphasis. These studies whilst perhaps appearing mundane and slow moving have in fact been very important for purposes of questioning the reliability of past methodologies and for the basic knowledge they have been conveying of the existing manpower structures in the modern sector of the Nigerian economy. Whatever the technical shortcomings of the studies, the NMB has certainly given the leadership to a new way of thinking about education for manpower requirements.

However, even though these later studies provided evidence to discredit past forecasting procedures, the Board was still utilizing 'Harbison rules-of-thumb' in 1969. By 1970 and the new Development Plan however, manpower forecasting was placed on a new and more sophisticated basis. The unfortunate feature of this new approach for Nigeria is that it is absolutely essential to have accurate knowledge of the actual manpower structure over a number of years before any projections are made since the approach basically depends on the extrapolation of time-series data. Whether or not responsibility can legitimately be completely placed on the disruption caused by the civil war, the lack of any bench mark survey which is sufficiently comprehensive and uses reliable classification systems represents a grave omission in Nigeria's manpower forecasting history. After this has been rectified, there will still be problems concerning the estimation of changes in labour productivity and occupational structures over time. Finally, for manpower forecasting to have any relevance for educational planning, much more knowledge must be gleaned of occupational—educational relationships. Even if emphasis is given to quantifying these relationships it will probably be many years before they can be used to provide accurate forecasts.

Finally, it is useful to recall the rough breakdown of the total labour force by productivity levels given at the beginning of this chapter in relation to the whole forecasting effort. Prior to the 1970—74 Development Plan, the most comprehensive report, *Nigeria's High Level Manpower 1963—70*, covered 174,000 people, or just under 1 per cent of the total labour force. As previously stated, there are good reasons to be concerned with high level manpower, for instance the drive for 'Nigerianization', but to put the whole of the forecasting effort in this area cannot be justified. This exclusion of the vast majority of the labour force may in general be the most important, negative consequence of detailed manpower forecasting techniques in developing countries. In their most sophisticated forms, a great deal of data are needed and since these do not generally exist for the labour force as a whole, emphasis is directed at the modern sector which is easier to survey. When the forecasting techniques are not even reliable this may result in much wasted effort. It is an attribute of the Second National Development Plan that this appears to have been realized. The aim now as the NMB itself recognizes, must be to build upon the knowledge of the manpower structure in agriculture and small-scale non-agricultural enterprises together with analysis of investment—employment relationships and surveys of apprenticeship and non-formal training schemes.

Appendix A6
Studies of the National Manpower Board, Nigeria

No. 1. *Manpower Situation in Nigeria*, was a first report aimed at bringing together all known information concerning the labour market and educational output.

No. 2. *High Level Manpower Survey 1964—70*, was an attempt at comprehensive manpower forecasting for 1970 and a presentation of the actual manpower situation in 1963.

No. 3. *Professional Manpower in Selected Occupations 1964*, was designed as a first step in an attempt to compile a complete register of professional manpower, analysing country of training, age, working experience and income.

No. 4. *Sectoral Manpower Survey 1964*, gives basic employment data for the manufacturing, mining, construction and electricity sectors.

No. 5. *Professional Manpower in Selected Occupations 1966*, had the same scope as No. 3 but in relation to 1966.

No. 6. *A Study of the Manpower Content of Capital Projects 1966*, was based on an enquiry of capital projects which had the aim of forecasting future manpower requirements of future projects.

No. 7. *A Study of the Education and Training Content of Occupations 1966*, was aimed at acquiring knowledge of the education and training of employees in 126 occupations, and also the requirements for potential entrants.

No. 8. *Management in Nigerian Industries*, a pilot study aimed at producing details of the distribution, age, salaries and performance of Nigerian management.

No. 9. *Health Manpower Survey 1965*, provides data on the existing manpower stock in health institutions throughout Nigeria.

No. 10. *A Survey of Labour Requirements 1965*, extends study No. 4 and embraces eight sectors.

7. Engineers in India

by Maureen Woodhall

For over 20 years the Indian government has been producing periodic forecasts of the economy's future requirements for skilled manpower. Even before the preparation of the First Five Year Plan it was recognized that 'the education and the training of the man-power required should be the sheet-anchor for every plan of national development' (Ministry of Education, 1949). Since the setting up of the Planning Commission in 1950, there have been a number of working groups on manpower, technical education and general education, and in 1956 a special Manpower Division was set up in the Planning Commission, which was later merged with the Perspective Planning Division. On the basis of their recommendations, the Five Year Plans established enrolment targets for each level of education and, in particular, the expansion of technical education was planned in accordance with forecasts of requirements for scientists and engineers. Similarly, the Education Commission, which reported in 1966, based its recommendations for expansion of enrolments in secondary and higher education upon specially prepared forecasts of demand for matriculates and graduates in 1976 and 1986 in the expressed belief that 'estimates of future manpower needs form a useful basis for regulating enrolment patterns above the primary level' (Government of India, 1966, p. 92).

The Third Five Year Plan announced the setting up of an Institute of Applied Manpower Research (IAMR), which has existed since 1962, and has undertaken research on supply and demand for different categories of manpower, including a calculation of the stock of engineering manpower, estimates of the demand for engineers, doctors, nurses and certain other occupations, and studies of costs and wastage in technical education.

Manpower considerations have been emphasized in India ever since Independence, and a fairly elaborate machinery has been created for collecting information about manpower, preparing forecasts and

157

formulating manpower and educational policy.[1] The main focus of the forecasting activity has been on requirements for specific key occupations, particularly engineers, but also doctors and other medical personnel, agricultural specialists and managers. However, more recently, the work of the Education Commission, and the general concern about educated unemployment, have stimulated a number of forecasts of demand for matriculate and graduate workers in general. The Indian government is deeply committed to the use of manpower forecasting, both as a necessary part of economic planning and as a guide for educational planning, and at the same time can draw upon far longer experience of manpower forecasting than most developing countries.

All the main problems of manpower forecasting in India can be illustrated from the experience of forecasting demand for engineers and this experience is particularly interesting because of the marked changes that have taken place in the labour market for engineers in the past 20 years. All the early forecasts, from 1949 onwards, were dominated by the problem of overcoming shortages of engineers. But the focus of manpower forecasting has gradually shifted and recent forecasts have emphasized the need to cure the problem of unemployment of engineers. Reports of unemployment of graduate engineers and diploma holders were mentioned in several forecasts during the 1960's, and by 1969 the Institute of Applied Manpower Research estimated that there were 56,700 unemployed engineers, including 10,000 graduates and 46,700 diploma holders. This represented 7.5 per cent of the total stock of graduate engineers, and 23.6 per cent of the stock of diploma engineers (IAMR, 1969, p. 11). How is it that, having geared the development of engineering education over 20 years to forecasts of the requirements for engineers, India should find itself in 1969 with almost one in five of its engineers unemployed? This is the central puzzle of the Indian experience, and the central purpose of this chapter is to throw light on this question.

---

[1] For descriptions of the machinery of planning in India, see:
B. N. Datar, 'Manpower Planning in India', *International Labour Review*, July 1958; G. Tobias and R. S. Queener, *India's Manpower Strategy Revisited, 1947—67*, New Delhi, 1970; J. P. Naik, *Educational Planning in India* (Bombay: Allied Publishers, 1965); UNESCO, *Educational Planning in Asia* (Bangkok: UNESCO Regional Office, 1967); J. A. Laska, *Planning and Educational Development in India* (New York: Teachers College Press, 1968).

A brief summary of the organization of educational planning in India is given in Blaug, Layard and Woodhall (1969), pp. 48—51.

Before turning to a detailed examination of particular forecasts, we give a brief catalogue of all the main forecasts of engineers in the past 20 years. A useful review was carried out by the Institute of Applied Manpower Research in 1963 (IAMR, 1963B, Part II; see also Srivastava, 1964). This dealt with forecasts produced for the periods of the First to the Fourth Five Year Plans by the Scientific Manpower Committee, set up in 1947; the Engineering Personnel Committee in 1956; the Perspective Planning Division of the Planning Commission, which produced forecasts of requirements of engineers in manufacturing industry and electrical supply undertakings, in 1957; and the Working Group on Technical Education and Vocational Training, whose forecasts for the Third and Fourth Plan were published by the Planning Commission in 1960. All these forecasts were official forecasts and formed an integral part of the general planning activity of the Planning Commission. Since producing this review of past forecasting methods the IAMR have themselves produced a number of forecasts, in 1963, 1965, 1967 and 1969 (IAMR Working Papers No. 7/1963, Part 1; No. 2/1965; No. 1/1967; No. 11/1969). In addition, the Education Commission requested a forecast of manpower requirements, including requirements for engineering personnel, from a joint project team from the Indian Statistical Institute, the Unit for Economic and Statistical Studies on Higher Education at L.S.E. (now the Higher Education Research Unit), and the Perspective Planning Division of the Planning Commission (Burgess et al., 1968). This means that there are forecasts of demand or requirements for engineers, both at the graduate and diploma level, stretching from 1952 to 1986.

The Scientific Manpower Committee and the Engineering Personnel Committee

We look first at the two earliest official forecasts of engineering requirements which deal with the periods of the First and Second Five Year Plans. The establisment in 1947 of the Scientific Manpower Committee predates the First Plan and was an early recognition of the key role that scientists and technologists would have to play in the economic development of the country. The purpose of the Committee was to assess the requirements for different grades of scientific and technical manpower over the next 10 years as a guide for educational expansion in that area. The forecasts covered only scientific and engineering manpower with formal qualifications at

159

degree or diploma level. During 1947 and 1948, the Committee sent out questionnaires to different branches of industry, government departments and educational institutions to collect facts about the employment of scientists and engineers, current levels of production and planned expansion, the views of employers on the adequacy of formal education, the availability of on-the-job training, as well as the annual intake, output and wastage in scientific and technical education. The Committee sent out 3,000 questionnaires and received 1,019 replies, which represented a high rate of response from government departments and educational institutions but a low response from industry. The Committee also sent out a questionnaire to individuals, designed to measure the extent of wastage, measured in terms of unemployment and 'drift' (employment of qualified manpower in non-scientific or non-technical posts). The Committee received 8,000 replies and concluded that overall wastage of qualified manpower amounted to 'less than 10 per cent which does not seem to us high' (Ministry of Education, 1946, p. 52).

On the basis of this information about current employment and output levels, the Committee tried to estimate 'production: personnel ratios' for different sectors, industries and government departments, taking into account such factors as variations in size of establishments, production techniques and conditions obtaining in similar industries in other countries. The Committee then estimated the future development of each industry or department; their estimates took into account the 'planned expansion' recorded in the questionnaires and the targets of the 'Industrial Panels', which had been recently set up by the Government. Thus, the estimates of future output upon which the manpower forecasts were based reflected both the predictions of employers and the targets of government policy. The Committee recognized that these targets might be criticized as over-ambitious but believed that 'in the matter of industrial development of a country like India, whose potentiality is great and the need for development urgent, plans have to be ambitious and planners adventurous'.

The Committee's forecasts of future demand for scientists and technologists simply assumed that the 'production: personnel ratios' would remain constant in the future and applied these ratios to the target output for each industry to give an estimate of additional requirements, classified by grade of engineer (junior or senior) and by category (chemical, electrical engineer, etc.). These estimates were not intended to be precise, but simply to indicate 'the broad magnitude of demand over the next five or ten years'. The forecasts of

160

demand were then compared with estimates of the increase in supply over the same period at the prevailing levels of input, output and wastage. This exercise revealed 'wide gaps between the possible requirements and the anticipated output . . . even on stretching the 5-year requirements to the next 10 years' (Ministry of Education, 1949, p. 61).

The work of the Committee was the first real attempt in India to collect information about the current stock of engineers and to estimate future needs. It was based on extremely inadequate data about current employment, since no accurate estimate of the stock of engineers was available and the response rate to the Committee's inquiries was fairly low; to overcome this deficiency, the Committee recommended setting up a National Register of Scientists, Engineers and Technologists. Another weakness of the forecasts was the inadequacy of information from which to calculate 'production: personnel ratios'. Since this was the first time such an analysis had been attempted, there was no way of testing whether the ratios in different industries were comparable, or whether they were likely to change over time. Still less was there any possibility of determining whether the ratios were in any sense optimal. Similarly, there was no way of testing the feasibility of the output levels assumed in the future. Indeed, the Committee adopted an ambiguous attitude towards these output figures, sometimes suggesting that they were unduly optimistic and elsewhere implying that they were perfectly feasible. But the ambiguity is understandable, since the Committee believed that the Government's new industrial policy heralded 'a new era'. Therefore, despite the inadequacy of data on the current situation, the Committee felt confident in identifying a shortage of engineering manpower and recommending a large-scale expansion of education and training facilities. This recommendation was accepted and between 1949 and 1955 there was a very marked expansion of engineering education. In 1946—47 the outturn of graduate engineers was only 950 and the outturn of diploma holders 1,150. Admissions in the following year rose to 2,520 and 3,150 respectively and by 1954—5, admissions had increased to 5,468 for degree level engineering courses and 8,313 for diploma courses. This expansion was considerably influenced by the manpower forecasts of the Scientific Manpower Committee and by the first Five Year Plan (1951—55), although some expansion would have taken place in any case, since the Committee had noted, in 1949, that all engineering institutions were planning to expand.

By 1955, however, the Planning Commission reported 'acute

161

shortages' and therefore set up the Engineering Personnel Committee to estimate the probable requirements of engineers for the Second Plan period and to make recommendations to ensure an adequate supply over the next 15 years. Although the forecasts covered the whole of India, the Committee made the comment that 'in any over-all assessment of this kind, a reasonable measure of regional mobility is implied. Under existing conditions in our country, this assumption is of doubtful validity . . .' The Committee, therefore, made separate assessments of demand for different regions of the country, although the report did not attempt to suggest how regional mobility could be increased. The forecasts also show a breakdown of requirements by speciality but no separate estimates were attempted for different industries. The Committee's first task was to estimate the extent of shortages in 1955 and it sent out a standard questionnaire to the main employers of technical manpower, asking for information on current shortages, as well as estimates of future demand. The replies to the questionnaires indicated shortages of 1,808 graduate engineers and 3,640 diploma holders, but the Committee did not make clear whether this 'shortage' was based on unfilled vacancies, or the application of personnel 'norms'. The forecasts of future demand were based on standard norms, suggested where possible by the Committee as a result of 'discussions with the Ministries', current staffing policy and past experience. These norms assume a fixed relationship between new investment, or production targets, and employment of engineers. Thus, the forecasts of the Engineering Personnel Committee were an attempt to spell out the manpower implications of the investment targets of the Second Five Year Plan, rather than predictions about future levels of employment. The forecasts for the private sector were based on estimates by the Ministry of Commerce and Industry and so, like the public sector forecasts, these represent a statement of the implications of official policy, rather than simple predictions about future employment.

In fact, the forecasts for the private sector were, in part, an expression of hope, rather than a prediction of future employment policy. The Committee observed:

'The existing pattern of engineering employment in the private sector reveals an inadequate complement of graduate engineers as against a disproportionately large number of personnel with lower levels of training. Except where precision work is involved, the private industrialists prefer to recruit men at the supervisor's level on low salaries and utilise their services for higher executive work as well, after giving them practical training . . . This was probably because men who came from the ranks were cheaper, stuck to their jobs better, and were more amenable to contractors' discipline' (Planning Commission, 1956, p. 10).

The Committee dismissed this policy as 'a heritage of the past', and envisaged that private employers would, in the future, employ proportionately more graduate engineers. Accordingly, their demand estimates for the private sector were based on an assumption of a change in policy, rather than on the existing pattern of graduate employment. The forecasts also assumed an expansion of research activity, which would increase the demand for engineers in the private sector. The Committee, therefore, admitted that these estimates might be less reliable than the public sector forecasts and indeed the Institute of Applied Manpower Research has since suggested that they were inflated, on the grounds that they did not take into account 'the prevalence of small and medium-scale establishments, in which the need for graduate engineers is small, and the large amount of available Western knowledge and techniques', which tends to reduce the need for research engineers.

The Committee compared their demand estimates with estimates of supply, based on the proposals for expansion in the Draft Outline of the Second Plan. This showed that by 1960—1 there would be a deficit of 1,800 graduates and 8,000 diploma holders per year. The Committee, therefore, recommended that additional facilities should be provided, in order to meet the entire deficit of graduates and 60 per cent of the diploma holders, on the assumption that the remaining 40 per cent of the deficit could be met by on-the-job training. At first sight, it would seem to be a comparatively easy matter to judge the validity of these forecasts by comparing them with actual additions to the stock of engineers between 1956 and 1960, and by comparing actual with planned investment. Unfortunately, it is difficult to find reliable estimates of the stock of engineers, and even more difficult to find estimates of the stock of working engineers.

Certainly the Committee itself did not have a reliable estimate. The Report estimated that the total pool of working engineers was about 22,000 degree holders and 29,000 diploma holders, and at the same time it attempted to estimate the extent of unemployment among engineers. It was said by some that the large numbers of engineers on the Live Register of Employment Exchanges indicated a problem of unemployment, but an enquiry had shown that 49 per cent of the engineers on the Live Register were already employed full-time and registered only to 'improve their prospects'; the Committee concluded, therefore, that unemployment among engineers was not significant, except among engineers of less than one year's standing, who were waiting to find their first job. If we assume that the whole of the 1955 output of 3,500 graduates and 4,500 diploma holders (the estimates of the Committee) still had to find jobs, this would give a total stock of 25,500 graduates and 33,500 diploma holders. We may assume, therefore, that the Committee's forecasts of additional requirements were based on an estimated total stock of not more than 60,000 engineers. However, other estimates of the stock of engineers in 1955 differ substantially from this. The IAMR has, at various times, quoted four different estimates of the total stock of engineers in 1955:

(a) an estimate by the Planning Commission of 71,900 engineers, consisting of 31,200 graduates and 40,700 diploma holders (IAMR 1963A, p. 28).

(b) an estimate based on the outturn of qualified engineers from institutions in previous years, after allowing for migration and mortality, of 74,500 engineers, of which 33,300 were graduates and 41,200 diploma holders (IAMR 1963A, p. 30).

(c) a total of 90,000 engineers, consisting of 39,000 graduates and 51,000 diploma holders (IAMR, 1965, p. 10).

(d) a fourth estimate, based on a survey by the Planning Commission, of a total stock of 79,200 engineers, of which 34,600 were graduates and 44,600 diploma holders (IAMR 1967, p. 9, and IAMR 1969, pp. 27 and 60).

Thus, we are left with estimates of the stock of engineers in 1955 differing by as much as 30,000. When we come to compare the 1955 figures with the stock at the end of the Second Five Year Plan (1960—61), we are in no better a position. The Working Group on Technical Education and Vocational Training (1960) took the Planning Commission's estimate of 71,900 engineers in 1955 as an estimate of the total stock at the beginning of the Plan, and estimated the institutional outturn, between 1955 and 1960, which gave a total stock in 1960—61 of 131,000 engineers, of which 58,000 were graduates and 73,000 diploma holders (IAMR 1963A, p. 32). The IAMR more recently has taken the alternative estimate of 79,000 engineers in 1955 and estimated the stock in 1960 to be 133,000, of which 58,000 were graduates and 75,000 diploma holders (IAMR 1969, p. 60). Both these estimates are derived from estimates of the net out turn between 1955 and 1960. However, if we try to check these against figures from independent sources, the result is more confusion. Although the National Register of Scientific Personnel, recommended by the Scientific Manpower Committee, had in fact been set up, the rate of registration by engineers was as low as 42 per cent in some specialities, and so this cannot be used as an independent check. The IAMR's *Stock Taking of Engineers* in 1963 compared three different sources of data for 1961: (1) the Census; (2) the Directorate General of Employment and Training's surveys of employment in 1961; and (3) institutional outturn figures. These three sources give estimates of the total stock of engineers in 1961 of 146,000, 110,000 and 150,000 respectively. The discrepancy between the DGE&T figures and the other two can easily be accounted for, since the employment surveys covered only 'professional, technical and related workers', but the discrepancy between the Census and the net outturn figures remains and is even larger if we consider the distribution between graduate and diploma engineers. The Census estimate of 146,000 is broken down into 52,000 graduates and 94,000 technicians, but the institutional outturn figures provide estimates of 65,000 graduates and 85,000 technicians. The IAMR assume that the net outturn figure is the more reliable and conclude that 'the Census estimate is a net undercount of graduate engineers and an overcount of engineering technicians' (IAMR 1963A, p. 74).

All this emphasizes the difficulty of evaluating the forecasts of the Engineering Personnel Committee for 1960—61 simply by means of a comparison of forecasts with actual data on the stock of engineers. Estimates of the stock of engineers in 1955 and 1960 are too unreliable to provide a simple index of success or failure for the forecasts, and data on the stock alone tell us nothing about the degree of utilization of the stock of engineers. In any case, the Committee's forecasts were intended to spell out the manpower implications of the investment proposals in the Second Plan on the assumption of a constant relationship between new investment and employment of engineers, and to serve as a guide for educational expansion, rather than to be predictions about future employment. The increase in the stock of engineers between 1955 and 1960 reflects the expansion of facilities that took place as a result of the forecasts, and does not provide an independent measure of 'requirements'. To evaluate these estimates of 'requirements', we need to examine the validity of the assumption of a fixed investment—

engineer ratio and to look at evidence on the utilization of engineers, as well as to compare the forecasts of additional requirements with actual increases in the stock.

However, a comparison of the forecasts and the actual increase in stock does show to what extent the forecasts influenced the supply of engineers. The Committee estimated that the requirements of additional engineers during the Second Five Year Plan would be about 26,500 graduates and 50,000 diploma holders. The Working Group on Technical Education in 1960 estimated that the stock of engineers increased between 1955 and 1960 by 26,308 graduates and 32,508 diploma holders. The more recent IAMR estimates show a similar increase of 23,400 and 30,500. The IAMR has also estimated that between 1955 and 1961, the total stock of engineers grew at a cumulative annual rate of 11.6 per cent, although in another publication the IAMR estimated an annual growth rate between 1955 and 1960 of 7.8 per cent for graduates, and 7.7 per cent for diploma

TABLE 7.1

FORECASTS OF ADDITIONAL REQUIREMENTS OF ENGINEERS, BY THE ENGINEERING PERSONNEL COMMITTEE, COMPARED WITH ESTIMATES OF ADDITIONS TO THE STOCK, INDIA, 1955—60

Specialism	Graduate engineers			Diploma holders (Engineering technicians)		
	(a) Forecasts of additional requirements	(b) Working group estimates	(c) IAMR estimates	(a) Forecasts	(b) Working group estimates	(c) IAMR estim
Civil	11,114	9,794	8,600	25,705	16,802	16,0
Mechanical	5,166	4,745	5,300	12,041	4,781	5,6
Electrical	5,473	4,615	4,000	10,421	3,626	4,6
Chemical	2,256	1,060	1,300	806	32	—
Metallurgical	693	475	800	204	232	1
Mining	469	697	400	692	589	4
Telecom-munications	1,320	723	400	562	550	3
Other	—	4,199	2,600	—	5,896	3,5
Total	26,491	26,308	23,400	50,431	32,508	30,5

Source: (a) Planning Commission (1956), p. 47; (b) IAMR (1963A), pp. 31 and 32; (c) IAMR (1969), p. 60.
— = nil or negligible.

166

holders (IAMR 1963A, p. 69 and 1965, p. 10). Table 7.1 compares the forecasts of the Engineering Personnel Committee with the actual additions to the stock, as estimated by the Working Group on Technical Education and Vocational Training in 1960, and the IAMR in 1969.

These figures suggest that the increase in the stock of graduate engineers was broadly in line with the Committee's estimate of additional requirements of 26,500, although the distribution between specialties differed considerably, but only about 60 per cent of its estimate of 50,000 additional diploma holders was actually achieved. This means either that there was an acute shortage of technicians in 1961, or that the Committee's assumptions about the engineer—technician ratio were unrealistic. In fact, the question of the right balance between graduate and diploma engineers has been a matter of considerable controversy in India during the last 20 years and a number of alternative policy proposals have been put forward. The forecasts of the Engineering Personnel Committee reflected the prevailing view that the ratio of technicians to graduate engineers should be increased. Actual outturn figures indicate that it did slowly increase but by much less than the Committee had envisaged. Leaving the question of the optimum ratio between degree and diploma holders aside for the moment, there is still the question of how much the increase in supply was actually utilized by employers. To answer this we need to look at data on the employment and unemployment of engineers, to assess the magnitude of underemployment, and to analyse data on the salaries of engineers. This we do later in the chapter.

We have spent some time examining the methods and conclusions of these first two official forecasts, because in some important respects they set a pattern which has been followed subsequently. Both were statements about the implications of official output or investment targets, rather than predictions about the future. Although both sets of forecasts were based on questionnaires to employers, they were not employers' forecasts in the usual sense but rather attempts to spell out the manpower implications of official targets, using information supplied by employers, largely in the public sector. Both were concerned with the problem of preventing shortages and aimed to influence the supply of engineers by recommending faster expansion of facilities than was already planned. The forecasts were based on the assumption of a fixed relationship between capital investment or output and employment of engineers, and no productivity changes or substitution between capital and labour were envisaged. Both Committees produced their forecasts on the basis of very inadequate data about the existing stock of engineers, both asserted that there were current shortages of engineers on the basis of employers' statements, but without adequate information about the utilization of existing manpower. Neither Committee made any reference to the costs of their proposals, although they were intended to form the basis for official policy on educational expansion. Nor was there any reference to the salaries of engineers, although the Scientific Manpower Committee did collect some information about salaries from employers. The terms manpower 'demand' and 'requirements' were used in a strictly technological, rather than an economic sense, implying that a shortage of engineers would impose physical bottlenecks which prevented the attainment of desired output levels. Finally, there is little concern about the possibility of creating excess supply. The situation of shortage of engineers was believed to be so severe that over-supply was not seriously considered, although the Engineering Personnel Committee did recognize that 'possibilities of both shortages and over-supplies require to be guarded against ... and in a country which is in short supply of finance, over-expansion of any activity is likely to thwart progress elsewhere, and can only be construed, to some extent, as a negation of planning'. But the qualification 'to some extent' indicates how little the Committee regarded a surplus of engineers as a serious threat.

These forecasts represent the first crude attempts to overcome 'bottlenecks' by examining the demand for technical manpower on the basis of official targets and very simple assumptions about the relationship between manpower and output or physical investment. Whether these assumptions are justified in the Indian context is the crucial question, and it is one which will be examined in more detail below. Whatever the validity of the assumptions, however, no forecasts can serve as useful guides for educational planning if they are based on inaccurate or inadequate data on the current manpower situation. Both Committees were aware of their deficiencies in this respect and emphasized the need for 'a continuing information programme' on manpower questions. We turn now to the attempts of the Planning Commission and its various Working Groups to provide such information, as well as to forecast future requirements of engineers.

The Planning Commission

The Engineering Personnel Committee was set up by the Planning Commission, and after its report the newly created Manpower Division of the Planning Commission carried out a number of studies of engineering manpower and tried to assess the long-term demand for engineers. But first, the Perspective Planning Division tried to estimate the current stock of engineers by analysing the annual outturn figures of universities and other technical institutions, the number of engineers actually employed by government and teaching institutions and the number and distribution of engineers employed in manufacturing industry in 1954 and electricity supply undertakings in 1955.

The study of engineering manpower in manufacturing industry included the first attempt to calculate engineering requirements for particular industries, and its results have been used for subsequent forecasting exercises. The object of the study was to calculate the ratio between employment of engineers and total employment in different manufacturing industries, to estimate the distribution of engineers by industry and by specialism, and to estimate additional requirements of engineers in manufacturing industry during the Second Five Year Plan (Planning Commission, 1957). Information relating to 890 manufacturing establishments employing at least 20 workers, was derived mainly from records in certain government departments. These data showed that the ratio of engineers to total employment varied from under 1 per cent in a number of industries to about 10 per cent in machine tools and hydro-electric undertakings. These ratios were then used to calculate the total number of engineers employed by specialism and by industry in 1954. The study estimated that there were 6,444 graduate engineers and 6,594 diploma holders employed in manufacturing. Thus, the overall ratio between graduate and diploma engineers was 1:1, although the ratio varied between industries.

This study provided the most detailed information available on the actual deployment of engineers in 1954. It was used by the Planning Commission as the basis for forecasts of additional requirements of engineers during the Second Five Year Plan (1955—60). These forecasts took the 1954 estimates of the number of engineers as the minimum number of engineers at the beginning of the Second Plan period. Thus, the forecasts were based on detailed but probably out of date information about the current stock, and the basic assumption that the number of engineers employed would increase in direct proportion to total output in each industry. The output targets of

169

the Second Five Year Plan were used as the basis of the forecasts, so that the forecasts represent what we have called 'policy-conditional forecasts'. The Planning Commission estimated that in order to achieve the output targets, the additional engineering requirements during the Second Five Year Plan would be 13,400 graduate and 13,300 diploma engineers.

To evaluate these forecasts, we need to know whether the output targets were achieved in practice, and whether the actual growth of engineering employment did correspond to the increase of production in each industry. It is easy to apply the first test but it is impossible to test the assumption of a constant engineer: production ratio, because even now there is no comprehensive information on the number and distribution of engineers in manufacturing industry. The IAMR has collected detailed information about the employment of mechanical and electrical engineers, but no data are available for other engineers.

However, if we accept the assumption of a constant engineer: output ratio and estimate what the actual growth of output between 1956 and 1961 would mean in terms of engineering employment, we find that differences between target and actual production at the end of the Second Five Year Plan would have reduced the additional requirements of graduate engineers from the Planning Commission's forecast of 13,398 to 12,106, a difference of about 10 per cent. This is because the actual increase in production during the Second Plan was higher than the target figure in four industry groups but lower than the target in the remaining five industries, and the combined effect of these differences is to reduce demand for additional engineers by 1,300.

Reviewing these forecasts in 1963, the verdict of the IAMR was that the approach was 'more comprehensive, and accordingly more appropriate than that of the Engineering Personnel Committee', and that marginal errors of forecasting could be explained by the following factors: '(a) engineering employment and increase in industrial production can hardly be related in a simple one to one ratio; (b) the proportions used for giving break-up of estimates by type of engineers based on data in the year 1954 cannot remain valid for major industries in succeeding years; and (c) the assumption that the employment of engineering personnel in April, 1956, could be equal to the numbers in 1954. These possible sources of error have not affected the validity of the broad estimates of the study' (IAMR, 1963B, Part II, p. 18). Unfortunately, this confident assessment is not supported by any evidence. Since there are no accurate data on the actual employment of engineers in different branches of manufacturing in 1961, we cannot judge whether errors were in fact marginal. While it is true that these forecasts were based on estimates of the actual pattern of employment in 1954, the IAMR itself pointed out in another report that the study was 'based on data from very few establishments is each industry, not selected according to any statistical principles' (IAMR, 1963A, p. 22). Therefore, although the forecasts were intended to be 'realistic illustrations of the use of a method' rather than precise predictions, we cannot even evaluate the method in the absence of data to test the basic assumption of a constant engineer—output ratio.

The next attempt by the Planning Commission to forecast engineering requirements was made by the Working Group on Technical Education and Vocational Training. The Working Group estimated requirements for the Third and Fourth Five Year Plans and these were published by the Planning Commission in 1960. The Working Group based its forecasts on a number of different assumptions, and therefore produced a range of alternative estimates. All the assumptions involved official targets for growth of national income, investment and production, but different relationships were assumed between engineering manpower and economic indicators. Whereas the Scientific Manpower Committee and the Planning Commission's study of manufacturing industry had both based their forecasts on engineer: output ratios, and the Engineering Manpower Committee had adopted investment—personnel ratios, the Working Group based its forecasts on three different relationships:

(a) the ratio of engineering manpower to output;
(b) the ratio of engineers to new investment; and
(c) the ratio of engineering employment to total employment.

In addition, it made estimates based on output targets for the economy as a whole and on separate targets for each industry. The various assumptions of the Working Group, together with its forecasts of engineering requirements in the Third and Fourth Plan periods, are summarized in Table 7.2.

For the first time, forecasts were produced which showed a range of estimates of additional requirements; however, this range was still based on single target figures for investment and output and can therefore be regarded as a series of checks rather than an examination of the effects of alternative hypotheses about the future growth of the economy. In fact, the Working Group combined these various estimates when making recommendations about the future growth of

171

TABLE 7.2

ASSUMPTIONS AND FORECASTS OF THE WORKING GROUP ON TECHNI-
CAL EDUCATION AND VOCATIONAL TRAINING, INDIA, 1960 AND 1965
(thousands)

| | Estimated additional demand for engineers | | | | | |
| | Third Plan | | | Fourth Plan | | |
	Degree	Diploma	Total	Degree	Diploma	Total
(i) Constant engineer—output ratio						
(a) Global estimate	45	90	135	..	..	..
(b) Sectoral estimate	45	80	125	..	..	..
(ii) Constant engineer—investment ratio of 24: Rs. 20 million	..	..	120	67	118	185
(iii) Ratio of engineers-total employment of 1 : 100	40	70	110	80	120	200

Source: IAMR (1963B), Part II, pp. 20—2.
.. = not available.

supply during the Third Plan and chose figures roughly in the middle
of the range, namely 45,000 and 80,000, as the final estimates of
additional requirements of graduates and diploma holders. On the
basis of this estimation of demand, the Working Group recommended targets for expansion of engineering education, and these
recommendations were accepted and used by the Planning Commission in fixing enrolment targets in the Third Plan.

In 1963, three years after the start of the Third Plan, a 'Mid-Term
Appraisal' was published by the Planning Commission. The year
1963 was dominated by the emergency caused by the outbreak of a
border dispute with China, which resulted in a large-scale expansion
of defence expenditure. This caused the government substantially to
increase the targets for engineering education in order to satisfy
defence needs. Immediately after this mid-term appraisal was published, the IAMR re-examined the demand and supply position in the
light of the new expectations for the Third Five Year Plan period
(IAMR, 1963B, Part II, pp. 23—31). It was apparent that although
the investment targets of the Plan would probably be achieved, the
production targets would not: during the first three years of the

172

Plan, national income grew by only 2.5 per cent a year, instead of the 5 per cent target. The IAMR therefore concluded that the demand for engineering manpower would be 20 per cent lower than the Working Group estimated. On the other hand, the IAMR argued that the increase in defence requirements compensated for this, so that over-all requirements for engineering manpower would be only slightly lower than the Working Group estimates. However this conclusion gave no support to the *increase* in enrolment targets: a comparison of these new demand estimates with the estimated additions to supply which would result from the expansion of engineering facilities that had already taken place, suggested that there would be a surplus of 7,025 graduates and 1,109 diploma holders by 1966, and a surplus of 8,705 and 12,028 respectively at the end of the Fourth Plan in 1971. The IAMR therefore concluded that 'the demand and supply position has taken a new turn . . . The position now warrants some change in order to reduce the large supply of engineering graduates. We are now confronted with the problem of their likely unemployment. In order to avoid this unhappy situation in the near future, it is imperative at this juncture that intake capacity at the degree level . . . should be checked' (IAMR, 1963B, Part II, p. 30). The IAMR therefore recommended a three-year 'Expansion Pause' for engineering education.

This was the first time that any report on engineering manpower had called for a halt to expansion. Previous forecasts of demand for engineers had emphasized a shortage of engineers and had always recommended expansion of the annual intake of degree and diploma courses. The response had been to expand enrolment from 4,119 at the degree level and 5,903 at the diploma level in 1950, to 17,667 and 29,924, in 1962—63. What, therefore, was the response in 1963 to the suggestion that expansion should now be halted? The intake figures for 1964 and 1965 continued to show large increases. It could be argued that it takes time to cut back the rate of expansion of enrolments. However, what actually happened was that expansion was accelerated because of the defence emergency, so that the original targets for enrolment suggested by the Working Group were exceeded by a large margin. The IAMR has compared what would have been the annual intake during the Third Plan if the Working Group recommendations and phasing had been adopted with the actual intake. The two sets of figures are shown in Table 7.3.

Thus, although the actual rate of growth of the economy was less than the Third Plan targets, so that it had become obvious at the time of the mid-term appraisal of the Plan that the Working Group

173

TABLE 7.3

ORIGINAL INTAKE TARGETS, COMPARED WITH ACTUAL INTAKE, INDIA, 1960—65

	Degree level		Diploma level	
	Original targets	Actual intake	Original targets	Actual intake
1960—1	13,500	13,692	25,000	23,736
1961—2	14,600	15,497	27,400	26,525
1962—3	15,700	17,667	29,800	29,924
1963—4	16,800	20,744	32,200	37,822
1964—5	17,900	22,214	34,600	41,645
1965—6	19,000	23,315	37,000	43,984

Source: IAMR (1969), pp. 24, 34.

forecasts based on an annual rate of growth of 5 per cent would prove too high, expansion of enrolments nevertheless went ahead even faster than was originally planned. Because of the Government's estimates of the needs of the defence sector, and the subsequent raising of targets by the end of the Third Plan, the Planning Commission's original targets for admission were exceeded by 34,000. The results of this policy are now apparent in the serious unemployment of engineers, and the IAMR used these figures to assess the demand. and supply situation in 1968 and to analyse the causes of unemployment. This is crucial to any evaluation of forecasts of engineering requirements and will be discussed in detail below; but before looking at the IAMR research on the employment and unemployment of engineers, we turn to the successive forecasts of engineering requirements produced by IAMR.

The Institute of Applied Manpower Research

One of the first pieces of research undertaken by the IAMR after its creation in 1962, was a *Stock Taking of Engineering Personnel*, that is a review of past experience of forecasting requirements for engineering manpower and the calculation of a new set of estimates for the Fourth and Fifth Plans, using official investment targets and a 'crude global yardstick' based on the ratio of '10.67 units of engineering manpower' for every 10 million rupees of investment.

The review of past forecasting experience is interesting but not

174

very critical, even though the IAMR recognized that the shortage of engineers, which had been proclaimed by all previous committees or working groups, was rapidly turning into a surplus. The review of past experience suggested to IAMR that, on the whole, all was well with forecasting methods. In any case, the IAMR stated, in connection with its own forecasts, that 'it cannot be emphasized too often that the data thus presented do not purport to be prophecies. They are the arithmetical results of various assumptions', and presumably the same line of defence would have applied to earlier forecasts.

As we have already seen, the assumptions of the forecasts were usually of a direct proportional relationship between output or investment and the number of engineers employed, and these assumptions had never really been put to the test. The 'norms' or 'yardsticks' which had been used by the Engineering Manpower Committee assumed a given relationship between investment and engineering manpower based on past experience but the Committee admitted that these were very crude calculations and the experience on which they were based was very limited. The Working Group on Technical Education had also assumed a relationship between investment and the number of engineers employed, and had used the ratio of 24 engineers to Rs. 20 million investment to calculate engineering requirements, but this was arrived at in a fairly arbitrary way. The IAMR tried to estimate the investment—personnel ratio for the First and Second Plan periods, and for the first three years of the Third Plan, and concluded that a comparison of investment outlay with estimated growth of engineering manpower did show a 'reasonably consistent pattern' and that over the past 15 years, net additions to the stock of engineers of 10 for every 10 million rupees of Plan investment had been sufficient to match the demand created by that investment (IAMR, 1963B, Part I, p. 11).

This estimate of a ratio of 10:10 million is lower than the Working Group's earlier assumption of 12:10 million. The IAMR gave two reasons why the ratio might change over time. In the first place, a high proportion of investment expenditure in any Plan period is used to create new assets; this means that the manpower used to create the new assets will be available in later Plan periods for maintenance and operation of these assets, which suggests that quite a marked decline in the ratio of engineers to new investment is likely in succeeding five year periods. On the other hand, the composition of investment may change in favour of industries employing a relatively high proportion of engineers. Taking these two considerations together, the IAMR concluded that a fairly constant ratio of 10.67:10

175

million (measured in terms of constant prices) was the best assumption for its first forecasts of requirements in the Fourth and Fifth Plans. However, subsequent research of the IAMR analysed this investment-personnel ratio in more detail, and compared this ratio as a basis for forecasts with the two other ratios that had been used in previous forecasts: the output—personnel ratio and the ratio between engineering and total employment.

The purpose of this study by IAMR in 1967 was to compare forecasts of engineering requirements based on these three ratios and also to compare global forecasts, with separate forecasts for each major sector. This represents a considerable step forward in Indian manpower forecasting. Previous forecasts had usually represented global estimates of demand for the entire economy, based on one assumed relationship between manpower and a single economic indicator. Only the Working Group in 1960 had used three different ratios, and this was to provide a set of checks rather than a systematic comparison of assumptions. However, the IAMR study recognized that 'the various sectors of the economy differ considerably from one another in matters like output per engineer, investment needed per engineer, and ratio of engineers to total work-force. Similarly, a simultaneous consideration of all the related factors, viz. output, investment, work-force and engineering manpower, is necessary to ensure consistency and feasibility of the assumptions and results' (IAMR, 1967, p. 2). The purpose of the study was to estimate the three ratios at the start of the First, Second and Third Plan periods for eight economic sectors, and use these as a basis for forecasts of requirements in 1970 and 1975.

The first problem was, of course, data. We have already seen that it is difficult to obtain reliable estimates for 1955 and 1960 even for the stock of engineering manpower. It is obviously more difficult to estimate its distribution between sectors. In 1964—65 the IAMR carried out a detailed study of the distribution of electrical and mechanical engineers but no information is available on other specialisms. There were also many deficiencies in the data on output, investment and work force — for example, sector-wise breakdowns were rarely available — and there were no estimates of investment and output in terms of constant prices.

The final estimates of output, investment, total work force and engineering manpower by sectors in 1955, 1960 and 1965 are therefore based on a large number of different sources of data, some of which are unreliable, or even conflicting. Even so, the data are not sufficiently detailed for the purposes required and certain assumptions had to be made by IAMR. In the circumstances, it is unfortunate that the study gives no more information than 'pooling all these sources together, the data on employment of engineers have been worked out', or 'approximations have been made'. The compilation of these tables showing sector-wise distribution of engineers, output, investment and work force in 1955, 1960 and 1965 was obviously a major task but the reliability of the results is very much open to question.

Having compiled these basic data, the IAMR calculated the average ratio between the number of engineers and output, investment and total work force in different sectors in the three years and then estimated regression equations, taking the number of engineers employed in a sector as the dependent variable and the other three parameters as the independent variables. The problems of non-comparability of data over time are frequently mentioned and so is another problem: 'Since ours is a demand study, the data on the number of engineers in different years should more or less correspond with the demand curve for engineers. In a situation of shortage . . . the employment figures of engineers reflected mainly the supply position, and not so much the demand position, because there were a number of unfilled vacancies of engineers . . .' (IAMR, 1967, p. 23). This crucial point is not really developed, nor is the related problem, that since the supply of engineers has been heavily influenced by successive forecasts of demand, which *assume* a certain relationship between output or investment and engineering employment, the resulting picture of employment in relation to these factors cannot be used as independent confirmation of that assumption.

Nevertheless, despite all these difficulties, the results of the IAMR study are extremely interesting. Table 7.4 shows the results of their calculation of the output—engineer ratio, investment—engineer ratio, and engineer—work force ratio in different sectors of the economy for the three years, 1955, 1960 and 1964.

This table shows a fairly consistent pattern throughout the sectors. The ratio of output per engineer shows a steady decline over time in almost all the sectors. A number of reasons are suggested for this, including a shift from small and medium term industries to larger-scale, engineer-intensive industries, the replacement of foreign engineers by Indians, but also 'it may indicate that initially engineers were in short supply and gradually this shortfall is not only being bridged but in some cases may be tending towards over-employment' (IAMR, 1967, p. 14). This finding is considerably at variance with the assumption of many of the previous forecasts that the output—

177

TABLE 7.4

RATIO OF ENGINEERS TO OUTPUT, INVESTMENT AND TOTAL WORK FORCE, BY SECTOR, INDIA, 1955—65

Sector	Output per engineer (Rs. 10,000)			Investment per engineer (Rs. 10,000)		Engineers per 1,000 workers		
	1955—56	1960—61	1964—65	1955—60	1955—64	1955	1960	1964
1. Mining, manufacturing and utilities	72	55	38	153	118	13.74	20.10	33.06
2. Construction	17	15	14	140	135	87.84	100.00	108.87
3. Transport and communications	92	61	59	282	311	21.74	33.33	36.79
4. Educational services	30	19	13	27	25	30.30	67.61	97.83
5. Government, administration, trade, commerce and other services	104	81	75	30	37	13.50	18.88	21.62
6. Agriculture	11,720	6,890	4,973	2,584	3,040	0.04	0.08	0.12
Total	148	107	82	125	120	4.79	7.65	11.05

Source: IAMR (1967), pp. 33—35.
Notes: (1) Output is measured in terms of value added, at constant prices.
(2) The average values of the investment—engineer ratio have been calculated by considering net increments over the base year, 1953—56.

engineer ratio would be constant over time.

The trend in the ratio of engineers to total work force also shows that the number of engineers per thousand workers had risen steadily since 1955, but the IAMR emphasize the problem of interpreting this, given the unreliability of the data on total employment and the existence of underemployment. The only other estimate of this ratio was made by the Working Group on Technical Education in 1960. The Working Group calculated that the ratio of engineers to total employment in the non-agricultural sector had risen from 0.12 per cent to 0.16 per cent in 1955 and 0.24 per cent in 1960. For purpose of the Working Group's forecasts, it was assumed that this ratio would continue to rise to 0.41 per cent in 1965 and 0.55 per cent in 1970. These IAMR calculations also suggest a ratio of about 0.16 per cent in 1950 to 0.16 per cent in 1955 and 0.24 per cent in 1960. For purposes of the Working Group's forecasts, it was assumed that this ratio would continue to rise to 0.41 per cent in 1965 and 0.55 per cent in 1970. These IAMR calculations also suggest a ratio of about 0.16 per cent in 1955 and 0.24 per cent in 1960, but then 0.33 per cent in 1965, and the IAMR forecasts would imply 0.45 per cent in 1970. However, the IAMR point out that no 'systematic and reliable' sets of figures are available on the size and distribution of the work force, so that 'no special claim can be made for this method under Indian conditions'. No great importance should, therefore, be attached to the differences between the IAMR and the Working Group estimates of this ratio.

problem arises in interpreting this trend, however, since it was impossible to estimate investment in terms of constant prices. The assumption made by the Working Group on Technical Education of 12 additional engineers per Rs. 10 million is higher than this ratio of about 8 engineers per Rs. 10 million, and IAMR's previous assumption of 10 engineers per Rs. 10 million also appears high in relation to this study, but the absence of any obvious trend and the problem of non-comparability of prices make it difficult to draw any confident conclusions about the relationship between investment and engineering manpower.

In addition to these calculations of trends in the three ratios, the IAMR estimated three regression equations with the number of engineers in each case as the dependent variable. The study gives very little information about the regression equations; it notes that 'although the number of degrees of freedom available to us for each sector is extremely small, the fit (between engineers and output) is surprisingly good because we have witnessed a steady growth in the

179

employment of engineers as well as output in each of the non-agricultural sectors' (IAMR, 1967, p. 15); nothing is said about the fit between engineers and investment or total work force and the equations themselves are not given, but simply used to calculate engineering requirements for the period 1970—1 and 1975—6. Two different definitions are adopted of 'engineering manpower'. Most of the previous studies we have described confined their forecasts to requirements of graduate and diploma engineers. However, several studies had shown that when 'engineer' is defined in terms of job function, a significant proportion of workers in engineering occupations did not possess a formal qualification in engineering but instead had gained practical experience on the job. Many previous forecasts had ignored these 'practicals', as they are called in India, but the Planning Commission had estimated that in 1955 there were 23,000 engineering 'practicals' compared with 79,000 graduates and diploma holders, and the IAMR estimated that in 1964. there were 41.000 'practicals' (IAMR, 1967, p. 17).[2] Their forecasts, therefore, distinguish between demand for graduates and diploma holders, on the one hand, and demand for total engineering manpower, on the other. This second forecast assumes that 'practicals' will continue to grow in absolute terms but will constitute a steadily declining proportion of qualified engineers.

The study calculates a wide range of alternative estimates of engineering requirements for 1970 and 1975. For each year, there are nine estimates of requirements for engineering graduates and diploma holders, and a further nine for total engineers, including practicals. The three different regression equations were used, together with target figures for output, investment and work force suggested by the Perspective Planning Division of the Planning Commission; in addition, separate estimates were made using global, two-sector and a full sectoral breakdown of output, etc. (IAMR, 1967, pp. 10—12[3]. Table 7.5 shows the full range of estimates for

---

[2] A more recent report by IAMR (1969, Table 10, p. 42) gives an entirely different estimate of 74,000 for 1964. There are certain discrepancies between the table and the figures quoted in the text and the latter appear to be in error. If the percentage of 26.5 per cent as given in the table is correct, this estimate is much higher than the earlier IAMR estimate.

[3] The figures are derived from *The Fourth Five-Year Plan: A Draft Outline*, and *Notes on Perspective of Development, India, 1960—61 to 1975—76*, prepared by the Planning Commission. After the latter was published, the recession caused the targets for 1975 to be lowered, and the IAMR used these lower figures in its calculations.

TABLE 7.5

RANGE OF FORECASTS OF ENGINEERING REQUIREMENTS, INDIA, 1970—71 (thousands)

Approach	Degree and diploma holders based on:			Total (including 'practicals') based on:		
	Output	Investment	Work force	Output	Investment	Work force
(i) Sectoral	403	411	356	456	464	409
(ii) Two-sector	395	354	341	448	407	394
(iii) Global	371	325	333	424	378	386

Source: IAMR (1967), p. 29.

1970, based on these alternative approaches.

This comparison reveals differences of up to 86,000. Requirements are consistently higher if the sectoral composition of output, investment and employment are taken into account, and on the whole, the estimates based on output are highest and those based on work force are lowest. A difference of 86,000 is significant in a period of only five years, when total requirements are estimated to be 350,000 to 400,000. The IAMR concluded that sector-wise forecasts were feasible and worthwhile but, because of the difficulty of obtaining reliable data, they should be attempted only in conjunction with global forecasts; furthermore the use of three independent variables was preferable to the use of a single factor, which would 'involve the risk of making projections which are out of tune with development in the factors left out of consideration'. However, we are left with the problem of reconciling the different estimates. Should we take a simple unweighted average, or should greater weight be attached to one approach? On this, the IAMR study is non-committal: 'To answer this question in a more definitive way than has been done in this paper, it is necessary to make a deeper study of the various issues . . . with more precise data covering a longer period of time'.

A final exercise was attempted by IAMR, which was to compare these estimates with other forecasts for the same year, prepared by other organizations. The comparison, shown in Table 7.6, was between:

(i) The nine different estimates by IAMR, for 1970 and 1975.

(ii) The Working Group on Technical Education and Vocational

181

TABLE 7.6

IAMR'S GLOBAL LEVEL COMPARISON OF ESTIMATED REQUIREMENTS OF ENGINEERS WORKED OUT BY DIFFERENT ORGANIZATIONS AND APPROACHES, INDIA, 1970—71 AND 1975—76 (thousands)

Approach/organization	Degree and diploma holders based on:			Total (including practic● based on:		
	Output	Investment	Work force	Output	Investment	Wo● for●
1	2	3	4	5	6	7
1970						
A. *Sectoral*						
IAMR	403	411	356	456	464	40●
B. *Two-sector approach*						
IAMR	395	354	341	448	407	39
C. *Global*						
1. IAMR	371	325	333	424	378	38
2. Planning Commission, Directorate of Manpower and Ministry of Education	420	422	..	434	436	.●
3. Working Group on Technical Education and Vocational Training	..	440	450	..	..	.●
1975						
A. *Sectoral*						
(i) IAMR	703	676	521	766	739	5●
(ii) Burgess, Layard and Pant	878	..	..	..	..	.
B. *Two-sector approach*						
IAMR	694	650	486	757	713	5●
C. *Global*						
(i) IAMR	615	581	470	678	644	5●
(ii) Planning Commission, Directorate of Manpower and Ministry of Education	720	..	..	732	..	.

Source: IAMR (1967), p. 29.
· · = not available.

Training's estimates for 1970, which were based on a global approach, involving two factors, investment and work force.

(iii) Forecasts prepared for 1970 and 1975 by a joint team from the Planning Commission, Ministry of Education and Directorate of Manpower, based on a global approach, involving output and investment.

(iv) The forecasts prepared for the Education Commission for 1975 by Burgess *et al.*, (1968), which were based on a sectoral breakdown of output, and assumed that demand for engineers would increase in each sector in proportion to increases in output.

The comparison of various forecasts shows clearly that the IAMR forecasts are consistently lower than other forecasts but the study does not attempt to analyse why these differences occur. In some cases the differences arise because of different assumptions about the relationship between engineers and economic variables but in other cases, it is different targets for economic growth that give rise to different estimates of manpower requirements.

For example, the only other estimate of engineering requirements based on a sectoral approach is the Burgess, Layard and Pant forecast, which was carried out in 1965 for the Education Commision (Burgess *et al.*, 1968, p. 23). This forecast was based on the assumption of a constant output—engineer ratio and the requirements for engineers in each sector in 1975 were calculated by applying target rates of growth of output, as suggested by the Perspective Planning Division of the Planning Commission, which at that time assumed a target of Rs. 369,000 million total output in 1975—6. But by 1967, when the IAMR made its own forecasts, the recession had caused the Planning Commission to revise its targets for output and investment, and the IAMR forecasts were prepared on the basis of only Rs. 231,000 million. Therefore, the difference between the two sets of forecasts results partly from different assumptions about the productivity of engineers and partly from different output targets. For example, Table 7.7 shows the difference between the two sets of assumptions regarding output targets in 1975 and the output:engineer ratio, together with the forecasts of engineering requirements in just one sector, the construction industry.

This shows that the two assumptions have a counter-balancing effect: Burgess, Layard and Pant assume a higher value for output but also assume higher productivity of engineers, so that their final estimate of requirements for engineers is higher than the IAMR forecast and lower than if the IAMR productivity assumption had been adopted. The actual difference between the two assumptions is

TABLE 7.7

COMPARISON OF ASSUMPTIONS ABOUT OUTPUT TARGET, OUTPUT–
ENGINEER RATIO AND ESTIMATED REQUIREMENTS FOR ENGINEERS
IN CONSTRUCTION INDUSTRY, INDIA, 1975

	IAMR forecast	Burgess, Layard and Pant
(1) Total output (Rs. abja = 1,000 m.)	9.1	15.2
(2) Output: engineer ratio (Rs. 10,000)	13	16
(3) No. of engineers (1,000)	70	95

Source: IAMR (1967), Tables 5, 8 and 14; Burgess *et al.*, (1968), p. 23.

25,000 but the difference between forecasts which assumed high
output and low productivity, and vice versa, would be 60,000. It is
difficult to explain the difference in the two forecasts purely in
terms of the two different assumptions because of the interaction
between the two. If we adopt the 'analysis of sources of change' used
by Hollister in his technical evaluation of the MRP (Hollister, 1966,
pp. 89–90), and apply it to the difference between the forecasts in
Table 7.7, the result is as follows.

TABLE 7.8

ESTIMATED CONTRIBUTION OF TWO FACTORS TO DIFFERENCE BE-
TWEEN FORECASTS OF REQUIREMENTS OF ENGINEERS, INDIA, 1975

Total difference	Output assumption	Productivity assumption	Interaction
25,000	46,900	−13,100	−8,800

Source: See text.

The influence of the lower target figure is considerably stronger
than the influence of the productivity assumption. The same is
almost certainly true in the case of most of the other differences
between IAMR's forecasts and those of the other organizations
shown in Table 7.6. Thus, these differences cannot be used to support or question the methods adopted by IAMR. For the forecasts
were all produced on the basis of official figures, so that there is no
question of a more or less feasible prediction of future output: the

184

purpose of all the forecasts was to spell out the implications of the output targets in the Fourth Plan and, therefore, the factor that most influenced the forecasts was the lowering of output targets due to the recession in 1965. What is useful in the IAMR exercise is the demonstration of the wide divergencies between various forecasts of engineering requirements. Previous forecasts had produced, on the whole, single-valued estimates of manpower requirements, based on official output targets and a single assumption about investment:engineer ratios. Now, for the first time, the conditional nature of all these forecasts is clearly seen.

The latest forecasting exercise by IAMR has, to some extent, continued the approach of comparing forecasts based on different methods and assumptions. Separate forecasts were made on the basis of assumed relations between engineers and national income, on the one hand, and engineers and investment, on the other, but all the forecasts are global in nature. The purpose of the study, published at the end of 1969, was to review the current demand and supply position and to produce long-term forecasts of engineering requirements up to 1979 (IAMR, 1969). The Fourth Plan, which was originally prepared for the period 1966—7 to 1970—1, was postponed because of the recession in 1965 and three separate Annual Plans were prepared for 1966—8. Therefore, the forecasts are, like their earlier ones, concerned with the Fourth and Fifth Plan periods but this time the forecasts are for the years 1973—74 and 1978—79.

The forecasts are based on linear regression equations for engineering manpower and national income, estimated from data for the period 1950 to 1968. During this period there was a change from a shortage of engineers in the 1950's to a near surplus in 1964, which became a significant surplus after 1964, so six separate regression lines were fitted for different periods, for example, 1950—60, 1950—64, 1955—64 and 1960—68. The IAMR concluded from this that there was a good relationship between the growth of national income and the employment of engineers (a correlation coefficient of 0.98), and that the fit of the regression line for 1955 to 1964 was better than the others.[4] This was used, therefore, to establish a relationship between engineering manpower and national income, which formed the basis of the forecasts.

---

[4] However, no tests were made for serial correlation. It is easy to produce spuriously high correlation coefficients between any two economic time series in a growing economy. Nor does the study give the actual regression equations calculated, or the standard errors of the coefficients.

There was an attempt to produce alternative forecasts and the study calculated separate regression equations for engineers and total national income, income in the non-agricultural sector and income in the engineering-intensive sector; in addition, separate regression lines were fitted to data on all engineering manpower (including 'practicals') and engineering graduates and diploma holders separately. But no attempt was made to make separate forecasts using a segmental approach, despite the recommendation of the earlier study by IAMR, because it was now felt that although a disaggregated method was in principle preferable, the data problems were too formidable. The only real comparison of methods was a comparison between forecasts based on the regression equations and a forecast based on the relationship between engineers and investment in the First, Second and Third Plans.

Figure 7.1 shows the regression lines for total national income and engineering manpower, both including and excluding 'practicals'. These separate estimates of the relationship between national income and engineers were used to produce two different forecasts of the requirements of engineering graduates and diploma holders in 1973. In the first case, data on qualified employed engineers, based on institutional outturn figures adjusted for unemployment, were related to national income and the demand for graduates and diploma holders in 1973 was calculated directly from the regression equation.

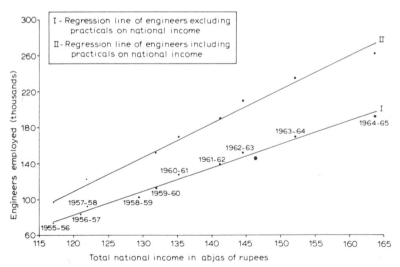

Figure 7.1. Relationship between growth of stock of engineers and total national income, India 1955/1956—1964/1965.
Source: IAMR (1969), p. 44.

186

In the second place, an estimate was made of total engineering manpower including 'practicals', using the findings of the Planning Commission and IAMR that the proportion of the total stock of manpower employed in engineering occupations without a degree or diploma had risen from 22.5 per cent in 1955 to 26.5 per cent in 1964. These figures for total engineering manpower were then related to national income and demand for all engineers including practicals was estimated for 1973; subsequently, the estimated number of 'practicals' was subtracted to yield the requirement of graduate and diploma engineers. The two methods gave estimates of 374,000 and 384,000 respectively and the IAMR concluded that a variation of 10,000 engineers, which is only 2.6 per cent of the range of 374–384,000 engineers, was not significant. The study decided, because of the importance of 'practicals' in the labour market, to adopt the latter approach. The justification was that 'we cannot ignore the number of engineering practicals, who form a constituent of the engineering manpower system . . .' (IAMR, 1969, p. 41). This is a strange argument, since it neglects the question of the reliability of the data. It is undeniable that practicals are a significant feature of the engineering labour market in India but estimates of their numbers are based on only three sample surveys: the Planning Commission's in 1955 and two surveys by IAMR, of employment of electrical and mechanical engineers in 1965 and civil engineers in 1968. This means that the estimate of total engineering manpower including practicals is fairly unreliable. Therefore, to forecast the demand for graduate and diploma engineers by first *adding* the estimated number of practicals, then relating this combined figure to national income, and finally *subtracting* the number of practicals to give the required number of qualified engineers, seems a most circuitous way to achieve the desired result. If truly independent estimates of engineering manpower including and excluding practicals had been available, the IAMR method would have been understandable but as it is, the unreliability of the data makes their choice very questionable indeed.

The other comparison, between forecasts based on total national income, non-agricultural income, and national income in engineering-intensive sectors, together with the forecast based on investment, showed that the forecasts for 1973 ranged from 325,000 (based on investment) to 384,000 (based on total national income). The IAMR concluded that the lowest estimate was unsatisfactory, since it excluded requirements for such sectors as defence, which are not included in the Five Year Plans. As for the other methods, the study concludes that variation between the estimates is less than 5 per cent (which is well within the margin of statistical differences

187

involved in the computation of data); since long-term targets are generally available only for total national income, this method was adopted which, incidentally, is the one yielding the highest forecasts.

The regression equation for total engineering manpower including practicals and total national income is therefore used to obtain estimates of the demand for engineers in 1973 and 1978, on the assumption of three different growth rates for national income: a low rate of 4.8 per cent (the actual rate of growth achieved between 1960 and 1964), a medium rate of 5.5 per cent between 1969 and 1973 and 6 per cent between 1974 and 1978 (the rates of growth postulated in the Draft Fourth-Year Plan), and a high rate of 7 per cent throughout the period (which corresponds to the target, originally proposed in the Third Plan). The range of forecasts is shown in Table 7.9.

TABLE 7.9

ALTERNATIVE ESTIMATES OF DEMAND FOR ENGINEERS, INDIA, 1973—74 AND 1978—79 (thousands)

Growth assumption	1973		1978	
	Total (including practicals)	Graduates and diploma holders	Total (including practicals)	Graduates and diploma holders
Low	493	357	711	513
Medium	530	384	824	593
High	607	439	989	710

Source: IAMR (1969), p. 49.

The IAMR study also estimated the future growth of supply, on the basis of existing enrolment patterns, and the assumption that future admissions would be maintained at the 1968 level. Allowance was made for wastage, retirement, death, emigration, etc. A comparison of these supply projections with the alternative estimates of demand showed that even if admissions are held constant at the 1968—9 level, there would be a significant surplus of engineers by 1973, whichever growth assumption is adopted. If the rate of growth suggested in the Fourth Plan is achieved (the medium assumption), the surplus in 1973 will be 100,000. If this medium assumption is adopted, demand and supply will be in balance by 1978, but if only the lower growth rate is achieved, there would still be a surplus of

188

71,000 in 1978. Therefore, the conclusion of the study is that there is an imbalance in the employment market in 1968—69, which is likely to extend over the next seven to eight years; it therefore recommends no increase in the admissions to engineering colleges and polytechnics to cure the existing imbalance between demand and supply by the end of the Fifth Plan. The extent of this imbalance is the subject of the next section.

Demand and supply in 1968

The first question is how many engineers were unemployed. Unfortunately data on unemployment are very inadequate. The returns of the Live Registers of Employment Exchanges can provide a first estimate but these figures need to be corrected to allow both for those who are employed but who register in order to seek a better job, and those who are unemployed but not registered. A few case studies in particular states reveal that, on average, 50 per cent of graduates and 35 per cent of diploma holders who are registered already have jobs, but at the same time recent rounds of the National Sample Survey suggest that 46 per cent of the educated unemployed are not registered at Employment Exchanges (IAMR, 1969, p. 9).[5] No separate data are available for engineers and data on registration do not distinguish between qualified engineers and 'practicals'. The IAMR has estimated the number of unemployed engineers in 1968 but given the nature of the estimates the data are very approximate. However, even if we assume that they are over-estimates, there is still evidence of a sharp rise in the number of graduates and diploma holders who are unemployed between 1955 and 1968. The IAMR estimate that 600 graduates and 4,200 diploma holders were unemployed in 1955, which represented 6 per cent of the total stock of qualified engineers. But by 1968, they estimate that 10,000 graduates and 46,700 diploma holders were unemployed, which was 17 per cent of the total stock (IAMR, 1969, p. 11).

The unemployment up to 1964 is dismissed as 'frictional'. The

---

[5] Earlier attempts to use NSS data to correct employment exchange data were unreliable, because the NSS and the Employment Exchanges produced widely differing estimates of the total number registered, which suggested that NSS respondents were not giving accurate replies (Blaug *et al.*, 1969, pp. 65—7). There may have been improvements between the 17th and the 19th and 20th rounds of the NSS but unless this is so, the IAMR's correction factors are unreliable.

Engineering Personnel Committee commented in 1956 that most unemployed engineers were newly qualified and that lack of experience was the main cause of their unemployment. Up to 1964, the number of engineering vacancies notified to employment exchanges during each year was roughly equal to the number of engineers on the Live Registers, so that although some sort of imbalance clearly existed, it seems to be an imbalance between the experience of job-seekers and the expectations of employers, rather than a true imbalance between demand and supply. The Engineering Personnel Committee had commented in 1956: 'We feel that too much stress on experience as a prerequisite for employment is unfair to engineering personnel coming out of technical institutions. We shall be moving in a vicious circle, if for want of engineers our work suffers, and for want of employment engineers do not gather the necessary experience' (Planning Commission, 1956, p. 21). To a large extent this 'vicious circle' does seem to explain the situation in the 1950's and early 1960's when declared shortages of engineers existed side by side with unemployed engineers. However, after 1964, the number of engineering vacancies notified to employment exchanges began to decline, whereas the annual outturn of newly qualified engineers increased steadily, so that the number of engineers registered at employment exchanges rose sharply in 1965 and was for the first time higher than the number of notified vacancies. By 1966 the number of registered unemployed was more than double the number of vacancies, and in 1967 it was almost four times as high.

These figures demonstrate the marked rise in the number of unemployed after 1965 but the IAMR estimates that the number of engineers who were 'underemployed' was even more striking.[6] The study measures under-employment by using the regression equation, fitted to engineering manpower and national income data for 1955 to 1964, to calculate the number of engineers 'required' to produce the achieved level of national income. This equation is estimated as $W_n = 3.7528\ P - 340.8436$, where W_n is the number of employed engineers and P represents national income. This equation is used to estimate the 'real demand' for engineers after 1964 and the differ-

---

[6] The definition of underemployment adopted is that of the ILO: 'underemployment exists when persons in employment, who are not working full-time would be able and willing to do more work than they are actually performing or when the income or productivity of persons in employment would be raised if they worked under improved conditions of employment, or transferred to another occupation, account being taken of their occupational skills' (ILO, 1964).

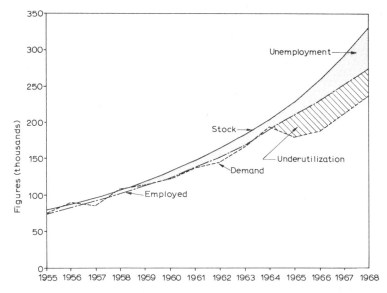

Figure 7.2. Unemployment and under-utilization of engineers, India, 1955–1968.
Source: IAMR (1969), p. 21.

ence between these figures and the number actually employed provides a measure of 'underemployment'. Figure 7.2 shows the results of these calculations for 1955 to 1968. This suggests that in 1967 there were 41,000 more engineers employed than the level of output required, and in 1968 the excess was 37,000.

This method is, of course, open to the objection that there is no evidence that the number of engineers given by the regression equation is in any sense optimal. The number of engineers employed between 1955 and 1964 is the result of the interaction between demand and supply and, therefore, the regression equation cannot be used to identify 'real demand'. All that this calculation shows is that in terms of the degree of utilization between 1955 and 1964 (when, for most of the period there were reported shortages), the number of engineers employed after 1964 is high in comparison to national income. Thus, it certainly suggests under-utilization after 1964 but does not provide a precise measure of the degree of underemployment.

The IAMR also uses the regression equations, which formed the basis for forecasts of future requirements and estimates of underemployment, to analyse the causes of unemployment. Basically, the study suggests there were two causes of unemployment of

191

engineers after 1964: the recession, which resulted in a very small increase in output and a corresponding slackening in the demand for engineers, and the increase in admission capacity during the Third Plan period in excess of the original targets, as a result of the defence emergency. The IAMR tried to estimate the relative influence of these two factors by using the regression equation to calculate the demand for engineers after 1964 if the rate of growth from 1964 to 1968 had equalled the target rate set in the Third Plan, namely, 5.5 per cent a year. Under these conditions, it is estimated, demand for engineers would have been 305,000 in 1968—69. However, what actually happened was that national income, which rose by 4.8 per cent between 1960 and 1964, declined by 4.7 per cent 1965—6 and then rose slightly but by much less than the target rate, so that national income by 1968—69 was about Rs. 175,000 million rather than Rs. 203,000 million, the Third Plan target. This meant a demand for engineers of only 275,000 in 1968 instead of 305,000, which in turn implies that the recession would account for unemployment of 30,000.

In addition, the fact that the original admission targets laid down in the Third Plan were exceeded meant that the supply of engineers in 1968 was 332,000, instead of the original target of 299,000. The

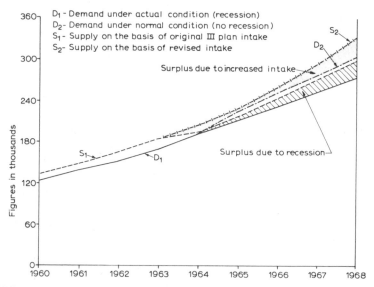

Figure 7.3. Extent of unemployment due to recession and on account of increased intake, India, 1960—1968.
Source: IAMR (1969), p. 25.

192

IAMR estimate that demand for engineers without the recession would have been 305,000, so that even under 'normal' conditions the increase in supply would have caused unemployment of 27,000 engineers.

This suggests that 53 per cent of the total unemployment of engineers in 1968 was attributable to the recession and 47 per cent to the increased intake in engineering institutions; this is shown in Figure 7.3. The final conclusion of this analysis is that without the 1965 recession, and the increase in admission capacity due to the defence emergency, supply and demand would have been roughly in balance by 1968. However, the combined result of these two factors was a serious over-supply of engineers in 1968, resulting in unemployment of 56,700 graduates and diploma holders and underemployment of a further 37,000.

Conclusions

The successive forecasts which have been examined have all been attempts to spell out the manpower implications of official targets for national income growth, output in particular sectors, and investment. They cannot, therefore, be evaluated simply by comparing forecasts with actual employment, since they were not intended to be 'onlooker forecasts' and in almost every case the actual pattern of output and investment was different from the targets laid down in the Five Year Plans. They must, therefore, be judged in terms of their influence on policy, and the validity of their methods and assumptions.

It is difficult to assess the influence of the forecasts on policy. Up to 1964 every organisation involved in forecasting recommended expansion of engineering facilities and these recommendations were translated into targets in the Five Year Plans. Since 1950, there has been a dramatic increase in enrolments, and yearly intake has risen from 4,119 at the degree level and 5,903 at the diploma level in 1950 to 24,237 and 42,935 in 1967—8. This can be interpreted as a sign that manpower forecasts have greatly influenced enrolment policy. However, this would ascribe too great an influence to the forecasts, since there was powerful independent pressure for expansion of engineering facilities. What actually happened was that admission targets, which reflected official forecasts and policy, were exceeded in both the Second and Third Plan periods, as shown in Table 7.10.

It is clear, therefore, that the manpower forecasts succeeded in

TABLE 7.10

TARGETS AND ACHIEVEMENTS IN THE FIRST THREE FIVE-YEAR PLANS, INDIA, 1955-56 to 1965-66 (thousands)

		Engineering degree intake	Engineering diploma intake
1955—56	target	no specific target	no specific target
	actual	5.89	10.48
1960—61	target	11.14	20.53
	actual	13.82	25.80
1965—66	target	19.14	37.39
	actual	24.70	49.90

Source: Blaug *et al.*, (1969), p. 46.

TABLE 7.11

INTAKE IN ENGINEERING DEGREE AND DIPLOMA COURSES, INDIA, 1967—69 (thousands)

Year	Intake	Degree	Diploma	Total
1967—68	Actual	24.2	42.9	67.1
1968—69	Recommended by Ministry of Education	15.5	37.2	52.7
1968—69	Accepted by State Governments	16.8	33.2	50.0
1968—69	Actual	17.5	26.4	43.9

Source: IAMR (1969), p. 31.

underwriting the pressure that already existed for expansion. This is borne out by experience after 1964, when the IAMR forecasts emphasized the need for a halt to expansion and, later, a reduction in intake. This has now been implemented and the intake in 1968—69 was considerably lower than the previous year's, but it proved more difficult to reverse the policy of expansion after 1964 than to speed up the rate of expansion. Intake continued to rise between 1964 and 1966, despite the forecasts of an impending surplus of engineers. Even the reduction in intake in 1968—69 cannot be explained simply in terms of the influence of official policy. For, as Table 7.11 shows, actual intake was higher than recommended by the Ministry of Education in the case of degree level engineers, but lower at the diploma level. This illustrates how difficult it is to measure the relative influence of official policy, which determines the sanctioned intake of engineering colleges, and labour market conditions which affect the actual demand by students.

Nevertheless, it is clear that the provision of facilities in engineering colleges and polytechnics has been considerably influenced by forecasts of manpower requirements, and the fact that the employment situation has changed from a shortage to a precarious balance and finally to a surplus reflects, in the first place, official policy and, latterly, the recession and the official panic about defence requirements.

The effect of the recession emphasizes one of the main weaknesses of Indian forecasts. With the exception of the latest IAMR exercise, the forecasts have tended to be single-value forecasts, based on only one target for economic growth. These targets have frequently been very optimistic, which has resulted in forecasts of requirements twice as high as alternative forecasts, based on the assumption of a lower rate of growth. This is illustrated clearly in Table 7.12, which shows the influence of alternative growth rates on forecasts for 1973—78.

TABLE 7.12

RANGE OF ESTIMATES OF ENGINEERING REQUIREMENTS, BASED ON DIFFERENT ASSUMPTIONS OF ECONOMIC GROWTH, INDIA, 1973—78 (thousands)

Forecast and growth rate assumption	1973	1975	1976
(1) IAMR (4.8 per cent, 1969—78)	357	.	513
(2) IAMR (5.5 per cent, 1969—73) (6.0 per cent, 1974—78)	384	.	593
(3) IAMR (7 per cent, 1969—78)	439	.	710
(4) Burgess, Layard and Pant (6.5 per cent, 1961—75)	.	878	.

Source: IAMR (1969), Table 13, p. 49. Burgess *et al.*, (1968), Table 20, p. 24.
. = not applicable.

When we attempt to evaluate the assumptions of the forecasts, we find that data are still not available for testing the assumptions of constant output—engineer or investment—engineer ratios. The IAMR has suggested that both these ratios have declined since 1960, indicating declining productivity and increasing engineer-intensiveness in both the pattern of investment and production. But the unreliability of much of the data means that further research is needed before the validity of these assumptions can really be tested. However, it is obvious that the period of time during which these ratios are assumed to remain constant in India is very long, which casts some doubt on the feasibility of the assumption. For example, Burgess, Layard and Pant produced forecasts of engineering requirements in manufacturing industry in 1985 on the assumption of constant engineer : output ratios in every industry group since 1955. The assumptions of constant productivity and technology during a five-year period may be quite reasonable, but to assume that they will remain constant over 30 years in a country like India seems a most remarkable assumption.

One problem that recurrs again and again in any assessment of manpower forecasting in India is the lack of satisfactory data. Even the estimates of the total stock of engineers vary between sources. Information on such questions as unemployment, or the proportion of workers in engineering occupations without formal engineering qualifications, is even more unreliable. When we look at economic indicators the situation is slightly better, but it is difficult to obtain estimates of investment at constant prices, or of the sectoral breakdown of the labour force. Time after time, the recommendations of the Planning Commission's Working Groups or Committees has been that more adequate information is needed about the current situation. Much has been achieved, for example by IAMR, but much more needs to be done if the search for new and improved forecasting techniques is not to run ahead of data availability.

The greatest lack of all is information about current utilization patterns. The statement of Burgess, Layard and Pant that their forecasts 'do not involve any judgement on the degree of utilization of the present stock' could be repeated for every other forecast. The early forecasts by the Engineering Personnel Committee and the Working Group on Technical Education emphasize the seriousness of the shortage of engineers, but this is based upon general statements by employers about unfilled vacancies, not a detailed analysis of the utilisation of employed engineers. At the same time, none of the forecasts makes any calculation of the costs involved in satisfying manpower 'requirements'. The implicit judgement which underlies all the forecasts is that a shortage of engineers would create such a crucial bottleneck to development that the question of relative costs and benefits does not arise, despite the fact that engineering education is the most expensive type of education in India. Yet recent estimates of the rate of return to education in India suggest that the social rate of return to engineering degree and diploma courses,

196

though higher than to other forms of higher education, is nevertheless only marginally above alternative rates of return for social investment (Blaug *et al.*, 1969, pp. 218—25).[7]

There are a number of questions for which earnings data, or better still, estimates of rates of return, might be illuminating, for example, the question of the appropriate balance between engineering graduates and diploma holders. The forecasts of the Engineering Personnel Committee reflected the attitude that the ratio of diploma holders to graduates ought to be increased and later forecasts also emphasized the need to change this ratio, which was 1:1 in 1955, according to the Planning Commission's survey of industry. The Working Group on Technical Education and Burgess, Layard and Pant assumed a ratio of 1:1.5 graduates to diploma holders, whereas the draft outline of the Fourth Five Year Plan suggested a ratio of 3:4, and the Education Commission advocated a ratio of 1:2.5. This wide range of values raises the question of the optimum value for this ratio. The IAMR have studied this problem fairly extensively and they concluded in 1965 that the 'required' ratio was 1:1.6, although recognizing that 'In one sense, of course, this change is predetermined by our forecast of the future growth of supply. The employers will have to use the degree holders and diploma holders in the manner in which they are actually produced by the engineering institutions' (IAMR, 1965, p. 51).

Later studies by IAMR, however, suggest a different conclusion. In the first place, an examination of the recent trend in the ratio of diploma holders to graduates shows that although the ratio of diploma holders in the total *stock* of engineers has increased from 1:1.3 in 1962 to 1:1.5 in 1968, the ratio of employed diploma holders to graduates has remained constant throughout this period at 1:1.2 (IAMR, 1969, p. 50). In other words, the assumption that 'employers will have to use degree and diploma holders in the manner in which they are actually produced' has proved unfounded and high rates of unemployment of diploma holders have resulted; the IAMR estimates that 23.6 per cent of the total stock of diploma holders was unemployed in 1968. Secondly, the IAMR now concludes that the attempt to change the ratio on the assumption of some 'required' ratio is misguided on the grounds that:

---

7 The estimates of the social rate of return to an engineering degree range from 10 to 12.5 per cent, and to an engineering diploma from 10 to 15 per cent. The authors estimated the alternative social rate of return to be 12.5 per cent, so that engineering education appears to be profitable but only just.

(a) The technician—engineer ratio is a concept based on the occupational structure of employment of engineering manpower rather than on educational qualifications,

(b) The ratio varies from country to country and, within a country, among sectors of employment, individual industry groups and among types of activity;

(c) The ratio also depends upon the definition of a technician in terms of his employment and education status and/or the informal/formal methods of education and training at this level;

(d) Taking the Indian structure, it seems that industry has not been able to use a higher proportion of diploma-holders probably because of (i) deficiencies in the present technician courses, (ii) low standards of instruction and training and (iii) limitations of the employment structure in industry (IAMR, 1969, p. 51).

This is a considerable improvement on earlier pronouncements on this question, since it does take into account actual patterns of employment. But this is surely one problem on which information on relative earnings of graduates and diploma holders might throw some light?

What then must be our final assessment of Indian forecasting of engineering requirements? The statement by IAMR, already quoted above, that 'employers will have to use degree and diploma holders in the manner in which they are actually produced' is very illuminating. It illustrates one of the fundamental problems of manpower forecasting and, unfortunately, no Indian forecast has yet come to terms with it. The problem is one of identifying the level of demand for engineers when the only data that are available reflect both supply and demand. Indian forecasting started in a situation which everyone recognized was non-optimal. Successive forecasts have been produced on the basis of largely untested hypotheses about the relationship between employment of engineers and output or investment and these have formed the basis of official policy. Hence, supply has been largely determined by the assumptions of the forecasts. And it is this supply which is reflected in recent statistics on the employment of engineers, which become in turn the basis for forecasts of future demand. For example, between 1955 and 1964, there was a massive increase in the supply of engineers, partly as a result of forecasts which assumed that engineers must increase in proportion to output. In the event, output rose less rapidly than the target figures in the Five Year Plans. Therefore, when IAMR tried to estimate the trend in the output—engineer ratio, it was found that this ratio had declined from an average of Rs. 1,480,000 per engineer in 1955 to

Rs. 1,070,000 in 1960 and Rs. 82,000 in 1964. This means declining productivity and it might be supposed that the IAMR would recommend a reversal of this trend in the future. On the contrary, it became the basis for the IAMR forecasts of future requirements and if these forecasts for 1970 and 1975 were to prove correct, the output per engineer would continue to fall to Rs. 570,000 in 1970 and Rs. 460,000 in 1975. There is no hint in the IAMR study that this will not represent an optimal situation.

It is the neglect of the question of the utilization of engineers, and the assumption that the past employment pattern which reflects supply can be used simply as a measure of demand, which are the main weaknesses of Indian forecasting of engineering requirements. The question of alternative strategies, of substitutability of different types of labour, or of informal and formal training, have received little attention. For example, it is a recurrent theme of the forecasts that the number of 'practicals' needs to be reduced in proportion to qualified engineers, but this is assumed without reference to relative salaries. This means that forecasts have been produced for 20 years of 'requirements' or 'demand' for engineers without any reference to the price that has to be paid. Indian forecasters are aware of this. For example, the IAMR, in its 1963 review of demand forecast methodologies, distinguishes between demand in the economic sense of 'a relationship between quantities of labour and a series of possible wage rates' and demand in the technological sense, but adopts the latter definition of demand on the grounds that the economic concept would require 'knowledge of, or at least assumptions about, the future pattern of relative salaries for various types of engineer' (IAMR, 1963B, Part II, p. 4). It is interesting that IAMR is prepared to make assumptions about many things in the future but not about that!

This neglect of cost-benefit considerations is particularly apparent in the tendency of forecasts to over-estimate on the grounds that a shortage is always more dangerous than a surplus. Since the tendency has been, in any case, for enrolment targets to be raised rather than lowered and to be exceeded rather than under-attained, while the economic targets on which the forecasts were based have for the most part not been achieved, the result has been increasing unemployment. The belief that 'the risk involved in over-estimation is comparatively less than in under-estimation' has influenced all the forecasts of engineering requirements and it also influenced the Education Commission, which recommended enrolment targets for all levels of education. Even so, the Commission recommended restriction of 'the unplanned and uncontrolled expansion of general, secondary and higher education, if massive educated unemployment is to be avoided' (Government of India, 1966, p. 97). Unfortunately, the Parliamentary Committee which discussed the Report of the Education Commission disregarded this recommendation, stating that 'we believe that every effort should be made to provide admissions to institutions of higher education to all eligible students who desire to study further' (quoted in Blaug *et al.*, 1969, p. 58). This illustrates clearly one of the striking lessons from manpower forecasting experience in India: where there are strong private pressures for educational expansion, manpower forecasts are likely to be welcomed when they justify existing demands for expansion but neglected when they advocate a reduction of enrolments. Indian experience shows that educational policy-makers are almost always more optimistic than even the most optimistic economic forecaster.

8. Engineers in Sweden[1]

by Kenneth Gannicott

Swedish experience of manpower forecasting dates from the 1930's when deteriorating employment conditions for university graduates created fears of a serious excess supply. Manpower forecasting in the modern sense of trying to relate educational decisions to the needs of the economy can be said to date from the mid-1950's. At that time forecasting was carried out in the Labour Market Board and even a casual glance at its publications demonstrates the extraordinary quantity and variety of its work. A summary of its activity between 1957 and 1961 described forecasts for 16 different occupational groups (Döös, 1961), and this was by no means a comprehensive survey. The forecasting programme was nothing if not ambitious: apart from predictions for such familiar groups as engineers, doctors and teachers, forecasts of supply and demand for kitchen and serving staff in restaurants, horticulturists and library personnel also appear in the list of publications.

The culmination of this work came in 1960, when the Swedish Parliament voted a five-year plan for the expansion of the universities and institutes of technology based on the estimates of future needs for highly qualified manpower put forward by the 1955 Educational Commission. The Commission had in turn relied very heavily on the many forecasts made by the Labour Market Board, supplemented by some special surveys. Since the forecasts indicated that the main lines of development required that this expansion lay stress on science and technology, these faculties were to have the most rapid growth; vocational counselling in the upper secondary schools was to be

[1] The research for this chapter was carried out during a visit to Stockholm in the spring of 1970. Mr. B. Eriksson of Stockholm University translated all the Swedish documents; Mr. Gunnar Bergendhal and Mrs. Désirée Stahle-Edmar of the Ministry of Education, and Mr. Göran Svanfeldt and Mr. Lars Abelin of the Forecasting Institute of the Central Bureau of Statistics provided every possible help. None of them is responsible for any errors or for the conclusions.

intensified; post-secondary professional education encouraged; and the Forecasting Section of the Labour Market Board expanded and moved to the Central Bureau of Statistics where it could, it was hoped, draw upon improved data and techniques. The stage seemed set, therefore, not only for the implementation of a thorough going manpower requirements approach to planning higher education but for its future expansion and refinement.

Within two years the forecasts put forward by the 1955 Commission had been criticized as misleading guidelines for planning in the 1960's. The criticism came from two different directions. One line was argued cogently by the Ministry of Education, which showed that the 1960 expansion programme was being rapidly overtaken by events. The 1955 Commission had paid little attention to the private demand for education, and the estimates for the supply side of its manpower forecasts were based on the trend in the output of graduates during the period 1930—55: this showed that 'the more probable alternative (was) that the transfer frequency from upper secondary school to higher education would decrease slightly during the 1960's rather than that it should stay at the present high level' (Educational Commission, 1959, p. 130). The Ministry demonstrated that a closer analysis of the factors affecting that transfer frequency (the post-war expansion in the birth-rate, the rising standard of living, the reorganization of the upper secondary school) led inevitably to the conclusion that the Commission had underestimated the number of students seeking higher education in 1970 by almost 20 per cent.[2]

Although the Ministry made many recommendations for the future based essentially on new enrolment projections, this did not mean that their critique of the Commission's forecasts extended to manpower forecasting as such. They concluded rather that 'although available forecasts . . . cannot serve as the sole basis for organising and determining the capacity and structures of higher education . . . they are a valuable support in the assessments that must be made of the future' (Ministry of Education, 1962A, p. 8).

Nevertheless, the doubts planted by the Ministry received powerful reinforcement in the following year with the publication of the report by a Working Group which the Labour Market Board itself

---

[2] Even the Ministry's projection turned out to be a serious under-estimate. Its prediction of 85—90,000 students enrolled at the universities and institutes of technology in 1970 was exceeded by 1967/68. The latest projection of total enrolment in 1970/71 gives 136,000 students (Central Bureau of Statistics, 1970A, Table 4).

had set up. The report was an appraisal of manpower forecasting in Sweden, emphasizing the theoretical problems involved. Since no English version of the report appeared until 1967 (and then only in very summarized form)[3], it is not surprising that it went unnoticed outside Sweden. This is a pity, since it preceded and was more comprehensive than Hollister's 1966 evaluation of the MRP for OECD; it thus ranks as a major contribution to literature on the economics of manpower forecasting.

The Report suggested that the forecasts of the Labour Market Board were unreliable because they had hardly considered the problems of substitutability, occupational—educational relationship and the measurement of shortage and surplus. It also pointed out that 'to try to plan the size of education in . . . a society by taking as an objective that supply and demand of different types of labour should balance is of course quite meaningless: the balance is created automatically at any educational capacity'. Moreover, 'it can be questioned whether forecasts for educational categories which in a lot of fields can easily be substituted for each other have any great interest. The possibilities of substitution mean that flexibility is great and that the number of persons with the education in question can vary within wide limits without a shortage or surplus symptom manifesting itself' (Labour Market Board, 1963, pp. 19 and 35).

It is not surprising that the result of these two reports was to undermine faith in manpower forecasting as a tool for planning the overall size of the higher education sector, and to emphasize the necessity for 'social demand' projections. Nevertheless, the Swedish authorities describe their present position as one in which manpower forecasts are still used for judging the distribution between faculties (see OECD, 1967, p. 208). The latest Educational Commission, that of 1968, has started work on deriving planning targets for the late 1970's and 1980's, and its brief consists of nothing less than an attempted synthesis of manpower forecasting, 'social demand' projections and rate of return analysis. It thus amounts to an attempt to plan the structure of higher education in the 1980's according to a consistent set of principles, rather than simply repeat the somewhat haphazard expansion of the 1960's. The construction of forecasts for various categories of manpower will play a prominent part in the Commission's work but the signs are not propitious. The latest forecast of engineers, the result of four years' work, is so comprehensive that it is practically a Cook's Tour through the different

---

[3] The English summary appears as Appendix II in OECD (1967).

methods of forecasting manpower requirements, yet it is widely conceded in Sweden to be a complete failure as a planning tool.

The time is thus ripe to take stock of the state of the art of forecasting in Sweden. It is neither possible nor desirable to be comprehensive. Instead, we shall try to illustrate the basic history outlined above by analysing a series of forecasts for one particular occupational group — that of engineers. We shall start with the forecast made by the Swedish Federation of Industry in 1957, which was a special forecast prepared for the 1955 Commission, and whose results were implemented in the 1960 legislation. The second major forecast was carried out by the Labour Market Board in 1962, and was an attempt to meet the criticism that the method used by the Swedish Federation in 1957 had underestimated the need for engineers (Labour Market Board, 1962). The final part of the chapter will consist of an analysis of the latest forecast for engineers, which was undertaken in the wake of the previously mentioned reappraisals of manpower forecasts (Technical Group, 1970).

Before turning to these forecasts, one point of definition must be made clear. In Sweden the term 'engineer' is applied not only to graduate engineers but also to those who in Britain would be termed 'technicians'. Within the general term 'engineer', Sweden distinguishes between various levels such as 'civilingenjör', 'institutsingenjör', and so on, according to the level of educational qualification. While the term 'civilingenjör' corresponds precisely to graduate engineer, it is not easy to translate the other terms directly into English equivalents, and though it may seem pedantic to refer constantly to the Swedish terms, it is less misleading to do so. The position with engineering qualifications is particularly complicated by the changes in secondary education during the 1960's. The qualifications are:

(1) Civilingenjörer: graduate level engineers.

(2) Läroverksingenjörer: those who have qualified from the former technical gymnasium and have since gained considerable practical experience.

(3) Institutsingenjörer: those who after some years practical work have attended courses for two years at an institute of engineering.

(4) Gymnasieingenjörer: those who after completing compulsory education at 16 follow a four-year course in the technical line of the new gymnasium.

(5) Fackskolieingenjörer: specialized professional school engineers; they have taken a two-year secondary education with basically tech-

nical subjects from 16—18; practical experience is required for completion of the second year.

Because of the changes in secondary education, the term 'läroverksingenjör' is not now used. It will be seen that the first two forecasts we examine refer to 'civil' — 'läroverks' — and 'institutsingenjörer'. The third forecast applies to all the categories with the exception of the 'läroverks'.

The Swedish Federation of Industry's forecast of engineers, 1957

As we have said, this forecast was carried out for the 1955 Educational Commission; one of its purposes was to check whether one could find 'meaningful and stable relationships which had existed in the past between the total number of engineers and any reasonable indicators of economic activity' (OEEC, 1960, p. 52). The methodology of the forecasts has been described elsewhere (OECD, 1962) but it is well worth a further review, since it is now possible to compare the first stage of the forecast with the actual outcome in 1965.

The data for the forecast were derived partly from historical statistics on the number of engineering graduates between 1935 and 1950 and partly from a questionnaire which was reckoned to cover about 90 per cent of employed engineers. Companies and organizations were asked to give details of the number of total employees, white-collar workers and engineers employed in 1950 and 1955, and the numbers expected to be hired in 1965. Respondents were also asked to estimate their anticipated yearly increase in production between 1955 and 1965. By combining all these data, the following relationships were derived:

(i) within the industrial sector, output per employee in constant prices had increased at an average annual rate of 1.5 per cent between 1935 and 1955; during the same period engineering density, that is, the proportion of engineers in the labour force, had increased at an average annual rate of 4.1 per cent. The survey of employers seemed to indicate that this relationship could be extrapolated linearly;

(ii) within national and local government from 1935 to 1955 there was a linear relationship between total expenditure per employee and engineering density;

(iii) for the rest of the economy, no stable relationship between the number of engineers and any indices of economic activity could be derived.

For the industrial sector, the change in productivity per employee can be derived once we have specified the changes in industrial production and the size of the labour force; we can then derive the corresponding engineering density by applying the linear relationship described above and multiplying this by the total number of employees to derive the future number of engineers. The Federation carried out this procedure for two yearly rates of production increase, 3 and 3.5 per cent. Since the latter figure corresponded closely to the mean prediction of the survey companies themselves (3.4 per cent), this was adopted as the main alternative.

For the government sector, an exactly analogous procedure was followed. The two basic assumptions were that GNP would increase from 1955 to 1965 at an annual rate of either 3 or 3.5 per cent, and that the proportion of GNP taken by government expenditure would remain at the 25 per cent level which had prevailed from 1935 to 1955. The procedure for the rest of the economy was even simpler. The forecast increase in working population in this sector was derived as a residual from the other sectors and the engineering density extrapolated using a linear trend: the two were then multiplied together to derive the number of engineers in 1965 and 1975.

The forecast is thus immediately recognisable as a 'policy-conditional forecast' of the number of engineers required to attain a 3 or 3.5 per cent yearly increase in GNP. The method is a variant of the density-ratios technique already described in Chapter 1. The economic rationale for the method is straightforward: it is implicitly assumed not only that the number of engineers employed in the past has been a cause of the output achieved, but also that there is a stable relationship between output and engineering employment which can be used for purposes of projection. The first implies that productivity should be treated as a dependent variable: a company is believed to employ engineers with the intention of increasing the productivity and output of the firm, at least in the long-run. But this does not allow for the two-way interaction of productivity and engineering employment, for it is equally plausible that increased productivity in a firm may increase the demand for engineers for R & D so that the higher productivity can be maintained in the future. The second assumption implies that the production function is of the fixed-proportions type. Our analysis of the actual predictive performance of this forecast supports these doubts about the useful-

206

ness of assuming a simple linear relationship between productivity and engineering density. We present below the results of the forecast, analysed by major sector.

Industrial sector

The forecast for the industrial sector was based on the assumption that 961,000 workers would be employed in this sector in 1965, and on the two alternative yearly increases in industrial production (3 and 3.5 per cent). In the event, both the number of workers and the rise in production were under-estimated by the Federation. The actual number of industrial employees in 1965 was 1,074,000, a 10.5 per cent projection error[4], and the average annual increase in industrial production was 6 per cent per year. More interesting is the finding that even if the Federation had correctly predicted the change in the exogenous variables, the linear model would still not have accurately forecast the number of engineers employed in industry in 1965. Using the density method explained above, a production increase of 6 per cent per year and an industrial labour force of 1,074,000 give a production value per employee of Kr. 20,000. This corresponds to an engineering density of 5.85 per cent, or 62,800 engineers.[5] Since the actual number of engineers employed in industry in 1965 was 53,000, the forecast would have overestimated the actual figure by almost 20 per cent. Table 8.1 below summarizes these data. The top line shows the original (main alternative) forecast of the Federation; the lower line ('revised') shows the manpower forecast that would have resulted with a perfect forecast of the exogenous variables.

Public sector

GNP grew by 4.1 per cent per year, and the proportion of public expenditure to GNP increased to 29 per cent by 1965 (as against the forecasts of 3 or 3.5 per cent and 25 per cent, respectively). The

---

[4] Percentage projection error $= 100 \left(\dfrac{\text{Predicted} - \text{Actual}}{\text{Actual}} \right)$

[5] Although the forecast is based on a linear relationship between productivity and density, the Committee does not seem to have made any test of the statistical validity of the relationship. As we shall see, the model is extremely sensitive to minor deviations in the observations. However, for the present purpose of obtaining an approximate comparison of prediction and outcome, we have used the average annual increases in productivity and density given earlier.

TABLE 8.1

FORECAST AND OUTCOME IN THE INDUSTRIAL SECTOR, SWEDEN, 1965

	Production increase per year (percentage)	Number of employees	Production value per employee (1935 prices) (Kr.)	Engineering density (percentage)	Forecast number of engineers
Original	3.5	961,000	17,500	4.68	45,000
Revised	6.0	1,074,000	20,000	5.85	62,800
Actual number	..	..	..	..	53,000

Source: Technical Group (1970), Section 2.6.2.2.
·· = not available.

TABLE 8.2

FORECAST AND OUTCOME IN THE PUBLIC SECTOR, SWEDEN, 1965

	Average yearly increase in GNP (percentage)	Number of employees	Cost per employee (1935 prices) (Kr.)	Engineering density (percentage)	Number of engineers
Original	3.5	536,000	11,000	3.82	20,500
Revised	4.1	685,000	10,800	3.74	25,600
Actual number	..	..	..	..	20,000

Source: As Table 8.1.
·· = not available.

third assumption, that the number of employees in the public sector would be 536,000 in 1965 underestimated the actual number of 685,000 by nearly 22 per cent. As in the industrial sector, even if the Federation had correctly predicted these changes, the manpower forecast would still have been wrong (Table 8.2). The correct GNP and employment figures would have forecast an engineering density of 3.74, which gives 25,600 engineers. Since the actual number employed in this sector in 1965 was 20,000, even a successful prediction

208

of the exogenous variables would have over-estimated the actual number of engineers by 28 per cent.

Rest of the economy

It is not surprising to find errors here, since the number of employees in this sector was derived as a residual, and we have already noted the errors in the labour force projections for the other two sectors. The number of employees was in fact 1,691,000 compared to a prediction of 1,800,000 (Table 8.3). The engineering density was assumed to extrapolate linearly in time to give a density of 1.63 in 1965: the actual density was 1.74 per cent. The result, even using the correct values for employment and density, would still have been an underestimation of the actual number of engineers by 13.5 per cent.

TABLE 8.3

FORECAST AND OUTCOME IN THE REST OF THE ECONOMY, SWEDEN, 1965

	Number of employees	Engineering density (percentage)	Number of engineers
Original	1,800,000	1.63	29,400
Revised	1,691,000	1.74	29,400
Actual number	..	..	34,000

Source: As Table 8.1.
·· = not available.

The forecasting errors thus arise because of errors in both the exogenous variables and the estimated relationships. We need not dwell on the errors in industrial production, GNP and the labour force, since it is well-known from other studies that forecasting even such aggregates as these is subject to large margins of error (Zarnowitz, 1968; Hajnal, 1955). In this instance, it is not surprising that there were considerable errors in forecasting industrial production, since the 3.5 per cent adopted as a main alternative by the Federation was approximately what the survey companies had themselves predicted (3.4 per cent) and no attempt was made to check that the survey responses were consistent with each other. There is, moreover, no evidence that the underestimation of GNP in this instance was due to cyclical fluctuations in economic activity. The long-term economic forecast for 1966—70 pointed out that a positive feature

209

of the 1960—65 period was 'the successful combatting of the —
admittedly very weak — recession that threatened early in this
period . . . the result has been a high and even average employment'
(Ministry of Finance, 1966, p. 18).

Nor is it true to say that the sectoral analysis presented above
exaggerates the overall errors in the forecast because of compensating
errors between sectors. To be sure, unless the educational system
trains graduates to work in one sector but not another, it is the
overall error which interests the education planner. But it would only
make sense to disregard the errors in individual sectors if we can
always rely upon errors in one sector to offset those in another; but
there is no *a priori* reason for expecting this to be so. Indeed, since
the Federation presumably carried out a sectoral forecast in the
belief that this would lead to a more accurate prediction, no postmortem would be complete without a test of that belief. Finally, a
quick test demonstrates that even if one chooses to concentrate on
the overall error of the forecast, the 10 per cent over-estimate[6] may
still be sufficient to lead to mistaken policy conclusions; it depends
of course on the policy in question (see Chapter 1). It will be recalled
that the objective of the forecast was to provide planning targets for
the number of engineers the educational system would have to
produce if a shortage of engineers were to be avoided. The result of
the Federation's calculations, which was accepted by the 1955 Educational Commission, was to forecast a shortage of 2,570 graduate
engineers in 1965 on prevailing supply trends.[7] Accepting for the
moment the Federation's judgement that 19 per cent of the forecast
number of engineers should be graduates, we derive graduate requirements of 22,400 in 1965. Supply in that year was predicted to be
15,400, so the forecast shortage would have been 7,000. In short,
even a 10 per cent over-estimate of the total number of engineers
required is sufficient to increase the predicted shortage of graduates

---

[6] This is calculated by comparing the actual number of 107,000 engineers in
1965 with the number that would have been predicted if the Federation had
correctly forecast the exogenous variables, i.e. 118,000 engineers (See footnote
on p. 207).

[7] It must be borne in mind that the term 'engineer' in Swedish covers all
engineering qualifications from lower technician to postgraduate. The Federation did not attempt to forecast the shortage of *all* engineers, as it found no
reliable statistics on the supply of the lowest engineering qualification, the
'institute' engineers. We shall examine the distribution of engineering needs by
educational qualification in a subsequent section; for present purposes, it is
proposed to concentrate on graduate engineers.

by a factor of almost three. Since intake capacity of new engineering enrolments in 1956 was only 900, it is of some importance to determine whether a future shortage is expected to be 2,600 or 7,000.

Thus, the crucial question is how far the errors in the various sectors affect the usefulness of the forecast. In terms of its own explicit objective, the forecast must be judged a complete failure. To give the forecast the best possible run for its money, let us suppose that the Federation made a perfect forecast of the actual number of engineers in the public sector and 'rest of the economy' in 1965; suppose further that it made a perfect forecast of the number of workers in industry in 1965, and that its only error was to under-estimate the value of industrial production by 7 per cent, i.e. one-third of its actual error. A 7 per cent under-estimate gives a production value per person of Kr. 20,000; substituting this into the linear model gives an engineering density of 5.8 per cent, or 62,000 engineers in industry. Adding this number to our perfect forecast of the other sectors gives a total engineering need of 116,000. Assuming, as before, that 19 per cent of these should be graduate engineers, we find a forecast requirement of 22,000 graduate engineers in 1965. Since supply in that year was predicted to be 15,400, the result would be a forecast shortage of 6,600 graduate engineers. This is two-and-a-half times the shortage predicted by the Federation. Of what possible use to the educational planner is a forecast where the predicted shortage of engineers is extremely sensitive to changes in output and productivity which are well within the margin of error of predicting these variables?

Nor is the sensitivity of the forecast merely a function of the difficulties of predicting output and productivity. A close examination of the linear model itself suggests some of the reasons for the severe over-estimate of the actual number of engineers in industry and the public sector. As we have said, the model used by the Federation was based on a linear relationship between productivity and engineering density derived from five observations. Four of these were based on historical data of productivity and engineering density up to 1955, while the fifth was derived from the survey answers for 1965. Presumably, the questionnaire answers were included in the model because the fact that the answers lay close to the same linear trend shown by the historical data alone served to increase confidence in using them together. But having asked employers how many engineers they expected to employ in 10 years' time, the Federation should either have accepted the employers' estimate as being the

211

'best guess' available, or, if it did not have sufficient faith in their answers to rely on them exclusively, it should have shown how their use improves the reliability of other data, rather than lessens it. If the proof of the pudding is in the eating, then discarding the employers' survey altogether would have slightly improved the success of the forecast. Applying the Federation's main alternative productivity value of Kr. 17,500 to the historical data alone gives a forecast density of 5.1 per cent in 1965 (49,000 engineers) compared to 4.7 per cent (or 45,000 engineers) if the survey answers are included in the data. The difference might seem small: after all, both equations severely under-estimate the actual number of engineers. But a difference in the total number of engineers of 4,000 is sufficient to increase the forecast shortage of graduate engineers by 28 per cent. The apparent linearity of productivity—density obscures a marked sensitivity to whether the survey answers are included or not. In fact, the point here is a more general one than the correctness of including the survey answers: the important question is whether it is sensible to base an educational plan on four or five observations when quite minor deviations in those observations can so greatly alter the educational planning implications.

A second feature of the linear model is the inclusion in the 1955 engineering density of an estimated shortage of engineers in that year. According to the questionnaire answers there was a shortage of 1,685 engineers then. This figure was added to the actual employment of 25,650 and the engineering density was calculated from the total of 27,334 engineers. The reason for this is clear: if one projected forward an overall shortage, one would merely be projecting present disequilibrium into the future. But in its (justifiable) anxiety to ensure that the existing stock of engineers was optimal relative to the level of economic activity, the Federation may have fallen into the same trap as some other manpower forecasters. As Rado points out in his postmortem on East African manpower surveys, 'some vacancies are relevant to a *future* as yet unattained output: were they to be filled output would be higher . . . such "vacancies" are automatically counted in a projection of manpower needs as a function of output, and treating them as *present* vacancies therefore involves double counting . . . the only vacancy that should be counted is one which *until recently* was filled . . .' (Rado, 1967, p. 11). The Swedish data do not permit a separation of vacancies in this way, so it is not possible to quantify the impact on the forecast; but since any reduction of the 3.2 per cent engineering density to its 'true' level will have the effect of raising the slope of the regression line, the result would be a higher prediction for future years. More specifically, there may very well have been an even greater over-estimate of the actual number of engineers in the industrial sector than the 20 per cent recorded earlier.

Finally, we turn to an analysis of the problem which we have so far taken for granted, the classification and definition of engineers. As we have seen, the Federation asked employers to state the number of engineers they had employed in 1950 and 1955, and to forecast the number they expected to employ in 1965. All levels of engineer — graduate, higher technician and lower technician — were rigidly defined by educational qualification. The assumption that companies kept such good personnel records that the number of lower technicians they employed five years previously could be classified by their educational specialization is a doubtful one. But there is a more fundamental problem than this. Döös pointed out in one of the earliest OECD seminars that 'the "second step" in manpower forecasting — the occupational breakdown — has not so far played any part in practical manpower forecasting work in Sweden' (Döös, 1962, p. 32). He went on to admit the desirability of using an occupational breakdown, since this came closer to the realities of industry. It would certainly have been desirable in this case. By its stress on an educational classification for engineers, the Swedish Federation has made precisely the same error as the Jackson Committee in Britain (see Chapter 9).

Employers evidently found the question as hard to answer as one would expect, for their estimates of engineers required by educational level and discipline were considered so unreliable that they were discarded. Instead, the distribution of graduate engineers and higher and lower technicians existing in 1955 — 19, 34 and 47 per cent respectively — was assumed to remain constant throughout the period 1955—75. The implicit assumption must be that the scale and composition of output requires this particular combination of levels of engineering skills in the productive process. It is not clear why the 1955 distribution should be so regarded. The past trend of engineering employment had been as shown in Table 8.4.

It would be hard to deny that some of these changes in the relative distribution (and hence the 1955 distribution) were as much the outcome of the supply of these categories in the past as of the demand for engineers with various levels of qualification. The question of whether these engineering levels stand in strict complementarity to each other, in a manner determined by technological requirements, is one to which we shall return in a subsequent section.

TABLE 8.4

PERCENTAGE DISTRIBUTION OF ENGINEERING LEVELS, SWEDEN, 1940—55

	1940	*1950*	*1955*
'Civil' engineers	31	20	19
'Läroverk' engineers	45	33	34
'Institute' engineers	24	47	47
All engineers	100	100	100

Source: Calculated from Tables 8, 9 and 10, Swedish Federation of Industry (1957), pp. 38 and 39.

As a curtain-raiser to that section, we simply note that a comprehensive survey in 1966 conceded that 'it has been hard to find examples of positions in the companies for which one and only one type of technical education is suitable' (Technical Group, 1970, Section 5.3.3).

The Labour Market Board's forecast of engineers, 1962

We have already commented that the chief criticism of the Federation's forecast when it appeared was that it was felt to underestimate the future need for engineers. It was against this background of dissatisfaction with the Federation's estimates that the 1962 forecast was made. This was carried out by the Labour Market Board and was a frank attempt to try a different method so as to derive higher estimates than the Federation's. Just as the Federation had attempted to derive numbers of (primarily) graduate engineers for the 1955 Educational Commission, so the Labour Market Board in 1962 was seeking to provide estimates for the Gymnasium Committee. This Committee had been set up in 1960 to examine ways of reorganising the gymnasium, or upper secondary school. The gymnasium was at that time divided into three quite separate streams, the general academic, the technical and the commercial[8], and 'the pur-

---

[8] In 1964, following the Committee's recommendations, the three separate gymnasiums were replaced by a single, integrated gymnasium offering five alternative lines of study, liberal arts, social science, economics, natural science and technology. A full description of these changes can be found in Orring (1967).

pose of the Gymnasium Committee has been as far as possible to shed light on the future recruiting need for technically-trained personnel in relation to the size of the technical gymnasium and the size of the science stream of the general gymnasium seen from a labour market point of view' (Labour Market Board, 1962, p. 9).

But if both forecasts share similar objectives, their methods could not be more different. The Federation's estimate was easily identified as a 'policy-conditional forecast' of engineers required to attain an explicit economic growth target: the Labour Market Board's work is more accurately described as an 'onlooker forecast', since it is largely a prediction of what will happen as a result of past trends of labour force and engineering density. In fact, it is not clear whether it amounts to a prediction of what will happen or what should happen, since the extrapolations were frequently modified by assumptions about both the probable and the desirable future. Nevertheless, it is, in essence, different from the Federation's forecast and we shall refer to it as an 'onlooker forecast'.

The economy was divided into four sectors: (i) manufacturing industry; (ii) building and construction; (iii) public services; and (iv) rest of the economy. The terminal year of the forecast was 1980, but as estimates were given in five-yearly intervals, we can check the outcome of the first five years up to 1965.

Manufacturing industry and building construction [9]

Manufacturing industry

The basic premise of the method used for this sector was that a highly disaggregated projection of total employment would lead to more meaningful predictions of engineering density than the aggregate figures of the labour force used by the Federation. The steps in the calculation were as follows. From a projection of the total labour force, the number of employees in manufacturing industry was estimated; the proportion of the manufacturing labour force in white-collar jobs was derived and these were divided into those with

---

[9] In Swedish Census statistics 'manufacturing industry' includes manufacturing, mining, small craft and building, and this was the convention followed in the Federation's forecast. Because of the different industrial statistics used by the Labour Market Board, building and construction was estimated separately. When checking the actual outcome in 1965 we shall have to use the (mainly) Census figures of employed engineers that we used when assessing the Federation's forecast. As these figures do not show building separately, we combine the projections of manufacturing and building for this stage. See also Appendix A8.

215

technical occupations and those with other jobs; the proportion of engineers among this technical group was calculated and finally an allowance was made for the upgrading of engineers. The calculation is summarised in the following identity:

Total labour   ×   Proportion employed   ×   Proportion of white-collar
force   in manufacturing   workers employed in manufacturing

   Proportion of technical   Proportion of engineers   Proportion of qualified
× personnel among white- × among technical person- × engineers among total
   collar workers   nel   engineers

= The number of up-graded engineers among technical personnel in the white-collar group of the labour force in manufacturing employment.

Table 8.5 shows the actual data on which the forecast was based. Even a casual glance at Table 8.5 makes it clear that it is essentially an exercise in trend extrapolation, which proceeds conventionally from a projection of industrial employment to an occupational breakdown (via the intermediate variable of white-collar workers) and finally to an educational classification. However, the outcome of the first five years suggests that this method has been no more successful than the Federation's. Before documenting that assertion, we briefly describe the estimates for the building industry.

Building and construction

Two methods were used for estimating the future number of engineers in this industry. The first was based on a simple labour—output ratio. Investments in building and construction — which comprise this sector's total gross production — were Kr. 12,500 million in 1960, and 10,000 engineers were employed, giving a ratio of 1 : 1.25 million kronor. Based on an average annual increase in the value of output of 4.5 per cent during the 1950's, an increase of 5 per cent was assumed for the 1960's. This gives a total value of Kr. 20,000 million for 1970, with 16,000 engineers required to produce it at a constant labour—output ratio. This method belongs more to the Federation in spirit but the second method followed very closely the Labour Market Board's calculations for the other sectors. The starting point was the actual 1960 engineering density of 3.6 per cent out of 286,000 employees. It was then assumed that the density would increase by 1970 to the same percentage as for the rest of manufacturing (6.2 per cent). This gives a total engineering requirement of 19,200 on a projected number of employees of 310,000. Since it was considered that 'it is reasonable to believe that the engineering density per invested million kronor ought to go up with

216

TABLE 8.3

ENGINEERING NEEDS IN MANUFACTURING INDUSTRY, SWEDEN, 1930–80 (thousands)

	Actual					Forecast			
	1930	1940	1950	1955	1960	1965	1970	1975	1980
(i) Total labour force	2,756.0	2,968.0	3,105.0	3,152.0	3,266.0	3,431.0	3,502.0	3,523.0	3,561.0
of which									
(ii) Employees in manufacturing industry	(28.3) 781.0	(29.6) 878.0	(32.9) 1,023.0	(33.5) 1,055.0	(33.8) 1,104.0	(33.9) 1,164.0	(33.9) 1,186.0	(33.5) 1,181.0	(32.4) 1,155.0
of which									
(iii) White-collar workers	(6) 51.5	(9) 83.3	(14) 148.8	(16) 173.3	(18) 198.1	(21) 245.0	(23) 277.5	(25) 301.2	(27) 317.2
of which									
(iv) Technical personnel		(22) 18.3	(25) 37.3	(26) 46.2	(30) 60.1	(31) 76.2	(33) 92.4	(35) 106.9	(37) 119.9
of which									
(v) Engineers				(64) 29.7	(61) 36.7	(65) 49.5	(70) 64.7	(70) 74.8	(70) 83.9
of which									
(vi) With engineering education				(73) 21.8	(76) 28.0	(80) 39.6	(85) 55.0	(90) 67.3	(95) 79.7
(vii) Plus 'Other engineers'				9.4	13.5	16.7	18.9	22.1	25.5
Row (vi) + (vii) = total need for									
(viii) Engineers in manufacturing industry				31.2	41.5	56.3	73.9	89.4	105.2

Source: Labour Market Board (1962), Tables 7, 8, 12 and 16.

Notes: (1) Some of percentages shown here (for White-collar workers and technical personnel) differ from those in the published tables. This is simply because much of the data presented in the forecast is a reconciliation of figures from the 1950 and 1960 Censuses, 'Sv. arbetsgivareföreningen' (SAF) salary statistics, and 'kommerskollegium' industrial statistics, and purely for ease of presentation we have omitted some of the intermediate steps in the calculation.
(2) Similarly the penultimate row, 'Other engineers' is a compression of Tables 13, 14 and 15. The method of calculating 'Other engineers' is exactly the same as for the majority of engineers and to avoid repetition we have simply given the final totals 'Other engineers' are differentiated from 'engineers' in the published forecast and in this table simply because of the different occupational coverage of the various sources.
(3) The figures in brackets are percentages.

TABLE 8.6

PREDICTION AND OUTCOME IN INDUSTRY AND BUILDING, SWEDEN,
1960 AND 1965 (thousands)

	Manufacturing industry		Building and construction		Total industry	
	Employees	Engineers	Employees	Engineers	Employees	Engine
1960 Actual	1,104	41.5	286	10.0	1,390	51.5
1965 Projection	1,164	56.3	303	14.5	1,467	70.8
1965 Actual	1,155	..	335	..	1,490	53.0
Percentage projection error $\frac{P-A}{A} \times 100$	−0.8	.	−9.5	.	−1.5	+33.5

Source: Labour Market Board (1962), Table 17; Technical Group (1970),
Section 2.6.2.2; Ministry of Finance (1966), Table 5.6; see also Appendix A.
· = not applicable; ·· = not available.

respect to expected rationalisation measures in building' (Labour
Market Board, 1962, p. 26), the latter figure of 19,000 was adopted
for 1970. The Board then interpolated the 1960 and 1970 figures to
give a projection of 14,500 engineers in 1965.

We show, in Table 8.6, the results of the projections for manufacturing and building and construction.

Public sector and rest of the economy

To conclude this summary of the method and outcome of the
Board's forecast, we present below a summary table showing the
prediction and outcome in the public sector and the rest of the
economy. The estimates for both sectors were simple: the number of
employees was extrapolated and an assumption was made that the
engineering density would change at a rate roughly parallel to the
change calculated for manufacturing industry.

Summarizing the data from Tables 8.6 and 8.7, we find that
compensating errors between sectors make the overall error very
much smaller than individual errors: the total labour force was
over-estimated by only 1.1 per cent and the number of engineers was

TABLE 8.7

PREDICTION AND OUTCOME IN THE PUBLIC SECTOR AND REST OF THE ECONOMY, SWEDEN, 1960 AND 1965

Public sector			Rest of the economy			Both sectors		
Emplo-yees	Engi-neer densi-ty	Engi-neers	Emplo-yees	Engi-neer densi-ty	Engi-neers	Emplo-yees	Engi-neer densi-ty	Engi-neers
1960 Actual								
429	2.3	10.0	1,477	1.9	28.0	1,876	2.0	38.0
1965 Forecast								
482	3.0	14.6	1,482	2.2	32.6	1,964	2.4	47.2
1965 Actual								
515	..	..	1,390	..	..	1,905	2.8	54.0
Percentage projection error								
−6.4	..	..	+6.6	..	..	+3.0	−14.5	−13.0

Source:

Labour Market Board (1962), Tables 27 and 29; Technical Group (1970), Section 2.6.2.2.

Note:

See Appendix A8.   ·· = not available.

over-estimated by 10.2 per cent. As before, it is pertinent to ask whether we can always rely upon sectoral errors to be self-cancelling. In any event, we showed earlier that an over-estimate in the number of engineers of 10 per cent was sufficient to destroy the usefulness of the Federation's forecast for planning, and the Labour Market Board achieved this same error after only five years, compared to the Federation's ten-year forecast. Furthermore, it is important to remember that this assessment is made at only the quarter stage of the forecast. The latest forecast of employees in manufacturing and building suggests that 1,565,000 will be employed in 1970, compared to a prediction by the Board of 1,497,000 (Ministry of Finance, 1966, p. 73). If the latest prediction is realized, the Board will have again under-estimated the actual number but this time by a larger margin — 68,000, compared to the 23,000 under-estimate in 1965. Since the Board seriously over-estimated the number of engineers in 1965 on a very small population error, the result in 1970 is likely to be a massive over-estimate of the actual number of engineers.

But if the labour force estimates were not too badly wrong in 1965, what then accounts for the error in projecting the number of engineers in that year? It is not possible to quantify the sources of error, since there are insufficient data to carry out a postmortem on all the variables in Table 8.5. Nevertheless, there are many *a priori* reasons why we should not be surprised that the forecast was inaccurate. Let us concentrate on the sector with the largest error, manufacturing.

A crucial source of error must have arisen through the use of the 'intermediate variable' white-collar worker density. The projected increase in this density sprang from the same concern that motivated many American forecasts at this time: the anticipated consequences of automation. The implicit belief was that there was a simple relationship between productivity increases and employment changes. It was alleged that 'the maintenance and upkeep of more complicated machinery must be done by better and better educated personnel, so to a greater extent than previously workers will have to have a theoretical-technical education, a process that sometimes transfers them into the white-collar category' (Labour Market Board, 1962, p. 14). Even if this is true, it is not clear that 'white-collar workers', as measured by SAF industrial statistics[10], is an appropriate index of this. The term 'white-collar worker' is a convenient shorthand for delineating those workers who frequently have different salary, holiday and hiring and firing arrangements from those on the factory floor, the blue-collar workers. While this is a useful distinction in many respects, it is of no help in manpower forecasting unless the shifts in measured white-collar worker density are in fact related systematically to the shifting structure of tasks in an industry. The Labour Market Board itself realized that 'it would have been of great

[10] SAF = Sveriges Arbetsgivareföreningen (Swedish Employers' Organisation).

value to be able to shed light on the development of certain tasks, irrespective of whether they were done by white-collar workers or not' but admitted that with these particular statistics this could not be done (Labour Market Board, 1962, p. 10). Moreover, even if the statistics did measure shifts in job function, it is doubtful if they would show the simple productivity—employment relationship assumed by the Board. American evidence suggests that during the 1950's and 1960's, changes in occupational composition resulted from changes in the industrial mix rather than as a consequence of one skill level replacing another one.[11] There is no reason to expect Swedish experience to parallel exactly that of America, but these findings are at any rate sufficient to cast doubt on the simple process that was assumed in this projection.

An examination of the subsequent stages of the calculation sheds even greater doubt on the methodology. The next step after calculating the white-collar worker density was to estimate the proportion with technical tasks. In its introductory comments, the Board showed itself well aware that even the minimum requirement of defining precisely which tasks are technical is no easy matter. Faced with the fact that 'there is no statistical source showing to what extent technical education is an actual demand for a position' (Labour Market Board, 1962, p. 10), the Board simply extrapolated the technical personnel density up to 1980 (see row iv, Table 8.5). Such an extrapolation may well be a sensible procedure, but it is impossible to judge this, since the Board nowhere states precisely which occupational categories constitute the technical group. We know from a footnote that it includes, among other things, laboratory assistants, technicians of various kinds, maintenance personnel and senior managers. Any classification which ranges from laboratory assistant to senior manager is clearly very heterogeneous and must be treated with caution: these doubts are magnified once it is realized that the apparently occupational category of 'senior manager' is defined entirely in terms of the educational profile of people most commonly observed in that occupation (Labour Market Board, 1962, p. 15).

---

[11] One study of the impact of technology on jobs concluded not only that 'the rate of change in output per worker contributes little toward explaining changes in occupational composition', but that 'even in these industries . . . undergoing the most rapid technological changes, one-half to three-quarters of the manual workers had less than a high school education (suggesting) that modern advancing technology does not necessarily require workers to have more formal schooling' (Jaffe and Froomkin, 1968, pp. 78, 89).

A further source of error must have been in the derivation of engineers from the technical personnel group. From row (v) of Table 8.5 it can be seen that the proportion of engineers in the technical group fell from 64 per cent in 1955 to 61 per cent in 1960. The Board commented that 'the decrease is probably connected with the shortage of supply of engineering-educated personnel, which has forced the employers to hire people without engineering education for more and more purely technical tasks' (Labour Market Board, 1962, p. 21). If this process really had taken place, it completely invalidates the attempt to derive the demand for educated engineers. If engineering vacancies have been satisfactorily filled by graduates from other disciplines, in what sense can there be said to have been a shortage of engineers? To concede that the occupational category of engineer can be adequately filled by a variety of educational disciplines is to undermine completely the theoretical rationale of the projection.

Notwithstanding this, the Board projected the 1965 figure to the higher 1955 level, since 'it cannot be denied that a great shortage of engineers prevailed in 1960 . . . and in 1955 industry also had a shortage of engineers' (Labour Market Board, 1962, p. 21). A definition of shortage, plus some evidence in the form of vacancy rates, starting and median salaries, etc., would have helped us to judge the validity of this assertion. Was the evidence of shortage in 1955 derived from the Federation's survey of employers' opinion? If so, it is quite probable that the Board has built an over-estimate into its projection in precisely the same way as the Federation.

The last stage of the calculation (row vi of Table 8.5) was to derive the number of qualified engineers in the occupational category of engineering. In view of the tendency of the Board to think of the occupation and education of engineer as being one and the same thing, it is not surprising that the Board should try to allow for an increased frequency of qualified engineers. Thus in 1960, 76.2 per cent of engineering personnel had engineering education, and this was projected to rise to 95 per cent in 1980 as a result of the increasing diffusion of better educated people among the working population. The Board explained the 1960 figure of 76.2 per cent as being partly the result of under-reporting in SAF statistics and partly because 'it is probably correct that a number of persons have engineering positions without having an engineering degree' (Labour Market Board, 1962, p. 20). If this *is* true, it suggests a degree of substitutability between educational disciplines sufficiently great to render pointless the attempt to derive the demand for one particular skill.

222

Moreover, the Board failed to explain the really interesting fact that the percentage of qualified engineers among the total remained remarkably constant around the 77—78 mark during the only five years for which we have data, 1955—60. During this time the total number of employed engineers rose from 59,000 to 71,000 (OECD, 1962, Table 1) and since this was also a period of rapid educational change, new entrants can be assumed to have been considerably better educated than those already in the profession. Yet the proportion of qualified engineers remained virtually constant. One plausible interpretation of this paradox is that there must have been substantial movement of better-educated engineers during this time, as they made their way into line management and supervisory functions. That the Board did not light upon this interpretation of the admittedly fragile evidence is surprising, as we have already noted that it devoted considerable attention to the large number of qualified engineers observed in the occupational category of 'senior manager'.

Yet its failure to consider this interpretation is precisely because it nowhere sufficiently distinguishes occupation from education. The rationale of the projection is the alleged technical complementarity between engineering education and engineering jobs, and the Board did not realize that the process we have described above represents the very essence of labour market adjustments. The Board has in fact made exactly the same error that we saw in Chapter 3. As Hansen pointed out in connection with the leading American forecast of engineers, 'in view of our tendency to think of engineers as having the education and training provided by the completion of four years of college work, it is not surprising that the role of non-degree people has been slighted in the projections. We tend to be impressed by the tremendous rate of growth of the engineering profession, but this growth has been made possible only by a large and continuous flow of non-degree entrants . . .. Moreover, when demand is expected to be higher than supply . . . then employers are going to be ever more willing to hire non-degree engineers and other non-engineer people as well' (Hansen, 1967, p. 206). The Labour Market Board paid for its failure to recognize this fact with a 33 per cent over-estimate in the industrial sector alone.

The Technical Group's forecast of engineers (1965)

We have been highly critical of the forecasts so far considered: their record of error speaks for itself, and an analysis of the methodology has suggested some reasons for those errors. No Swedish reader will be surprised by these findings, for the forecasts we have been assessing belong to what might be termed the 'naive era' of Swedish manpower forecasting when a pressing need for results was felt despite the crudity of methods used. Many of the criticisms we have made of the two engineers' forecasts have in fact been specific applications of the general comments made by the Ministry of Education and Working Group of the Labour Market Board. As we showed in the introduction, their analysis of the early Swedish forecasts centred around the problems of substitutability, occupational—educational relationships and the measurement of shortage and surplus, an analysis which was sufficient to discredit totally the overall manpower requirements approach to planning that had been tried in the late 1950's and early 1960's.

It is not surprising, therefore, that in the first major manpower forecasting exercise after the Working Group's report — a survey of the requirements and supply of engineers up to 1980 — a major part of the work should be case studies of substitutability and educational usage. This forecast was carried out by a Technical Group of the Central Bureau of Statistics between 1965 and 1970 and 'it was intended that this survey should provide a basis for a review of the specialisation of technical education according to the various levels and also provide a basis on which the resources allocated to technical education can be weighed against those allocated to other types of education' (Central Bureau, 1970B, p. 13).[12] This brief reflects the shift in the objectives of forecasting after the criticisms of the early 1960's and the movement away from overall manpower planning towards the forecasting of requirements for planning the size of individual faculties. But it is the attempt to tackle the problems of substitution and the actual utilization of educational knowledge that differentiates this latest work from the rather crude forecasts discussed earlier. We show below that the results of the studies were disappointing but in concept at least they were pioneering efforts. Since the two studies were intended to be the cornerstone of the forecast, we turn first to these before describing how the forecast itself was constructed.

---

[12] A summary of the forecast was published by the Central Bureau of Statistics in its 'Forecasting Information' series, and this is the reference cited here. The complete forecast, together with all the working papers, is available only in stencilled form under the title, 'The Labour Market for Technical Personnel: Report from the 1965 Technical Group'. For ease of reference, we have distinguished the two titles.

The substitution study

The basis of the substitution study was an interview and question-naire survey carried out in 41 Swedish companies in 1966. The survey was a pilot study of what was hoped to be a very wide-ranging inquiry into Swedish companies. The intention was to develop a questionnaire technique that would not only be useful for straight-forward manpower data collection but would also shed light on the substitutability of various types and levels of engineer. Thus, one third of the pilot questionnaire was devoted to questions about the existing number of employees, the distribution of engineers by educational level, and so on; a further third asked the companies to forecast (for five years ahead) the number of engineers, the distribution of white-collar workers among technical and other tasks, and similar questions; and the final section of the questionnaire aimed at eliciting information about substitutability and shortages of various types of engineer. The questions for this final section were relatively straightforward. Question 16, for example, asked whether the company had noticed a shortage, balance or surplus of engineers in recent years. Question 20 inquired into the circumstances in which a new recruit with a lower engineering qualification than was 'ideally desired' would be acceptable. And Question 22 asked companies to give an example of a position in the company for which one and only one type of technical education was suitable.[13]

The results were mixed. On the one hand, the Group concluded that 'it became apparent . . . that the firms generally did not have a planning basis in the form of quantitative data which could be used for estimating their need for technically qualified manpower even as little as five years ahead' (Central Bureau, 1970B, p. 17). Indeed, so disappointing were the results that the plans to follow up the pilot study were abandoned. On the other hand, such empirical informa-tion as did emerge has radical implications for manpower forecasting. The Group admitted that 'practically nothing was found to bear out the view that a certain speciality is so generally useful that the members qualifying in it should be increased or that the reverse was true of any other speciality, with the consequent necessity of avoiding an increase in its capacity' (Central Bureau, 1970B, p. 17). Such an admission suggests that the elasticity of substitution be-

---

[13] These examples are sufficient to give to flavour of the questionnaire. The full schedule of questions is given in the unpublished version of the forecast (Tech-nical Group, 1970, Section 5.3).

tween various types of engineer is considerably greater than zero, a finding which is supported by the evidence from Question 22 that 'it has been hard to find examples of positions in the companies for which one and only one type of technical education is suitable' (Technical Group, 1970, Section 5.3, p. 23).

These admissions, if based on reliable evidence, would make meaningless all attempts to derive the number of engineers required to fill a given occupational function. But the Technical Group's decision not to place too much reliance on the findings of the survey was probably the correct one. British and American experience, not to mention Sweden's own record with the Federation's forecast in 1955, should have warned the Technical Group that the chances of extracting reliable objective information from a survey of employers' opinions were not good. In the event, the Group discovered for itself that it is 'improbable that you get a true picture of the actual relationships by letting different people judge for themselves their own substitutability' (Technical Group, 1970, Section 5.3.3, p. 5).

But instead of dwelling in the general area of attitude surveys, let us turn to the much more fundamental criticism that the entire attempt to measure substitution in this way seems to have been based on a misconception. The aim of the survey was to examine 'in what fields engineers can replace, or be replaced by, other categories' (Central Bureau, 1970B, p. 16). In other words, the aim was to examine the extent to which various types of educated manpower can fill the same job. The way the survey was conducted seems to betray an implicit assumption that occupational requirements are determined by technical considerations and that educational requirements come later in the chain of causation because men have to be fitted to a predetermined occupational structure. Discover the feasible range of this fit, the survey is saying, and you will discover a coefficient that will translate occupation into education far more meaningfully than the crude methods used to date. This is a plausible hypothesis, but as we pointed out in Chapter 3, it is almost as plausible to assume that employers hire workers to fulfil a given set of tasks and then develop a job structure to suit the labour they have hired, rather than the other way round. It is even possible that occupation and education are simultaneously determined in the recruitment process. This latter alternative would explain why the Group was disappointed in its search for generally applicable principles of engineer substitutability, and why 'the people interviewed emphasised that no general rules could be given as regards the vocational specialities that were interchangeable with certain other

226

specialities' (Central Bureau, 1970B, p. 17). As a recent Canadian attempt at measuring engineer substitutability pointed out, functional substitution and educational substitution are often related because 'the substitution between people with different educational qualifications requires simultaneous adjustment of technology or job design. Moreover, educational substitution may require training on the job. If this training is considerable then the process is less one of substituting one category of labour for another than of transferring a *person* of one category to a different category' (Skolnik, 1969, p. 3).

The Technical Group's attempt to estimate the substitution of engineers was a radical innovation in practical manpower forecasting. That the attempt failed was because fundamentally it took for granted the traditional forecasting concept of the fit between occupation and education. What is needed is an even more radical attempt to rethink this relationship.

The survey of educational utilization

The substitution study had been intended to show the usefulness of engineers in different types of activity compared with other types of labour: enough was said above to indicate that it yielded some interesting impressionistic judgements but no solid evidence. The survey of the usage of engineering education was intended to approach the question of the precise relationship between education and occupation in quite a different way. The objective was to study the 'gearing' between the amount and type of technical education an engineer received and the amount and type of technical knowledge his job required. Such a study is the key to more successful forecasting. Many manpower forecasts have foundered at the point of translating occupation into educational requirements, and Swedish forecasters, as we have seen, have fared no better than others. As with the previous survey, an acknowledgement of a pathbreaking attempt is called for. To be sure, Eckaus in 1964 had utilized the *Estimates of Worker Trait Requirements for 4,000 Jobs*[14] to try to compare 'required' with 'actual' amounts of education in the U.S. labour force, but he failed in the attempt to translate periods of learning into school grade equivalents (Eckaus, 1964; Ross, 1966). In Sweden there had been an even earlier attempt to measure the

---

[14] This publication by the U.S. Department of Labor summarizes for 4,000 jobs the judgements of experienced labour placement specialists as to the attributes required for an average level of success in the job.

utilization of electrical engineers (OECD, 1967, pp. 201—10) but the Technical Group's project is, so far as we are aware, the only attempt to carry out a survey of educational utilization as an integrated part of a manpower forecast.

The method was straightforward. The discipline chosen was mechanical engineering, and the object was to test the utilization of the technical components of an education in this field. The necessary degree of disaggregation of the components had been determined after a pilot study. This was carried out at what might be termed the third level of disaggregation: out of the main field of mechanical engineering one component subject was selected ('machine-elements') and from this subject the course in 'cog-gears' was chosen. The same level of disaggregation was chosen for the main study and the subjects comprising the technical education in mechanical engineering are listed in Table 8.8. (The various courses which make up each subject are not stated in the forecast.) Which subjects were to be included, their relative weight and differences between educational institutions were settled after discussions with teachers, practising engineers and textbook authors. The courses and subjects were classified by a simple points system. Thus, from Table 8.8 it can be seen that physics accounts for 9 points, mechanical heating 11 points, and so on. The total number of points in the applied technical education of a mechanical engineer is 83.

Let us turn now to the measurement of the utilization of this education. The method of testing was by interviews: a sample of 60 employed engineers was asked how many of the points compiled above they needed to do their jobs. The greater the correspondence between the points an engineer had learned in any subject and the points he needed to know to carry out his job efficiently, the greater the degree of utilization of his education. The results of the survey are shown in Tables 8.8 and 8.9. Table 8.8 classifies the results by functional field, Table 8.9 by level of responsibility. Thus, we see from Table 8.8 that graduate engineers working in research needed 18 per cent of the knowledge they had acquired in physics in order to do their job properly. Similarly, Table 8.9 indicates that engineers working at senior management level (2) used only 3 per cent of their total knowledge of physics, and so on.

The paramount feature of the tables is the very low level of utilization of technical education. A caveat should immediately be entered that in some categories the number of engineers was so small that the answers are not significant, but the broad conclusion of both tables is the extent to which educational knowledge acquired by

228

TABLE 8.8

THE UTILIZATION BY ENGINEERS OF THE TECHNICAL SUBJECTS IN MECHANICAL EDUCATION, CLASSIFIED BY FUNCTIONAL FIELD, AND EXPRESSED AS A PERCENTAGE OF THE OPTIMAL UTILIZATION OF THE RESPECTIVE SUBJECTS, SWEDEN, 1966

Subject	Total points of educational attainment	Research				Construction				Other technical tasks				Technical sales				Total			
		T	C	G	I	T	C	G	I	T	C	G	I	T	C	G	I	T	C	G	I
Maths	22	40	61	24	23	27	29	26	26	22	29	27	8	18	25	11	9	27	35	23	20
Physics	9	13	18	8	11	6	6	6	7	14	4	22	4	21	20	22	22	11	12	13	8
Mechanics	10	45	68	28	20	36	45	33	31	7	7	8	3	8	12	5	–	27	37	22	21
Strength of materials	9	39	60	28	11	44	51	40	40	7	–	15	–	13	20	–	33	31	39	26	27
Mechanical heating	11	52	49	55	–	30	39	25	30	31	30	45	3	42	55	23	55	36	49	34	21
Machine elements	7	26	29	21	29	46	54	51	41	15	10	19	14	10	14	4	14	30	29	31	32
Industrial economics	9	8	9	8	6	5	11	4	–	25	41	24	11	27	31	14	44	13	20	12	6
Industrial organization	6	12	13	13	17	22	42	18	6	32	50	42	11	33	43	21	33	24	34	23	10
Total	83	33	47	24	14	27	32	25	23	19	20	25	6	21	27	13	25	25	33	23	19
Number of engineers	.	11	5	4	2	27	8	11	8	12	3	6	3	10	5	4	1	60	21	25	14

Key: T = Total; C = Civilingenjör; G = Gymnasieingenjör; I = Institutingenjör.
Source: Technical Group (1970), Section 5.4, Appendix 2.
. = not applicable; — = nil or negligible

TABLE 8.9

THE UTILIZATION BY ENGINEERS OF THE TECHNICAL SUBJECTS IN
MECHANICAL ENGINEERING EDUCATION, CLASSIFIED BY LEVEL OF
RESPONSIBILITY, AND EXPRESSED AS A PERCENTAGE OF THE OPTIMAL
UTILIZATION OF THE RESPECTIVE SUBJECTS, SWEDEN, 1966

Subject	Total points of educational attainment	Position Level					
		2	3	4	5	6	2—6
Maths	22	31	28	27	26	29	27
Physics	9	3	13	12	13	—	11
Mechanics	10	30	27	21	30	53	27
Strength of materials	9	28	42	26	27	52	31
Mechanical heating	11	25	52	36	33	24	36
Machine elements	7	29	40	29	24	57	30
Industrial economics	9	50	19	15	5	—	13
Industrial organization	6	58	48	26	9	—	24
Total	83	30	32	24	22	28	25
Number of engineers		4	10	19	24	3	60

Key: Position-levels defined according to SAF's code for the level of responsibility in a firm.
Level 2 = Executive managers in smaller firms and managers of large departments in big industrial firms.
Level 3 = Heads of smaller departments and heads of divisions in big industrial firms.
Level 4 = Heads of sections or corresponding in industrial firms.
Level 5 = Younger engineers in industrial firms.
Level 6 = Junior engineers.

Source: Technical Group (1970), Section 5.4, Appendix 2.
· = not applicable.
— = nil or negligible.

mechanical engineers is under-utilized in their jobs. As the survey
itself concluded, 'most of the educational components in the technical subjects were only to a very limited extent part of the demands
for knowledge of the jobs. Furthermore, the knowledge required to
carry out the jobs often included special technical components that
had not been included in the basic education of the employee'
(Technical Group, 1970, section 5.4.2).

If these findings are reliable the implications for manpower forecasting are dramatic. The essence of manpower forecasting is the
alleged link between education and occupation. Even the firmest

230

advocates of this approach to educational planning take care to point out that in the majority of occupations we observe a considerable spread of educational qualifications (see, for example, Parnes, 1962). Nevertheless, the fundamental rationale of the manpower approach is the notion that there is a definite connection between occupation and education. Nowhere is this better seen than in the two forecasts analysed earlier. The forecasts of both the Swedish Federation and the Labour Market Board implicitly assumed that the occupation and education of engineers were synonymous, and that the number of qualified engineers required to be produced by the educational system could be directly inferred from a specification of the number of engineering jobs in the economy. If there really is such a loose gearing between engineering education and engineering jobs as this survey suggests, the attempt to specify the occupational requirements from which the appropriate number of educated engineers can be derived would seem to be a futile activity.

But how reliable are these findings? One major drawback (which the report itself acknowledges) is that the survey did not measure the educational demands of various job positions: instead, it measured the educational demands put upon the existing incumbent of that position. After our comments about the substitution survey no more need be said here other than that this raises grave doubts about the reliability of the findings. In part, the answers may reflect not the educational demands put upon the job-holders, but the way the job-holder has managed to tailor the job to suit his particular knowledge. Particularly as job specification is intimately bound up with salary grades, a ranking of people rather than of jobs may be nothing more than the rationalization of the salaries and qualifications of the employees currently occupying different jobs. The rationale of this study is that the 'objective list of abilities' can be implicitly translated into 'equivalent educational standards' by the respondent: his inability to do so may well account for a significant part of the poor match between knowledge acquired and knowledge used.

If the findings of the substitution survey and the study of educational utilization could be taken at face value they would represent a formidable indictment of the manpower forecasting approach for deriving engineer requirements. But it is clear from the preceding pages that the two special studies, though admirable in concept, do not offer unambiguous empirical results, and we have taken care to emphasize their shortcomings and the tentative nature of the conclusions. It is at this point that we reach a curious feature in our story. We have shown so far that the predictive performance of the two

231

leading forecasts for engineers was so poor as to make them useless for their declared objective of providing a basis for educational planning. We have shown how a pathbreaking study published in 1963 strongly criticized the theoretical rationale of manpower forecasting, and how it urged empirical studies of substitution and educational utilization. We have shown, finally, how these studies, despite considerable misgivings about their methods, in many ways explain the failure of the earlier forecasts by showing that employers do not care about a perfect fit between occupation and education but about the trade-off between jobs and men. It follows that the simple, costless, technological requirements approach needs vast modification. This was the position that the Technical Group found itself in at the end of 1967. It had been given a wide-ranging brief by the Chancellor's Office[15] to 'start a survey of the future labour market for technically trained labour' so as to 'give guidance for a continued check of the distribution of resources to different disciplines and levels of technical education' (Technical Group, section 2.1). The cornerstone of this work was to be the two special studies which it was hoped would usher in a new era of 'sophisticated' forecasting. But the dilemma confronting the Group at the conclusion of the special studies in 1967 was a curious one. The evidence of the earlier forecasts and the findings of the special studies were sufficient almost to guarantee the failure of a forecast constructed in the old, 'naive' way: but the special surveys did not yield sufficiently operational principles of substitution and utilization to be able to build them meaningfully into any future forecast.

The way out chosen by the Group was effectively to ignore the findings of the special studies, but to try to reduce the margin of error of forecasting by using a variety of different methods of estimating engineering requirements in 1980. The feeling was that even if one of the crude methods was unreliable, a combination of methods (if they all pointed in the same direction) would increase faith in the projected estimates.

This assumption was not borne out by the projected estimates. Table 8.10 shows all the alternative methods for the various sectors. We shall analyse some of these methods, but for the present let us concentrate on the range of estimates. The Technical Group chose to assume that the maximum alternative in each sector was the most

---

[15] The Office of the Chancellor of the Universities (Universitetskanslersämbetet) is constituted and functions in a similar manner to the U.G.C. in Britain.

realistic, and this gives a total of estimated maximum requirements of 212,000 engineers in 1980. But the choice of these maximum requirements was based on nothing more than the judgement of the Group. Having calculated what were presumably thought to be plausible alternatives, it is misleading not to point out that an equally probable outcome in 1980 could be requirements of only 172,000, i.e. by choosing the minimum alternative in each sector.

Since the supply of economically active engineers in 1980 was estimated to be 224,000, the Group concluded that the result would

TABLE 8.10

REQUIREMENTS FOR ENGINEERS BY SECTOR, SWEDEN, 1980

Sector	Number of engineers
Manufacturing industry	
Alternative (i)	95,000
(ii)	75,000
(iii)	78,000
(iv)	82,000
Building and construction	21,000
Electricity, gas and water	3,000
Trade	22,000
Communications	8,000
Public sector	
Alternative (i)	16,000
(ii)	18,000
(iii)	21,000
(iv)	21,000
Business and professional services	
Alternative (i)	26,000
(ii)	31,000
(iii)	41,000
Other activities	1,000
Estimated maximum requirements	212,000

Source: Central Bureau (1970B), pp. 21—27; Technical Group (1970), section 6.1.1, Table 6.
Note: See text for description of alternatives.

be a rough balance between supply and demand. Using the minimum requirements figure, however, the result could be a surplus of over 50,000. In fact, even this range flatters the forecast. The Group candidly admitted that the supply estimates were very tentative. In part, this is because of the reorganization of the gymnasium, and 'there is so far no reference material showing how big a proportion of gymnasium freshmen reach the grade of 2.3 (the university qualifying grade) and therefore this has to be estimated out of the blue' (Technical Group, 1970, section 4.2.2). In part, it is because the Census statistics combine gymnasium and university educated engineers, and an arbitrary allowance has to be made for those gymnasium engineers who are thought subsequently to obtain a degree. And, finally, it is because an entirely new type of education for engineers, 'fackskolor', or specialized professional school for engineers was started during the 1960's, and there are no data on their impact on the labour market or transition into higher education.[16] Unfortunately, no alternative supply projections were given, so it is not possible to assess the sensitivity of the 224,000 estimate to different assumptions. Nor do we know if the supply figure given is a mean, minimum or maximum estimate. All we can say is that if the variance in the supply estimate is as great as that for requirements, the range of possible outcomes in 1980 is vast.

By way of illustration, let us assume that the supply estimate is a mean figure; let us further assume that it can be expected to vary to the same extent as the estimate of requirements, i.e. by 224,000 ± 20,000. We then derive the following results:

Maximum surplus = Max. supply − Min. requirements = 224,000 −172,000 = 72,000.
Maximum shortage = Max. requirements − Min. supply = 212,000 −204,000 = 8,000.

A possible range of 80,000 on a forecast of total requirements of the order of 200,000 is sufficient to destroy completely the notion that a combination of methods would lead to more precise and reliable estimates than one method alone.[17]

---

[16] The 'need' estimates calculated earlier exclude the possible impact of this new category of engineers. Allowance can be made for this either by adding to the need or reducing the supply. We have chosen the latter alternative. This does not alter the fact that the amount of the adjustment is imprecise.

[17] It must be emphasised that these figures are only illustrations. We do not know whether the Group's supply estimate is a mean figure, nor whether the variance is similar to that for requirements. The reader is invited to test alternative assumptions of his own: he will see that they make no difference to the general conclusion that the range of possible outcomes is huge.

No useful purpose would be served by analysing in detail the method of estimation of all the different sectors, but some interesting light can be shed upon the forecast if we look at some selected aspects of the estimates. In manufacturing industry, for example, the alternatives were:

(i) to forecast those occupations which in the past had employed, and in the future could be expected to employ, varying proportions of engineers, and to allow for an increased density of engineers in those occupations in 1980;

(ii) the same as (i), but to apply the observed 1967 frequency of engineers to those occupations;

(iii) to apply a weighted average of the observed engineering density in best-practice companies in 1967 to the forecast occupational distribution in 1980;

(iv) the same as (iii), but to apply an unweighted average density.

(There was also a fifth estimate, which was to apply the observed engineering density in manufacturing industry in the USA in 1960 to the employment forecast for Sweden in 1970. As estimates were not made for 1980, we have not considered this method).

On a closer look, it soon emerges that alternative (i) is simply a variant of the method tried by the Labour Market Board in 1962. Like the Board, the Technical Group projected the number of white-collar workers, derived the proportion with technical tasks and allowed for an increased frequency of engineers in these tasks. It will be recalled that the result of the Board's projection was a massive over-estimate of the actual number of engineers in 1965; it is not surprising, therefore, that this alternative gives by far the largest estimate of the four methods for manufacturing industry.

Alternative (ii) can be quickly dismissed: of all the lessons to emerge from the substitution survey and the study of educational utilization, the most prominent is that multiplying the projected occupational structure by the numbers of educated people observed in those occupations in the base year will give misleading results.

Alternatives (iii) and (iv) are more interesting. Salter's and Kendrick's evidence on the irregularity of productivity advances and the diffusion of best-practice techniques in the economy of the US and UK should have warned the Group that the chances of success were slim (Salter, 1966; Kendrick, 1961). In the event, despite attempts to compare various firms on the basis of capital intensity, engineer density, productivity and costs, the Group conceded that they had failed to come up with an operational definition of a best-practice company. The solution adopted was to ask various 'sector experts' to state their opinion about which companies were best-practice, which is a total abandonment of the belief in scientific forecasting.

That is a harsh judgement, and it may be thought by some, too harsh in view of the Group's willingness to explore the implications of various methods. Certainly, no praise is too high for their pioneering attempts to measure substitution and educational utilization. These were pathbreaking studies. But the final judgement on the forecast surely hinges on the use that was made of these findings. Because the studies in practice turned out to be less generally applicable than was hoped, the compromise of ignoring the findings but of compiling the future estimates by several different methods was worth the try. Where the Technical Group deserves censure is in not making it clear that the various methods, so far from all pointing in the same direction, furnished such a range of estimates as to be quite useless for education planning. In particular, to choose the 'maximum requirements' forecast (using a method which in the case of manufacturing industry had already been thoroughly discredited) on no more than the collective wisdom of the Group is to arrogate to itself a view of the future which is impervious to rational criticism.

The widespread criticism and dissatisfaction which greeted the Group's Report is some evidence that this judgement is shared by many Swedish planners. We showed in the introduction that Sweden has moved from using manpower forecasting as a tool for general educational planning in the late 1950's to a position during the 1960's in which forecasts were thought useful for allocating the faculty balances. But this seems to be an *ex post* rationalization of the way expansion has actually proceeded. It is true that social demand projections have been used to determine the overall numbers in higher education (the 1963 Education Act adopted the Ministry of Education's projection and proposals virtually without amendment). It is also true that the 1963 University Commission and the 1965 Education Act took the view that forecasts for various categories of specialized manpower were both feasible and desirable. Such forecasts have continued to be made by the Forecasting Unit of the Central Bureau of Statistics, but it is doubtful whether they have actually been used except in the most general sense of indicating a continuing 'unmet need' for engineers, doctors, dentists, etc. In practice, the distribution between faculties seems to have been determined by simple budgetary constraints. The high cost per student place at the engineering and medical faculties in particular has meant that the planners have permitted only a moderate expansion in enrolments. Since there has been excess demand for places in these faculties, with consequent bidding-up of the grade requirements for entry, the result has been that much of the demand has instead been channelled into the 'free' faculties[18], where the much less rigid complementarity between space and equipment and the number of students means that places can be expanded relatively quickly and cheaply.

This policy has certainly ensured that all those who wanted a university education have obtained it, at least cost to the exchequer. Moreover, the combination of allowing students a free choice in deciding the level of education they desire but of regulating the subjects they study within that level makes sense if students' subject choices are not closely related to the differential economic benefits of one subject or another (see Blaug, 1970, pp. 180–82). But there is no evidence that this has been the case in Sweden. Both manpower forecasts of 'need' and labour market indicators of vacancies and earnings have pointed to a desirable expansion of the 'restricted' faculties. The result has been restrictions on the supply of those groups of manpower in greatest demand in the labour market and the expansion of those with frequently quite severe employment prospects.

It is easy to point out the economic irrationality of such a policy: by foregoing the education of engineers and doctors whose training costs and contribution elsewhere are less than their social return to the economy, Sweden loses potential output. Swedish educational planners well appreciate this, and are now eagerly awaiting the findings of the 1968 Educational Commission. The Commission is fully aware from past experience that 'as regards both the labour market requirement of skilled manpower and the students' demand for education there is considerable uncertainty even in the short-term view' (Educational Commission, 1968, p. 1). Certainly, the construction of manpower forecasts and social demand projections will play a large role in the Commission's work, but the major investigation concerns the way in which the output of and the demand for manpower with higher education are adjusted to each other. The sort of questions the Commission will be attempting to answer are: How are choices of subject made? What are the mobility patterns of highly

---

[18] The high-cost faculties of medicine, engineering, dentistry and pharmacy, where physical constraints of laboratory space and equipment limit the number of students, are collectively termed the 'restricted' faculties. The other faculties of law, humanities, social science and theology are known as the 'free' faculties.

qualified manpower and how are they related to education? What is the reaction of an employer to a shortage or surplus situation? Finally, the Commission will attempt to relate all these questions to an examination of the social rate of return to education. It is an exciting list of projects.

Appendix A8

The figures for total employees shown in Table 8.6 differ from those in Table 8.1 because of the different coverage of various statistical sources. Part of the difference arises because the Federation mainly relied on a sample inquiry which excluded most of the building industry. Another important difference is that 'Kommerskollegium' industrial statistics exclude companies with less than five employees. Finally, the Census and industrial statistics use different definitions of labour force participation. All this means that not too much reliance should be placed on precise changes when comparing the Federation's and the Labour Market Board's work. In particular, while the estimates of 'actual number of engineers in 1965' are likely to be reasonably accurate when used in conjunction with the Federation's total employment figures, they are much less reliable as a guide to the outcome of the Board's prediction. Mainly because of the differences in accounting the construction industry between the Federation and the Board, the total of 53,000 engineers may very well understate the actual number on a Labour Market Board basis. Similarly, because the definitions of 'public sector' and 'rest of the economy' used by the Board do not correspond precisely with those used by the Federation, we have not attempted to separate 'actual number of engineers' by sector in Table 8.8. However, as the Swedes themselves seem happy to make a direct comparison between engineers and employees according to both sources (see Technical Group, 1970, Section 2.6.2.2 and Ministry of Education, 1962B, Table 2.2.15) we offer Table 8.7 so as to give an order of magnitude.

9. Scientists and Engineers in Britain

by Kenneth Gannicott and Mark Blaug

No one predicting the future of scientific manpower forecasting in Britain in the early 1960's could have foreseen the wealth of papers and reports which have flowed from official committees in the last few years. The Committee on Scientific Manpower had been extremely successful during its 14 years of existence in persuading the Advisory Council on Scientific Policy and the University Grants Committee to expand science and technology places in higher education. But its influence on policy was out of all proportion to the quality of its forecasts, in which almost everyone had lost confidence by 1964 or thereabouts. Moser and Layard, in reviewing the work of this Committee, expressed severe misgivings about its techniques over both the medium and the long-term and, in particular, questioned the value of three-year forecasts based on unconditional estimates by employers (Moser and Layard, 1964, pp. 503—4). Furthermore, the Robbins Report, in adopting a 'social demand' approach to the planning of higher education in 1963, justified itself by noting the primitive state of manpower forecasting in Britain. Indeed, one of the bases of its dismissal of manpower forecasting must have been the evidence of the chairman of the Scientific Manpower Committee, Sir Solly Zuckerman (now Lord Zuckerman), who placed himself in the somewhat curious position of defending both his proposals for expanding the colleges of advanced technology and the Committee's long-term forecast which predicted a *surplus* of scientists and engineers by 1970. In his oral evidence, Sir Solly not only abandoned all claims to faith in his own forecasts but also gave the strong impression that, despite the variety of techniques which had been tried since 1946, his Committee was really no nearer to developing a reliable forecasting technique for scientists and engineers. He said, for example:

'I must indicate again that I myself am not prepared to die in the

240

ditch for any one of these figures. I could not agree with you more that the precision with which some of these figures are given seems rather remarkable when one remembers that we are predicting ten years ahead.'

And again:

'I would like to re-emphasise that it (the 1961 forecast) was one of a series of four reports . . . in which different methods have been used . . . Each time a different method has been used. No doubt, if there is a fifth report, yet another method would be used.' (Committee on Higher Education, 1963, *Evidence*, Part One, Vol. B, pp. 431, 433.)

Far from suffering a rapid demise, however, the Zuckerman Committee was replaced in 1965 by the Committee on Manpower Resources for Science and Technology under the chairmanship of the late Sir Willis Jackson (Lord Jackson of Burnley) with vastly increased scope and influence. In its first report, the Jackson Committee made it clear that it interpreted its brief 'to advise . . . on manpower resources for science and technology' in the widest sense, and boldly set out a programme of work covering 'such matters as statistical sources; factors affecting the choice of a scientific or technological career; preparation for employment in the context of a rapidly changing technology; (and) the better utilisation of scientific and technological manpower' (Jackson Report, 1965, para. 4). The Committee fulfilled almost the whole of this programme: not only did it continue to conduct triennial surveys of manpower requirements, but its reports — on science study in schools (Dainton Report, 1968), the 'brain drain' (Jones Report, 1967), the growth of postgraduate studies (Swann Report, 1968) and the proposals for industrial training schemes (Arthur, 1965; Bosworth, 1965) — received wide publicity and favourable attention from both the popular and the scientific press. The Committee in fact succeeded in erecting a comprehensive view of scientific manpower problems in Britain, resting on four central propositions: (i) that the existence of a long-term shortage of scientists, technologists and engineers in Britain has been empirically established; (ii) that universities tend continuously to denude industry and school teaching of the best talent; (iii) that there exists a high rate of emigration of scientific manpower; and (iv) that there is a strong swing away from science study in secondary schools, foretelling even greater shortages in the future.

241

Now that the Jackson Committee has itself been wound up, the time is ripe for a postmortem on its work. A recent similar attempt, although critical of some aspects of the Committee's work, congratulated it for creating an atmosphere in which 'controversies on scientific and technological manpower have been frankly and ably ventilated' (Hall, 1969, p. 28). Our conclusions are different. We contend that, instead of making out a convincing case for a shortage of scientists and technologists, with due attention to the 'swing from science' and the 'brain drain' which may have intensified it, the Jackson Committee's effort to develop an integrated picture of scientifically qualified manpower is simply a series of contradictions. Using no better forecasting techniques than those discredited a few years earlier, indeed the very same which Sir Solly had found wanting, the Committee dismissed reasonable criticism of its methods and apparently accepted the proposition that the country 'needs' more scientists and technologists as an axiom in all their work.

Methods of forecasting

We begin by examining the Committee's case for the existence of a shortage of scientists and technologists. The amount of space devoted in the 1966 Triennial Survey to 'Problems of Interpretation' leaves no doubt that the Jackson Committee was aware of some of the technical criticisms of the forecasts of the Zuckerman Committee. Whereas terms like 'demand', 'needs' and 'requirements' had been used interchangeably and confusingly in earlier forecasts, the Jackson Committee drew a distinction between 'demand', as defined 'with respect to the community's and in particular the employers' willingness and ability to pay', and 'needs', nowhere precisely defined, emphasizing that its surveys of employers' intentions measure the former (Triennial Survey, 1966, para. 35). We shall show in a moment that, despite this terminological distinction, the Jackson Committee continued to confuse 'demand' with 'needs'. Nevertheless, it is important to grasp the fact that its forecasts were intended to measure observable market demand, independently of anyone's normative judgement. That is to say, it is possible at least in principle to test the accuracy of the Committee's forecasts.

The method used to measure future demand was quite simple. The Ministry of Labour circulated a questionnaire to all educational establishments, government departments and a sample of industrial

242

firms stratified by sectors of activity, asking them to give, by discipline and type of work done, the numbers of qualified scientists and engineers employed, the number of vacancies and 'the number of persons you aim to have in your employment in 3 years' time', assuming 'that the required number of persons will be available'.[1] Thus, given actual employment in 1965 and predicted demand for 1968, net additional demand was obtained by simply subtracting the former from the latter. Similarly, net additional supply was derived by adding the actual net increments up to 1964 and the predicted net annual additions over the period 1964—8 to the total active stock (as given by the sample inquiry into scientific and technological qualifications in the 1961 population census).

Presumably the rationale for this method is that the three basic analytical problems of manpower forecasting — effects of the composition of demand, substitutability between inputs, and productivity changes — are solved implicitly by the employer who provides the estimates. Both Peacock (1963, p. 10) and Moser and Layard (1964, p. 503), however, have pointed out that an unconditional survey of employers' demand invites inconsistent replies. Unless some target rate of output or a market share is specified, how can we be sure that an automobile manufacturer's assumptions are consistent with those of the steel manufacturer who supplies him? Sir Solly Zuckerman, who had accumulated a good deal of experience with this type of survey, testified that 'we discovered in our successive inquiries that one of the least reliable ways for finding out what industry wants is to go and ask industry' (Committee on Higher Education, 1963, *Evidence*, Part One, Vol. B, p. 432). Moreover, it is a fallacy to assume that employers can take account of 'foreseeable fluctuations arising from scientific and technological developments' (Triennial Survey, 1966, para. 32). Although one might think that businessmen are good at predicting the likely trend of technical developments in their own industry, there is abundant evidence that productivity improvements, in the form of the diffusion of 'best practice' techniques throughout an industry, are quite irregular, even in the short run (see Salter, 1966). The Jackson Committee was aware of this: it conceded that 'the quality of employers' estimates is likely to depend on the size of the firms and on the degree of sophistication in their manpower planning'. But it simply assumed away all further doubts with the assertion that 'cumulatively these estimates are

---

[1] The questionnaire, the sectors surveyed and the definitions are available in the Appendix to the Report on the 1965 Triennial Survey.

useful in giving guidance on short-term trends in demand' (Triennial Survey, 1966, paras. 31, 32).

The Committee drew pessimistic conclusions from its survey for the period 1965—8: 'Returns from employers in the sectors surveyed indicate that they expect to employ by 1968 a further 50,400 scientists, technologists and engineers than in 1965. This represents an increase of 24 per cent, or 7.4 per cent annually, and exceeds the expected rate of growth of stock estimated at some 14.6 per cent (or 4.6 per cent annually)', (Triennial Survey, 1966, para. 33). Table 9.1 illustrates this: given the size of demand in the surveyed sectors, the predicted supply in 1968 would be sufficient to meet the forecast demand in these sectors only if employment in the *un*surveyed sectors decreased, an unlikely possibility given the trend between 1962 and 1965.

This kind of comparison between stock and demand may make some sense if both are unambiguously defined in the same terms, but this is manifestly untrue in the case of the Triennial Survey. Despite the chapter entitled 'Terminology and Definitions', the survey nowhere came to grips with the fundamental problem that scientists, technologists and engineers can be classified either in terms of qualifications attained or of job carried out. Consider the following phrase, intended to show how manpower should be classified:

TABLE 9.1

STOCK OF AND DEMAND FOR SCIENTISTS, TECHNOLOGISTS AND ENGINEERS, BRITAIN, 1962—68

| | 1962 (thousands) | 1965 (thousands) | 1968 forecast (thousands) | Percentage growth | |
				1962—65	1965—68 (forecast)
Total active stock	273.2	313.0	358.7	14.6	14.6
Employment in sectors covered by surveys	183.2	211.2	261.6	15.3	23.9
Balance available for employment in unsurveyed sectors	90.0	101.8	97.1 (residual)	13.1	−4.6 (residual)

Source: Triennial Survey (1966), Table VI, p. 16.

244

'the technologist is frequently several steps ahead of the scientist in the breadth of his knowledge and in his awareness of the potentialities within his field of inquiry but he is likely to be less concerned with full understanding of the underlying scientific relationships' (Triennial Survey, 1966, para. 10).

Even the apparently quite straightforward method of adding annual increments to the 1961 census stock becomes seriously misleading when it is remembered that 'total active stock' represents a very mixed bag of age groups, new and outdated qualifications and trained and untrained personnel. The Committee showed itself fully aware of this when it declared that a direct comparison with demand cannot 'reveal the kind of balance between supply and demand which has previously been inferred from it' (Triennial Survey, 1966, para. 41). This statement was apparently designed to disclaim the Zuckerman Committee's long-term forecast in 1961, predicting a surplus by 1970 on the grounds that total active stock would exceed predicted demand in that year (Zuckerman Report, 1961). The Jackson Committee was right to be sceptical of such a crude comparison, but apparently absolved its own forecast from taking account of the same criticism. If stock and demand cannot be directly compared, what possible meaning can we give to Table 9.1? If 'total active stock' is a thoroughly ambiguous notion in this context, then the third row, derived as a residual, is equally ambiguous.

The terms in which future demand was expressed were no less ambiguous. Respondents were asked in the questionnaire to indicate 'present and future requirements of qualified scientists, engineers and technologists, irrespective of the type of work done' (Triennial Survey, 1966, page 44). Superficially, this provides a clear-cut forecast in terms of educational disciplines required, but a closer look suggests that the results are as dubious as the forecasts of active stock. Employers may not be interested in the educational qualification of, say, mechanical engineering: their concern may be the number of people carrying out a mechanical engineering function, which is not at all the same thing. The two are identical only if no other educational discipline but mechanical engineering can adequately supply the demand for jobs with a mechanical engineering function, and if the occupational category of mechanical engineer is a technically indispensable input into production which cannot be contributed at any price by other job functions. In short, the Committee's method is a viable technique for forecasting the demand for educational disciplines only if there is a very low degree of

245

substitutability both within and between occupations — an untenable assumption for a Report which admits that 'it is unrealistic to press distinctions between disciplines too far' (Triennial Survey, 1966, para. 53). The Committee nowhere drew the obvious conclusion from this admission: if industry's stated demand for 'mechanical engineers' can in fact be satisfied by people trained in a whole range of educational disciplines, it makes little sense to inquire into the demand for the educational discipline of 'mechanical engineering', unless of course we have reasons to think that mechanical engineers are more effective per unit of cost in any job than people with different qualifications.

None of these criticisms is new: they have all been made before by critics of the Zuckerman Committee. But whereas Sir Solly came in the end to recognize all the difficulties of surveying employers and attempting to fathom their intentions, the Jackson Committee refused to believe that 'technical problems in estimates of this type' affect the results more than marginally (Triennial Survey, 1966, para. 31). Indeed, so confident was the Jackson Committee of both its own results and those of the Zuckerman Committee that it simply linked together all the three-year forecasts made since 1956 to demonstrate that they formed part of a consistent long-term pattern of shortage. Figure 9.1 derived from Figure 1 of the 1965 survey summarizes this exercise.

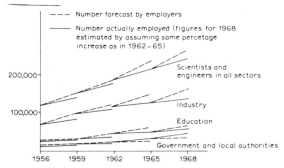

Figure 9.1. Growth of employment and demand, by sector, Britain, 1956—1968.

Source: Triennial Survey (1966), Figure 1.
Note: Surveys changed in coverage in 1959 and 1962.

It is easy to see from the graph how the Jackson Committee arrived at its alarmist conclusions about the employment of scientists and technologists in Britain. The implications of the graph would seem to be (i) that there has been a long-term failure of supply to

246

meet demand and (ii) that industry has suffered most from this shortage, while the education sector has much more nearly achieved its forecast. Apparently the fact that 'actual' employment has consistently been below 'forecast' employment constitutes sufficient evidence for a shortage. Nowhere in any of the reports is there any suggestion of an alternative explanation: that the forecasts of shifts in the demand curve were simply mistaken. This possibility does not seem to have occurred to the Committee because it defined 'shortage' in such a way as to preclude errors in forecasting. It will be recalled that employers were asked in the questionnaire to state the number of qualified people they would aim to employ in three years on the assumption 'that the required number of persons will be available' (Triennial Survey, 1966, p. 44). The very phrasing of this invites the interpretation that an employer ought to be able to hire as many people as he wants (at identical salaries?); if actual employment falls short of such aspirations, then by definition the cause is an overall shortage.

It seems obvious that, in spite of assertions to the contrary, the Committee invoked the term 'demand' in a purely physical sense: the uncritical acceptance of employers' estimates, the way the question of future demand was posed, and the talk of forecasts being 'achieved', all point to a prediction of future demand totally devoid of economic content. The concept the Committee seems to have had in mind is one where relative prices play no part: earnings are not mentioned in the questionnaire, and indeed any consideration of their role is emasculated by the assumption of 'available supply'. It is a concept where, if the employer can predict his future output with some degree of accuracy, technical requirements dictate his demand for labour. On the supply side too, relative earnings play no part. As earnings are nowhere mentioned, the assumption must be that the supply of scientists and technologists is price-inelastic and is a function simply of the number of places made available for the study of scientific subjects. The costs of education may apparently be ignored: if it is 'required' by the technological nature of the output, the cost of producing it is irrelevant. In short, demand is fixed without regard to possible supply; supply is fixed independently of demand and there is no common, automatic mechanism for ever bringing the two into equilibrium.

A further reason why the Committee was loath to raise the possibility of an inaccurate forecast was its view that demand estimates represent only a minimum target: we ought really to try to produce enough scientists and technologists to meet the 'needs' of

247

the country. The 1966 Triennial Survey report declared that 'the present output . . . is still deficient in relation to ascertainable short-term demand, let alone to need', and the Swann Report in 1968 suggested that 'if we are to achieve new and more productive patterns of utilisation and employment, manpower policy must attempt to cover long-term need as well as short-term demand' (Triennial Survey, 1966, para. 94; Swann Report, 1968, para. 64). Indeed, one of the reasons why the Jackson Committee dismissed previous criticisms of manpower forecasts was its belief that all such criticism misses the point: the notion is that even if demand forecasts are unreliable, one cannot go far wrong in putting them forward as minimum estimates, since the real 'needs' must exceed them.

What precisely does it mean to assert that there is always an unsatisfied 'need' for scientists and technologists, even if there is no market shortage? The Committee evidently found it easier to state the problem than to solve it. The 1965 Survey offers little guidance on this problem: a crude international comparison suggests that 'the combined technological resources of the European Economic Community are well ahead of our own', but no evidence that the EEC is actually being rational or efficient in allocating this proportion of its total resources to science and technology is actually provided.[2]

The only clue the Committee gives us is the statement that '. . . at any time the scale and composition of a country's productive activity . . . give rise to a postulated need for highly qualified skills if economic, technological and cultural progress is to be sustained' (Triennial Survey, 1966, para. 35). But this, as we have seen, is precisely the belief underlying the Committee's concept of demand. Conceptually, therefore, 'demand' and 'need' seem to be treated as identical: the only difference is that 'demand' is what employers say they require, 'need' is what the Committee thinks employers ought to require.

A possible justification for the Committee's belief that 'need' always exceeds 'demand' is the notion that scientists and technologists in Britain are systematically under-utilized. That is to say,

2 Britain's 'need' for more scientists and engineers is established by a large number of emotive statements, of which the following is a random sample: 'Some examples are the need for technological viability in our aircraft, ship-building, machine-tool and computer industries, for better standards of design and means for the training of larger numbers with design skills, for better utilisation of scientific knowledge of materials, for better standards of mensuration and calibration, and for the more scientific exploitation and conservation of our limited national resources' (Triennial Survey, 1966, para. 49).

employers are inefficiently utilizing them in occupations that could be just as effectively carried out by less educated individuals: if they were efficiently utilized, there would be a greater demand for them. This argument may well be correct but it has some far-reaching consequences for the rest of the Committee's work. If one really believes that employers malutilize educated manpower, one clearly cannot put much faith in forecasts of demand based on employers' opinion. Furthermore, malutilization of labour implies a high degree of substitutability between labour with different educational qualifications, albeit at a cost, in which case one must allow for the differential earnings that are associated with demand for different kinds of educated labour, something that the Committee has never done.

If this much is accepted, two things follow: (i) if employers fail to perceive optimum 'needs', it seems pointless to rely exclusively on their so-called estimates of demand as the basis for forecasting; and (ii) if 'needs' as perceived by the Committee are so remote from the actual structure of job opportunities that employers cannot reasonably be expected to perceive them, any attempt to increase the supply up to this target will, in the absence of compulsory direction of labour, result in the unemployment or emigration of scientists and engineers. It is, of course, possible that employers' demands are not a good guide to national needs, since the salary which employers are prepared to pay, and hence the numbers of scientists and technologists they are prepared to employ, may not reflect the external economies which result from educating more of them. But this type of argument can be used to support an increase in the amount of virtually any highly qualified skill: one could just as easily assert on these grounds that the recent economic performance of Britain indicates a 'need' for more economists. How do we choose between economists and scientists?

Yet, so far from accepting the logic of these propositions, the Committee did not consider the first and expressly rejected the second with the statement that '... employers can be expected, when there is a better educational supply, to revise their views about the importance of employing new skills, and also because *the emergence of such skills duly creates its own demand*' (our italics) (Triennial Survey, 1966, para. 37). But if the supply of highly educated manpower creates its own demand — a modern version of Say's Law — there never can be a surplus of manpower. We cannot go wrong, the Committee is saying, by producing too much. Apparently, however, the argument is asymmetrical: demand does not create its own supply, so there can be shortages. But how are all possible increments in supply absorbed into employment, if a given supply leads to a determined demand? Clearly, the Committee has suddenly ceased to believe in the low substitutability of educated manpower, in which case why worry about shortages? If demand and supply are not independent of each other, forecasts of demand are meaningless, and in asserting Say's Law for scientists and technologists, the Committee has in fact abandoned its entire theoretical rationale.

All this adds up to the conclusion that the Committee has failed to make its case for a long-term shortage. Its measure of demand not only ignores the realities of the labour market, but relies on dubious surveys and misleading classification techniques. 'Needs', the umbrella term under which the inadequate demand forecasts were supposed to take shelter, turns out on examination to be nothing more than an assertion of a value judgement that more scientists and technologists would benefit the country. This has nothing to do with the art of manpower forecasting and is simply the special pleading of a science and engineering lobby.

Surveys of policy problems

If the Committee failed to make a case for a chronic shortage of scientists and technologists, some of the alarmist talk about 'the swing from science' and the 'brain drain' seems misplaced. In the absence of a reliable criterion for judging where manpower 'ought' to go, there is no reason to assume that the 'swing' in secondary schools or the growth of postgraduate education represents a misallocation of resources. Even so, it is highly instructive to examine the policy reports dealing with these phenomena, for they illustrate the way in which the Committee's dependence on crude forecasts left it without any analytical framework to explain the educational problems with which it concerned itself after the Triennial Survey of 1965.

According to the Committee, the basic factor that ties together all the problems investigated by Dainton, Swann and Jones is the rigid and specialized nature of the British educational system and the irrelevance of science teaching in schools and universities. The result, it is alleged, is to produce a group of narrow specialists who 'emerge with little knowledge of . . . the problems of the society in which they are to become responsible members', and who 'see little place for themselves except in the specialities in which they have been trained'. 'Are they to be blamed', so the argument runs, 'for preferring the academic world here or abroad to industry or school-teaching in this country'? (Swann Report, 1968, para. 158).

This type of explanation is most clearly seen in the Dainton Report on the 'swing from science' in schools. This report was concerned to explain why there had been a movement away from science subjects both at 'O' and 'A' level in upper secondary schools since 1960, with the consequence that entrants into science and technology faculties in universities had fallen from 45.9 per cent of total admissions in 1962 to 40.6 per cent in 1966. A corollary to this was 'a tendency towards acceptance of candidates for science and technology of lower grades of "A" level achievement than those applying for arts and social studies' (Dainton Report, 1968, para. 56, 31).

Much of the Report is an excellent analysis of the way in which specialised university entrance requirements percolate down and dictate a rigid pattern of specialisation comparatively early in a secondary school career. In particular, the Report correctly demonstrates that the irreversible decision for or against specialised science study is made at the point in secondary schools when mathematics ceases to be taught. As a result, one of Dainton's central recommendations was that broad courses of sixth form study should replace the present emphasis on two or three specialised 'A' levels; mathematics, the key to increased flexibility, would be the norm for the majority of sixth formers, who would thus be able to postpone the fatal choice for or against science. Universities in turn could assist this process by altering their entry requirements so as to encourage a broad span of studies in the sixth form.

Whatever the genuine merits of these proposals, it is mistaken to suggest that an early choice of subject specialisation is in itself a cause of the swing from science. To be sure, the Report recognises that its proposals will not necessarily influence pupils' preferences in the direction of science, but it goes on to imply that they are very likely to because older pupils will not fail to appreciate the glories of science: 'It is in the individual's interest that he should not be required to take these critical decisions at a relatively immature stage, before he has had opportunity to appreciate something of the true significance of science and technology as intellectually satisfying pursuits in themselves, or to see them more roundly in their social context' (Dainton Report, 1968, para. 174).

But to imply that universities will thereby have a wider range of applicants for science study is totally to confuse necessary and sufficient conditions for an increase in the number of science and

251

technology students. One of the more distressing features of the Dainton Report is the manner in which it is shot through with generalizations of the type just quoted, whose only purpose is to glorify science and technology. One more example must suffice: 'few students can be aware . . . of the extent to which science ultimately unifies knowledge and makes learning easier by giving a structural framework of concepts that brings diverse facts into relationship' (para. 150); or 'the study of science requires intellectual rigour; indeed it is one of the cardinal characteristics which distinguish it from mere speculation and experiment. For the gifted pupil this can be a positive attraction. But most young people are now able to choose apparently less rigorous alternatives and have to be encouraged, if not persuaded, to face the discipline of science' (para. 149).

After thoroughly exploring and conclusively rejecting the hypothesis that the quality of science teachers is responsible for the swing, the main influence the Report identified was the school science curriculum; it called for an urgent move '. . . to infuse breadth, humanity and up-to-dateness into the science curriculum' so that something of that 'satisfying and regenerating intellectual curiosity along ever-widening boundaries' can be transmitted to children (Dainton Report, 1968, para. 181). There is little question that the science curriculum *is* out of date: as early as 1960, the Advisory Council on Scientific Policy commenting on the Crowther Report, said that 'school science curricula were in need of a thorough re-examination' (Advisory Council, 1961A). But this can hardly be the main explanation of the swing, since the Dainton Report itself pointed out that 'science, engineering and technology gained ground in school and higher education from about 1945 to the late fifties' (para. 145), and presumably much the same curriculum was in use then.[3]

---

[3] Nowhere is the alarm with which the Jackson Committee approached its task better seen than in its attitude to science teachers. Even after Dainton had rejected the hypothesis that the quality of science teaching is responsible for the swing, the Swann Report recommended that 'local authorities should consider re-employing specialist teachers who have recently retired' (para. 141). If the curriculum is really as important a factor in the swing as Dainton contends, how can Swann think that to employ teachers with obsolete qualifications would improve the swing? Perhaps such inconsistency is only to be expected from a report which asserts in one and the same breath that '. . . the demand for graduate scientists and technologists of high academic ability to teach in schools cannot at present be quantified, though there is evidence of acute shortage'; or again: 'we have no means of saying how many (top—level graduates) the schools ought to have, (but) . . . the evidence of shortage is indisputable' (para. 63, 82).

Specialized education and an out-of-date curriculum may be bad for all sorts of reasons, but they do not explain what is essentially a change during the last few years: vast generalizations about educational structure and the 'public image' of science are hardly convincing when what one is trying to explain is a movement of very recent origins. Dainton's long-term projection that 'on present trends by 1971 only about one quarter of the 'A' level students in the first year of the sixth form would be found in the Science Group' (p. 8), should not blind readers to the fact that the acute pessimism of the Final Report represents a complete turnaround from the 'qualified optimism' of the Interim Report a mere two years earlier.

The Swann Report saw an exactly analogous process, for similar reasons, occurring at the higher education level. The main theme of the report was the apparently worrying trend that graduates and postgraduates were preferring to remain in the 'higher education and research' sector rather than seeking employment in industry or in school teaching. Even more worrying was the tendency of this sector to cream off the more able graduates: 'almost three-quarters of scientists and half of technologists obtaining "firsts" have proceeded to postgraduate work, together with substantial proportions of those gaining "upper seconds" . . . Industry and Schools (including teacher training colleges) recruit less than one tenth of science "firsts", and the proportion entering Schools has declined over the last five years' (para. 104). The Report was in no doubt about the cause: university degrees were not oriented to the real 'needs' of industry, and graduates were being produced who believed that the only worthwhile activity was academic research. Reinforcing this trend was a Ph.D. system which was even more remote from the vocational training which industry required (Chapter VII).

One feature of Swann's analysis is immediately obvious: by focussing attention exclusively on trends among *university* graduates, the Report completely neglects the fact that almost one-half of engineers in Britain qualify through degrees of the Council for National Academic Awards or through membership of professional institutions. Since industrial experience is a requirement for the qualifications of professional institutions, the supply of these engineers is related very closely to industrial demands. Therefore, even if Swann's analysis of the trends among university graduates is correct, it follows that what Dainton identified is not necessarily a general swing from science. Although Swann quoted Dainton approvingly in support of his own analysis, it makes little sense to accept both explanations at face value. If the uninteresting curriculum, the early specialization and the poor image of science add up to a swing away from science study among fifth and sixth formers, why do we observe such high proportions of scientists at university level only too keen to remain active in specialized scientific research? Is it that science becomes interesting only after it has been studied up to first degree level? If the trends noted by Swann and Dainton do have a common cause, that cause is certainly not a general social drift away from science. If it lies in the structure of the educational system, then apparently it has to do with poor teaching of science in secondary schools and the superb teaching of science in universities and technical colleges. This may be the right explanation, but, if so, it still awaits demonstration.

The failure of the Committee to provide a comprehensive explanation of these phenomena is nowhere better seen than in the Jones Report on the brain drain. This Committee was charged with explaining the specific problem of 'an increasing net loss in recent years of qualified manpower arising from an upsurge in emigration with no marked change in immigration . . ., from a near numerical balance in 1961 . . . to a position in 1966 which represented a net loss equivalent to nineteen per cent of the 1963 output of newly qualified engineers and technologists and nine per cent of the scientists' (Jones Report, 1969, para. 34).

The Jones Committee professed to be unperturbed by the upward trend for scientists, since 'most scientists who go abroad do so on a temporary basis for further research and study', but took fright at the emigration of engineers and technologists, since these groups were seeking permanent employment abroad (Jones Report, 1967, para. 28). Nowhere does the Report offer an analytic resolution of these differences in the behaviour of scientists and of engineers. Part of the answer lies in the figures which the Report itself presents, showing that a substantial proportion of emigrant engineers and technologists came from the aircraft and associated industries, which at this time were going through an acute phase of uncertainty, provoked by doubts about the future of Concorde, the cancellation of the TSR—2, HS1154 and HS681, and the heavy redundancies at Bristol, Preston and Luton. These figures were supplied to the then Ministry of Technology by a North American recruiting agency, and although not comprehensive, give an illustrative picture of those registered and those hired by subject of qualification. They indicate that 'three-quarters of those hired were under 35, and that most of them come from design and development jobs in aeronautical engineering, electronics and control systems' (Jones Report, 1967, para. 33). The report noted that 'the uncertainty of the air-craft industry . . . can be

254

held responsible for much of the loss of aeronautical and allied engineers in late 1965 and 1966', but failed to recognize that such essentially short-term problems have to be carefully distinguished in an assessment of long-term trends. It preferred to write emotively about the 'loss of seed-corn' and the 'disastrous consequences for British industry and the economy within ten to twenty years if it were to continue at the present rate' in a way that suggests that Britain's prime shortage is not of engineers but of competent economists (Jones Report, 1967, para. 143, 36).

Not surprisingly the result of this exercise is another airing of the explanation we have seen before: the British educational system produces graduates who are biassed against employment in industry and who in turn have received such a specialized, theoretical education that they are of little use to industry. The fault for this 'lies as much with university curricula in science as with those who do the teaching, and we must look for the solution here in a change of emphasis in the curricula towards the needs of industry' (Jones Report, 1967, para. 177). If the curriculum really does produce narrow specialists, imbued with the ideal of pure research and biassed against employment in industry, one wonders why the bias apparently disappears when contemplating employment in America; nor is American industry complaining that the skills produced by British education do not match its 'needs'. And even if the allegations about the nature of the curriculum and of the graduates produced are true, these long-term factors manifestly cannot explain such a recent phenomenon as the upsurge in emigration in the mid-1960's. If a key role in this turnaround is assigned to the demands of the space programme and the defence industry, it still has to be shown how these 'pull' factors alone could operate so successfully in a situation of alleged shortage of scientists and technologists in Britain.

The policy recommendations are as mixed as the analysis. For example, the Committee placed under 'non-acceptable remedies' the very key to the problem. It was scornful of the idea that 'since the rate of emigration of certain types of specialist can be held to imply their overproduction, the educational system should be adjusted to match the annual output more closely to the immediate national demand. This argument may well hold true in the case of some specialist disciplines which may be fading into obsolescence . . . but it is fallacious as a general proposition in the face of large domestic demand for talented engineers, technologists and scientists' (Jones Report, 1967, para. 137). What *is* fallacious is the Report's abrupt dismissal of this line of argument: it provides yet another example of the way in which reliance on a bogus concept of 'shortage' leads to the total lack of analysis of labour market adjustments: the brain drain is precisely one indicator of behaviour which can support or refute a manpower forecast of a current or impending shortage.

An economic analysis of manpower shortages

The subject of this chapter has been the lack of economics in the work of the Jackson Committee. The essence of our criticism was that the Committee ignored the operations of the labour market: relative earnings, prices, and costs were not even mentioned, much less analysed. Even the Jones Report, which came nearest to an assessment of the role of earnings and costs failed to integrate them in its examination of the brain drain. The last chapter of this book argues for a new approach to educational planning in which relative earnings and costs are brought together in an optimizing model. In the United States, Hansen (1965; 1967) has demonstrated the explanatory power of comparing rates of return on investment in different educational qualifications. Rates of return are a summary statistic combining those variables of earnings and costs which the Jackson Committee consistently ignored in assessing manpower shortages.[4] This is not an over-simple rejection of all non-economic factors: the assumption is simply that, on the margin, students implicitly calculate the net financial advantage of choosing one career rather than another.

Armed with this tool, the problems which Dainton, Swann and Jones failed to explain satisfactorily fall neatly into place. The behaviour they noted is precisely what would be predicted from a relatively low or declining rate of return, or a *surplus* of scientists and technologists. The essence of the swing is a decline in the relative number and quality of entrants into science and technology. While many factors can help to explain this, one of the most obvious is that the yield on this training has declined, and this decline in turn indicates the appearance of a surplus. Similarly the preference for lengthier postgraduate research by scientists and technologists may

---

[4] Two more recent articles have attempted to examine the hypothesis of a shortage of scientists and engineers in Britain in terms of changes in vacancy rates and relative earnings (Peck, 1968; Richardson, 1969), but both attempts founder on the use of *median* salary levels, which are known to conceal continual adjustment by age and so fail to bring out the impact of short-run changes in starting salaries.

be motivated not by the 'academically-oriented values' of the students but by their perception that they will now have to undergo a lengthier training period than colleagues in relatively scarcer disciplines in order to secure equally remunerative employment. Dainton pointed out that 'in chemistry . . . we are already moving towards the situation where the Ph.D. is the professional qualification pursued by nearly half of those attaining a first degree' but merely noted that 'if a degree course in science or technology took much longer than in other subjects this would act as a discouragement' (Dainton Report, para. 191, 192). He failed to realize that the lengthier training period for chemists raises the private costs and so lowers the rate of return to chemistry education. The alternatives to this, in a situation of a surplus of chemists, are for the B.Sc. chemist either to accept an offer of employment unrelated to his skill as a chemist, or to take a job at a lower level of skill than his training fits him for.

Such an interpretation sheds an entirely different light on the other problems that worried Swann. In these circumstances of course it is the lower quality of graduates who will go into industry immediately after their B.Sc., and of course the curriculum, both in schools and in universities, will remain oriented to academic values. Swann's recommendation to shift postgraduate education from the traditional types of courses to something more 'vocational' misses the point that the undergraduate curriculum and the structure of the Ph.D. *are* vocational: they are vocational just as long as students perceive that the rational choice is to undertake research for a higher degree.

The most recent data from OECD yield an interesting perspective on this analysis. The report on *Gaps in Technology: Comparisons between Member Countries* demonstrates that Britain is training 40 per cent more technologists in relation to the size of the age group than the USA, and a higher proportion of pure scientists than any OECD country but the USA (OECD, 1970). In contrast to the Jackson Committee's belief that we cannot have too many scientists and technologists, the OECD evidence suggests that the United Kingdom may well be investing too much in the production of high level scientists and technologists particularly in view of her relatively low rate of economic growth.

In the earlier analysis we assumed that pupils and students were acting as if they were making perfectly rational decisions in a world where they are well informed and where demand for educated manpower is transmitted smoothly through the price mechanism. Ultimately, we should expect to see a change in the pattern of research work and emigration for scientists and technologists as the recent 'swing' in the schools works its way through the education system and out into the labour market. That is to say, Dainton, Swann and Jones were witnessing nothing more disturbing than the operation of a supply/demand adjustment process. This is not to imply that we can simply rely on this process to bring us to equilibrium in the near future. Arrow and Capron discuss all the factors on the demand side which inhibit a rapid labour market clearance (Arrow and Capron, 1959) and in Britain this process is considerably worsened by the slow response on the supply side. The result is that although the market is functioning, it is not necessarily completely clearing the market in any one period. Thus, by the time the 'swing' has worked itself through the schools, the labour market may well be attempting to employ more scientists and technologists. The fear of cobweb cycles is the classic justification for manpower forecasting, but these very imperfections in the education and labour markets mean that the outcome of an inaccurate forecast, as the OECD Report implies, can be a disastrous misallocation of resources.

The successors of the Jackson Committee can best address themselves to analysing the operation of the labour market for highly qualified manpower in Britain. What is needed is not more employers' surveys, but an analysis of the nature of market responses. We list below some of the questions it should attempt to answer.

What changes in earnings and numbers of entrants are likely to occur in the short and long-term, given shifts in the demand curve for different types of qualified manpower?

What factors account for the lags between the short and long-term?

How might government policy help to reduce these lags and what are the costs of doing so?

What are the alternative methods of increasing the supply of qualified manpower?

What are the costs and benefits of these alternatives? What is the cost to the economy of a shortage of any particular skill?

The adoption of this agenda for research will not have an immediate pay-off in the kind of dramatic conclusions to which we have become accustomed after 14 years of the Zuckerman and four years of the Jackson Committee. But it may mean that manpower policies can at last be conducted in an atmosphere free from partisan prejudice.

Fortunately, there have been signs of an official change of heart. The UGC, so long persuaded by manpower forecasts to expand science and technology places and restrict those in the arts and social sciences, has reluctantly bowed to the probability that 'pressure of demand for places in undergraduate courses requiring science-based entry qualifications was unlikely to increase', while 'on the other hand, pressure of demand for undergraduate places in arts and social studies . . . would continue to increase'; in the circumstances, it was 'these two considerations (which) largely determined our planning figures for the distribution of undergraduate places during the quinquennium' (UGC, 1968, para. 331—35).

However, the UGC did not entirely lose faith in the Jackson Committee. Although individual preferences were the guideline for undergraduate places, at the postgraduate level it proposed to implement Bosworth's 'matching sections'[5], in spite of Arthur's evidence of little industrial interest in that type of course (Arthur, 1965), and in spite of the fact that postgraduates have shown themselves to be in favour of more academic research. If we are right in our supposition that individual preferences for research have reflected the existence of a surplus of scientists and technologists, we can almost guarantee the failure of Bosworth's scheme: postgraduates are almost certain to seek to convert 'matching sections' into more academic type courses. If individual preferences can be allowed to guide undergraduate places, why is it that postgraduates cannot be allowed the same choice?

This plea for individual choice is not a plea for *laissez-faire*. On the contrary, it implies a massive increase in vocational counselling, counselling that is, firmly rooted in actual job opportunities, not in the metaphysical world of 'needs'. Clearly the government has to take a look into the future, since the provision of science and technology places means that specialized and indivisible investment decisions have to be made, but forecasting with a view to providing for likely trends in enrolment is a very different matter from persisting in the fiction that a forecast of 'manpower requirements' can tell us how many scientists, technologists and engineers the educational system ought to produce.

---

5 'Matching sections' are short bridging courses, designed to expunge 'academically oriented values' from the graduate and convert him into an effective industrial technologist.

259

Postscript

In the two years since this chapter first appeared, its findings have been generally corroborated by an increasing weight of evidence. The 'Committee for Manpower Resources', which we assumed would succeed the Jackson Committee, has not in fact materialized, and the new Triennial Survey (1971) was carried out under the aegis of the Department of Trade and Industry. The latest report has supplemented the actual Survey data with an analysis of the 1966 Sample Census, with startling results. So far from there being a long-term shortage of scientists and engineers, it emerges that their rate of unemployment doubled between 1961 and 1966: in 1966 the unemployment rate for scientists was equal to the national rate, and the unemployment of engineers was expected to rise to the national percentage by 1968 (Triennial Survey, 1971, pp. 34, 35). The report also usefully demolishes the myths of the 'brain drain'. During the decade 1958—68, Britain was actually a net importer of scientists: those returning from overseas, plus immigrants from other countries, more than outweighed the emigrants. Although Britain was a net exporter of engineers during those years, the yearly peaks of emigration add some evidence to our earlier suggestion that this was largely induced by the cancellation of major aircraft projects.

But by far the most startling aspect of the report is its manner of presentation, for there is not a single sentence on the implications of its findings. To be sure, we pleaded earlier for a less partisan approach to the planning of scientific manpower, but to say nothing at all about possible causes of recent unemployment, about the differences in migration patterns of scientists and engineers, about past planning of student numbers, and to fail to explore at least some of the alternative strategies for future policy, is to carry neutrality to a *reductio ad absurdum*. Nowhere is this better seen than in the Survey itself. It devotes several pages to such trivial matters as the date on which postal reminders were dispatched and the transfer of returns to punch-cards and then merely notes that 'frequently there will be very inadequate data on which to base a forecast three years ahead' (Triennial Survey, 1971, p. 64). All the tables from the Survey are then presented without a word of comment. If the authors of the report had so little faith in what they were doing, why did they publish it?

10. Teachers in England and Wales

by Bashir Ahamad

The need for efficient planning of the supply and distribution of primary and secondary school teachers has long been recognized in England and Wales. More than 20 years ago, it seemed clear that there was a substantial shortage of qualified teachers and that some schools found it impossible to recruit enough teachers to eliminate oversize classes. The Minister of Education realized that additional pressures would be created in the 1950's and he therefore set up the National Advisory Council on the Training and Supply of Teachers to advise him on policy for ensuring that the country's schools would be adequately staffed.

The Council tried to discharge this responsibility by undertaking a few studies of special groups of teachers, but many of their later reports were confined to planning an increase in the supply of teachers through the expansion of the colleges of education. The Council made projections of the future demand for teachers using pupil—teacher ratios which would apparently allow the elimination of oversize classes. The supply of teachers was projected on the basis of assumptions about recruitment and wastage, that is, loss through mortality, retirement and occupational mobility. The differences between supply and demand were then interpreted as shortages (if negative) and surpluses (if positive), and these were used for making recommendations about the future number of teachers to be trained.

The methods and recommendations were subject to some criticism both inside and outside the Council. It was pointed out that the Council had failed to consider the possibility of removing existing shortages by the redistribution of teachers or pupils. It had moreover implicitly assumed that distributional shortages would automatically be removed if the total supply of teachers were increased in accordance with its recommendations.

But the Council did explicitly recognize that its models were unsatisfactory and that its forecasts were subject to substantial error.

261

In its Ninth Report it recommended that the '. . . methods of formulating objectives of staffing policy should be re-examined urgently . . .' (DES, 1965 p. 40). Curiously, however, it did not take account of some of the shortcomings in its analyses and made its recommendations as if its forecasts were in fact fairly precise.

Since the publication of the Ninth Report in 1965, the Council has apparently ceased to exist. But its methods have now been adopted by the Department of Education and Science (DES) which has recently published revised projections for the period to 1986 (DES, 1969A). This seems to suggest that projections of the future demand and supply of teachers will continue to exert a strong influence on government policy on planning the distribution and recruitment of teachers.

For this reason, it seems important that we should try to evaluate the forecasts of demand and supply of teachers made by the National Advisory Council. To do so we shall examine some of the methods and assumptions used by the Council. We shall also compare the projections with observations to obtain an indication of the empirical performance of the model.

Forecasting demand

The three sets of forecasts made by the Council used the same basic methodology though they differed slightly in coverage. The Ninth Report included all qualified teachers, together with a small number of uncertificated and supplementary teachers with specially protected service agreements, in maintained primary and secondary schools; but in the Fifth and Seventh Reports, the coverage was limited to full-time teachers only. In none of the reports was an attempt made to forecast demand by subject, or by geographical area.

The Council defined demand to mean the number of teachers required to achieve the objectives of staffing policy. In other words it calculated a pupil—teacher ratio which it assumed would allow the elimination of oversize classes and simply multiplied this by the projected number of pupils in a given year.

In the Fifth and Seventh Reports, demand was calculated separately for two groups of students — juniors and seniors. For juniors, the pupil — teacher ratio which would eliminate classes over 40 was assumed to be 27.0:1, while for seniors the ratio required to eliminate classes over 30 was assumed to be 16.0:1. These ratios included only full-time teachers and they were subsequently revised to 26.3 and 15.7 respectively for use by the Robbins Committee.

Pupil—teacher ratios in the Ninth Report

The Council noted in its Seventh Report that the above pupil—teacher ratios '. . . have been used for many years now but it should not be assumed that they are immutable. Some of the factors underlying the calculations have changed' (DES, 1962, para. 29). These doubts were particularly strong for seniors, and a survey of secondary schools was undertaken on January 23, 1964 to provide data for calculating revised ratios for this group. But the Council continued to use the figure of 26.3 (and 19.7 for eliminating classes over 30) for juniors despite the doubts expressed in the Seventh Report: there it had noted that even a small decrease from 27.0 (the figure for full-time teachers) to 26.5 would have increased the demand for teachers by 3,000 (para. 29).

The report divided seniors into two groups: (i) pupils in the first five years of secondary school and (ii) sixth form pupils. The revised pupil-teacher ratios for pupils in the first group were derived from the survey data in a rather complicated manner. The starting point was the identity,

$$\frac{P}{T} = \frac{P_t}{n} \left(\frac{T_t}{T} \times \frac{P}{P_t} \times \frac{n}{T_t} \right)$$

Where P = total number of pupils,
      T = total number of teachers,
      P_t = number of pupils in class at the time surveyed,
      T_t = number of teachers teaching at the time surveyed,
      n = number of classes.

This equation simply says that the pupil—teacher ratio depends on the average size of class, the proportion of teachers actually teaching, the proportion of pupils actually being taught and the average number of teachers per class.

The Council then assumed that the proportions in brackets would all remain constant so that the pupil—teacher ratio could be related to the average size of class by the simple equation,

$$\frac{P}{T} = K \left(\frac{P_t}{n} \right)$$

263

where K is a constant.

No attempt was made to justify the use of the assumed constant proportions and indeed it is not difficult to think of reasons why this may appear to be unreasonable. For example, it seems logical to assume that the proportion of teachers actually engaged in teaching at a given time (T_t/T) will depend on the subjects being taught at that time: the proportion can therefore be expected to change as the structure of subjects changes. Similarly a change in the proportion of pupils being taught (P_t/P) will, *ceteris paribus*, generate a change in the average size of class (P_t/n), and vice versa; it is to be expected then that the proportion will tend to fall as the average size of class falls. Thus it seems reasonable to question the validity of the simple relationship given in the equation above.

The second step was to derive the average size of class required to eliminate classes with more than 30 pupils. Here the Council assumed that elimination of oversize classes would mean that a small proportion (assumed to be 5 per cent) of classes with more than 30 pupils would continue to exist '. . . in circumstances which make it impracticable to secure any further reduction in size' (DES, 1965, Appendix C, para. 10). This assumption is clearly a contradiction of the Council's basic objective of measuring demand in terms of assumed staffing standards. If classes with more than 30 pupils continue to exist then this surely means that the aims of staffing policy have not been met and that a shortage in the Council's sense still exists. The assumption was necessary, however, to predict the fall in the average size of class as oversize classes are eliminated: the Council assumed that the mean would fall at the same rate as the 95th percentile. For example, for pupils under 15, the 95th percentile in 1964 was 38 pupils: as the 95th percentile fell to 31 and hence classes with more than 30 pupils were eliminated it was assumed that the average size of class would fall in the ratio 31:38.

In effect the Council assumed that the size of *all* classes would fall at the same rate. It did not therefore consider the possibility of altering the existing distribution by reducing the size of only those classes with more than 30 pupils: if it had done so, the average size of class necessary to eliminate oversize classes would have been somewhat larger than assumed.

Values of the average size of class (P_t/n) were calculated in this way separately for pupils under 15, and for pupils of 15 and over but not in the sixth form. These were multiplied by the respective values of K to give the projected pupil—teacher ratios. These turned out to be 16.7 for pupils under 15 and 14.5 for pupils of 15 and over but not in sixth form. The pupil—teacher ratio used for sixth form pupils was taken directly from the 1964 survey. The Council considered that the complicated calculations carried out for the pupils in secondary schools who were not in sixth form were unnecessary in the case of sixth form pupils '. . . since the elimination of oversize classes does not arise' (DES, 1965, Appendix C, para. 10). However, data from the 1964 survey given in Appendix C of the Ninth Report show that 2.3 per cent of classes for pupils in the sixth form still exceeded 30. The Council again clearly assumed that complete elimination of oversize classes was impossible and that the distribution in 1964 — with nearly 1 per cent of classes with more than 40 pupils — was acceptable.

To summarize, the ratios actually used in the Report are collected together in Table 10.1. We have also calculated projected ratios for secondary school pupils for three types of schools using the data and methods in Appendix C of the Ninth Report.

The figures show that there is clearly a wide variation between the three types of school but the Council did not apparently try to discover the reasons for it. The differences are too large to be attributed solely to sampling variability and they would seem to reflect a systematic difference in the structure of different types of school: they might have arisen because of differences in the number of pupils in remedial classes, or in the subjects taught, or in the ability of students, and so on. But whatever the reasons, it is clear

TABLE 10.1

PUPIL—TEACHER RATIOS, ENGLAND AND WALES, 1964

Age group	Projected for use in Ninth Report	Projected for secondary schools using data in Ninth Report		
		Modern	Grammar	Comprehensive
Juniors (i)	26.3	.	.	.
(ii)	19.7	.	.	.
Pupils 14 and under	16.7	16.6	18.4	16.9
Pupils 15 — but not in sixth form	14.5	13.1	16.4	14.5
Sixth form	10.6	9.2	10.9	9.1

Source: Based on data from DES (1965).

Note: (i) To eliminate classes over 40; (ii) To eliminate classes over 30.
. = not applicable.

that the weighted average used in the Ninth Report included an implicit assumption that these differences would continue to exist and that the distribution of schools by type would remain constant over time.

The pupil—teacher ratios used in the Ninth Report were based not on calculated norms or on technological optima but simply on the manipulation of observed statistics. It is clear that substantially different projections of demand would have been obtained if different pupil—teacher ratios had been employed. For example, if the Council has adopted the pupil—teacher ratios in grammar schools as desirable targets, the demand for teachers in secondary schools, except in sixth forms, would have been smaller by about 10 to 15 per cent. The Council clearly recognized the limitations of basing demand projections on such pupil—teacher ratios. For example, it noted that 'this approach may be too narrowly based and may not allow sufficiently for the effects of educational and social factors on the relationship between class sizes and pupil—teacher ratios' (DES, 1965, Appendix 6, para. 10).

Despite the Council's warning, the DES has used the ratios in the Ninth Report in its revised projections for the demand of teachers to 1986 (DES, 1969A). Indeed, the DES noted there that 'recent events have cast doubts on whether it is any longer possible to identify a particular limit on size of class with a particular pupil—teacher ratio', and that 'the proportion of primary classes which are oversize has diminished more rapidly than might have been expected, given the change in the pupil—teacher ratio, but the reverse has been true of secondary classes' (DES, 1969A, p. 77). The DES, therefore, appears to be well aware of the severe weaknesses of using rigid pupil—teacher ratios for forecasting the demand for teachers.

Pupils in schools

Projections of pupils in school were derived using population projections by age group which had been prepared by the Government Actuary. It is well known that population projections are generally subject to wide margins of error mainly because of the difficulty of forecasting fertility and migration. This was recognized in the Ninth Report where it was noted that the use of alternative (high and low) projections prepared by the Government Actuary would have changed the projected demand for teachers in 1976 by ± 10,000.

266

Although the methods used for projecting the number of pupils were not described in the Fifth Report, we can nevertheless compare the projections with actual estimates in order to illustrate the substantial errors which may arise. Percentage projection errors have been calculated for the period 1956—68 and these are shown in Figure 10.1.

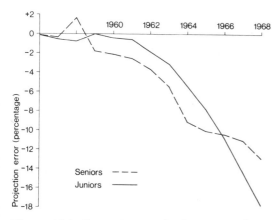

Figure 10.1. Percentage projection errors for pupils in school, England and Wales, 1956—1968.

Source: Projections: Ministry of Education (1957); actual: DES (1969).

Note: Percentage projection error = $\left(\dfrac{\text{Projected} - \text{actual}}{\text{Actual}} \right) 100$

The graph shows that the projections were in almost all cases under-estimates of the actual numbers of pupils in school. For juniors, the figures became noticeably less accurate from about 1962. This is probably due to the fact that the projections before that year were based on children already born: errors in forecasting births therefore dominated the projection errors in the period 1963—8. For seniors, the figures gradually became less accurate over the entire period: here the errors might have arisen because of errors in forecasting the proportion of pupils staying on at school after the school leaving age.

In the Ninth Report, the methods used to obtain the projections of pupils in the maintained schools were described in detail. Here the Council started with population projections for children of 5 and over but below the school leaving age which were equivalent to the projected numbers of pupils in *all* schools. For those below 5 and those at about the school leaving age, however, assumptions had to be made about the proportion entering and staying on at school: the

267

Ninth Report assumed that the proportion of 4-year-olds in school would rise from 17.66 per cent in 1963 to a maximum of 25 per cent in 1977, and that there would be a constant annual increase in the proportion of each age group staying on after the school leaving age. Note that an adjustment was also made for the raising of the school leaving age to 16, but that no attempt was made to allow for the secondary effects of the change, that is, for any significant increase in the proportion of children over 16 staying on at school.

Projections of the pupils in maintained schools were derived by making projections of pupils in 'non-maintained' schools and subtracting these from those for all schools. These 'non-maintained' schools included independent schools, direct grant schools, special schools, maintained nursery schools, and so on.

The assumptions which were used to provide these projections were quite detailed and they were generally different for different age groups and for different kinds of school. For example, for direct grant schools, it was assumed that the 'numbers in school aged 10 and under will remain constant, and numbers aged 11 to 15 will increase by 12,000 (16 per cent) between 1963 and 1990' (DES, 1964, p. 2); similarly the 'percentage of five year old children who are in independent schools will fall from 4.28 per cent in 1963 to 2.24 per cent in 1990' while the numbers of entrants '. . . aged 6 to 11 and (the) net numbers of leavers aged 12 and 13 will grow in

TABLE 10.2

PERCENTAGE PROJECTION ERRORS IN NUMBERS OF PUPILS IN SCHOOL, ENGLAND AND WALES, 1964—68

Year	Infants		Other juniors		Seniors 14 and under		Seniors 15 and over	
	(i)	(ii)	(i)	(ii)	(i)	(ii)	(i)	(ii)
1964	1.1	1.4	0.3	0.3	0.1	0.2	3.8	3.4
1965	1.2	1.6	0.6	0.3	—0.8	—0.2	1.9	2.0
1966	1.7	2.2	0.9	0.9	—1.1	—0.8	—0.3	0.2
1967	2.3	2.6	0.9	1.1	—1.1	—0.8	—3.6	—2.3
1968	2.2	2.8	0.9	1.3	—1.0	—0.5	—7.9	—5.9

Source: Based on data from DES (1964) and (1969B).
Note: (i) Maintained primary and secondary schools; (ii) All schools.
Percentage projection error = $(\frac{\text{Projected}-\text{Actual}}{\text{Actual}}) 100$.

proportion to the growth of population in the relevant age-groups'. It is not clear however that assumptions of such detail will necessarily reduce the projection errors.

Percentage projection errors have also been calculated for the period 1964—68 for the figures used in the Ninth Report; these are shown in Table 10.2 for the four groups of pupils distinguished, and separately for maintained and for all schools.

The projection errors for infants and for seniors of 15 and over are the most interesting. For infants, the projections consistently over-estimated the actual numbers probably because of an over-estimate in the proportion of 4-year-olds in school. For seniors of 15 and over, the errors are larger, and an original over-estimation error has now been removed by an increasing under-estimation bias. This increasing trend is moreover very marked and clearly arises because of under-estimation of the proportion staying on at school after the school leaving age. This error will probably be much smaller for future projections since the DES have now fitted exponential (rather than linear) trends to the proportions staying on at school after 15 (DES, 1969B, p. xix).

The figures also show that the percentage projection errors for the maintained schools are of roughly the same size as those for all schools. However, since the projections of pupils in the maintained schools were obtained as residuals, it is interesting to compare the errors here directly with those for all schools. Pupils in maintained primary and secondary schools represented over 92 per cent of pupils in all schools in 1963 so that the projection errors there should be expected to form roughly that proportion of projection errors for all schools. The figures in Table 10.3 show that this has not been the case.

TABLE 10.3

PERCENTAGE PROJECTION ERRORS OF NUMBER OF PUPILS IN MAIN-TAINED SCHOOLS AS A PERCENTAGE OF THOSE FOR ALL SCHOOLS, ENGLAND AND WALES, 1964—68

Year	Infants	Other juniors	Seniors 14 and under	Seniors 15 and over
1964	81.1	82.9	48.9	147.3
1965	69.7	172.5	388.6	78.5
1966	74.0	83.7	118.9	−169.2
1967	62.7	77.0	129.7	129.3
1968	74.3	66.5	166.1	111.7

Source: Based on data from DES (1964 and 1969B).

For infants and other juniors, the errors for the maintained schools were (with one exception) proportionately smaller than would have been expected. This means that errors for the 'non-maintained' schools were in fact in the same direction as those for all schools so that the errors for the residual maintained schools were therefore improved. For seniors however, the reverse was true: the errors for the 'non-maintained schools' were generally in the opposite direction to those for all schools so that the errors for maintained schools became worse than would have been expected.

Projected and 'actual' demand for teachers

We can extend this type of empirical assessment and try to determine the effects of these errors in the projections of pupils on the projected demand for teachers. Thus we define 'actual' demand for teachers to mean the projected pupil—teacher ratio divided into the actual number of pupils, and we compare these with the published projections.

TABLE 10.4

PROJECTED AND ACTUAL DEMAND FOR TEACHERS, ENGLAND AND WALES, 1956- 68 (thousands)

Year	Fifth Report			Ninth Report		
	Projected	Actual	Error	Projected	Actual	Error
1956	302	303	− 1	.	.	.
1957	309	311	− 2	.	.	.
1958	315	316	− 1	.	.	.
1959	322	325	− 3	.	.	.
1960	324	328	− 4	.	.	.
1961	326	332	− 6	.	.	.
1962	322	332	−10	.	.	.
1963	314	329	−15	.	.	.
1964	308	333	−25	342	339	3
1965	305	335	−30	342	341	1
1966	302	338	−36	345	346	−1
1967	301	344	−43	351	351	0
1968	299	353	−54	359	361	−2

Source: Based on data from Ministry of Education (1956), DES (1965) and (1969B).
Note: Actual = Actual number of pupils divided by pupil—teacher ratio.
· = not applicable.

The figures in Table 10.4 show that the errors in the projected demand of teachers which arose because of errors in the projections for pupils were fairly small for about the first five years of the projection period. The projection errors in the Fifth Report rapidly increased from 1962 and by 1968 the error was roughly 15 per cent. This illustrates clearly that the erroneous forecasts of births have generated substantial errors in the projected demand for teachers.

The question which arises is this: in view of the effects of the large errors in the population projections on the projections of teacher demand, was it worth making a forecast? The question is difficult to answer positively, but we can go some way towards an answer by comparing the errors with the errors which would have arisen if no forecast had been made at all. Thus in Figure 10.2, we compare the time path of errors in the Fifth Report (Model I) with those which would have arisen if it had been assumed that population — and hence teacher demand — would remain at the level observed in 1955 (Model II). The graphs show that Model I did appreciably better than Model II, for about the first eight years of the projection period, but that afterwards there was little difference between the two. Thus as the length of the projection period increased, the forecasting errors increased so much that the errors became as large as would have been obtained if no forecast had been made.

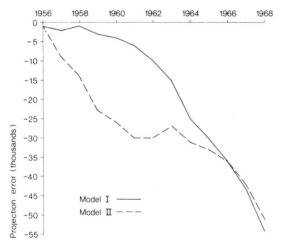

Figure 10.2. Comparisons of errors in demand for teachers using two different models, England and Wales, 1956—1968.

Source and note: Model I is based on projections in Ministry of Education (1956); Model II is based on the observation for 1955 only (see text).

271

Supply forecasts

Supply was used by the Council to mean the stock or employment of teachers, and forecasts were derived by separately projecting annual changes through recruitment and wastage (that is loss through mortality, retirement and occupational mobility). In the Fifth Report the methods used were simple: annual recruitment and wastage were assumed to remain constant at 14,000 and 7,000 to 8,000 respectively, that is at roughly the levels observed in the years preceding the report. An attempt was also made to take account of the effects of introducing the three-year training course on the assumption that the intake of the colleges of education would remain constant.

The assumptions about recruitment and wastage turned out to be disastrously wrong, mainly because of the Council's later recommendations to expand the intake of the colleges of education. For the year ended March 1967, recruitment was roughly 35,000 while wastage was about 29,000. The Fifth Report thus substantially under-estimated both annual recruitment and wastage. But the forecast of the net gain, the difference between recruitment and wastage, was almost exactly right.

In its later reports, the Council increased the detail of the supply forecasts enormously. For example, in the Ninth Report, projections of recruitment and wastage were made separately for full-time and part-time graduates and for full-time and part-time non-graduates; but within each of these four groups, different assumptions were made for each sex and for different age groups. The process of disaggregation has been extended by the DES and its revised forecasts were based on separate projections for 16 groups of teachers; within these groups different assumptions were made for many more sub-groups.

The presentation here would be rather complicated if we were to consider all of these detailed assumptions. For this reason, we have restricted our examination to the methods used in the Ninth Report for projecting full-time non-graduate teachers. This group represented slightly more than 75 per cent of the total supply of qualified teachers in maintained primary and secondary schools in 1963, and the projections suggest that in 1986 they will still form more than 70 per cent of the total. Projection errors here will therefore be relatively more important than those in the other groups.

Annual recruitment was derived by separately projecting entrants from colleges of education and other institutions together with the

TABLE 10.5

STUDENTS ADMITTED TO INITIAL TRAINING IN COLLEGES OF EDUCATION, ENGLAND AND WALES, 1965—68 (thousands)

Year	Recommended by Robbins Committee	Recommended in Ninth Report	Actual
1965—66	24.6	.	29.6
1966—67	25.0	26.0	34.0
1967—68	26.4	27.5	36.2

Source and notes: Figures include art training centres and colleges of education (technical). Figures in Robbins and Ninth Report recommendations are taken from DES (1965), para. 73 and 118. The actual figures obtained from DES (1969A) differ for the years 1960—1 and 1964—5 from the actual figures cited in the Ninth Report. It is not clear why this should be so but it appears to be connected with the double-counting of students admitted in January and April. The actual figures here are therefore probably not strictly comparable with the recommendations but they serve to illustrate the degree of under-estimation.

. = not applicable.

number of re-entrants, that is, the number of persons previously employed in the schools. For entrants from colleges of education, the recommendations of the Robbins Committee were used together with assumptions about the in-course and end-of-course wastage, which varied by type of course and sex. At this point it is interesting to note that in the Ninth Report the Council made recommendations about the expansion of the colleges of education on the basis of comparison of its demand and supply forecasts. Since its recommendations exceed those of the Robbins Committee its supply forecasts would automatically be invalidated if its recommendations were accepted.

The figures in Table 10.5 show that the actual expansion in the student intake of the colleges of education has exceeded not only the recommendations of the Robbins Committee but also those of the Ninth Report. From the comparison it is clear that the assumptions made in the Ninth Report about the expansion of the colleges of education will have introduced a substantial under-estimation bias in the supply forecasts.

The Report also assumed that the sex balance of students admitted to the colleges of education would be changed in an effort to reduce in-service wastage. The proportion of male students was expected to increase from the then current level of about 30 per cent

273

to 36 per cent by 1970 and to 39 per cent by 1974. In practice the proportion has not increased and in 1967 it was still only 29.5 per cent. Since wastage rates are much higher for women than for men, the projection error in the sex composition of entrants would have introduced an over-estimation bias in the supply forecasts, but this error will probably only be important for the forecasts near the end of the projection period.

Separate assumptions about re-entry were made for men, single women and married women. The Council recognized that the number of re-entrants may be related to the pool of qualified teachers no longer engaged in teaching but because of lack of data, cruder methods had to be used. For men and single women, the number of re-entrants at each age group was expressed as a proportion of the intake of the colleges of education and this proportion was projected forward. For married women, the report cited the Kelsall survey (1963) which suggested that women who return to teaching do so at roughly equal rates over the 20-year period after their first break of service. This prompted the Council to use the ratio of returners in any one year to the average annual wastage of women under 40 for the preceding 20 years, to forecast re-entry. The ratio was 0.70 in 1961—62, the only available observation year, and the Council assumed that it would fall to 0.55 in 1985—86 because of increasing opportunities for part-time service. On this basis the number of married returners was projected to increase from 4,000 in 1961—62 to 10,000 in 1985—86. It is clear that the assumption about the size of the ratio would have had a substantial effect on the number of returners projected: for example, if the ratio had been assumed to remain at 0.70 instead of falling to 0.55, the number of returners in 1985—86 would have been 12,700 instead of 10,000.

Wastage during service has often been described as the heart of the supply problem but no attempt was made to investigate the effects of alternative wastage rates on the supply forecasts. This weakness has now partly been corrected, and recent projections (DES, 1969A) include two alternative assumptions about the course of wastage rates: that wastage rates will increase linearly (i) until 1969—70 and (ii) until 1973—74, and remain constant thereafter. This alone has generated a difference of 34,000 in the supply of teachers projected for 1986.

In the Ninth Report, the Council argued that the growth of opportunities in the further education sector had been an important cause of the observed increase in wastage rates for men below 60. Since its calculations suggested that the growth of further education

274

would slacken noticeably, it assumed that the wastage rates for 1961—62 would apply throughout the period to 1986.

For women under 35, the method used is not completely clear. The Council apparently started with an association observed between wastage rates and the product of the marriage rate and the fertility rate for first births. This association together with the Government Actuary's projections of the marriage and fertility rates suggested that wastage rates would decline over the period. However, the Council decided to adopt a cautious approach and assumed that the rates would continue to increase though as a somewhat lower rate than in the years immediately preceding the Report. It is therefore not clear that the observed association between wastage rates and product of the marriage and fertility rates — which might well have been spurious — was in fact used for projecting wastage rates. For women aged 35—39, wastage rates were assumed to remain at the levels of 1962—63 while for men and women over 60, the rates for 1961—62 were applied.

Wastage rates for the years since the Report have all been substantially higher than those projected by the Council. This is illustrated in Table 10.6 where the actual observations for 1967 are compared with the Council's projections. In fairness to the Council it should be

TABLE 10.6

WASTAGE RATES BY AGE AND SEX (NON-GRADUATE TEACHERS), ENGLAND AND WALES, 1966—67 (per cent)

Age group	Men		Women	
	Assumed	Actual	Assumed	Actual
24 and under	3.3	7.5	..	16.2
25—29	5.2	7.5	..	23.1
30—34	3.4	5.1	..	14.5
35—39	2.3	3.9	6.2	8.6
40—44	1.8	2.7	4.1	5.4
45—49	1.5	2.2	3.0	4.0
50—54	}1.6	1.9	}2.8	3.6
55—59		2.4		5.0
60 and over	23.5	23.7	29.6	34.4

Source: DES (1965) and (1969A).
Note: Projections for women in the first three age groups were not published in the Report.
.. = not available.

noted that there was a break in the continuity of the series between 1962 and 1963 so that the two sets of figures are not strictly comparable. But the rates appear to fluctuate markedly from one year to the next and it is difficult to establish clear trends.

These examples for full time non-graduates are sufficient to demonstrate the detailed calculations used in the Ninth Report in forecasting the supply of teachers. The Council's implicit assumption, which has apparently also been made by the DES, was that this level of detail would necessarily improve the accuracy of the forecasts. This is a question to which we now turn.

Projected and actual supply

TABLE 10.7

PROJECTED AND ANNUAL SUPPLY OF FULL-TIME TEACHERS, ENGLAND AND WALES, 1956—68 (thousands)

Year	Projected	Actual	Percentage projection error
1956	247	247	
1957	254	252	0.8
1958	261	256	2.0
1959	268	262	2.3
1960	272	268	2.6
1961	282	273	3.3
1962	288	278	3.4
1963	284	277	2.5
1964	287	280	2.5
1965	290	284	2.1
1966	293	291	0.7
1967	295	296	—0.3
1968	298	304	—2.0

Source: Projected: Ministry of Education (1956); actual: Ministry of Education (1961) and DES (1969A and B).
Note: Projections assumed introduction of the three-year training course for teachers in 1960.
· = not applicable.

In the Fifth Report, projections of supply were published for each year from 1956 to 1968. These are compared in Table 10.7 with

TABLE 10.8

PROJECTED AND ACTUAL SUPPLY OF FULL-TIME TEACHERS, ENGLAND
AND WALES, 1965 (thousands)

	Non-graduates		Graduates		Graduates non-graduates		
	Men	Women	Men	Women	Men	Women	Total
Projected	84.8	136.5	41.5	21.6	126.3	158.1	284.4
Actual	84.1	140.9	37.5	21.4	121.6	162.3	283.9

Source: Projected: Ministry of Education (1962); Actual: DES (1969A).

actual estimates of teachers in full-time service.

The projection errors are remarkably small even for 1968. As we
noted above, the errors in recruitment and wastage almost cancelled
each other so that the forecast net addition to stock was almost
exactly correct.

In the later reports, supply projections were presented only for
selected years so that only limited comparison is possible. The only
year for which the projections in the Seventh Report can be compared with observations is 1965: this is done in Table 10.8. The
forecast for the total number of teachers is remarkably close to the
actual number in service in that year. But when we examine the
separate groups shown, we see that the projection errors for female
non-graduates and for male graduates more or less compensated for
each other in the projected total number of teachers.

Estimates of teachers in full-time service in 1968 are compared in
Table 10.9 with the forecasts for that year published in the Ninth

TABLE 10.9

PROJECTED AND ACTUAL SUPPLY OF FULL-TIME TEACHERS, ENG-
LAND AND WALES, 1968 (thousands)

	Non-graduates		Graduates		Graduates and non-graduates		
	Men	Women	Men	Women	Men	Women	Total
Projected	97	148	43	22	140	170	310
Actual	89	145	39	23	128	168	297

Source: Projected: DES (1965); actual (1965): DES (1970).

Report. The figures suggest that there were substantial errors in the projections in the Ninth Report for both graduate and non-graduate men. Thus there appears to be a change in the pattern of projection errors observed for 1965. The errors were moreover apparently in the same direction so that the total number of teachers also seems to show substantial error. But it is also clear that there was some cancelling out of errors at the various stages of the exercise. For example we noted above that the Council had seriously *under-estimated* the expansion of the colleges of education; but the errors in the aggregates are *over-estimation* errors, thus suggesting that there was an over-compensation for errors in the projections of students entering the colleges.

These errors suggest that in the long run the more detailed methods will not perform appreciably better than those used in the Fifth Report. The most important source of error undoubtedly lies in the projection of future wastage. Wastage rates vary enormously by age, and disaggregation into several age groups may be expected to improve the accuracy of the projections if the age structure of the teaching force were to change substantially. But it is clear that any gains from disaggregation may be quickly swamped by errors in the predicted course of wastage rates for each of the age groups.

It is obvious that detailed models of the type used by the DES may be necessary for some purposes. But they seem to introduce an unnecessary complexity in obtaining projections for fairly broad aggregates: this complexity tends, moreover, to create the mistaken impression of high statistical reliability. Aggregate models are simple and more easily understood and, until we know more about why wastage rates change over time, they may not prove appreciably less accurate than more detailed models.

Recommendations by the Council

Throughout its reports the Council seemed to recognize that the forecasts of demand and supply were subject to substantial error. This was explicitly emphasized in the Ninth Report but the Council nevertheless chose to present the forecasts '. . . with a greater degree of precision than they can properly claim' since it allowed '. . . the balance between demand and supply . . . to be more easily compared . . .' (DES, 1965, para. 13). This approach in fact allowed the Council to make its recommendations as if the projections could be expected to be fairly accurate, and as a result it failed to recognize

278

TABLE 10.10

DEMAND AND SUPPLY FOR TEACHERS,
ENGLAND AND WALES, 1956—68 (thousands)

Year	Demand	Supply
1956	302	247
1958	315	261
1960	324	275
1962	322	288
1964	308	287
1966	302	293
1968	299	298

Source: Ministry of Education (1956).
Note: The predictions assume the introduction
of the three-year training course in 1960.

the necessity for flexibility in planning the supply of teachers.

The comparison of demand and supply in the Fifth Report (reproduced in Table 10.10), suggested to the Council that the existing shortage of teachers would be substantially reduced in the early part of the 1960's and indeed that a surplus would tend to develop towards the end of that decade. The Council therefore concluded that the three-year training course could be introduced about 1959 or 1960 without much effect on the shortage of teachers or class sizes.

In retrospect, this turned out to be a very bad time for introducing the change. The lengthening of the training period caused a reduction in the supply of teachers from 1962 and hence at exactly the time that the under-estimation errors in the demand projections became substantial. The Council's recommendation therefore served to increase the shortage of teachers and caused a worsening of staffing standards.

If the Council had tried to allow for the presence of projection errors in its forecasts, it might well have made a less disastrous recommendation. For example, if it had allowed for a small margin of error of ± 5 per cent — which is not unreasonable when judged in terms of its methods — this would have been enough to suggest a shortage of up to 30,000 in 1968 instead of the predicted balance between demand and supply.

Despite these mistakes, the Council continued to compare its demand and supply forecasts to obtain projections of shortages and

TABLE 10.11

FORECASTS OF DEMAND AND SUPPLY OF TEACHERS, ENGLAND AND WALES, 1963—86 (thousands)

Year	Demand		Supply	Shortage (—) or Surplus (+)	
	(i)	(ii)		(i)	(ii)
1963 (actual)	334	·	280	— 54	·
1968	358	·	324	— 34	·
1972	420	·	380	— 40	·
1976	461	530	440	— 21	—90
1978	477	545	479	+ 2	—66
1981	491	562	540	+ 49	—22
1986	508	581	636	+128	+55

Source: DES (1965), p. 19.
Note: (i) Assumption that junior classes over 40 eliminated.
(ii) Assumption that junior classes over 30 eliminated.
· = not applicable.

surpluses. The comparison for the Ninth Report showed that the existing shortage of teachers would not be eliminated until the later 1970's or early 1980's. The Council expressed dismay at the slow improvement of staffing standards implied by its forecasts and it therefore recommended a minimum speeding-up of the Robbins Committee's proposals for the expansion of the colleges of education. Curiously, however, the Council did not recommend a *reduction* in the Robbins recommendations for the late 1970's even though the comparison showed that a substantial surplus would develop by 1986 (see Table 10.11).

It is again interesting to consider the effects of projection errors on the derived shortages and surpluses assuming an error of ± 5 per cent in the demand and supply forecasts. This margin is sufficient to generate a shortage between zero and 68,000 in 1968 and a surplus of between —6,000 and 185,000 in 1986. These variations are substantial and they must clearly raise some doubts about the validity of the Council's recommendations.

The Council was concerned here with planning the right scale of expansion of the student intake of the colleges of education. It did however explicitly recognize that the colleges of education provide only one — though, of course, the most important — source of supply of teachers, and hence that the existing shortages could be partially relieved by increased part-time service, by increased encouragement to qualified teachers to return to teaching, by reducing wastage, and so on. But it nevertheless placed the full burden of adjustment to the shortage only on the expansion of the colleges and took no account of efforts to increase supply from other sources.

Summary and conclusion

In the late 1940's the National Advisory Council on the Training and Supply of Teachers was set up by the Minister of Education to advise him on the training, recruitment and distribution of teachers in England and Wales. The Council tried to discharge this responsibility by studying the demand for special types of teachers, but its most ambitious work was concerned with forecasting the future demand and supply of teachers in maintained schools. It interpreted the differences between supply and demand as shortages (if negative) and surpluses (if positive) and on this basis it made recommendations about the adoption of the three-year teacher training course (Fifth Report) and the expansion of the colleges of education (Seventh and Ninth Reports).

Demand was defined by the Council as the number of teachers required to achieve the aims of staffing policy and was expressed in terms of desired pupil—teacher ratios. Although this is not demand in the economic sense of the number of teachers who will be offered employment at a given wage rate, it may nevertheless be useful for planning purposes because of the unique role of the government in regulating both the level of wages and the number of jobs available. But such targets are operationally meaningful only if they are measured in terms of the costs of achieving them. The Council recognized that its demand projections might have implied the use of too large a share of the country's resources but it considered that such questions were outside its terms of reference.

The target pupil—teacher ratios were derived by assuming, first, that the pupil—teacher ratio depends on the average size of class and, second, that the average size of class would fall at the same rate as the proportion of over-size classes. These simplifying assumptions meant the Council could relate demand directly to the elimination of over-size classes and hence to a highly desirable objective of educational policy.

It is easy to see that a decrease in the pupil—teacher ratio will not necessarily lead to a reduction in the average size of class or in the proportion of over-size classes. If the pupil—teacher ratio falls, any

281

extra teachers who become available may be used to increase the number of remedial classes, or to broaden the range of subjects taught, or in pursuing educational objectives other than the elimination of over-size classes. Evidence for recent years suggests that this has indeed been the case in secondary schools and that the proportion of over-size classes has fallen more slowly there than the Council had anticipated.

In trying to measure demand in this way, the Council merely confused the question of the future demand for teachers with the question of the elimination of over-size classes. These are quite separate though related issues and they obviously require quite different policies. Thus it may be possible to eliminate over-size classes by simply redistributing the existing supply of teachers. This may be encouraged by differential wage payments or by decree as in the 1969 circular to this effect (Ministry of Education, 1969).

The Council recognized that its methods were not really appropriate for forecasting demand, and that uncertainty about the future numbers of pupils in school would have introduced additional errors in its projections. Comparison of the projections with observations shows that the Council's doubts have been confirmed: the errors in the projections of pupils in school have tended to increase over time mainly because of increasing errors in the forecasts of the number of births.

On the supply side, forecasts were obtained by estimating annual changes in employment through recruitment and wastage (that is, loss through mortality, retirement and occupational mobility). In the Fifth Report, the model used was simple and fairly crude and recruitment and wastage were each assumed to remain roughly constant. In practice, these assumptions have turned out to be very substantially wrong; recruitment has increased enormously mainly because of the later recommendation by the Council to expand the intake of the colleges of education. But wastage appears to have kept pace with recruitment so that the net addition to employment has remained almost constant. It almost seems as if the enormous expansion of the colleges of education has made no contribution at all towards reducing the teacher shortage.

The Council considerably increased the detail of its supply projections in the Seventh and Ninth Reports. Thus, separate estimates were made for several different groups of teachers and wastage rates were projected for different age and sex groups. Only limited empirical assessment of these projections has been possible so far, but it does not appear that this level of detail has improved the accuracy of the forecasts. The reason for this is probably that the gains from disaggregation are being swamped by large errors in forecasting the future course of wastage rates.

The Council was well aware of these limitations in its forecasts and it repeatedly emphasized this throughout its reports. Curiously, however, it chose to present them, and indeed to make its recommendations, as if they could be expected to be accurate. If it had allowed for a small margin of error of ± 5 per cent in its projections this would have been sufficient to suggest that many of the projected shortages could in fact turn out to be surpluses, and vice versa. This uncertainty would, moreover, have implied quite different planning policies for the future. For example, it might have become clear that the introduction of the three—year teacher training course should have been spread over a number of years, or that the intake of the colleges of education should have been expanded at the same time, to allow for the possibility that the actual shortage might have turned out to be greater than expected.

Since the publication of the Ninth Report in 1965, the Council has apparently ceased to exist. However, its forecasting work has been continued by the DES which has recently published revised projections to 1986. On the demand side, the pupil—teacher ratios derived by the Council have again been used although the DES has explicitly stated that they may not be meaningful for planning purposes. On the supply side, the Council's methods have also been used but the DES has now introduced a slight improvement by including two alternative projections of wastage rates.

In principle it seems clear that these forecasting models can be considerably improved by detailed investigation of the utilization of teachers. If optimal pupil—teacher ratios exist, then they can be determined only by studying the technology in the education sector and by analysing the variation between the ratios for different subjects, institutions, geographic area, and so on. Similarly a thorough analysis of the factors affecting wastage and re-entry will provide better guidance for decision-making. Wastage remains the heart of the supply problem, and if the future course of wastage rates can be at all influenced by government policy — for example through relative wages or conditions of employment — this may provide a far less costly means of increasing supply than the expansion of the colleges of education.

In practice, planning cannot be delayed until we have built completely satisfactory and realistic models and crude models have to be used in the meantime. But crude models should be kept simple so their limitations may be more easily understood. In addition it is important to examine the sensitivity of the projections to changes in the basic assumptions in order to identify the necessity for flexible planning.

The models currently used by the DES are crude but, because of the level of detail used, they create the false impression of high statistical reliability. The demand projections are moreover couched in terms of the elimination of over-size classes even though achievement of this desirable educational objective cannot be guaranteed if the projected demands are met. Rigid planning based on these models has already led to a worsening of staffing standards in the schools; and if they continue to be used for decision-making in the same way, the costs in terms of the country's human resources may turn out to be higher still.

11. Doctors in Britain, Canada and the United States

by Bashir Ahamad

The interest in forecasting the number of doctors needed to ensure the provision of adequate medical services has had a somewhat longer history than general manpower forecasting. Poor health has long been considered to be a matter of bad luck and hence there has always been strong support for arguments that medical treatment should be available to all in need; indeed, the medical profession has always insisted that their services are available to all persons in need irrespective of their ability to pay. But in recent years, economic arguments have played an important part in strengthening the case for planning the supply of health services. Poor health often means lower productivity and hence benefits are lost both to individuals and to society. In addition a large and growing proportion of the national income is being allocated to the health sector and it seems important that these resources should be utilized in the most efficient way.

It is not surprising that in many of the attempts to plan the provision of adequate health services, doctors have been the focus of attention. They have traditionally played the central role in the provision of health services, and there has been a widespread belief that there is little room for the substitution of other types of health manpower for doctors. Moreover, the training period is long so that it seems clear that shortages of doctors — and hence of medical services — will tend to develop in the absence of planning. It has also been argued that it is fairly easy to forecast the number of doctors necessary to achieve given medical standards and to compare this with the number expected to be available on the basis of existing enrolments in medical schools, since membership of the profession is closely regulated by both legal and institutional controls. The case of doctors is also often quoted in the literature on manpower forecasting as an example of the close link between education and occupation and hence as an example of one area in which the

285

manpower forecasting approach to educational planning is clearly valid (Parnes, 1962, p. 18).

For these reasons, it is particularly appropriate that we should critically examine some of the methods used to forecast the number of doctors. We shall be looking at forecasts in Britain, Canada and the US and we shall try to compare the methods used in the three countries. A comparison of this type is interesting since the countries differ considerably in their social, political and economic structures. For example, in Britain education — and hence the expansion of training facilities for doctors — comes under the direct control of the central government; on the other hand, in Canada and the US education is controlled by the provincial and state governments and hence it cannot be directly influenced by the federal governments.

The markets for medical services in the three countries also differ. In Britain, medical services are available under the National Health Service at almost no direct cost to the individual; however, in the US, and in Canada until recently, medical services for most of the population are priced in the market like other services. Prices are often related to ability to pay, and although part of the cost of medical care can be covered by a health insurance scheme, prices will tend to play their usual role in equating demand and supply. Under both systems, the individual must first recognize the necessity for medical care but in a free market this medical need must be translated into effective demand by willingness to pay. Thus, *ceteris paribus*, the demand for medical care will tend to be lower in a market pricing system. This also suggests that the income-elasticity of demand for medical services may be higher in such a system so that expenditure on health services will tend to rise faster than income.

Finally, because of differences in the geographical structure of the three countries, special planning problems may arise. In Britain, the costs of providing medical services may be relatively smaller than those in Canada and the US because of the sheer physical size of the latter: because of the lower density of population in rural areas, medical services may therefore be offered at a higher price, or at a lower quality, in the latter.

Experience in Britain

In Britain, several attempts have been made to estimate the necessary expansion of medical schools on the basis of manpower forecasts. In 1941, the Interdepartmental Committee on Medical Schools (the Goodenough Committee) was set up to ' . . . enquire into the organisation of Medical Schools particularly in regard to facilities of clinical training and research . . .' (Ministry of Health, 1944). The Committee found it impossible to forecast the demand for doctors, but on the basis of their analysis, an annual student intake of 2,500 or 2,600 seemed to be desirable.

However, in the early 1950's, there was growing concern in the medical profession at the apparent difficulty young doctors faced in getting employment and hence pressure was brought to bear for a reassessment of the desired student intake. The Committee to Consider the Future Numbers of Medical Practitioners and the Appropriate Intake of Medical Schools (the Willink Committee) was duly appointed, and they recommended in 1957 that the annual student intake should be reduced to about 1,760 by 1970. The recommendation of the Committee thus corresponded closely with the prevailing view in the medical profession that too many doctors were being trained.

But only a few years later, various authorities argued that a severe shortage of doctors appeared to be developing in Britain. Growing public concern and increasing dissatisfaction in the medical profession itself led to the setting up of the Royal Commission on Medical Education ' . . . to review medical education . . . and in the light of national needs and resources . . . advise Her Majesty's Government on what principles future development . . . should be based . . .' (Royal Commission, 1968, p. 19). Manpower needs or demand where not specifically mentioned in their terms of reference but the Commission's initial investigations led to an urgent recommendation made in an interim memorandum that the annual intake of the medical schools should be increased without delay by at least 1,100. In their main report they further recommended that the annual average intake should be 2,600 in the period 1965–9, and that this should be almost doubled over the following 20 years.

On the face of it, the recommendations of the various bodies have been so contradictory and have apparently created such unsatisfactory manpower imbalances, that we may be tempted to dismiss the usefulness of such forecasts for planning and policy. But, as we shall see in a closer examination of these studies, the various bodies appear to have had more confidence in their recommendations than can be justified on the basis of their analyses and on available data. In addition, it seems clear that the recommendations were adopted for planning and policy without taking sufficient account of the qualifications attached to them by the bodies concerned.

The Goodenough Committee

The Goodenough Committee sensibly recognized that forecasts of the demand and supply of doctors could only be highly speculative because of the effects of the war on both the supply of civilian medical manpower and on the demand for medical care. This was particularly true in the case of demand since the Committee thought that large changes in the productivity of doctors seemed likely because of changes in the organization and size of practice and in the use of ancillary manpower. For these reasons, the Committee felt that it was impossible to make meaningful quantitative projections of demand and they concentrated their attention on investigating the effects of different student intakes on the future supply of civilian doctors.

These were derived in a fairly crude way. From specially collected data, the Committee estimated that: (a) 87.5 per cent of the annual student intake would eventually graduate; (b) 81.5 per cent of these would set up practice in Britain; (c) these new British graduates would represent 91.5 per cent of the number of doctors setting up new practices in Britain each year, the remaining 8.5 per cent coming from Ireland and from other countries.

These calculations are illustrated in Table 11.1 for two values of student intake: thus the Committee's assumptions suggested, for example, that an annual intake of 2,500 would be necessary to generate 1,950 new doctors in practice.

TABLE 11.1

ANNUAL INCREASE IN DOCTORS EXPECTED FROM A GIVEN STUDENT INTAKE, BRITAIN

Intake	Graduates i.e. (1) x 0.875	Setting up practice i.e. (2) x 0.815	Total new practices i.e. (3) ÷ 0.915	Net loss of graduates i.e. (2) − (4)
(1)	(2)	(3)	(4)	(5)
2,000	1,750	1,425	1,560	190
2,500	2,190	1,785	1,950	240

Source: Based on data from Ministry of Health (1944), p. 258.
Note: Net loss includes transfer to the armed forces.

288

These projections of the number of doctors estimated to be available, which in our terminology in Chapter 1 are 'policy-conditional forecasts', are highly sensitive in numerical terms to changes in the various assumptions. Thus, for example, if we assume that 85 per cent (instead of 87.5 per cent) of the intake will eventually graduate, and that all other figures are the same as in Table 11.1, then the number of new practices turns out to be 1,893 instead of 1,950 for an intake of 2,500.

The projected annual increases of doctors in practice, plus the existing stock, were then corrected for attrition in service through mortality and retirement. Three separate assumptions were made about the proportion of doctors in each age—sex group actively engaged in practice: one of these assumed that the proportions would all remain constant, while the other two assumed that they would decline at different rates after the war. On this basis, the Committee estimated the annual number of new practices — and hence of new students — necessary (i) to maintain the existing stock (45,400); (ii) to increase the stock to 50,000 in ten years; (iii) to increase the stock to 50,000 in 15 years and so on. In effect, the Committee derived forecasts of the annual student intake necessary to ensure a given number of doctors in practice at different points in time.

The figures in Table 11.2 illustrate two of the many projections made by the Committee. These suggested, for example, that if the stock of doctors in practice were to be increased to 55,000 by 1958, then the annual number of new practices necessary would lie be-

TABLE 11.2

ESTIMATED ANNUAL INCREASE OF DOCTORS IN PRACTICE TO ENSURE DIFFERENT STOCKS, BRITAIN, 1944–63

Stock	(a) 45,400 (existing stock)		(b) 55,000 by 1958	
Period	Projection (i)	Projection (ii)	Projection (i)	Projection (ii)
1944—48	1,650	1,650	1,650	1,650
1949—53	912	1,111	1,844	2,043
1954—58	1,007	1,045	2,049	2,086
1959—63	1,149	1,228	1,210	1,283

Source: Ministry of Health (1944), p. 255.
Note: The two different projections are based on different assumptions of proportions active.

tween 1,650 and 2,086. This meant in turn that the annual student intake would have to be between 2,000 and 2,500 or 2,600 (Table 11.1).

It is important to note that the Committee did not make a specific recommendation about the required size of the student intake. Their calculations simply demonstrated the effects of different assumptions about some of the relevant parameters on the stock of doctors in practice. In fact, the Committee explicitly noted that '. . . improvements in the health service implied in the Government's plans may necessitate . . . a larger number of doctors in practice . . . but also that it was . . . very doubtful . . . whether a final verdict can be made' (Ministry of Health, 1944, p. 112). Moreover, they recommended that '. . . a cautious policy on the question (of expanding training facilities) is the wiser course at the present time, particularly with regard to the establishment of new medical schools' (Ministry of Health, 1944, p. 113).

This was a sensible recommendation not only because of the difficulty of forecasting demand but also because of the sensitivity of the projections of the stock of doctors to changes in the relevant assumptions. However, it appears that despite the warning by the Committee, a decision was taken by the government of the day to expand the annual student intake to 2,500 or 2,600. Thus, although the Committee recognized the limitations of their projections, it appears clear that the planning authorities did not.

The Willink Committee

The methods used by the Willink Committee to '. . . estimate . . . the number of medical practitioners likely to be engaged in all branches of the profession in the future, and the consequential intake of medical students required' (Ministry of Health, 1957, para. 1), were quite different to those described above for the Goodenough Committee. This was understandable because of the different demand and supply conditions in peace-time and also because of the introduction of the National Health Service in 1948. There were three separate steps in the Committee's work: (i) an estimate of the number of doctors active in 1955, and of the number of doctors required to offset attrition through mortality and retirement in the existing stock; (ii) a forecast of the number of doctors necessary to meet the increased demand for services; (iii) an estimate of the student intake required to satisfy these demands.

In step (i), the estimated replacement demand for doctors was

290

derived by making assumptions about mortality and retirement. Step (ii) was rather more complicated and separate forecasts were made for different sectors of the health service: general practice, hospitals, local authorities, armed forces, and so on. In many cases, the Committee estimated current demand by current employment plus vacancies, and they then assumed that this would remain constant over time. But in other cases, rather complicated — but often arbitrary — assumptions were made; for example for general practice, it was assumed that the average number of persons per 'principal' should be 2,500 in urban areas and 2,000 in rural areas, and that the number of 'assistants' and 'trainee assistants' would be constant over time. [1]

In this way the Committee obtained precise numerical estimates of the future demand for doctors. In doing so they assumed implicitly not only that there is a simple and direct relationship between the number of doctors and the provision of medical services, but also that existing standards were optimal or, at least, desirable. Thus the Committee made no attempt to study the complex inter-relationship between the various parts of the National Health Service and between different types of health personnel, in the provision of medical care. It is also interesting to note that they took no account of expected changes in the productivity of doctors which the Goodenough Committee had considered to be so unpredictable that meaningful quantitative demand projections could not be made.

Of course, the Committee recognized that their projections were subject to large errors because of the uncertainty of the future. But they made their recommendations *as if* the projections were numerically precise. Thus their demand projections suggested that over the seven-year period 1955—61 the additional number of doctors required would be 12,720, which was slightly less than the estimated number of new doctors (12,985) expected on the basis of current enrolments. The Committee argued that the excess of 265 doctors would have gone some way towards eliminating the shortage of 625 principals in general practice estimated in 1955, and that the balance of this shortage would be more than met by a proposed reduction of 1,060 doctors in the medical staff of the armed forces. It therefore seemed likely to the Committee that a surplus of doctors would develop after 1961 if the student intake were maintained at the existing level. For this reason, the Committee recommended that the

---

[1] Principals own the capital of the practice and hence share in the profits. Assistants and trainee assistants are qualified doctors who are salaried employees of the practice.

annual student intake should be reduced to about 1,760, so that annual graduations would fall to about 1,655, that is, to about 170 less than output expected for the period 1955—61.

Shortly after the publication of the report, it became clear that the Committee had seriously under-estimated the demand for doctors. As a result their recommendations were severely criticized both inside and outside the medical profession. But most of the criticisms centred on the assumptions made by the Committee rather than on the methods used to forecast the demand for doctors. For example, it was argued that the Committee had substantially under-estimated both the growth of population — and hence the 'expansion' demand for doctors — and the emigration of doctors. These arguments have been borne out by the experience of the 1960's. Thus, by 1965 total population had grown by 11.5 per cent or about three times as fast as had been assumed by the Committee. Similarly, a comprehensive study on the emigration of doctors (Abel-Smith and Gales, 1964) showed that actual emigration was about twice as high as the level assumed by the Committee; the rise in the number of immigrant doctors over the same period has however reduced the projection error in the net loss of doctors by migration.

The Royal Commission: Projections to 1975

The Royal Commission made projections of doctor requirements for the period to 1975 using broadly the same methods as the Willink Committee. But the two sets of projections could hardly have been

TABLE 11.3

PROJECTED DEMANDS FOR DOCTORS (ANNUAL AVERAGES), BRITAIN, 1965—75

Source of demand	Royal Commission (1965—75)	Willink Committee (1965—70)
To maintain existing stocks	1,350	1,230
General practice	500	75
Hospitals	830	160
Net emigration	180	70
Other	210	100
Total	3,070	1,635

Source: Royal Commission (1968), and Ministry of Health (1957).
Note: Net emigration includes overseas service.

292

more different (Table 11.3): the Royal Commission projected the annual average number of doctors demanded over the period 1965—75 to be 3,070, while the comparable figure estimated by the Willink Committee was only 1,635 (for the period 1965—70).

The differences in each of the categories shown in Table 11.3 are all large, but the differences in general practice and hospitals alone account for more than 70 per cent of the total difference. For general practitioners, the difference is somewhat inflated since the Commission's figure included an adjustment for an estimated shortage of 1,000 principals in 1965, which was derived on the assumption that the desired number of patients per principal should be 2,180 — the lowest ratio ever observed (in 1961). But this only differed marginally from the Willink Committee's assumption of 2,500 in urban areas and 2,000 in rural areas. As we noted above, the erroneous population projections used by the Willink Committee also played a part in the difference.

However, the bulk of the difference in the projected requirements for general practitioners arose because of the different assumptions made about the growth of assistants and trainee assistants. The Willink Committee assumed that the *number* of such assistants would remain constant, while the Commission assumed that the *ratio* of assistants to principals should remain constant, after being restored to the 1955 level: the latter assumption implies that the number of assistants should increase as fast as the number of principals. On this basis the Commission projected requirements for an additional 1,700 doctors by 1975, that is, for 170 additional doctors per annum.

The Commission's assumption that the number of assistants should grow as fast as the number of principals followed naturally from their recommendation that prospective general practitioners should undertake a three-year period of professional training as assistants before becoming principals. But they failed to take account of this increase in assistants on the requirements for principals. A principal can increase the length of his patients' list by employing an assistant, so that an increase in the number of assistants will lead to an increase in the average number of patients per principal, and hence to a reduction in the requirements for principals. Thus the Commission's assumption treated assistants and principals as complements, rather than the substitutes they are, in the production of medical services, and this will probably mean that they have overestimated the requirements for general practitioners in 1975.

The difference in the projections of requirements for doctors for the hospital service was largely due to the way in which the two

projections were derived. The Willink Committee made their forecasts fairly arbitrarily and assumed a decline in annual requirements —
from 320 p.a. for 1955—65 to 160 p.a. thereafter — on the basis of
the scanty evidence available since the introduction of the National
Health Service. On the other hand, the Royal Commission used
estimates of doctor requirements made by the Health Departments
on the basis of the recommendations of the Joint Working Party on
Medical Staffing Structure in the Hospital Service (1961). However,
the Working Party had merely suggested several broad principles
which should be, kept in mind, rather than any hard and fast
rules, for determining doctor requirements in hospitals. As a result,
the estimated shortage in 1965 — 6,200 doctors — included in the
Commission's projection, was based in fact on the judgement and
subjective assessment of staffing needs by the various regional hospital boards.

To sum up, the projections made by the Willink Committee and
by the Royal Commission differed substantially mainly because of
the differences in the basic assumptions made by the two bodies. The
large differences between the two sets of projections illustrate that
the projections are extremely sensitive to changes in these assumptions. It therefore follows that unique projections may lead to
mistaken policy advice — as was the case in the Willink Committee's
report. Since the future is uncertain, there is no way of ensuring that
the assumptions made by the Royal Commission will turn out to be
any more accurate than those made by the Willink Committee. Thus
there is a very real danger that rigid plans based on the Commission's
projections will lead to a repetition of the mistakes that were made
in the past.

The Royal Commission: Long-term requirements

The Commission argued that their recommendations for the expansion of medical education depend on the requirements for doctors in the longer term, that is beyond 1975, and they therefore
extended their forecasts to 1990. But they recognized that forecasts
over such a long period '. . . must inevitably be tentative and plans
based on them must be flexible enough to be modified as circumstances change and more information becomes available' (Royal
Commission, 1968, p. 131).

The Commission did not think it appropriate to base their long-
term projections on the specification of requirements in the separate
parts of the National Health Service, and they based them instead on

TABLE 11.4

PROJECTED REQUIREMENTS FOR DOCTORS, BRITAIN, 1975

Projection		Doctor—population quotient	Number of doctors required
(i)	Royal Commission	1,385	78,100
(ii)	Log-linear regression	1,342	75,700
(iii)	Linear regression	1,278	71,100

Source: Based on data from Royal Commission, 1968.
Note: The doctor—population quotient is the number of doctors per 1,000,000 population.

projections of the doctor—population quotient, that is, the number of doctors per million population. They found that the quotient had grown at an almost constant rate in the period since 1911, and that a rate of growth of 1.25 per cent p.a. not only forced the curve through their projection for 1975, but also reproduced the variation over the seven observations fairly well. This seems to be reasonable from the graph included in the report, but the Commission made no attempt to test the goodness of fit by using statistical methods. If we assume a constant rate of growth and estimate the slope of the relevant log—linear regression equation, the best statistical estimate turns out to be 1.24 per cent p.a.; but the statistical fit is no better than that obtained by fitting a linear regression equation, which implies a *declining* rate of growth.

It is interesting to compare the projections for 1975 obtained using the three different methods (Table 11.4). If we assume that the Commission's estimate for 1975 represents the 'best' estimate for 1975, then the statistical regression models provide quite poor estimates. The large discrepancy illustrates the dangers of using purely mechanical models based on the doctor—population quotient for obtaining forecasts.

The Commission recognized that because of the uncertainty of the future, their long-term projections could be used only as very rough indicators for planning purposes. They rightly argued that future demand would depend on the use of alternative types of health manpower, on greater efficiency in the organization of medical work, on the importance of group practice, and other such factors which are often not quantifiable or predictable. But they failed to recognize the full limitations of using the doctor—population quotient for planning the expansion of medical schools.

The doctor—population quotient is obviously only a crude indicator of standards of medical care since it takes no account of the different demands of different groups of the population, and of the organization and structure of medical practice. Observed quotients represent the results of the working of the labour market and the adjustment of both demand and supply: they reflect, for example, the effects of government expenditure on the health services as well as the effects of enrolments in medical schools. For these reasons they may not represent optimal or even desirable standards of health service provision.

The direct extrapolation of the observed trend in the doctor—population quotient moreover implicitly assumes that all of the factors affecting the structural relationships between the number of doctors and the size of the population will continue to change as they changed in the past. It implies, for example, that emigration and immigration, enrolments in medical schools, the development of new treatments, the utilization of ancilliary health personnel and the productivity of doctors will all continue to change as they did in the past. Thus extrapolation can at best indicate what seems likely to happen if structural changes follow past trends, and not what is likely to happen if changes in structure are contemplated: in other words, in our terminology, extrapolation provides 'on-looker forecasts' rather than 'policy-conditional forecasts'.

The Commission recognized these limitations of their method but they nevertheless recommended that '. . . long-term plans should be made with the aim of reaching an annual British resident medical student intake of 5,000 by 1990' (Royal Commission, 1968, para. 367). This represents an enormous expansion: it is about two-and-a-half times the average annual intake of the period 1960—64 and about twice that estimated for the period 1965—69. Of course, the Commission recognized that such plans should be flexible because of the uncertainty of the future, but it would probably have been more sensible to recommend a moderate expansion until better forecasts become available: the costs of under-expansion may be much lower than the costs of over-expansion.

The Commission also tried to assess the implications of their recommendation both in terms of students qualified to enter university and in terms of the cost of undergraduate medical education. In the case of the former, they recommended a change in student selection procedures to help the medical schools maintain their share of the total student intake. On the cost side, they estimated that the cost of undergraduate medical education would rise from about

£30—£35 million in 1965 to about £80 million (in 1965 prices) in 1990; but since these estimates were based on crude data, they may well be low. The Commission recognized that 'no nation can afford to spend such sums without proper consideration' (Royal Commission, 1968, para. 415), but their concern was apparently confined to the proper allocation of *these* funds, rather than to the more general question of the costs and benefits of medical education.

Other experience in Britain

Forecasts of doctor requirements have also been made in various other studies of health and welfare services in Britain. For example, in 1966 the National Institute for Social and Economic Research published a study of the existing state of health service provision together with projections of doctor requirements for 1980 (Paige and Jones, 1966). The methods used by Paige and Jones were basically the same as those already described for the Willink Committee and for the Royal Commission: the authors concluded that on the basis of existing enrolments in medical schools, requirements would exceed stock by 9,000 in 1980.

Peacock and Shannon (1968) have strongly criticized the methods used and the conclusions reached by Paige and Jones. They argue that the future course of population growth and of emigration of doctors is so unpredictable that the projections of doctor requirements are necessarily subject to large errors. Moreover '. . . the (doctor—population) ratio does not measure the services of doctors . . . concentration on the ratio[2] means that changes in productivity and in the technology and organisation of medicine will tend to be ignored' (p. 33). Peacock and Shannon suggest that it is only by focussing attention on the *services* provided by doctors and hence on the substitutability of different types of health manpower and on their relative costs in the provision of these services that manpower planning problems can be satisfactorily solved. They further argue that to do so we need an appropriate index of health services, based perhaps on the number of days of restricted activity caused by illness. Changes in such an index could then be related to changes in the methods of providing health services and to changes in the productivity of doctors.

Experience in Canada

In Canada, forecasts of doctor requirements were made in a study

[2] The doctor—population ratio is the reciprocal of the doctor—population quotient.

of medical manpower (Judek, 1964) carried out for the Royal Commission on Health Services. The Commission was appointed in 1961 to 'report upon the existing facilities and the future need for health services . . . and the resources to provide such services, and to recommend . . . measures . . . (to) ensure that the best possible health care is available to all Canadians' (Royal Commission, 1964, Foreword). The Commission interpreted these terms of reference in the widest possible way and they commissioned the preparation of 26 separate research studies on relevant topics — medical manpower, medical education, utilization of nurses, dental manpower, paramedical manpower, a model of Canadian economic growth, etc.

Judek's study of medical manpower was largely devoted to the existing utilization of doctors and it covered an impressively wide range of topics. Thus he discussed and described some of the factors affecting the earnings of medical practitioners, their hours of work, the variation in the size of practice, the location of first practice, and so on. His findings are far too complex and detailed to be discussed in the brief evaluation we are attempting here. But it is important to note that Judek made his projections in a fairly broad economic and statistical framework.

Judek used several criteria to investigate the possible existence of a shortage of doctors. He argued that the wide variation in the doctor—population ratio between provinces indicated an inadequate distribution of doctors by province; comparison of the doctor—population ratio of Canada with that of other developed countries also indicated that Canada was relatively worse off in its stock of doctors. Similarly the wide variation in physician—visits[3] per capita suggested the existence of distributional shortages. In economic terms, incomes of doctors and dentists had risen consistently over the period 1946—60, while those of other professional groups had varied with economic conditions. The average income of doctors increased by 110 per cent over the period while total personal per capita income increased by 75 per cent. Doctors' fees increased much faster than the consumer price index — by 50 per cent and 31 per cent respectively — and the share of national expenditure on personal medical services increased from 1.09 to 1.56 per cent. Judek argued that all of this evidence was consistent with the existence of a shortage of doctors.

---

[3] A physician-visit is defined as a consultation with a doctor either in person or by telephone, in his office, in hospital or in the patient's home, for examination diagnosis, treatment or advice (see Judek, 1964, p. 268).

TABLE 11.5

SOME ALTERNATIVE PROJECTIONS OF REQUIREMENTS OF DOCTORS,
CANADA, 1966–86

Annual net immigration	Assumptions		Required number of doctors		
	Doctor–population ratio	Physican-visits per capita	1966	1976	1986
(1) —	Constant	•	23,362	28,300	34,673
(2) —	Increasing	•	24,357	32,123	42,878
(3) 50,000	Increasing	•	24,691	33,421	45,520
(4) 50,000	•	Observed	23,764	29,545	36,935
(5) 100,000	Increasing	•	25,025	34,719	48,163
(6) 100,000	•	Observed plus 23 per cent	30,107	38,364	48,848

Source: Judek (1964), p. 268 and pp. 294—95.
— = nil or negligible; • = not applicable.

Projections of the future number of doctors required were made by Judek under a number of different assumptions. These were derived using (i) projections of the doctor–population ratio and (ii) projections of physician-visits per capita, together with projections of total population. Judek used two assumptions about the doctor–population ratio: (a) that it would remain constant at its observed level and (b) that it would increase at the rate observed in the period 1951—61. Similarly, he used two assumptions about physician-visits per capita: (a) that they would remain at their existing level and (b) that they would increase by 25 per cent if the economic barriers to medical care were removed. Finally, because of the importance of immigration in the population growth of Canada, Judek made five different assumptions about the average annual level of net immigration, and hence five different population projections. On this basis, he arrived at 20 different projections of doctor requirements for each projection year. Some of these are reproduced in Table 11.5.

These calculations provide 'policy conditional forecasts' since they illustrate the range of possibilities for different policy alternatives. The range in the projections is extremely wide and it increases as the projection period increases: for 1966 it is about 7,700, but for 1986 it is about 14,200. The highest projection (for the period shown) assumes a net immigration of 100,000 p.a. and a change in the pricing of medical services, while the lowest projection assumes zero net immigration and a constant doctor—population ratio. The lowest projection provides an effective lower limit on the projections since it seems unlikely that net immigration will in the foreseeable future reach zero. In addition, Judek's analysis of the existing demand and supply situation for medical services seemed to indicate the existence of a shortage of doctors and hence suggested that the maintenance of the observed doctor—population ratio would be undesirable.

On the supply side, Judek assumed that the annual output of Canadian medical schools would be 800 in the period 1961—65, 900 in the period 1966—70 and 950 thereafter. He also assumed that the number of doctors expected on the basis of net immigration would be 350 p.a. until 1971 and 250 p.a. thereafter. Unfortunately Judek did not derive alternative projections of stock on the basis of different assumptions about the number of immigrant doctors, but it is clear that if the recently high rates of immigration should fall, the future stock of doctors may be substantially lower than predicted. Judek then derived projections of the number of doctors in active service, assuming attrition in service due to mortality and retirement of 3.2 per cent p.a. (Table 11.6).

Comparison of the projected requirements in Table 11.5 with the projected stock in Table 11.6, suggests that in, say 1976, there will be a shortage, in a sense, of between 700 and 11,000 doctors. On the basis of such comparison, Judek concluded that '. . . existing educational facilities and certainly the present output of our medical schools cannot satisfy our future needs for physicians' (Judek, 1964, p. 270). But he made no attempt to forecast the numerical expansion necessary and he seemed to recognize that such decisions had to be taken in a wider context with due regard of the future pattern of government expenditure and of the general development of the health services sector.

Judek's projections are subject to many of the same criticisms which we noted in our discussion of forecasts of doctors in Brit-

TABLE 11.6

PROJECTED STOCK OF DOCTORS IN
ACTIVE SERVICE, CANADA, 1966—86

1966	1976	1986
23,489	27,759	30,335

Source: Judek (1964), pp. 269—70.

ain. Thus although he undertook a fairly thorough analysis both of the existing demand for medical services and of the utilization of doctors in the provision of such services, he did not directly incorporate the effects of these factors in his forecasting model. For example, he did not explicitly estimate the effects of variations in the organization of medical care and the increased incidence of group practice or of increases in government expenditure on medical facilities on the supply of medical services. But in fairness to Judek, we should note that he did implicitly try to allow for the effects of changes in relative prices and in other omitted variables by making alternative assumptions about the values of the fixed coefficients, thus emphasizing the extreme uncertainty about the future employment of doctors.

Judek's use of physician-visits per capita as a basis for making projections represents a considerable improvement over the crude doctor—population ratio. The visit rate provides a means of estimating the effects of changes in the population structure and in the price of medical care on the demand for services; it also provides a means of separating out the effects of changes in the productivity of doctors from the average work-load of doctors in the provision of medical services. However the definition of physician-visit as used by Judek is not satisfactory since it weights different types of consultation equally in the index of output: ideally, the weights should reflect the different costs involved in the different types of consultation.

It is difficult to assess the effects of Judek's study on the ultimate recommendations of the Royal Commission on Health Services. As we noted earlier, 26 separate studies were prepared for the Commission. These were all undertaken independently of one another although the different aspects of the health services are in fact closely inter-related: for example, the necessary expansion of medical schools is closely related not only to the future requirements for doctors but also to the structure of medical education, the future growth of the economy, the availability of ancilliary personnel, and so on. Thus, in arriving at their recommendations, the Commission had to co-ordinate and integrate these independent research results in order to ensure that they were consistent with one another and with their own objectives. For example, they had to ask questions of this type: What expansion of medical schools would be consistent with the growth of the economy? How would the requirements for doctors be affected by increases in ancilliary personnel? What would be the costs of introducing a system of comprehensive medical care? Thus the Commission's work provides an excellent example of the true complexity of adopting manpower forecasts for planning and policy, and of the importance of decision-making in a wider and more general social and economic context.

Experience in the US

In the US, forecasts of doctor requirements and resources have been made over a long period of time using a number of different methods. These have been critically examined in many recent works (Fein, 1967; Klarman, 1969; Hansen, 1969) and we limit our discussion here to a brief description of some of the methods used.

The earliest study of doctor requirements dates back to the 1930's when Lee and Jones (1933) attempted to forecast doctor requirements on the basis of professionally determined standards. Their method consisted essentially of forecasting (i) the incidence of specific diseases in the population, (ii) the estimated physician-time required to diagnose and treat these diseases, and (iii) the hours worked per physician. Thus Lee and Jones were concerned with the number of doctors required to satisfy the medical needs of the population, and not with the economic demand for medical care. It may be desirable that medical needs should form the proper basis for planning the expansion of medical services, but in a free market the financial means must be provided for these needs to be expressed in terms of effective demand. Lee and Jones took no account of the necessity for a change in the methods of financing the cost of medical care in order to ensure that the additional stock of doctors would be efficiently utilized.

The most difficult part of the Lee and Jones study was the estimation of adequate medical standards. This was carried out by canvassing members of the profession; it is clear that this involves enormous problems of definition and measurement, and that there may be very little agreement on the necessary treatment. In addition, it is clearly difficult to predict not only changes in technology — for example, the introduction of a new drug — but also the side-effects of such changes. It is probably for these reasons that the Lee and Jones study has not been repeated.

Projections of doctor requirements were made by the President's Commission (1953) for 1960 on the basis of assumptions about the doctor—population ratio. The Commission made six different assumptions about the size of the ratio: these ranged from the national ratio

302

observed in 1940 to the average ratio observed in the New England and Middle Atlantic States in 1949, that is, a ratio somewhat above the national average. The corresponding projections of doctor requirements varied between 227,000 and 292,000, thus illustrating the sensitivity of the projections to changes in the assumptions about the size of the ratio.

The Surgeon-General's Consultant Group (Bane Committee) also used projections of the doctor—population ratio to make projections of doctor requirements in 1975. But unlike the President's Commission, the Bane Committee derived only one projection of requirements based on the existing doctor—population ratio. The Committee argued that the existing ratio represented the *minimum* goal if the supply of medical services were to continue at the existing levels and hence that their forecast of 330,000 doctors required provided the minimum target for the stock of doctors in 1975. The Committee also projected the stock expected on the basis of existing enrolment trends in medical schools and this differed from the forecast requirements by 27,000. These calculations therefore suggested that the output of the medical schools should be increased from the existing level of 7,900 p.a. to 11,000 p.a. over the fifteen-year period.

More recently, the US Public Health Service (1967) published three forecasts of doctor requirements in 1975. The projections were based on (i) professional judgement (400,000 doctors required); (ii) the highest doctor—population ratio in the four major regions of the US (425,000 doctors required); and (iii) the input—output model being developed by the Bureau of Labor Statistics[4] (390,000). These projections are all strikingly higher than the Bane Committee's projection (330,000) for the same year, thus illustrating how sensitive projections of doctor requirements are to differences in the forecasting model used, and to differences in the assumptions adopted. The projected requirements all exceed the projected stock of doctors in 1975 (360,000) and for this reason, the report recommended that the student intake to medical schools should be increased from 9,300 p.a. to 15,000 p.a.

Projections of physicians' services

We have already pointed out the limitations of using the doctor—population ratio as a basis for forecasting doctor requirements and

---

4 See Chapter 3.

we therefore limit our discussion here to the methods of Fein (1967) based on the physician-visit rate. Fein first projected the demand for physicians' services and the expected stock of doctors in 1975: these were then compared and the implied changes in the productivity of doctors were examined in the light of observed productivity growth. The projected changes in productivity seemed reasonably likely and hence the author concluded that an expansion of medical schools did not really seem to be necessary.

Fein assumed that the real price of medical care would remain constant[5] and that the physician-visit rate per capita would remain constant for different sub-groups of the population; for example, he assumed that the physician-visit rate would remain constant for each age—sex group, for each educational level, for each income level, and so on. Thus Fein derived his projected requirements for medical services by applying these rates to the projected structure of the population in 1975.

The results of Fein's calculations suggest that the largest component of the increased requirements for physicians' services will arise from the growth of the population. Thus the projected requirements will tend to be very sensitive to changes in the assumptions made about population growth. Fein tried to allow for errors in the population projections by deriving a range — as shown in Table 11.7

TABLE 11.7

PROJECTED CHANGES IN PHYSICIAN-VISITS, US, 1965– 75

Source of change	Percentage increase in physician-visits
Population growth	12.2—14.6
Age—sex distribution	1.0
Region and residence	0.2
Colour	0.5
Income	5.5— 6.0
Education	1.5
Medicare	1.0— 2.0
Total	21.9—25.8

Source: Fein (1967), p. 38 and 60.

---

[5] His demand projections are thus really projections of requirements in the terminology we have adopted (see Chapter 1).

304

for the projections of physician-visits required; but he pointed out that if he had in fact included two other population projections available to him, the range in total requirements would have been 18.7 per cent to 28.1 per cent (Fein, 1967, p. 30).

It should be noted that Fein's calculations assumed that the sources of change in the physicians' services required were independent and hence he took no account of the interaction between them. Thus, for example, since age and income are highly correlated, the requirements for physicians' services estimated for either age or income will clearly include some (or all) of the effects of the other variables. Thus it seems clear that his estimates will be biased upwards. Fein however considered that the figures represent a lower limit since additional (non-quantifiable) requirements for physicians' services will arise because of new discoveries, changing tastes, increased availability of services, and so on. He also pointed out that changes in government expenditure on health programmes, or a fall in the price of medical care would create substantial additional demands.

Fein also projected the stock of doctors in 1975 and this suggested an increase of 19 per cent in the period to 1975. Comparison of this change with the projected changes in the requirements for physicians' services (21.9 per cent to 25.8 per cent) thus suggested that only 'nominal' increases (3 per cent to 7 per cent p.a.) in the productivity of doctors would be necessary to ensure that these requirements could be met with the projected stock. Fein argued that such increases in productivity were consistent with its growth in recent years and they seemed likely because of changes in the organization and structure of medical practice, in the increased use of new drugs and modern medical equipment, and in the greater utilization of other types of health manpower. He further argued that increasing the student intake of medical schools — and hence the expected stock of doctors — would seem to be necessary only if any unsatisfied current demand for medical care is to be made effective through, say, the implementation of a universal medical care plan, or if it were felt desirable that the US should draw less of its medical manpower through immigration (approximately 1,600 p.a.). Fein suggested that the far more pressing problems appeared to be the reduction of distributional shortages in the provision of medical services, and greater efficiency in the supply of such services.[6]

---

[6] Jones et al., (1967) took broadly the same approach as Fein and came to the same conclusions.

TABLE 11.8

DOCTOR—POPULATION RATIOS, US, 1955—75

Year	Doctors per 100,000 population	Basis
1955	152	Observed
1965	156	Observed
1975 (i)	159—168	(i) Projected stock
1975 (ii)	189—200	(ii) Projected requirements

Source: Observations for 1955 and 1965: Fein (1967), p. 68. Projected stock and requirements: US Public Health Service (1967). Population projections for 1975: Fein (1967), p. 30.

Since physician-visits per capita are closely related to the doctor—population ratio[7], it may be surprising that Fain's conclusions should differ so substantially from recommendations based on projections of the ratio. But the figures in Table 11.8 suggest that the differences arise because of differences in *assumption* rather than in method. Thus the projected stock of doctors in 1975 produces a greater change in the doctor—population ratio in the period 1965—75 than that observed in the period 1955—65: hence Fein's conclusions are consistent with a simple extrapolation of the ratio over time. However, the requirements projected by the US Public Health Service — based on the highest ratio observed in four regions in the US — generate substantially higher ratios and hence implicitly assume either a fall in the productivity of doctors, or a rise in physician-visits per capita.

Conclusion

The studies we have described in this chapter indicate that forecasts of doctors have been used in Britain, Canada and the US for planning the student intakes to medical schools. The forecasts have all referred to requirements and stock — rather than to demand and supply in the economic sense (see Chapter 1) — since no attempt has been made to incorporate the effects of changes in the earnings of

[7] $\dfrac{\text{Number of physician-visits}}{\text{Population}} \times \dfrac{\text{Number of doctors}}{\text{Population}} \times \dfrac{\text{Number of physician-visits}}{\text{Number of doctors}}$

306

doctors on the number of employed. The methods used in the three countries have been fairly similar, but there have been marked differences in the interpretation of the forecasts and in their application for planning and policy. In some cases, the forecasts were treated as exact indicators of future outcomes with the consequence that the plans adopted were rigid. In other cases, alternative projections of requirements were generated by making different assumptions about the relevant parameters in order to provide policy-makers with a range of likely outcomes. But curiously few attempts were made to investigate the effects of alternative assumptions on the projected stock; for this reason methods of altering the future stock of doctors by means other than the student intake — for example, through retirement rates, or immigration — have not been properly investigated.

Not surprisingly, the doctor—population ratio has been a popular method for projecting doctor requirements: the ratio is simple to apply and the necessary data are often easily obtainable. But the ratio is only a crude indicator of standards of care and it can at best be expected to provide only crude indicators of future requirements. Observed ratios are the results of demand and supply forces and, because of differences in the socio-economic characteristics of the population at different points in time, they may imply sub-optimal or even undesirable standards of medical care. Of course, *in the absence of better information*, projections based on observed ratios may provide useful guide-lines for planning and policy, since they do at least take account of the influence of the changing population size. If the population is growing very rapidly, the costs of over-investment in medical training because of, say, the improved productivity of doctors, may be far smaller than the ultimate cost of under-investment on the health and productivity of the population. But plans based on the use of the ratio must be flexible and subject to continuous revision as more up-to-date and better information becomes available.

In many of the studies we examined, we found that the ratio was used as if it represented a direct relationship between the demand for medical services and the number of doctors *necessary* to provide those services; consequently the projections were interpreted in a very rigid way for planning purposes. Hansen (1969) has rightly argued that this approach takes no account of the possibility of substituting other types of health personnel for doctors in the production of medical services. Peacock and Shannon (1968, p. 38) further argue that 'if we go on making estimates of needs of doctors which assume that the traditional professional training and occupation of doctors is sacrosanct, we encourage the expectation that there will always be funds available to allow the projected number of doctors to retain the economic and social status which they have enjoyed for so long'. Thus Peacock and Shannon believe that we encourage the maintenance of the institutional rigidities which exist in the training of medical manpower and in the provision of medical services if we continue to make forecasts of doctor requirements on the basis of the doctor—population ratio.

The use of physician-visits per capita is clearly preferable to the crude doctor—population ratio since the visit rate can be measured for different sub-groups of the population and hence the effects of the changing structure of the population can be taken into account. In addition it encourages us to investigate changes in the productivity of doctors which are necessary if forecasts of physician-visits are to be converted for planning purposes into forecasts of the demand for doctors. Changes in productivity are difficult to predict: large changes in productivity may be possible through greater use of ancilliary health personnel, through better organization of medical practice and hospitals, through the development of new treatments, and so on. Observed changes in productivity provide indicators of possible future changes in productivity, but some authorities argue that enormous changes would occur if some of the institutional controls in the provision of medical care could be relaxed.

However, physician-visits may provide only a poor indicator of the true medical needs of the population. Since individuals not only have to recognize the possible necessity for medical care but also to translate their needs into effective demand, medical needs may exceed total physician-visits. Moreover, the difference may be important in a market pricing system since physician-visits will be partly determined by the price of medical care. In such a case it would clearly by meaningless to plan to expand the supply of doctors to meet future medical needs unless the financial means were provided for translating these needs into effective demand. In a market pricing system, the usefulness of the visit rate will itself be limited unless estimates of the price elasticity of demand are available for different sub-groups of the population.

It is obvious that we know very little about the utilization of doctors and that there may be wide disparities in the provision of care between rich and poor, between ethnic groups, between areas, and so on: in this sense, shortages of doctors seem to exist, but these shortages will not necessarily be eliminated by simply increasing the supply of doctors. Any extra doctors who become available may move to the already well-stocked areas or may treat the already well-treated groups of the population. In such a case, adjustment of supply and demand may take place through the elimination of queues, or through an increase in the time spent per patient, or by a reduction of hours worked, or by an increase in the price of care, and so on. Thus we cannot solve the existing problems in the provision of health services by simply increasing the supply of doctors.

The models currently used for forecasting the number of doctors are clearly very crude. Health services can be provided by different types of health manpower (for example, by general practitioners or consultants) in a number of different organizational structures (for example, in hospitals or in health clinics) using different kinds of treatment (intensive care or surgery) and assisted by a wide variety of health personnel and medical equipment (medical technicians and X-ray machines). The cost of providing a service, and the quality of the service itself, will depend on the complex inter-relationships between all of these factors. Thus before we can build adequate forecasting models we must develop a better understanding of these relationships and of the substitution possibilities that exist in the provision of medical care.

Of course we realize that it will be extremely time-consuming and expensive to build a fully integrated model of the health services sector, and that planning decisions will sometimes have to be made before such a model can become operational. Thus it may be argued that crude models and limited data may provide the only basis for decision-making. If this is the case, then we must recognize that forecasts obtained from such models can only be very approximate and they may provide no clear policy signal for planning purposes. For example, Hansen (1969) has argued that the various projections for the US in 1975 suggest that there will be either a shortage or surplus of doctors in that year: thus it would not be wise in this case to alter enrolments in medical schools on the basis of the forecasts alone. But if we were forced to make crude forecasts, this should not divert our attention from studying at the same time the fundamental issues in the provision of medical care in order to build better models in the future. In the meantime, existing methods may provide useful indicators for planning but only if their limitations receive the consideration they deserve.

12. Conclusions

The future is uncertain and the point of making a forecast, whether of manpower or anything else, is to reduce the margin of uncertainty of future outcomes. We cannot expect any forecast to reduce the margin of uncertainty to zero — perfect accuracy in forecasting is an utopian ideal — but we can expect a forecast to improve on, say, the rolling of dice as a method of estimating future outcomes. The precise degree of accuracy that we are entitled to demand from a forecast depends entirely on the decision that follows from the results of a forecast. In short, to ask whether manpower forecasting is useful for educational planning is to ask whether educational decisions are typically insensitive to the actual errors involved in forecasting manpower demands.

We can now consider this question with the benefit of ten case studies, five of which concern all types of manpower in the economy as a whole and five of which deal with special categories of qualified manpower, such as, engineers, scientists, teachers and doctors. It must be frankly conceded that even this considerable body of evidence does not lead straightaway to a definite answer. The first difficulty is that we lack a precise statistical measure of the accuracy of manpower forecasts. Statistical methods for testing the empirical performance of a forecasting model have been developed in the growing literature on economic forecasting (Theil, 1966; Zarnowitz, 1967 and 1968; Mincer, 1969; Stekler, 1970). These methods assume that a certain number of past forecasts using a given model are available for statistical analysis; with the aid of such data, we estimate the mean and variance of a sample of observed discrepancies between forecasts and outcomes and then make a statistical inference about the value of the discrepancy in the population.

Unfortunately, this approach could not be applied to the manpower forecasts we have examined. Most of these were available for only one point in time. In addition, because of large changes in the definition and measurement of manpower data, current observations frequently differed radically from the data originally used in making the forecast. Many of the models used for manpower forecasting were not explicitly specified in quantitative form and sometimes the forecasts were stated in such a way as to virtually preclude empirical assessment. 'Policy-conditional' forecasts, for example, were often stated in the form: unless we take action A we get the (undesirable) result B; in consequence action A was taken, thereby invalidating forecast B. In all such cases, it would nevertheless have been possible to test the validity of the model if the assumed relationship between the forecast variable and the policy variable had been explicitly specified. But, most of the 'policy-conditional' forecasts we examined were not fully specified. For example, forecasts of the supply of doctors in Britain were made on the basis of existing enrolments in medical schools; these were compared with forecasts of doctor requirements, and enrolments were then altered to eliminate any discrepancy between the two. Hence the supply forecasts were automatically invalidated. But, what is more serious is that nothing like a real model of the interaction between enrolments and requirements lay behind the entire exercise. Similarly, forecasts of demand and supply of particular types of manpower were usually based on the implicit assumption that relative earnings would remain constant: thus since relative earnings invariably changed, the forecasts could not be checked because 'demand' in these forecasts was not assumed to be a function of earnings.

Our first major conclusion is that the manpower forecasts we examined could not be evaluated by statistical methods. This means that we could not determine how much of an observed discrepancy could be attributed to mere chance and how much to a mis-specified model. We believe that manpower forecasting models must be properly specified if we are to be in a position to evaluate them empirically and hence to improve their future performance.

On the basis of our case studies, we have nevertheless been able to draw some conclusions — which may not be statistically significant — about the degree of accuracy that has been actually achieved by manpower forecasts. We found that there was considerable variation in the errors of forecasts of employment by occupation, using models similar to the MRP approach. For example, many of the errors in French forecasts were smaller than 5 per cent but, in a few cases, the errors were greater than 20 per cent and in one case it even exceeded 60 per cent. The errors seem to have arisen partly because of the basic fixed-coefficients model that was adopted, but there

311

were also large errors in the projected levels of employment and productivity growth in the various sectors of the French economy.

Likewise, for single occupation/education forecasts, we found that there were often large forecasting errors in both the coefficient (density-ratio) and the assumed exogenous variable (output). Swedish forecasts of engineers are a case in point. In some cases, the errors in the various sectors were in opposite directions and hence they partly cancelled one another in the aggregate; in other cases, the forecasting errors were in the same direction and hence there were no cancelling effects.

As might be expected, we also found that forecasting errors tend to be greater, the longer the time horizon of the forecast. Moreover, our analysis of the attempt to forecast the demand and supply of teachers in England and Wales suggests that forecasting errors increase only slowly over the first few years but then accelerate rapidly as the time horizon lengthens.

The usefulness of manpower forecasting

Manpower forecasts serve a variety of purposes. Some of them, such as the American and Canadian forecasts, are designed to improve labour placement services and government training programmes and therefore tend to stop short of translating the forecast occupational distribution of the labour force into a projected educational distribution. Even those that are specifically geared to educational decision-making are rarely designed to answer some specific question but are instead addressed to the general problem of determining the appropriate balance of the educational system.

Each of the case studies has tried to ask what influence the forecasts actually had on policy in the particular country concerned but it was not easy to find definite evidence directly linking a forecast to an educational decision. In many cases, manpower forecasts provided additional support for educational expansion which appeared to be desired on political and social grounds: thus it was difficult for us to determine whether or not the forecasts had an independent impact on the decisions which were taken.

At the same time, we found some cases in which manpower forecasts gave support to what turned out to be a wrong decision. In the case of teacher demand and supply in England and Wales, manpower forecasts in the 1950's suggested that a surplus of teachers would develop in the 1960's; this prompted a decision to implement a planned increase in the length of the teacher training course in the early 1960's. But because of large errors in the population forecasts, teacher demand was substantially under-estimated and the projected surplus turned out to be a shortage: the introduction of the three-year teacher training course thus aggravated the shortage. Similarly, projections of doctor requirements for Britain made in the 1950's suggested that too many doctors were being trained, and this led to reductions in medical school enrolments. By 1960, however, it became apparent that a shortage of doctors was developing and rapid steps had to be taken to reverse the decision. Again, a whole series of forecasts of scientists and engineers in Britain purported to show that there were serious shortages of technically qualified people, on the basis of which scarce university places were allocated to students studying science and technology, even though there is counter-evidence which suggests that Britain was actually producing too many scientists and engineers.

We conclude therefore that the manpower forecasting methods in current use certainly can lead to erroneous policy decisions. It follows that it would be wrong to argue *a priori* that forecasting always improves policy decisions, or that some view of future developments is better than none.

Our case studies suggest that there are important weaknesses in the methods that have been used to make manpower forecasts and in the ways in which forecasts have been interpreted for planning purposes. On the demand side, forecasts of manpower requirements have been derived on the assumption that manpower inputs per unit of output are in some sense fixed parameters or coefficients. In some cases, for example in Nigeria, it was assumed that these coefficients were fixed over time and hence that the observed values of the coefficients could be used for making forecasts: however, recent evidence for Nigeria shows that the coefficients have changed substantially after only a few years. In other cases, for example in Canada, it was assumed that the coefficients were fixed for a given technology and that the values associated with future technologies could be obtained by the extrapolation of observed values over time although the main problem of technological forecasting is precisely that technical change is always something more than mere continuation of past trends.

The concept of fixed-coefficients may provide a good approximation for estimating the effects of changes in output on the manpower structure of an economy. But unless long-term rigidities exist in the economic system, the approximation can only be expected to hold in

313

the short-run. Adjustment of the demand and supply of manpower will normally take place through the pricing mechanism, so that observed coefficients are as much the result of demand effects as of supply effects. The basic question here concerns the substitutability of one type of manpower for another and of other factors of production for labour. But this important question has received very little attention in the studies we examined. One exception was a recent study of the utilization of engineers in Sweden: the evidence here suggests that there is only a loose link between engineering education and engineering jobs, so that substitution possibilities apparently do exist.

Even if we rejected the economic arguments about the flexibility of the manpower structure in the production of goods and services, there are other good reasons for expecting that observed coefficients are subject to large statistical variation. Thus observed coefficients include the effects of business cycle fluctuations as well as seasonal and other short-term variations. Similarly they reflect the average effects of existing technology and these include the effects of the existing distribution of firms by size and technology: hence in times of rapidly changing technology or rapid economic growth, observed coefficients may provide poor approximations for planning purposes.

For all these reasons, it seems sensible to assume that observed coefficients cannot be regarded as unique or exact in a numerical sense. But few of the studies have explicitly recognized this, and in only a very few cases — for example in the forecasts of doctors in Canada — were projections derived on the basis of different assumptions about the size of the fixed coefficients.

This type of deterministic thinking extended to the treatment of the variables assumed to be exogenous in the different forecasting models. Thus few attempts were made to estimate the effects of alternative assumptions about the projected values of the exogenous variables despite evidence that forecasts of manpower requirements are extremely sensitive to such assumptions. For example, forecasts of engineer requirements in India in 1978 varied between 513,000 and 710,000 because of an increase in the assumed rate of growth of output from 4.8 per cent per annum to 7.0 per cent per annum in the period 1969—78.

Of course, in most of the studies described, it was explicitly recognized that, because of the uncertainty of the future, the forecasts could not be regarded as unique or exact indicators for planning purposes. But we found that recommendations were often made as if the forecasts were unique and hence as if the future were predictable

314

with perfect certainty.

So far we have talked of manpower demand or requirements forecasts, but the same conclusions hold for manpower supply or stock forecasts. Forecasts of manpower stock were generally derived using existing enrolments in the educational system together with assumptions about retirement, mortality and mobility to other occupations or regions. But as in the case of the requirements forecasts, very few attempts were made to estimate the effects of alternative assumptions about the parameters or about the exogenous variables.

In almost all of the studies, it was assumed that future manpower supplies could be directly influenced by the state and hence that appropriate planning should be undertaken to ensure that the projected requirements would be met. In some cases, the projected stock was simply subtracted from the projected requirements to provide an estimate of the projected manpower shortage or surplus: recommendations were then made to alter the level of enrolments in the relevant part of the educational system in order to ensure that the imbalance would be eliminated. For example, shortages of scientific and technical manpower in Britain were estimated by subtracting the projected stock from the requirements projected by employers, and these were used as a basis for recommending an expansion in enrolments in scientific and engineering courses at universities. Some of the studies recognized that the supply of manpower can be altered by means other than through the expansion or contraction of parts of the formal education system. But no attempt was made to investigate the possibility of eliminating the predicted shortages or surpluses by altering retirement or wastage rates.

It will be clear that manpower shortages or surpluses derived in this way may be subject to large errors because of the uncertainty of future values of both the parameters and the exogenous variables. But since the projected requirements and stock were often treated as if they were numerically exact, few attempts were made to investigate the effects of different assumptions on the predicted shortages or surpluses. Our case studies show that these imbalances are in fact very sensitive to changes in these assumptions and that different policy advice would probably have been given if allowances had been made for this sensitivity. For example, in the forecasts of teachers in England and Wales, allowance for a small margin of uncertainty of ±5 per cent in the demand and supply projections would have been sufficient to change a predicted balance to a shortage of 30,000 teachers: hence a different recommendation about the introduction of the three-year teacher training course might well have been made

315

if the uncertainty of the forecasts had been explicitly taken in account.

The performance of different forecasting models

The forecasts of manpower requirements we examined were obtained using a number of different models. In some cases forecasts were made simultaneously for all occupation/education groups using the basic MRP approach, but there were substantial differences between the various applications. For example, in the applications for the U.S. and France, an inter-industry input—output model formed the basis for the output projections, while in other cases output projections were mainly obtained by trend extrapolation. Similarly, in some cases the model was applied fairly mechanically, while in other cases an attempt was made to co-ordinate informed opinion about future developments; a particularly important example of the latter is the French model in which the projections were obtained by an iterative process in which adjustments were made by different groups of experts.

One of the main advantages of the MRP approach is that it ensures that the manpower projections are consistent with one another in the sense that their sum for any industry equals the total employment projected for that industry; in addition, it provides a means of investigating some of the effects of the growth of output on the manpower structure of the economy. But because of its basic fixed-coefficients structure, it can only be expected to provide reasonable approximations over the short-term since the importance of supply effects and hence of substitution possibilities will become important as the time horizon lengthens. The French have tried to overcome this defect by using experts' judgement to incorporate supply effects; but this is clearly not a completely satisfactory procedure since some of the supply effects may be complex and difficult to estimate without quantitative models.

The MRP approach is also extremely data demanding because observations on output by industrial sector, on employment by occupation and industry, and so on, are necessary for the application of the method. In the studies we examined, we found that forecasts were often based on only one or two observations and out-of-date observations at that. For example, in the French Fifth Plan, forecasts of employment by industry for 1970 and 1978 were translated into employment by occupation using projections of the occupational structure of each industry derived from occupation—industry ma-

316

trices observed in 1954 and 1962. Similarly, in Canada recently, projections of the occupational structure of each industry for 1975 were derived from observed occupation—industry matrices for 1941, 1951 and 1961.

One way of improving forecasts based on the MRP approach is to allow for substitution possibilities by making a variety of projections based on different assumptions about the fixed coefficients. In this way we can investigate the sensitivity of the forecasts to changes in the estimated parameters. But this has seldom been done in applications of the MRP method: one reason for this is that the number of calculations increases rapidly as the size of the occupation—industry matrix and the number of alternatives adopted increase.

It appears that the MRP approach is mainly useful as an experimental model to provide approximate planning indicators in the short-run. The applications of MRP to developed countries suggest that informal judgement has played an important role in the interpretation of forecasts based on such models. For these reasons, it seems to us that if the model were applied in a purely mechanical way, its forecasts would not be sufficiently accurate for providing answers to the questions normally asked by educational planners — particularly in underdeveloped countries.

The single occupation/education models we investigated also varied substantially from one forecasting exercise to the other. The most popular method was the density-ratio or physical norm method: it was applied in making forecasts of doctors in the U.S., teachers in England and Wales, scientists and engineers in the U.S., and engineers in India. In some cases, existing density-ratios were used in making the forecasts: for example, constant density-ratios were assumed in some of the forecasts of engineers in India. In other cases, a projected coefficient was obtained by the extrapolation of observed trends in the coefficient. One such application was made for engineers in Sweden; but the number of observations was only five and these covered a period of 20 years (1935—55). But even here no attempt was made to include the effects of variation in the coefficients.

Single occupation/education forecasts were also obtained by the international comparisons approach and by means of employers' forecasts. The latter method proved to be popular in Britain and a whole series of forecasts of scientists and engineers were obtained on the basis of employers' forecasts. Our investigation suggests that such forecasts were often inconsistent with one another and that the results were wrongly interpreted for policy purposes.

The conclusions we draw about the single occupation/education forecasting models we examined are roughly the same as those for the MRP model. We feel that such models have not proved sufficiently reliable to be applied purely mechanically for educational planning purposes: as we noted earlier, we have found evidence that forecasts based on the fixed-co-efficients single occupation/education models were misinterpreted for policy purposes.

Our conclusion on manpower forecasting

The reason why manpower forecasts have been made in practice is to avoid 'bottlenecks' in economic growth arising from absolute shortages of educated manpower, or to reduce relative shortages of particular types of manpower co-existing with relative surpluses of other types. These imbalances arise because of the rigidities in both the labour market and in the production process. The usual model adopted for making manpower forecasts assumes that production processes are absolutely rigid and that labour markets are completely powerless to eliminate shortages and surpluses by variations in wages and salaries. Indeed, the term 'manpower requirements' has often been used to mean the amount of manpower necessary to achieve a given objective: the implicit assumption here is that an economic system requires educated manpower if it is to grow in the same way that an automobile requires an engine if it is to be driven. But of course even if there were absolutely no substitutes for educated manpower, it would still be possible to import it and hence to choose between growth with foreign-educated labour and no growth with domestically produced educated labour. Thus, as soon as we take a more realistic and less extreme view of the economy, the number of alternatives and hence the scope for choice rapidly increases. The fact is that economic systems are much more like organisms than like machines: it is not obvious that they 'require' educated manpower any more than they require steel, and hence particular types of manpower may not be indispensable elements in the process of economic growth.

It is true, however, that this notion of 'requirements' is the more justified, the more comprehensive the category of manpower we are talking about. If we preclude the importation of foreign labour, it seems reasonable to assume that economic development, particularly planned economic development, requires a minimum number of highly qualified people. But unless we are considering the case of an underdeveloped country which produces pratically no people with higher level education, such use of the term 'requirements' does not appear to be justified even when we are thinking of all people with higher education. When it comes to scientists, engineers and similar professional categories, the use of the term begs the very questions we want to ask. Are such people required in strict proportion to output, or at least in proportions that are confined within narrow limits? If so, there is literally no problem of choice once we have decided on an output target and the costs of educating them cannot influence our decision. On the other hand, if there is any variation, the problem is to choose the best manpower mix, that is, to optimize the structure of manpower for every level of output.

Once we have come this far, we must face the fact that the problem of optimization is more complicated than that of working backward from a given output to a resulting educational composition of the labour force; the educational composition may well have something to do with the average productivity of labour and hence the causal chain runs from manpower to output as well as from output from manpower. Forecasts that take account of this two-way process, such as French forecasts, are inherently more satisfactory than those that ignore it.

There is still no absolutely convincing evidence that manpower forecasters are wrong in assuming that the partial elasticities of substitution between tertiary and secondary educated manpower, and between educated manpower and physical capital, are zero or nearly zero; it is not even possible to show that they are wrong in making such an assumption about scientists, engineers, teachers and doctors. But once again, the weight of such evidence that we have is, generally speaking, incompatible with the hypothesis that elasticities are very nearly zero.

The fixed-coefficients model normally adopted by manpower forecasters implies either that various types of manpower are combined in rigid proportions to produce a given output, or that a given output dictates a particular occupational structure which in turn imposes definite minimum educational requirements. Furthermore, what is not always appreciated is that it also implies that the industrial composition of output is somehow rigidly determined independently of the pattern of consumers' demand; otherwise, a rise in the price of education-intensive products leads necessarily to a decline in the consumption and output of such goods, which thereby restores substitutability of manpower across the economy as a whole, even though there may be no substitutability within industries.

It is perfectly possible to take the view that elasticities of substitution for educated manpower are generally lower than those between capital and unskilled labour, or between different components of capital; that, in addition, labour markets are imperfect and that professional labour markets in particular are subject to long lags on both the demand and supply side, which impede and even prevent equilibrium adjustments. No doubt, the demand for labour is in some sense a function of earnings but until we learn how to estimate statistical demand curves for labour, there is no alternative to making approximate forecasts based on fixed coefficients if we want to frame policies that will help to eliminate chronic shortages and surpluses in labour markets. It is fair to say that this is the motive for making manpower forecasts in such countries as Canada and the United States. In this sort of context, we tend to concentrate on short-term and medium-term forecasts because the policies we have in mind are in fact those designed to influence the workings of the labour market in the immediate future. Unfortunately, the time lags involved in expanding educational facilities usually call for long-term forecasts (perhaps 10 years or more); but the concepts of low substitutability and non-functioning of labour markets become more and more implausible as we stretch the time horizon over which we are forecasting. It is conceivable that there may be no substitutes for production engineers or nuclear physicists over a short period but it seems implausible that no substitutes could be found in a period of several years. The labour market may not eliminate a shortage of doctors in a few years but it is unlikely that it will also fail to do so over the long term. And yet, as we have seen, rare indeed is the manpower forecast that aims modestly to predict requirements a few years hence. A large number of the manpower forecasts that have been made in different economies have looked ahead at least ten years and in some cases 20 years.

The problem of assessing the accuracy of forecasting over long time intervals is literally insuperable. As we know, manpower forecasts often start with an exogenously determined GNP growth target and then work out its implications for the occupational and educational structure of the labour force. But economists have so far had little success in accurately predicting the growth of GNP in an economy more than two to three years in the future;[1] for GNP growth targets over periods of five years or longer, there are hardly any cases on record of achieving such targets precisely. In most economies that have practiced GNP target-setting, the government only controls part of economic activity and far too little is known about the structure of economic systems to judge whether the failure to achieve GNP targets is due to imbalances in investment programmes, imbalances in manpower supplies, or to unforeseen changes in consumers' demand. Even the breakdown of GNP targets into output targets for individual industries presents considerable problems. The use of an input—output model to forecast value added in 27 sectors of the Dutch economy over a ten year period, given observed final demand in the economy as a whole, predicted better than a simple extrapolation of past trends for periods up to two or three years, but it predicted much worse for longer periods (Theil, 1966, ch. 6,7). In view of these results, is it plausible that the occupational distribution of labour in a sector, not to mention the educational distribution of labour, can be accurately projected ten or more years into the future? We think not.

'It would be a bold economist', one econometrician has said, 'who would claim to foresee economic conditions and the tempo of economic change more than a decade ahead in view of rapid technical and institutional changes' (Leser, 1969, p. 8). Manpower forecasters are, in that sense, 'bold economists'; mindful of the long gestation lags in providing additional educational facilities, they have

---

[1] The following succinct summary of present-day achievements in GNP forecasting in the USA is worth quoting to show how far we still have to go in accurately predicting GNP changes one or two years ahead: 'The record of economic forecasters in general leaves a great deal to be desired, although it also includes some significant achievements and may be capable of further improvements. According to the current NBER study, the annual GNP predictions for 1953—63 made by some three hundred to four hundred forecasters (company staffs and groups of economists from various industries, government, and academic institutions) had errors averaging $10 billion. Although this amounts to only about 2 per cent of the average level of GNP, the errors were big enough to make the difference between a good and bad business year. The average annual change in GNP in this period was approximately $22 billion. Hence the errors were according to absolute averages not quite one-half the size of those errors that would be produced by assuming that next year's GNP will be the same as last year's (since the error in assuming no change is equal to the actual change). Had the forecaster assumed that GNP would advance next year by the average amount it had advanced in the preceding postwar years, the resulting average error would not have been greater than S12 billion' (Zarnowitz, 1968, pp. 935—36).

not hesitated to forecast 10 and even 20 years ahead. Unfortunately, it does not appear that manpower patterns can be predicted ten years hence with the degree of accuracy required by educational planners and to pretend otherwise can only do a disservice to the cause of educational planning.

We do not say that manpower forecasts of the traditional type are useless. Fairly accurate predictions can be made over short periods of time (say, two to three years) and this is useful for an 'active manpower policy' that seeks to intervene in labour markets. Indeed, we feel that manpower forecasting should become much more of an on-going activity and that short-term forecasts should be made fairly regularly at short-term intervals. This would afford greater flexibility and would also give more scope for improvement of the models used. In time we may even learn to predict accurately further into the future. However, short-term forecasts seem to be less useful for educational planning than long-term forecasts: we are therefore driven to the central conclusion that manpower forecasting has not so far proved to be particularly useful for educational decision-making; we may even go so far as to say that it has on occasion been positively misleading.

Lessons for the future

How then can we make better manpower forecasts? Whatever the final answer to that question, it is clear that we must begin by repudiating the fixed-coefficients approach. The popularity that such manpower forecasting has enjoyed, and to some extent still enjoys, is easy to explain: it yields exact numbers in terms of which decisions can be defended and it does so by invoking the deeply comforting notion that the economy is just a sort of complicated machine. Any new departure has to start with the idea that planning is the deliberate activity of making choices among alternative actions, all of which are feasible but only one of which is best. Economic growth is compatible with a wide variety of manpower structures and therefore with a wide variety of educational decisions. Although these statements are obvious, they sometimes meet profound resistance in ministries of education because, in one sense, they reduce the role of the expert to that of delineating the feasible paths of action while throwing the final decision to choose the optimum path back to the minister. The merit of the manpower requirements approach was that it virtually made choice unnecessary and undoubtedly this has

322

been one of the secrets of its abiding appeal.

Of course the type of model we need will depend on the particular problems we wish to solve. For example, a fully specified econometric model of the economy, may of course forecast quite accurately and, by virtue of the fact that it is fully specified, it can be improved as time goes by to yield still better forecasts. Nevertheless, because it is non-optimizing, it can at best tell us what is likely to happen and not what we should do to maximize our objective. If a model is both non-optimizing and a partial rather than a total representation of the economy — and this is after all the typical manpower forecasting model of the past — we can have even less confidence in the guides it offers for policy. Ideally, forecasters should aim to state the odds which they attach to predicted outcomes, as is now becoming current practice in American weather forecasting, but in fact such probabilistic predictions are still rare in general economic forecasting and they are unheard of in manpower forecasting. Manpower forecasts are increasingly making use of sensitivity analysis, and in time this will produce estimates of the probability of various outcomes, but as such it brings the model no nearer to fully specified optimizing models.

Some of the case studies, such as those for Thailand, Sweden and Britain, contain constructive suggestions for educational planning that is not exclusively geared to manpower forecasting and one of us has tried elsewhere to sketch a 'doctrine of educational flexibility' (Blaug, 1970, ch. 7) that is grounded in our inability to look far ahead in the future. Others, for example, those for Canada and India, contain suggestions for improved forecasting models.[2] But whatever one may say about these suggestions for a new departure, it is clear that manpower forecasting as such must shed its reliance on the notion of requirements if it is to become a fruitful, scientific activity. It must move beyond the forecasting of shifts of demand at the same wage rate to predictions of both shifts in demand and changes in the quantity demanded. It must introduce the costs of education as a genuine decision-variable; it must aspire to making optimizing forecasts if it is to be relevant to educational planning. In other words we need to specify our objective in quantitative terms and then to maximise our objective within the constraints which limit our potential. This is an ambitious task and it may be a difficult one; but we must make a start in this direction if we are to contribute to educational decision-making.

---

[2] See also Layard (1971) and Crossley (1970) for an attempt to spell out a new approach to educational planning that combines manpower forecasting with cost-benefit analysis.

References [1]

GENERAL

Anderson, C. A. and Bowman, M. J. (1967). Theoretical considerations in educational planning. *World Yearbook of Education*, ed. G. F. Z. Bereday, J. A. Lauwerys and M. Blaug London: Evans Bros.

Arrow, K. J. and Capron, W. M. (1959). Dynamic shortages and price rises: the engineer-scientist case. *Quarterly Journal of Economics* (May).

Blaug, M. (1967). Approaches to educational planning. *Economic Journal* (June).

Blaug, M. (1970). *An Introduction to the Economics of Education*. London: Allen Lane Penguin Press.

Bowles, S. (1969). *Planning Educational Systems for Economic Growth*. Cambridge, Mass.: Harvard University Press.

Cairncross, A. (1969). Economic forecasting. *Economic Journal* (December).

Crossley, J. R. (1970). Theory and methods of national manpower policy. *Scottish Journal of Political Economy* (June).

Denison, E. F. (1962). *The Sources of Economic Growth and the Alternatives Before Us*, Supplementary Paper No. 13. New York: Committee for Economic Development.

Denison, E. F. (1964). Measuring the contribution of education and the residual to economic growth. *The Residual Factor and Economic Growth*. Paris: OECD.

Denison, E. F. (1967). *Why Growth Rates Differ : Postwar Experience in Nine Western Countries*. Washington, D.C.: The Brookings Institution.

Friedman, M. (1966). *Essays in Positive Economics*. Chicago: University of Chicago Press.

Frisch, R. (1961). Survey of types of economic forecasting and programming and a brief description of the Oslo channel model. *Seventh General Conference of the International Association for Research in Income and Wealth* (mimeo).

Goldstein, H. and Swerdloff, S. (1967). *Methods of Long-term Projections of Requirements for and Supply of Qualified Manpower*. Paris: UNESCO.

Hajnal, J. (1955). The prospects for population forecasts. *Journal of the American Statistical Association* (June).

Hansen, W. L. (1965). "Shortages" and investment in health manpower. *The Economics of Health and Medical Care*. (Ann Arbor: University of Michigan.)

Hansen, W. L. (1967). The economics of scientific and engineering manpower. *Journal of Human Resources* (Spring).

Hollister, R. (1966). *A Technical Evaluation of the First Stage of the Mediterranean Regional Project*. Paris: OECD.

[1] General references are used throughout the book, but in Chapters 1 and 2 in particular. Specific country sources are listed under the relevant chapter headings below.

Horowitz, M. A., Zymelman, M. and Herrnstadt, I. L. (1966). *Manpower Requirements for Planning : An International Comparison.* Boston: Department of Economics, Northeastern University.

Jaffe, A. J. and Froomkin, J. (1968). *Technology and Jobs : Automation in Perspective.* London: Praeger.

Kendrick, J. W. (1961). *Productivity Trends in the United States.* Princeton: Princeton University Press.

Layard, P. R. G. (1971). Economic theories of educational planning. In *Essays in Honour of Lionel Robbins*, ed. M. H. Peston and B. A. Corry. London: Weidenfeld and Nicolson.

Layard, P. R. G. and Saigal, J. C. (1966). Educational and Occupational characteristics of manpower : An international comparison. *British Journal of Industrial Relations* (July).

Layard, P. R. G. Sargan, D., Ager, M. A. and Jones D. J. (1971). *Qualified Manpower and Economic Performance : An Inter-plant Study of the Electrical Engineering Industry.* London: Allen Lane The Penguin Press.

Leser, C. E. V. (1969). *Can Economists Foretell the Future?* Leeds: University Press.

Mehmet, O. (1965). *Methods of Forecasting Manpower Requirements.* Toronto, Ontario: Department of Labour and Centre for Industrial Relations, University of Toronto.

Mincer, J., ed. (1969). *Economic Forecasts and Expectations: Analysis of Forecasting Behavior and Performance.* Columbia, N.Y.: National Bureau of Economic Research.

OECD (1970). *Occupational and Educational Structures of the Labour Force and Levels of Economic Development.* Paris: OECD.

Parnes, H. S. (1962). *Forecasting Educational Needs for Economic and Social Development.* Paris: OECD.

Psacharopoulos, G. and Hinchliffe, K. (1971). *Further Evidence on the Elasticity of Substitution between Different Types of Educated Labour.* Higher Education Research Unit, LSE (mimeo).

Rado, E. R. and Jolly, A. R. (1965). The demand for manpower: an East African case study. *Journal of Development Studies* (April).

Rado, E. R. (1967). Manpower planning in East Africa. In *The World Yearbook of Education 1967*, ed. G. Z. F. Bereday, J. A. Lauwerys and M. Blaug. London: Evans Bros.

Salter, W. E. G. (1966). *Productivity and Technical Change.* Cambridge: Cambridge University Press.

Skorov, G. (1966). *Integration of Educational and Economic Planning in Africa*, African Research Monograph No. 6. Paris: UNESCO—IIEP.

Stekler, H. O. (1970). *Economic Forecasting.* New York: Praeger.

Stone, R. (1970). *Mathematical Models of the Economy and Other Essays.* London: Chapman and Hall.

Theil, H. (1966). *Applied Economic Forecasting.* Amsterdam: North-Holland.

Tinbergen, J. (1963). Employment forecasting and planning: In *Employment Forecasting.* Paris: OECD.

Walters, A. A. (1968). *An Introduction to Econometrics.* London: Macmillan.

Zarnowitz, V. (1967). *An Appraisal of Short-term Economic Forecasts.* NBER, New York: Columbia University Press.

Zarnowitz, V. (1968). Prediction and forecasting, economic. In *International Encyclopaedia of the Social Sciences*, Vol. 12, ed. D. L. Sills. New York: Macmillan.

CHAPTER 2

Ahamad, B. (1969). *A Projection of Manpower Requirements by Occupation in 1975 : Canada and its Regions*. Ottawa: Queen's Printer.
Ahamad, B. (1970). *The Regional Distribution of the Canadian Labour Force 1961 by Occupation and Industry*. Ottawa: Queen's Printer.
Ahamad, B. and Scott, K. T. N. (1972). A Note on Sensitivity Analysis in Manpower Forecasting. *Journal of the Royal Statistical Society Series A Vo. 135, Part 3.*
Bertram, G. W. (1966). *The Contribution of Education to Economic Growth*. Ottawa: Queen's Printer.
Caves, R. E. and Holton, R. H. (1959). *The Canadian Economy — Prospect and Retrospect*. Cambridge, Mass.: Harvard University Press.
Denton, F. T., Kasahara, Y. and Ostry, S. (1965). *Population and Labour Force Projections to 1970*. Ottawa: Queen's Printer.
Economic Council of Canada (1965). *First Annual Review*. Ottawa: Queen's Printer.
Economic Council of Canada (1967). *Fourth Annual Review*. Ottawa: Queen's Printer.
Fellegi, I. R., Gray, G. B. and Platek, R. (1967). The new design of the Canadian labour force survey. *Journal of the American Statistical Association* (June).
George, M. V. and Gnanasekaran, K. S. (1966). Census data and recent population projections for Canada. Technical Memorandum, *Population Estimates and Projections Series No. 2*. Ottawa: Dominion Bureau Statistics.
Illing, W. M., George, M. V., Kasahara, Y. and Ostry, S. (1967). *Population, Family, Household and Labour Force Growth to 1980*. Ottawa: Queen's Printer.
Meltz, N. M. (1969). *Manpower in Canada 1931—61: Historical Statistics of the Canadian Labour Force*. Ottawa: Queen's Printer.
Meltz, N. M. and Penz, G. P. (1968). *Canada's Manpower Requirements in 1970*. Ottawa: Queen's Printer.
OECD (1966). *Manpower Policy and Programmes in Canada*. Paris: OECD.
U. S. Department of Labor (1968). *Canada Manpower Policy and Programs*. Manpower Research Bulletin No. 16 (November).

CHAPTER 3

Alterman, J. (1968). *The Use of Input—output Models in Economic Projections and Manpower Analyses by the Federal Interagency Growth Project in the United States*. Paper presented at the Fourth International Conference on Input—output Techniques, Geneva: (mimeo).
Boulding, K. (1953). An economist's view of the manpower concept. In *Scientific and Professional Manpower*, National Manpower Council. New York: Columbia University Press.
Bureau of Labor Statistics — National Science Foundation (1961). *The Long-range Demand for Scientific and Technical Personnel : A Methodological Study* Washington, D.C.: Government Printing Office.

Bureau of Labor Statistics — National Science Foundation (1963). *Scientists, Engineers and Technicians in the 1960s : Requirements and Supply*. Washington, D.C.: National Science Foundation.

Bureau of Labor Statistics (1969). *Tomorrow's Manpower Needs*. Washington, D.C.: Government Printing Office.

Cartter, A. M. (1966). The supply and demand for college teachers. *Journal of Human Resources* (Summer).

Cooper, S. and Johnston, D. (1965). Labor force projections for 1970—80. *Monthly Labor Review* (February).

Department of Labor (1955). *An Occupational Industry Matrix for the United States*. Washington, D.C.: Government Printing Office.

Department of Labor (1963). *Manpower Report of the President, 1963*. Washington, D.C.: Government Printing Office.

Department of Labor (1965). *Manpower Report of the President, 1965*. Washington, D.C.: Government Printing Office.

Department of Labor (1967). *Projections 1970, Interindustry Relationships, Potential Demand, Employment*. Washington, D.C.: Government Printing Office.

Department of Labor (1968). *Manpower Report of the President, 1968*. Washington, D.C.: Government Printing Office.

Engineering Manpower Commission of Engineers Joint Council (1964). *Demand for Engineers, Physical Scientists and Technicians — 1964*. New York: Engineers Joint Council.

Folger, J. K. (1967). Scientific Manpower Planning in the United States. In *World Yearbook of Education*, ed. G. F. Z. Bereday, J. A. Lauwerys and M. Blaug. London: Evans Brothers.

Folger, J. K. and Nam, C. B. (1964). Trends in education in relation to the occupational structure. *Sociology of Education* (Fall).

Folger, J. K., Astin, H. and Bayer, A. (1970). *Human Resources and Higher Education*. New York: Russell Sage Foundation.

Goldstein, H. (1963). Occupational trend projections : an appraisal. *Monthly Labor Review* (October).

Goldstein, H. (1966). Projections of manpower requirements and supply. *Industrial Relations* 5 (3).

Heller, W. L. (1966). The case for aggregate demand. In *The Manpower Revolution*, ed. Garth L. Mangum. New York: Anchor Books.

Harris, S. (1949). *The Market for College Graduates*. Cambridge, Mass.: Harvard University Press.

Kutscher, R. E. and Jacobs, E. E. (1967). Factors affecting change in industry employment. *Monthly Labor Review* (April).

Lecht, L. A. (1968). *Manpower for National Objectives in the 1970's*. Washington, D.C.: National Planning Association.

Lukaczer, M. (1968). Reflections on federal manpower projections. *Labor Law Journal* (April).

Mangum, G. (1969). *The Emergence of Manpower Policy*. New York: Holt, Rinehart and Winston.

March, G. B. ed. (1966). *Occupational Data Requirements for Educational Planning: Proceedings of a Conference at the University of Wisconsin*. Wisconsin: Center for Studies in Vocational and Technical Education.

327

Parnes, H. (1963). Manpower analysis in educational planning. *Planning Education for Economic and Social Development.* Paris: OECD.
Rivlin, A. (1961). The demand for higher education. In *Microanalysis of Socio-economic Systems: A Simulation Study,* ed. G. H. Orcutt, M. Greenburger, J. Korbel and A. Rivlin. New York: Harper and Row.
Rosenthal, N. and Hedges, J. (1968). Matching sheepskins with jobs. *Monthly Labor Review* (November).
Siegel, I. (1966). Productivity measures and forecasts for employment and stabilisation policy. In *Dimensions of Manpower Policy,* ed. S. Levitan and I. Siegel. Baltimore: Johns Hopkins Press.
Somers, G. G. and Wood, W. D., ed. (1969). *Cost-Benefit Analysis of Manpower Policies.* Kingston, Ont.: Queens University.
Wolfbein, S. (1967). *Education and Training for Full Employment.* New York: Columbia University Press.
Wolfle, D. (1954). *America's Resources of Specialized Talent.* New York: Harper.
Working Group on Manpower Projections (1967). *Report of the Working Group U.S. Department of Labor.* Washington, D.C.: Government Printing Office.

CHAPTER 4

Fourastié, J. (1963). Employment forecasting in France. In *Employment Forecasting.* Paris: OECD.
Vimont, C. and Dubrulle, N. (1966). La Prévision de l'emploi dans le cadre du Plan et de l'évolution réelle de l'emploi de 1962 à 1968. *Population* (Special Issue, February).
Vimont, C. and Dubrulle, N. (1966). 'La Prévision de l'emploi dans le cadre du Ve Plan en France, 2e partie: essai de calcul des besoins de recrutement par niveau et type de formation. *Population,* 5.
Vimont, C., Peslier, M. and d'Hugues, P. (1966). La Prévision d'emploi dans le cadre du Ve Plan en France, 1er partie: la repartition de la population active par professions en 1970. Hypothese de travail pour 1978. *Population,* 3.

CHAPTER 5

Adams, D., ed. (1964). *Educational Planning.* Syracuse: Syracuse University Press.
Hunter, G. (1967). *Higher Education and Development in South-East Asia,* Vol. III, Pt. 1, High-level Manpower. Paris: UNESCO—IAU.
ILO (1968). *Asian Employment and Training Projections. Report on Case Study on Thailand.* (Bangkok) (cyclostyled).
Joint Thai — US Task Force (1963). *Preliminary Assessment of Education and Human Resources in Thailand,* 2 vol. Bangkok: AID—USOM (cited as Task Force, 1963).
Muscat, R. J. (1966). *Development Strategy in Thailand. A Study of Economic Growth.* New York: Praeger.
NEC (1969). *Educational Statistics of Thailand 1957—67.* Bangkok: National Education Council.

NEDB (1967A). *The Second Social and Economic Development Plan 1967—71.* Bangkok: NEDB.

NEDB (1967B). *Methodology on Manpower and Employment Projection in the Second Plan of Thailand.* Bangkok: NEDB.

NSO (1968). *Final Report of the Labour Force Survey. All Municipal Areas.* Bangkok: NSO.

Research Committee on Secondary Education (SEM), (1966). *Current and Projected Secondary Education Programs for Thailand: A Manpower and Educational Development Project.* Bangkok: Ministry of Education.

Seal, K. C. (1970). *A General Review of Current Manpower and Related Statistics and Manpower Projections in Thailand.* Bangkok: ILO, Asian Manpower Team (mimeographed).

SEM (1966). See Research Committee on Secondary Education (SEM) (1966).

Silcock, T. H. (1967). *Thailand. Social and Economic Studies in Development.* Canberra: National University Press.

Task Force (1963). See Joint Thai—US Task Force.

Wronski, S. P. and Panich, K. S. (1966). *Secondary Education Manpower and Educational Development.* Bangkok: Ministry of Education.

CHAPTER 6

Archer Report (1961). *Educational Development in Nigeria 1961—70. A Report on the Phasing and Cost of Educational Development on the Basis of the Ashby Commission's Report on Post School Certificate and Higher Education in Nigeria.* Lagos: Federal Government Printer.

Ashby Report (1960). *Investment in Education. The Report of the Commission on Post School Certificate and Higher Education in Nigeria.* Lagos: Federal Ministry of Education.

Callaway, A. (1969). Expanding Nigeria's education: projections and achievements since independence. *Nigerian Journal of Economic and Social Studies* (July).

Callaway, A. and Musone, A. (1968). *Financing of Education in Nigeria.* African Research Monographs 15. Paris: UNESCO—IIEP.

Education and World Affairs (EWA) (1967). *Nigerian Human Resource Development and Utilisation. A Final Report Prepared for USAID.* New York: Education and World Affairs.

Eke, I. I. V. (1966A). The Nigerian national accounts — a critical appraisal. *Nigerian Journal of Economic and Social Studies* (November).

Eke, I. I. V. (1966B). Population of Nigeria 1952—63. *Nigerian Journal of Economic and Social Studies* (July).

Federal Ministry of Education (Annual to 1962). *Annual Abstract of Education Statistics.* Lagos.

Federal Ministry of Education (Annual from 1962). *Statistics of Education in Nigeria.* Lagos.

Federal Ministry of Information (1970). *Second National Development Plan 1970—74.* Lagos.

National Manpower Board (1964). *Nigeria's High Level Manpower 1963—70.* Manpower Study No. 2. Lagos.

National Manpower Board (1967). *Sectoral Manpower Survey 1964.* Manpower
Study No. 4. Lagos.
National Manpower Board (1969). *A Survey of Labour Requirements 1965.*
Manpower Study No. 10. Lagos.
Netherlands Economic Institute (1966). Financial aspects of the educational
expansion in developing regions: some quantitative estimates. *Financing of
Education for Economic Growth,* Part 1, B4. Paris: OECD.
Okigbo, P. N. C. (1962). *Nigerian National Accounts 1950—57.* Lagos: Federal
Ministry of Economic Development.

CHAPTER 7

Blaug, M., Layard, P. R. G. and Woodhall, M. (1969). *The Causes of Graduate
Unemployment in India.* London: Allen Lane The Penguin Press.
Burgess, T., Layard, P. R. G. and Pant, P. (1968). *Manpower and Educational
Development in India 1961—1986.* London: Oliver and Boyd.
Government of India (1966). *Report of the Education Commission
(1964—1966).* Delhi: Manager of Publications.
IAMR (1963A). *Stock Taking of Engineering Personnel.* Working Paper
No. 6/1963. Delhi: Institute of Applied Manpower Research.
IAMR (1963B). *Engineering Manpower Analytical Review of Demand Forecast
Methodology and Provisional Forecast of Growth.* Parts I and II. Working
Paper No. 7/1963. Delhi: Institute of Applied Manpower Research.
IAMR (1965). *Second Report on Engineering Manpower Survey — Demand and
Supply of Engineering Manpower (1961—1975).* Report No. 2/1965. Delhi:
Institute of Applied Manpower Research.
IAMR (1967). *A Sectoral Study of Engineering Manpower Requirements up to
1976, Based on Output, Investment and Work-force.* Report No. 1/1967.
Delhi: Institute of Applied Manpower Research.
IAMR (1969). *Employment Outlook for Engineers 1969—1979.* Working Paper
No. 11/1969. Delhi: Institute of Applied Manpower Research.
ILO (1964). *Employment and Economic Growth.* Geneva: ILO.
Ministry of Education (1949). *Report of the Scientific Manpower Committee.*
Delhi: Manager of Publications.
Planning Commission (1956). *Report of the Engineering Personnel Committee.*
Delhi: Planning Commission.
Planning Commission (1957). *Pattern of Engineering Employment in Manufac-
turing Industries in India.* Manpower Study No. 2. Delhi: Planning Commis-
sion.
Srivastava, R. K. (1964). *Projecting Manpower Demand: A Review of Method-
ology.* Delhi: Directorate of Manpower (mimeo).

CHAPTER 8[1]

Central Bureau of Statistics (Statistiska Centralbyran) (1970A). *Number of
Graductes at Universities and Colleges of Higher Education and Number of
Persons Holding Certain Degrees — Projections up to 1980.* (Examination vid

[1] All citations are given in English so as to correspond with usage in the text.
Where a reference has been translated from Swedish, the original title is given
immediately below the English citation.

330

Universitet och Högskolor Samt Antalet Personer med Vissa Examina Frams-kirvningar till 1980). Stockholm: SCB.

Central Bureau of Statistics (1970B). *Investigations Concerning the Labour Market for Engineers, A Summary.* (Utredningar Rörande Teknikernas Arbetsmarknad, Sammanfattning). Stockholm: SCB.

Döös, S-O (1961). *Some Recent Manpower Forecasts in Sweden.* Stockholm: Labour Market Board.

Döös, S-O (1963). Long-term employment forecasting. In *Employment Forecasting.* Paris: OECD.

Eckaus, R. S. (1964). Economic criteria for education and training. *Review of Economics and Statistics* (May).

Educational Commission (Universitetsutredning) (1959). *Universities and Specialised Colleges in the Society of the 1960's.* (Universitet och Högskolor 1960 — Talets Samhalle). Stockholm.

Educational Commission (1968). *The 1968 Educational Commission, An Outline of its Work.* Stockholm (mimeo).

Labour Market Board (Arbetsmarknadstyrelsen) (1962). *The Future Need for Engineers* (Det Framtida Ingenjörsbehovet). Stockholm: Labour Market Board.

Labour Market Board (1963). *Methodological Problems in Long-term Labour Forecasting.* (Metodproblem i Langsiktiga Arbetskraftsprognoser). Stockholm: Labour Market Board.

Ministry of Education (Ecklesiastikdepartementet) (1962A). *The Continued Expansion of Higher Education.* (Det Högre Utbildnings-Väsendets Forsatta Utbyggnad). Stockholm: Ministry of Education.

Ministry of Education (1962B). *Tendencies in the Labour Market for Graduates up to the 1970's, Statistical Appendix.* (Tendenserna pa Akademikernas Arbetsmarknad fram till Mitten av 1970-Talet, Statistiska Sammanställningar). Stockholm: Ministry of Education.

Ministry of Finance (1966). *The Swedish Economy, 1966—1970.* Stockholm: Ministry of Education.

OECD (1962). *Country Reviews, Policies for Science and Education, Sweden.* Paris: Organisation for Economic Co-operation and Development.

OECD (1967). *Educational Policy and Planning, Sweden.* Paris: Organisation for Economic Co-operation and Development.

OEEC (1960). Methods and techniques for forecasting specialised manpower requirements. In *Forecasting Manpower Needs for the Age of Science*, ed. S. Moberg. Paris: Organisation for European Economic Co-operation.

Orring, J. (1967). *School in Sweden.* Stockholm: National Board of Education.

Ross, D. A. (1966). Economic criteria for education and training: a comment. *Review of Economics and Statistics* (February).

Skolnik, M. L. (1969). *Skill Substitution, Technology and Supply Conditions: The Case of Engineers and Technicians in Canada.* Toronto: Ontario Institute for Studies in Education.

Swedish Federation of Industry (Sveriges Industriförbunds Teknikerkommittee) (1957). *The Need for Engineers in Sweden.* (Ingenjörsbehovet i Sverige). Stockholm: Swedish Federation of Industry.

Technical Group of the Central Bureau of Statistics (SCB Teknikergrupp) (1970). *The Labour Market for Technical Personnel, Report from the 1965 Technical Group.* (Teknikernas Arbetsmarknad. Rapport fran 1965 ars Teknikergrupp) (mimeo).

331

CHAPTER 9

Advisory Council on Scientific Policy (1961A). *Annual Report 1959/1960.* London: HMSO.

Advisory Council on Scientific Policy, Committee on Scientific Manpower (1961B). *The long-term Demand for Scientific Manpower.* London: HMSO, Cmnd. 1490 (cited as Zuckerman Report).

Arthur, H. (1965). *Enquiry into Longer-term Postgraduate Courses for Engineers and Technologists 1964—1965.* London: HMSO.

Blaug, M. (1966). An economic interpretation of the private demand for education. *Economica* (May).

Bosworth Report — see Committee on Manpower Resources for Science and Technology (1965B).

Committee on Higher Education (1963). *Higher Education, Report of the Committee under the Chairmanship of Lord Robbins 1961—1963.* London: HMSO, Cmnd. 2154.

Committee on Manpower Resources for Science and Technology (1965A). *A Review of the Scope and Problems of Scientific and Technological Manpower Policy.* London: HMSO, Cmnd. 2800 (cited as the Jackson Report).

Committee on Manpower Resources for Science and Technology (1965B). *Education and Training Requirements for the Electrical and Mechanical Manufacturing Industries.* London: HMSO (cited as the Bosworth Report).

Committee on Manpower Resources for Science and Technology (1966). *Report on the 1965 Triennial Manpower Survey of Engineers, Technologists, Scientists and Technical Supporting Staff.* London: HMSO, Cmnd. 3103 (cited as the Triennial Survey, 1966).

Committee on Manpower Resources for Science and Technology (1967). *The Brain Drain. Report of the Working Group on Migration.* London: HMSO, Cmnd. 3417 (cited as the Jones Report).

Committee on Manpower Resources for Science and Technology (1968). *The Flow into Employment of Scientists, Engineers and Technologists, Report of the Working Group on Manpower for Scientific Growth.* London, HMSO, Cmnd. 3760 (cited as the Swann Report).

Council for Scientific Policy (1968). *Enquiry into the Flow of Candidates in Science and Technology into Higher Education.* London: HMSO, Cmnd. 3541 (cited as the Dainton Report).

Dainton Report — see Council for Scientific Policy (1968).

Department of Trade and Industry (1971). *Persons with Qualifications in Engineering, Technology and Science 1959 to 1968.* London: HMSO (cited as Triennial Survey 1971).

Hall, M. (1969). Research v. industry. *Higher Education Review* (Spring).

Jackson Report — see Committee on Manpower Resources for Science and Technology (1965).

Jones Report — see Committee on Manpower Resources for Sciences and Technology (1967).

Moser, C. A. and Layard, P. R. G. (1964). Planning the scale of higher education in Britain: some statistical problems. *JRSS* Vol. 127. Reprinted in *Penguin Modern Economics: Economics of Education I*, ed. M. Blaug. London: Penguin Books 1968.

OECD (1970). *Gaps in Technology: Comparisons between Member Countries — An Analytical Report.* Paris: OECD.

Peacock, A. T. (1963). Economic growth and the demand for qualified manpower. *District Bank Review*, 146.

Peck, M. J. (1968). Science and technology. In *Britain's Economic Prospects*, ed. Richard E. Caves and Associates. Washington, D.C.: The Brookings Institution.

Richardson, V. A. (1969). A measurement of demand for professional engineers. *British Journal of Industrial Relations* (March).

Swann Report — see Committee on Manpower Resources for Science and Technology (1968).

Triennial Survey (1966) — see Committee on Manpower Resources for Science and Technology (1966).

Triennial Survey (1971) — see Department of Trade and Industry (1971).

University Grants Committee (1968). *University Development 1962—1967*. London: HMSO, Cmnd. 3820.

Zuckerman Report — see Advisory Council on Scientific Policy (1961B).

CHAPTER 10

Department of Education and Science (1964). *Statistics of Education, 1963*, Part 2. London: HMSO.

Department of Education and Science (1965). *The Demand for and Supply of Teachers 1963—1986, Ninth Report of the National Advisory Council on the Training and Supply of Teachers*. London: HMSO.

Department of Education and Science (DES) (1969A). *Statistics of Education, 1967*, Vol. 4. London: HMSO.

Department of Education and Science (DES) (1969B). *Statistics of Education, 1968*, Vol. 1. London: HMSO.

Department of Education and Science (DES) (1970). *Statistics of Education, 1968*, Vol. 4. London: HMSO.

Kelsall, R. K. — see Ministry of Education (1963).

Ministry of Education (1956). *Three Year Training for Teachers, Fifth Report of the National Advisory Council on the Training and Supply of Teachers*. London: HMSO.

Ministry of Education (1957). *Education in 1956*. London: HMSO., Cmnd. 223.

Ministry of Education (1961). *Education in 1960*. London: HMSO., Cmnd. 1439.

Ministry of Education (1962). *The Demand and Supply of Teachers 1960—1980, Seventh Report of the National Advisory Council on the Training and Supply of Teachers*. London: HMSO.

Ministry of Education (1963). *Women and Teaching*, ed. R. K. Kelsall. London: HMSO.

Ministry of Education (1969). Circular 16. London: HMSO.

CHAPTER 11

Abel-Smith, B. and Gales, K. (1964). *British Doctors at Home and Abroad.* Welwyn: Codicotte Press.

Fein, R. (1967). *The Doctor Shortage.* Washington, D.C.: The Brookings Institution.

Hansen, W. Lee (1969). *An appraisal of physician manpower projections* (mimeo).

Jones, H., Struve, A. and Stefani, P. (1967). *Health Manpower in 1975: Demand, Supply, Price,* National Advisory Commission on Health Manpower Report Vol. II. Washington, D.C.: Government Printing Office.

Judek, S. (1964). *Medical Manpower in Canada.* Ottawa: Queen's Printer.

Klarman, H. E. (1969). Economic aspects of projecting requirements for health manpower. *Journal of Human Resources* (Summer).

Lee, R. I. and Jones, L. W. (1933). *The Fundamentals of Good Medical Care.* Chicago: University of Chicago Press.

Ministry of Health and Department of Health for Scotland (1944). *Report of the Inter-departmental Committee of Medical Schools* (the Goodenough Committee). London: HMSO.

Ministry of Health (1957). *Report of the Committee to Consider the Future of Medical Practitioners and the Appropriate Intake of Medical Schools* (the Willink Committee). London: HMSO.

Ministry of Health and Department of Health for Scotland (1961). *Report of the Joint Working Party on the Medical Staffing Structure in the Hospital Service.* London: HMSO.

Paige, D. and Jones, K. (1966). *Health and Welfare Services in Britain in 1975,* Occasional Paper No. XXII, National Institute for Social and Economic Research. Cambridge: Cambridge University Press.

Peacock, A. T. and Shannon, J. R. (1968). The new doctors' dilemma. *Lloyds Bank Review* (January).

President's Commission on the Health Needs of the Nation (1953). *Building America's Health,* Vol. 2. Washington, D.C.: US Government Printing Office.

Royal Commission on Health Services (1964). *Report* Vol. I. Ottawa: Queen's Printer.

Royal Commission on Medical Education (1968). *Report.* London: HMSO.

Surgeon-General's Consultant Group on Medical Education (1959). *Physicians for a Growing America* (Bane Committee). Washington, D.C.: US Government Printing Office.

U.S. Public Health Service (1967). *Health Manpower, Perspective 1967.* Washington, D.C.: US Government Printing Office.

List of Tables

336

337

List of Figures

339

Author Index

341

Rosenthal, N., 62, 328
Ross, D. A., 227, 331
Royal Commission on Health Services, Canada, 298, 334
Royal Commission on Medical Education, U.K., 287, 292, 293, 294, 296, 297, 334

Saigal, J. C., 19, 123, 325
Salter, W. E. G., 12, 13, 235, 243, 325
Seal, K. C., 109, 329
Secondary Education Programs, Thailand, 117—19, 122, 325
Shannon, J. R., 297, 307, 334
Siegel, I., 53, 328
Silcock, T. H., 109, 110, 111, 329
Skolnik, M. L., 227, 331
Skorov, G., 2, 325
Somers, G.G., 48, 328
Srivastava, R. K., 159, 330
Steckler, H. O., 310, 325
Stone, R., 20—21, 325
Swann Report, 241, 248, 251, 252, 253, 333
Swedish Federation of Industry, 214, 331
Swerdloff, S., 14, 58, 324

Task Force, Thailand, 110—16, 122, 328

Technical Group, Sweden, 204, 214, 226, 229, 230, 232, 233, 234, 238, 331
Theil, H., 24, 25, 310, 321, 325
Tinbergen, J., 22, 325
Tobias, G., 158
Triennial Survey, U.K., 242, 243, 244, 245, 246, 247, 248, 249, 260, 333

UNESCO, 158
University Grants Committee, U.K., 259, 333
U.S. Public Health Service, 306, 334

Vimont, C., 79, 90, 94, 328

Walters, A.A., 10, 325
Wolfbein, S., 48, 328
Wolfle, D., 51, 328
Wood, W.D., 48, 328
Woodhall, M., 158, 330
Working Group on Manpower Projections, U.S.A., 50, 328

Zarnowitz, V., 73, 209, 310, 321, 325, 326
Zuckerman Report, 245, 333

Subject Index

Adult education, 118
Agriculture, 85, 106, 112

Birth rate, 111, 117, 128, *see* Population
Brain drain, 241, 242, 250, 254—55, 256, 260, 292, 297

Canada, 2, 26ff.
Capital-output ratio, 83
Class, size of, 264—66, 281, 282, *see* Pupil—teacher ratio
Cost-benefit analysis, 1, 47, 129, 199, *see* Rate of return analysis
Cost-effectiveness analysis, 25
Cost of education, 129, 247, 296—97

Developing countries, *see* Underdeveloped countries
Doctors, 2, 7, 17, 18, 21, 22, 87, 121
  definitions of, 291
  emigration of, 292, 297, 299, 300
  forecasts for, 122, 125, 285ff., 313, 314, 317
  population ratio, 295, 296, 298, 299, 300, 301, 303, 306, 307, 308
  productivity of, 291, 297, 304, 305, 308
  ratio of patients to, 293, 298, 301, 304, 306, 308
  wastage of, 290—91, 300

Eastern Europe, 2
Economic growth targets, 1
Economic planning, 1, 77—79
Economic theory, 4
Education,
  and economic growth, 19

classification of, 100, 113
  demand for, 1, 202
  specialization of, 7, 250—51
See Adult education, Enrolments, Higher education, Primary education, Secondary education
Educational flexibility, 323
Educational planning, 1, 2, 27, 51, 74, 106, 130, 322
  approaches to, 1, 203
Educational pyramid, 107
Educational structure, of labour force, 11, 15—16, 17, 32—33, 34, 76, 109, 153, 227, 231, 318
  forecasts of 57—60, 80, 87—88, 112, 113, 114, 118, 321
Elasticity of employment, 122, 134, 136, 143, 144, 146, 149—50
Employment forecasting, 82—83
Engineers, 2, 15, 17, 18, 95—96, 180, 314
  definition of, 204, 210, 213, 228, 245, 246, 253
  forecasts of, 63, 64—71, 125, 158ff., 204ff., 312, 313, 314, 317
  to employment ratios, 169, 171, 177—80, 205
  to investment ratios, 165—166, 168, 171, 174—85
  to output ratios, 160, 161, 162, 168, 170, 177—88, 190—91, 194—95, 198—99, 206—7, 211, 216, 320
  to technician ratios, 167, 198
  unemployment of, 189—93
Enrolments, 111, 120
  projections of, 125, 269, 270
  trends in, 126—29, 138—39, 202
Equilibrium in labour markets, 4—6, 247, 258

142, 221, 235, 316—17
    forecasts of, 14, 17—18, 28, 29,
      31—32, 33, 34, 35—36, 38—43,
      55, 57—58, 59, 60—62, 64, 80,
      85—87, 113, 118, 120, 152,
      317—18, 321

Planning, *see* Economic planning,
    Educational planning, Manpower
    planning
Population
    forecast of, 81, 82, 132—33,
      266, 267
    growth of, 34, 57, 111
Primary education, 113, 116, 128
Production functions, 10, 11, 19
Productivity of labour, 12—13,
    14—15, 16, 36, 47, 73, 83, 108—9,
    112, 120, 123—24, 142, 148, 206,
    216, 220, 320
Programming
    linear, 94, 130
    models, 22
Projections, *see* Manpower forecasting
Public employment, 109, 117, 120,
    121, 218
Pupil-teacher ratios, 262, 263, 265,
    266, 270, 281, 283, *see* Classes, size
    of

Rate of return analysis, 1, 94, 130,
    196—97, 203, 256

Say's Law, 250
Scientists, 2, 17, 18, 248, 251, 254,
    257
    forecasts of, 64, 242ff., 313,
      317, 320
Secondary education, 113, 114, 116,
    117, 129
Self-employment, 109
Sensitivity analysis, 15, 32, 35,
    39—42, 307, 317
Services, 85, 86, 120

Substitution,
    elasticity of, 6, 10, 11, 33, 225,
      320
    of commodities, 10, 319—20
    of factors, 5, 6, 9, 15, 16, 36,
      45, 73, 123, 203, 222, 224, 225,
      227, 241, 246, 249, 250, 297,
      314, 316, 319, 320
Substitutability, *see* Substitution
Supply, of manpower, 11, 247, 315
Sweden, 201ff.
Swing from science, 241, 242, 250,
    251, 252, 254, 258, *see* Scientists

Teachers, 2, 9, 17, 87, 92
    by sex, 273—74, 275
    forecasts of, 260—61, 270ff.
    graduate, 272
    length of training, 279
    wastage of, 260, 272, 274—75,
      277, 278, 282, 312—13,
      315—16, 317
Technical progress forecasting, 243
Technicians, 204
Technologist, 245, 257
Training programmes, 2, 3, 118

Uncertainty, of future, 8
Underdeveloped countries, 1, 2
Unemployment, 2, 26, 28, 108, 116,
    151, 164, 167, 173, 174, *see* Engi-
    neers
United States, 48ff.
University graduates, 115—16, *see*
    Higher education
Upgrading hiring standards, 112, 114

Vacancies, 5, 28, 108, 145, 146, 190,
    212, 243
Vocational counselling, 2, 3, 51, 259
Vocational schools, 122, 129

Wages, 5, 95, 248, 249

Books from the
Higher Education Research Unit

Elsevier Scientific Publishing Company — Amsterdam,
Studies on Education'

The Practice of Manpower Forecasting: A Collection of Case Studies by
B. Ahamad, M. Blaug and others (1973)
Returns to Education: An International Comparison by George Psacharopoulos
assisted by Keith Hinchliffe (1973)

In preparation

Demand for Social Scientists
Costs in Universities and Polytechnics
Economic and Social Aspects of the Academic Profession

Published by Allen Lane The Penguin Press
'L.S.E. Studies on Education'

Decision Models for Educational Planning by Peter Armitage, Cyril Smith and
Paul Alper (1969)
The Causes of Graduate Unemployment in India by Mark Blaug, Richard Layard
and Maureen Woodhall (1969)
Paying for Private Schools by Howard Glennerster and Gail Wilson (1970)
Policy and Practice: The Colleges of Advanced Technology by Tyrrell Burgess
and John Pratt (1970)
A Fair Start: The Provision of Pre-school Education by Tessa Blackstone (1971)
*Qualified Manpower and Economic Performance: An Inter-plant Study in the
Electrical Engineering Industry* by P. R. G. Layard, J. D. Sargan, M. E. Ager and
D. J. Jones (1971)

Published by Penguin Books

The Impact of Robbins: Expansion in Higher Education by Richard Layard,
John King and Claus Moser (1969)

Published by Oliver and Boyd

Graduate School: a Study of Graduate Work at the London School of Economics by H. Glennerster with the assistance of A. Bennett and C. Farrell (1966)
The Utilization of Educated Manpower in Industry by M. Blaug, M. Peston and
A. Ziderman (1967)
Manpower and Educational Development in India (1961—1986) by Tyrrell
Burgess, Richard Layard and Pitambar Pant (1968)
Educational Finance: its Sources and Uses in the United Kingdom by Alan
Peacock, Howard Glennerster and Robert Lavers (1968)
Education and Manpower: Theoretical Models and Empirical Applications by
Tore Thonstad (1969)

Published in collaboration with the
Directorate for Scientific Affairs, O.E.C.D.

*Statistics of the Occupational and Educational Structure of the Labour Force in
53 Countries* (1969)